DATE DUE

EXPLORATIONS IN MATHEMATICAL ANTHROPOLOGY

The MIT Press   Cambridge, Massachusetts, and London, England edited by Paul Kay

EXPLORATIONS IN MATHEMATICAL ANTHROPOLOGY

Copyright © 1971 by The Center for Advanced Study in the Behavioral Sciences

Set in Monotype Baskerville. Printed and bound in the United States of America by The Colonial Press Inc.

ISBN 0 262 11034 2 (hardcover)

Library of Congress catalog card number: 79–110229

Contributors

JOHN PAUL BOYD
University of California at Irvine

EDWIN BURMEISTER
University of Pennyslvania

ELIOT D. CHAPPLE
Richland State Hospital, Orangeburg, New York

BENJAMIN N. COLBY
University of California at Irvine

ROY G. D'ANDRADE
University of California at San Diego

HAROLD E. DRIVER
University of Indiana

WILLIAM H. GEOGHEGAN
University of California at Berkeley

JOHN P. GILBERT
Harvard University

HANS HOFFMANN
State University of New York at Binghamton

ROGER M. KEESING
University of California at Santa Cruz

ROBERT M. KOZELKA
Williams College

MARLYS McCLARAN-STEFFLRE
University of California at Los Angeles

GIANDOMENICO MAJONE
University of Rome and Carnegie-Mellon University

PETER REICH
University of Michigan

JOHN M. ROBERTS
Cornell University

A. KIMBALL ROMNEY
University of California at Irvine

PEGGY R. SANDAY
Carnegie-Mellon University

VOLNEY STEFFLRE
University of California at Irvine

RICHARD F. STRAND
Cornell University

IV
PROBABILISTIC METHODS

Preface

The present volume is the result of a three-part symposium on Mathematical Anthropology conducted at the annual meetings of the American Association for the Advancement of Science (Section H) held in Berkeley during the final six days of 1966. All of the papers contained in this volume were originally presented there orally except for those by Chapple, by D'Andrade, and by Majone and Sanday.

My gratitude is due Dr. Eleanor Leacock, then Secretary of Section H of the AAAS, for the invitation to organize and chair the symposium. The entire project has been highly educational for me.

The symposium and part of the publication cost of this volume were supported by a grant from the Mathematical Social Science Board from their National Science Foundation Grant No. GS-547. I wish to thank John M. Roberts of the Mathematical Social Science Board for encouragement and guidance in all phases of the project. Also the help of Preston Cutler of the Center for Advanced Study in the Behavioral Sciences on matters financial and legal is gratefully acknowledged.

Benjamin G. Blount and Katherine B. Branstetter furnished valuable editorial assistance, and Jill Varney typed much of the manuscript and an indefinitely large amount of correspondence.

Finally I wish to thank most deeply the contributors for their forbearance with the time it has taken me to get out the volume.

P. K.

EXPLORATIONS IN MATHEMATICAL ANTHROPOLOGY

Introduction: Mathematics in Anthropology

The stature of a science is commonly measured by the degree to which it makes use of mathematics

–S. S. Stevens (1962:1)

Mathematics in Anthropology: How better approach so broad a subject than with the standard queries: who, what, when, where, how, and why?

1. Why Mathematics in Anthropology?

Stevens's remark quoted above may typify to some anthropologists the kind of wrong-headedness that could inspire a volume on mathematical anthropology. Any attempt to make anthropology more precise will appear to many as presumptuous at best and at worst as evil antihumanism (cf. Berreman 1966). But such judgments, although they often live in the same heads as deep knowledge of anthropological data and deep understanding of anthropological problems, betray a profound ignorance of the history of Western thought in general and scientific thought in particular. Stevens is basically right, and although there are bound to be isolated errors of evaluation produced by criteria so sweeping as these, there are fundamental reasons why the intellectual community at large so frequently assesses the sciences in this way.

First, mathematics is the language *par excellence* in which it is difficult to say something you do not intend. To be sure, there are degrees of clarity in mathematical writing just as there are degrees of elegance of style, but the entire level of precision is many removes from anything that can be achieved in a natural language. For this reason, throughout Western history the sciences have pushed increasingly toward mathematical formulation as they have developed clearer understanding of their subject matter. Modern physics, the descendant of the earliest empirical science to break away from philosophy, would be literally unthinkable without mathematics. In fact, the histories of mathematics and the empirical sciences are inextricably intertwined, and the modern concept of pure mathematics, divorced from physics, is a quite recent invention. Empirical science has contributed just as often to mathematics in our intellectual history as the reverse. If at the turn of the eighteenth century an ethnographer had asked Newton if he considered himself primarily a mathematician or a scientist, the master would have been quite unable to answer. That contrast did not exist in his culture. Inventing the calculus and expressing his laws of motion in terms of it were to Newton not particularly distinct parts of the basic task of understanding the universe.

This fact is often noted by students of man and then discounted by the following argument. Given that physics and the other "natural" sciences have relied heavily on mathematics and have contributed substantially to that branch of learning, the study of human phenomena is qualitatively different from the study of "natural" phenomena. The former, so runs the argument, are inherently imprecise, and consequently any attempt to speak of such phenomena in a precise language imposes a spurious structure on phenomena that are by their nature vague. In this view, an honest search for precise relationships among human phenomena is doomed to failure at the start because such relationships simply do not obtain.

There have been enough facts around for quite a while to suggest that this view is untenable. Some of the clear advances of knowledge achieved in the more mathematical branches of economics and psychology should have convinced anthropologists, and indeed have convinced a few, that at least some gains might be made by an increased level of formalization. However, anthropologists have for the most part either ignored these sister fields entirely or focused on the excesses, the unnatural uses to which these sciences have sometimes put mathematics. I think it is a fair criticism of some parts of mathematical social science that extensive logicodeductive structures have been built on empirical assumptions that violate the rudiments of scientific common sense. However, this fact, which will enter our argument again, should not be focused on by anthropologists to the exclusion of all others in considering the possible relevance of mathematics to anthropology.

Recently the situation has changed. It is no longer merely the case that anthropologists who looked sympathetically at their sister social science disciplines might find there indications suggesting the value of mathematics to their own work. In the past decade there has developed in the subfield of anthropology that deals with the most uniquely human aspect of man, language, a revolution in theory, method, and general conception which is based largely on an attempt to specify mathematically the nature and goals of its subject matter. That there has in fact been a Chomskian revolution in linguistics can, I think, no longer be doubted. That the essence of this revolution is a *génial* application of mathematics to a very large segment of the entire field is attested by the fact that many linguists who consider themselves nontransformationalists admit freely, often enthusiastically, that the example of transformational-generative grammar—the kind of intellectual entity it is—has raised the general level of linguistic conception and discussion to a higher order. The lesson of this revolution, which has taken place squarely within the conceptual domain, if unfortunately not within the institutional domain, of anthropology can no longer be ignored. If ten years ago there was a possible justification for the notion that the most distinctively human phenomena are all and everywhere unamenable to precise discussion, no such possibility now exists. The development of a mathematical linguistics that has simultaneously revolutionized empirical linguistics must surely lay forever to rest the notion that discussion of things human can never be both precise and interesting. Truth and precision are not in complementary distribution.

2. When Mathematics in Anthropology?

Now, and increasingly in the future. A look at the anthropological literature over the past decades shows an increasing use of mathematical and quasi-mathematical methods in all phases of anthropological inquiry and in almost all substantive areas of anthropological concern. The relevant facts taken from a bibliography of mathematical, including statistical, articles appearing in the leading general anthropology

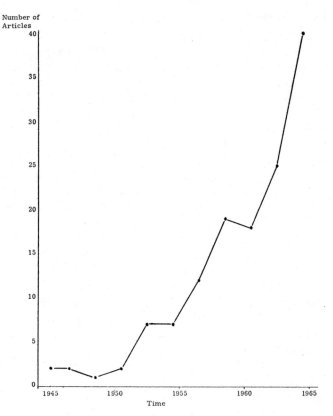

Figure 1. Number of mathematical and statistical articles appearing in selected anthropology journals by two-year periods (1945–1965) (source: Roberts 1966).

journals (*American Anthropologist, Ethnology, Human Organization, Southwestern Journal of Anthropology*) covering the two decades 1945–1965 are summarized in Figure 1 (Roberts 1966).

The phenomenal growth of mathematical methods in anthropology shown in the figure doubtless reflects to some extent the growth of the total anthropological literature during the period. Nevertheless, it seems apparent that we are just entering a period of exponential growth with respect to the mathematization of anthropology. The question is no longer whether anthropology will become increasingly formal but rather the direction which the formalization of anthropology will take. We will return to this question in section 6.

3. Who Mathematics in Anthropology?

Answer: anthropologists. Anthropology as a field cannot count on occasional recruitment of mathematicians or statisticians as consultants to tidy up this or that bit of research and can certainly not expect any persons, including mathematicians, who are not familiar with anthropological data to produce anthropological theory. Moreover, as many readers can doubtless attest from their own experience, when a mathematical or statistical consultant is called in to assist a research project after the data have been gathered, his most insightful comments frequently concern how the data should have been gathered. Anthropologists are becoming familiar with formal techniques of all kinds, and it appears that with each succeeding generation of students this is becoming increasingly the case. This already existing trend needs to be nurtured and encouraged if anthropology is to realize its full potential as a field devoted to the scientific understanding of man. We are now producing and must continue to produce a crop of students who exceed us in technical competence. A few graduate anthropology programs are beginning to give their students credit toward degrees for work in the fields of mathematics and statistics or in fields that rely heavily on mathematical methods such as linguistics and psychology. This is a healthy trend and one that will hopefully spread. In addition, students with undergraduate training in technical fields should be encouraged to enter anthropology, rather than being discouraged by entrance requirements stressing a too heavy concentration in anthropology.

4. Where Mathematics in Anthropology?

Almost everywhere in anthropology. Mathematical and statistical work in the fields of archaeology and physical anthropology is many-faceted but is not dealt with in this volume. Mathematics including statistics has been used in almost every field and subfield of social-cultural anthropology, and this trend will no doubt accelerate in the future. Increasingly emphasis is away from statistical tests of significance of purely associational hypotheses in the direction of precise statement of theories held to underlie the data. This is a healthy trend. Statistical tests of significance are never very informative, particularly when the variables found to be associated are not thoroughly understood in advance. Moreover, high significance levels are often misunderstood by the statistically naïve as measures of strength of association. In any case, where anthropology needs mathematics is not in establishing statistically that, say, pastoral nomadism is positively associated with patriliny; rather what is needed is a literally functional expression of the relationship between the two variables, if such a relationship in fact exists.

As shown by the papers in this volume, various mathematical techniques can be applied at all levels of methodology and theory to a wide range of problems of interest to anthropologists. Mathematics in anthropology must be at the service of the anthropologists, the problems being selected in terms of their substantive interest. Among some of the substantive anthropological problems treated in varying degrees, mathematically, in this volume are cultural systems as mental systems of identification, classification, evaluation, and action (Geoghegan, Keesing), kinship terminologies as logical systems (Boyd), relation of social structure to relational terminology

(D'Andrade), cultural systems as systems of knowledge and belief (Stefflre, Reich, and McClaran-Stefflre), folklore (Colby), genealogy (Gilbert), cultural continuity and culture change (Hoffmann), endogamy/exogamy (Romney), interinformant reliability, cultural distinctiveness in conceptual areas (Kozelka and Roberts), systemic culture patterns (Roberts, Strand, and Burmeister), interaction process (Chapple), and cross-cultural correlations (Driver and Sanday, Majone and Sanday).

The list of anthropological topics is by any standard impressive, and shows that even at this early stage mathematics and mathematically based techniques (e.g., computer technology, for which see Hymes 1965) can be of service to anthropologists with a wide range of interests.

5. What Mathematics in Anthropology?

Anthropologists are currently using many kinds of mathematics and mathematical techniques. No doubt in the future the variety of kinds of mathematics used will be even greater. It would thus be both presumptuous and premature to attempt now to foreclose on just what kinds of mathematics will become most useful to and most used by anthropologists. Nevertheless, since mathematical training for anthropology students is being more and more frequently discussed in anthropology departments where it does not yet exist, some very general observations on what sort of formal training will be most useful to future anthropologists may be in order.

Again, the papers presented in this volume display the major themes. The chief areas of mathematics and related fields that I think will in the future become of interest to anthropologists are, roughly in order of importance, (1) abstract algebra in a wide sense, including, for example, set theory, mathematical logic and axiomatic method, (2) computer technology, and (3) probability and statistics. Within the latter field I think we will, and should, see a slight deemphasis on correlational methods, a great deemphasis on tests of significance, and an increase both in uses of statistics to discover patterns and in stochastic processes as historical models. The emphasis on algebra, logic, and related discrete methods is dictated by the fact that anthropologists are seldom concerned with naturally continuous quantities. Computer methods for problems not concerned with continua can be learned without knowledge of the calculus if and when basic computer science courses do not presuppose this knowledge in their problem sets. Full understanding of probability theory cannot be attained by someone ignorant of the calculus, but a knowledge of probability concerned with finite sample spaces and processes can be so obtained, and such problems are all that are likely to be very important to anthropologists. There is little doubt that anthropology students would benefit if their probability and statistics training were more probability and less statistics. Almost certainly, the overwhelming emphasis on the testing of hypotheses is a less than optimal use of the small amount of time the social science student has to devote to formal training. In fact, this kind of training has not infrequently led to the incredible conception of science as a matter of "testing hypotheses."

The problem of how much calculus might ideally be required of a graduate anthropologist remains a knotty one. Its answer probably depends on how much and what kind of probability theory is thought necessary, since it seems unlikely that the calculus will ever find many anthropological applications in and of itself. For example, it is not clear in what sense, if any, one can understand a Pearson correlation or the normal distribution without some knowledge of calculus. In any case, the day at which the question of how much calculus to include in the training of professional anthropologists will become a practical issue appears sufficiently remote as to render detailed discussion unnecessary at this point.

As regards the kinds of mathematical techniques employed, the papers in this volume may be roughly and nonexclusively classified as follows: (1) algebra in the widest sense: Geoghegan, Keesing, Boyd, D'Andrade, Majone and Sanday; (2) computer methods: Colby, Stefflre, Reich, and McClaran-Stefflre, Gilbert; (3) probability and statistics with emphasis on derivation of pattern: Roberts, Strand, and Burmeister, Driver and Sanday, Majone and Sanday, Romney, D'Andrade, (4) probability and statistics with an emphasis on stochastic processes: Hoffmann, Romney. Kozelka and Roberts's paper is mainly concerned with statistical inference but, unusually in anthropology, starts out with a problem dictated by anthropological data and ends up making an original contribution to statistics. The same comment holds for Romney's paper. Chapple's paper is exceptional in that it is based on classical mathematical methods. The basic measurement strategies are inspired by the example of classical physics, and Chapple envisages the formalization of the results of his research in the form of deterministic equations such as those used in classical physics.

6. How Mathematics in Anthropology?

Briefly, anthropology needs mathematics, not because mathematics is glamorous these days, but because mathematics can help anthropologists solve the kinds of problems anthropologists want to solve. The ineluctable mathematization of anthropology that has already begun deserves the notice and guidance of all anthropologists· As things are beginning, we see a rather wide variety of mathematical techniques applied to a great diversity of anthropological problems. This is an excellent beginning, and the profession of anthropology must keep things developing in this way. So far, the substantive concerns of anthropologists are dictating what in anthropology gets studied mathematically and that must continue. What we have now is, not a school of mathematical anthropology, but increasing use of mathematical and quasi-mathematical methods by anthropologists with widely differing substantive interests. I think the contents of this volume amply demonstrate that point. We must avoid the development of a school of mathematical anthropology and continue the nascent trend to introduce greater precision into all anthropological discourse.

Paul Kay
Berkeley
August 1970

References

Berreman, Gerald E.
1966 "Anemic and Emetic Analyses in Social Anthropology," *American Anthropologist* 68: 346–357.

Hymes, Dell, ed.
1965 *The Use of Computers in Anthropology* (The Hague: Mouton and Company).

Roberts, John M.
1966 "Mathematical and Statistical Anthropology Bibliography (1945–1965)" (mimeographed), 13 pp.

Stevens, S. S.
1962 "Mathematics, Measurement, and Psychophysics," in *Handbook of Experimental Psychology*, S. S. Stevens, ed., (New York: John Wiley and Sons).

ALGEBRAIC METHODS

Introduction

Geoghegan's paper represents an original synthesis of some of the most recent results in ethnography and cognitive psychology. He presents an axiomatic theory of coding behavior in finite-dimensional cognitive domains. Among the advantages of Geoghegan's approach are the following:

1. In contrast to many formal theories of psychological process, this approach contains nothing counterintuitive. On the contrary, Geoghegan's results stem from intuitively clear primitives and highly plausible axioms. The outcome is a theory encompassing a precise synthesis of empirical results from both ethnography and cognitive psychology.

2. Substantively, Geoghegan's theory deals not only with the formal ("code") aspects of information processing systems but also with some of the real-time aspects of the cognitive processes involved. In the terminology current in linguistics and psychology, this theory makes a considerable advance in embedding an account of the subject's competence in a wider theory that includes noncompetence aspects of performance. In currently fashionable anthropological terminology, Geoghegan's formulation comes squarely to grips with the problems of so-called "psychological reality."

3. Geoghegan's method presents a distinct advantage over existing paradigmatic and taxonomic methods for representing cognitive/semantic domains (cf. Kay, P. 1966, *Current Anthropology* 7: 20–23) in that it presents a natural and explicit mechanism for expressing the relations among different domains. Geoghegan's recoding procedure, which allows the total formal structure of one domain (ordered rule) to serve as an item in the structure of another domain (assessment in another ordered rule), goes a long way toward solving the ethnographic problem of interrelation of semantic domains. Moreover, this achievement is attained by a formal device independently motivated by an impressive number of experimental findings in cognitive psychology [cf. Miller, G. A. 1956, *Psychological Review* 63: 81–97 and Miller, G. A., E. Galanter, and K. H. Pribram, 1960, *Plans and the Structure of Behavior* (New York: Holt, Rinehart and Winston)].

4. Formally, the paper can serve as an introduction to axiomatic method for anthropologists as well as an introduction to some of the basic concepts of naïve set theory and the theory of order relations. The endnotes contain sufficient information on mathematical prerequisites to enable a reader with two years of high school mathematics to follow the argument— although some readers who have had no contact with mathematics since the tenth grade may find it somewhat slow going.

Information Processing Systems in Culture
WILLIAM H. GEOGHEGAN

Introduction

Among the recent developments in anthropological theory, especially in ethno-science and the more psychologically biased variety of componential analysis, there has been a tendency to look upon the production of socially conditioned activity as the end result of a series of information processing operations performed by individual native actors. This orientation has been characterized by an interest in discovering and formulating sets of "rules" which account for culturally appropriate acts in terms of the situations that properly evoke them. Componential analysis, for example, can be conceptualized as a partially deductive, partially inductive technique used for discovering a rule that maps sets of distinctive features onto members of a complete set of lexemes at one taxonomic level. Insofar as the elements and structure of such a rule are held to be cognitively valid, it is felt that the rule constitutes an adequate model for certain cognitive processes as well as for the structure of a given semantic domain and the associated overt linguistic behavior. A rule of this kind exemplifies the class of models for one possible theory of information processing systems.

Speaking in more general terms, Frake (1964a) introduced his notion of the "cultural code" with the following remark: "The ethnographer ... seeks to describe an infinite set of variable messages as manifestations of a finite shared code, the code being a set of rules for the socially appropriate construction and interpretation of messages [socially interpretable acts and artifacts]" (1964a: 132). He characterizes such rules as follows:

If we want to account for behavior by relating it to the conditions under which it normally occurs, we require procedures for discovering what people are attending to, what information they are processing, when they reach decisions which lead to culturally appropriate behavior . . . it is not the ethnographer's task to predict behavior per se, but rather to state rules of culturally appropriate behavior. . . . The model of an ethnographic statement is not: "if a person is confronted with stimulus X, he will do Y," but "if a person is in situation X, performance Y will be judged appropriate by native actors." (1964a: 133)

To describe a culture, then, is not to recount the events of a society but to specify what one must know to make those events maximally probable. The problem is not to state what someone did but to specify the conditions under which it is culturally

This paper was originally presented in a somewhat simplified form at the Symposium on Mathematical Anthropology, Annual Meetings of the American Association for the Advancement of Science, Berkeley, California, on December 29, 1965. Since the preparation of the present version, research in native information processing systems has continued and has suggested a number of changes in the mode of presentation of the formal theory, in the method of analysis, and in the presentation of results. The suggested revisions, however, do not involve any major changes in the substantive content of the theory as expressed in this paper, and it has not, therefore, been altered since preparation. Forthcoming publications of subsequent research will include such recent revisions. I am indebted to H. C. Conklin, Roy D'Andrade, Charles Frake, Paul Kay, and A. Kimball Romney for many valuable criticisms and suggestions. Though none of these people necessarily agree with everything that is said here, the paper has benefited immeasurably from their assistance. Financial assistance for the author while this work was in progress was supplied by the National Science Foundation in the form of an NSF Cooperative Graduate Fellowship.

appropriate to anticipate that he, or persons occupying his role, will render an equivalent performance. (1964b: 112)

If the ethnographer's task is to describe the "code" of a particular culture in terms of its component rules, and if this description is to specify the content and structure of rules as they are actually used by native actors, then it is only logical to demand that we first develop some conceptualization of what naturally occurring IP (information processing) systems are like. That is to say, we should have in hand a theory that indicates the necessary and sufficient conditions for any logical entity (e.g., a particular ethnographic statement) to be a model for a naturally occurring information processing rule.

Although Frake's paradigm for an ethnographic statement ("if a person is in situation X, performance Y will be judged appropriate by native actors") does give us a starting point for such a theory, it leaves a number of relevant questions unanswered. Are we to postulate, for example, the existence of a different rule for each recognized situation and the action appropriate to it; or does a rule account for a set of contrasting acts, each of which is appropriate to one or more members of some *set* of situations? How are we to characterize a "situation" itself? Is it some kind of unitary indivisible phenomenon, or can it be factored into a number of discrete, and at least semi-independent, components? Is the result of applying an information processing rule always a "performance" (which seems to imply overt activity), or can it also be the receipt of additional information for a native actor's "internal" use? What is the nature of the information processing phenomenon itself; how is the information contained in a native actor's characterization of a particular situation operated upon to yield inferences concerning the appropriate output? And, finally, given the possibility that such rules can differ from one another in their degree of complexity, we can ask whether or not there exist any natural boundary conditions on the complexity of naturally occurring rules, arising, perhaps, from limitations on human information processing capabilities. These, and a number of related questions that will arise during the subsequent discussion, should be answerable in terms of an adequate theory of natural (or "cultural") IP systems.

It should be clear that the kind of phenomenon we are dealing with is cognitive as well as cultural, that information processing systems comprise part of the basic "mental apparatus" of individual native actors, and therefore that the elements of an adequate theory must represent classes of phenomena actually present in their cognitive maps. If all we desire is to account for the relationship between situations and performances as *we* define and conceptualize them, then there are any number of adequate theories (and models for these theories) which could be used to accomplish the task. Such an approach would go a long way toward summarizing data from the ethnographic record (and even teach us how to behave more or less unobtrusively within a given society), but it would not tell us very much about how the native actors themselves make culturally appropriate decisions. If, on the other hand, the adequacy of ethnographic description is to turn on whether or not it accounts for not only *what* a native actor does under certain circumstances, but also *how he decides* what to do, then we have to know what information *he* is operating with and how it is being processed.

This particular criterion of adequacy (with which we are in complete accord) links our problem directly with a large body of theory and research in cognitive psychology, where an information processing approach to human cognition has been receiving increasing emphasis in recent years. (See Reitman 1965 and Hunt 1962 for detailed summaries of work in this field.) Any theory of natural IP systems which hopes to meet a criterion of cognitive validity will have to take such work into account and be compatible with its established findings. Conversely, what we already know of natural IP systems through ethnographic research must enter into such a theory and its interpretation, and perhaps stimulate some needed reforms in the purely cognitive studies of complex systems.

In brief, the foregoing describes what we have attempted to do in this paper: namely, to propose a formal theory of natural information processing systems of one particular type and to provide it with an interpretation consistent with relevant findings from ethnographic and cognitive research.

The Structure of Information Processing Systems

In the most general sense of the term, an information processing system is a set of interconnected rules of inference, or information processing rules, each of which includes instructions for gathering and operating upon a body of data which becomes the rule's *input information*. Depending upon the nature of the situation being assessed in accordance with these instructions, the input information may take any one of a finite number of possible configurations. The rule also specifies a limited set of potential inferences, each one of which is a possible output of the rule. And finally, it contains a *mapping function* from the various configurations of the input information onto the set of possible outputs.[1]

This characterization of an IP rule covers a wide range of possible types, since we have specified neither the nature and internal structure of input/output information nor the type of operations called for. A rule for obtaining the product of two numbers, for example, would be consistent with this description if it told us how to arrange the input data and how to carry out the procedures necessary for getting an answer. Although such rules would certainly be relevant to a description of how the members of a particular society organize their scientific knowledge, we shall limit ourselves in this paper to a discussion of what we shall call *classification* or *code rules*.[2]

---

[1] A mapping from a set A *onto* a set B requires a function f such that (1) for every a_i in A there is exactly one b_j in B such that $f(a_i) = b_j$, and (2) for every b_j in B there is *at least* one a_i in A such that $f(a_i) = b_j$. A mapping from A *into* B requires a function such that only condition (1) must hold; e.g., there may be some b_j in B such that for every a_i in A, $f(a_i) \neq b_j$.
[2] During the remainder of this discussion, when we use the terms "information processing system" or "information processing rule," it is to be understood that we are referring to rules or systems of rules of the classification (code) type and not to other kinds of information processing behavior which are outside the scope of this paper.

The inputs and outputs of a code rule shall be referred to as *input situations* and *output situations*, respectively. A situation in general is one member of the set of all possible combinations of values on a finite set of variables, such that each combination includes exactly one value from each variable. A variable of the type used in such a rule (called an *assessment*) describes the set of possible correspondences between a given entity and the member categories of a particular classification scheme. The rule specifies the two sets of assessments which generate the potential input and output situations, and it includes a procedure for determining which of the possible inputs is actually in effect for any given application. It also contains the required mapping from the set of potential inputs onto the possible outputs. The applications of a code rule proceed as follows: The actual input situation is first discovered by following the specified procedure. The mapping then indicates which of the potential output situations should be in effect. The indicated output thus contains information inferred from the existence of a specific input situation.

Even though a classification rule may be used to determine the activity appropriate to a given situation, we should emphasize that the output of the rule is not overt behavior in any form; it is information concerning the classification of one or more entities (i.e., a situation). When we have to use an address term to an unfamiliar Alter, for example, a code rule may be used to determine which category of some classification scheme he corresponds to; the actual use of an appropriate term may be considered an overt behavioral realization of the inferred knowledge. Inferences obtained by applying a code rule of this type may also be put to purely internal use, perhaps in making judgments about the behavior of another individual, or in using a second rule which requires this information to define its input. In other words, a classification rule operates completely at the informational level, even though the inputs and outputs may ultimately be connected to activity of the senses and motor behavior.

Derivation of the Theory

The Structure of Axiomatic Theories In deriving the formal components of this theory, we shall be using the axiomatic method. This approach to theory construction usually involves four basic elements: (1) a specification of primitive notions, (2) a statement of the axioms, (3) a presentation of relevant definitions, and (4) the derivation of useful theorems.

The primitive notions of a theory are those elements that are not defined internally, that is, elements whose nature either is intuitively obvious or can be inferred from other theories taken as logically antecedent to the one being constructed. To state that a certain logical element is primitive does not prohibit us from describing or explicating it, but it does imply that such description or explication is external to the formal theory. Discussion of the primitive notions usually constitutes part of the theory's interpretation: the assignment of "meaning" to otherwise "meaning"-less logical entities.

The axioms of a theory constitute the set of basic propositions from which all other propositions are derived. They must be logically independent of one another and refer to no notions that cannot be reduced to primitive elements. The definitions and theorems form the set of derived elements, and they must be reducible to the axioms and primitive notions.

We have already mentioned the idea of an interpretation for a theory and have indicated that it gives "meaning" to statements contained in the theoretical corpus. It is a true but often overlooked fact that a theory by itself is simply a set of one or more logical statements that fulfill certain formal criteria, but which are "meaning"-less until given an interpretation (see Braithwaite 1962). For example, the statement $a^2 + b^2 = c^2$ may be logically correct as a theorem for some specific theory, but it has absolutely no link with the "real world" until the primitive notions and axioms of that theory are given a representation in terms of particular phenomena. Then, perhaps, we have a relationship true of things labeled "right triangles." Even though a theory and its interpretation are two completely different things, it is often the case that they are presented simultaneously, usually through a judicious choice of familiar terminology. This technique has a tremendous advantage over others when we are dealing with a theory of even moderate complexity; it certainly facilitates understanding on the part of the reader by providing him with ready-made concepts to which he can anchor the derivation. But it also has the disadvantage that ambiguities or contradictions in the interpretation will sometimes be used as an argument for rejecting the theory, when in fact the interpretation alone is at fault and should be corrected or abandoned. This drawback can often be overcome through a careful selection of the primitive notions and axioms. If they are chosen so as to minimize their number and complexity, and to reduce the possibility of ambiguous interpretation, then the derived entities will share this precision and lead to a generally straightforward interpretation of the entire theory. This is one of the principal advantages of a self-conscious, carefully done axiomatic derivation. By constructing an economical axiomatic basis for the theory, we can minimize the amount of interpretation required to make it meaningful, and thereby eliminate many of the semantic problems that might otherwise confront us in using the theory and constructing productive models for it.

Primitive Notions and Axioms[3] The first primitive notion of this theory is that of an *entity*, symbolized E_i. It shall be interpreted very broadly as referring to any phenomenon that possesses a set of properties. An entity specified in a code rule operates as a variable whose current value depends upon the particular circumstances in which the rule is applied. In a detailed example presented in the Appendix to this paper, one of the relevant entities is identified by the label "Alter," or "addressee." "Alter" might refer to different human beings at different points in time, but it must always refer to an individual fulfilling the specified role of addressee.

The second primitive notion, also broadly interpreted, has been labeled *categoriza-*

---

[3] Most of the notational conventions and formal terminology used here conform with that employed in Suppes (1957).

tion (K_j), and may be regarded as a classification scheme in terms of which some entity or entities may be classified. Any categorization K_p consists of a set of *categories* k_{pq}, each of which refers to one or more properties which an entity may possess. (The first subscript in the notation k_{pq} identifies the categorization as K_p; the second specifies the particular category.) The term "color," for example, might be the label of a specific categorization for native speakers of English, the constituent categories being referred to by the terms "blue," "green," "red," "yellow," etc. *Category* is the third primitive notion of this theory; and, although in the formal sense it may not be completely correct to propose two primitive elements that exhibit such strong interdependence, this state of affairs should present no difficulties in the present context, but will simplify the following discussion immensely.

The fourth primitive notion is that of a *correspondence* between an entity E_i and a category k_{pq}, which we shall represent by the ordered couple $\langle E_i, k_{pq} \rangle$.[4] We say that an entity corresponds to a particular category when it possesses some property or set of properties which allows it to exemplify that category. For example, an entity labelled "social occasion" will correspond to the category labeled "formal" if the attributes or properties of that occasion are such as to make it a "formal social occasion."

The fifth and final primitive notion concerns what we have called the assessment of an entity E_i in terms of a categorization K_p, represented by the ordered couple $\langle E_i, K_p \rangle$. This notion refers to a basic operation in any classification rule, that of determining the actual correspondence between an entity and some category of a relevant categorization. Under this interpretation, a correspondence may be regarded as the result of making an assessment.

The two axioms which constitute the propositional basis of the theory may be stated as follows:

Axiom 1 (Contrast)
Given an assessment $\langle E_i, K_p \rangle$ and categories k_{pq} and k_{pr} in K_p ($k_{pq} \neq k_{pr}$), if E_i corresponds to k_{pq}, then E_i does not correspond to k_{pr}.

Axiom 2 (Finite Membership)
For every categorization K_p there exists some positive integer $n \geqslant 2$ such that K_p has exactly n member categories.

---

[4] An ordered couple is a special case of an ordered *n*-tuple: specifically, the case in which there are exactly two elements. In general, an ordered *n*-tuple is a group of *n* elements in which *order* as well as *membership* is important. For example, while the set $\{A, B\}$ is the same as the set $\{B, A\}$, it is *not* the case that the ordered couple $\langle A, B \rangle$ is the same as the ordered couple $\langle B, A \rangle$, since two ordered *n*-tuples can be identical if and only if for every positive integer $i \leqslant n$, the *i*th element of the first is identical with the *i*th element of the second. Also, the same element may appear more than once in an ordered *n*-tuple, while this is not true of a set. For example, we could have an ordered triple $\langle A, B, A \rangle$; the *set* of elements in this triple would be $\{A, B\}$ (or $\{B, A\}$).

Axiom 2 is the simpler of these and can be disposed of quickly. It states that a categorization must have at least two member categories and that it must be finite in extension. If we could not discover a positive integer n, greater than or equal to 2, such that the categorization had exactly n members, then it must have either no members, just one member, or an infinity of members (i.e., no matter how large an n we selected, the set would always have more than n members). (See Suppes 1960: 98) For reasons which should be fairly obvious, we do not want to allow any of these three cases.

Axiom 1 requires that the possible results of making a given assessment must contrast with one another. That is, if one particular correspondence results, then no other correspondence may result simultaneously. Since we interpret an assessment as referring to a process that may be performed at different points in time, and since an entity is a variable that may take any of a limited set of values, we do not have to assume that Axiom 1 requires the result of an assessment to be the same every time the process is repeated. It does require, however, that in any given instance the resulting correspondence must be unique. The axiom therefore places several restrictions on specific models for the theory. We could not allow a case, for example, in which one of the assessments involved a categorization having categories like "formal" and "important" if it were possible for the entity (e.g., a "social occasion") to correspond to both categories simultaneously.

Definitions and Theorems In this section we shall present a series of definitions and theorems which characterizes the structural features of code rules and which has a direct bearing on data analysis, model construction, and testing methods relevant to empirical studies that involve this theory.

Definition 1 (State of an Assessment)
Given an assessment $\langle E_i, K_p \rangle$, an ordered couple $\langle E_i, k_{pq} \rangle$, where k_{pq} is a category in K_p, is a *state* of the assessment $\langle E_i, K_p \rangle$.

Under the interpretation we are proposing for this theory, *a state of an assessment is any possible result of that assessment; the actual result in a given instance is a correspondence.* Every state of an assessment is therefore a potential correspondence.

Theorem 1, which follows, is essentially a restatement of the contrast axiom.

Theorem 1 (Contrast between States)
Given an assessment $\langle E_i, K_p \rangle$ and states $\langle E_i, k_{pq} \rangle$ and $\langle E_i, k_{pr} \rangle$ ($k_{pq} \neq k_{pr}$) of this assessment, if $\langle E_i, k_{pq} \rangle$ is a correspondence, then $\langle E_i, k_{pr} \rangle$ is not a correspondence.

PROOF: The proof follows directly from Axiom 1 and Definition 1.

Definition 2 (Assessment Set)
A set A_u of assessments $\langle E_i, K_p \rangle$ is an *assessment set*.

An assessment set, as its name implies, is simply a specified set of assessments.

Definition 3 (State Set)
Given an assessment set A_u, a set S_{uv} of states is a *state set generated by A_u* if and only if for every assessment $\langle E_i, K_p \rangle$ in A_u there is exactly one state $\langle E_i, k_{pq} \rangle$ of $\langle E_i, K_p \rangle$ in S_{uv}.

In other words, by taking exactly one state of each assessment in A_u, and by combining these states into a single set, we obtain a state set generated by A_u.

Definition 4 (Situation)
Given an assessment set A_u and a state set S_{uv} generated by A_u, S_{uv} is a *situation* if and only if for every state $\langle E_i, k_{pq} \rangle$ in S_{uv}, $\langle E_i, k_{pq} \rangle$ is a correspondence.

That is, a situation (in the formal sense that we are using) is a state set, S_{uv}, such that every state in S_{uv} is also a correspondence. Recalling an earlier remark, a state of an assessment is interpreted as a potential result of that assessment, while a correspondence is the actual result. Or, in other words, an assessment is a kind of variable; its states are the values it may take; and a correspondence is its current value. We can extend this idea to the notions of state set and situation by noting that a state set refers to a possible result of making some *set* of assessments, while a situation refers to the actual result. In slightly more formal terminology, a situation is the set of current values taken by the members of a set of variables of the type we have called assessments. The following theorem extends the notion of contrast between states to contrast between state sets.

Theorem 2 (Contrast between State Sets)
Given an assessment set A_u and state sets S_{uv} and S_{uw} generated by A_u ($S_{uv} \neq S_{uw}$), if S_{uv} is a situation, then S_{uw} is not a situation.

PROOF: Since $S_{uv} \neq S_{uw}$, there must be at least one state $\langle E_i, k_{pq} \rangle$ such that $\langle E_i, k_{pq} \rangle$ is a member of S_{uv} and $\langle E_i, k_{pq} \rangle$ is not a member of S_{uw} (Definition 3). S_{uv} is a situation, and by Definition 4, $\langle E_i, k_{pq} \rangle$ must be a correspondence. Since $\langle E_i, k_{pq} \rangle$ is a state of some assessment in A_u and is not a member of S_{uw}, there must be some other state $\langle E_i, k_{pr} \rangle$ of that same assessment which is a member of S_{uw} (Definition 3). Since $\langle E_i, k_{pr} \rangle$ cannot be a correspondence (by Theorem 1), S_{uw} cannot be a situation (Definition 4). Q.E.D.

The following definition introduces the notion of *code segment*, which plays a central role in the derivation and interpretation of the remainder of this theory.

Definition 5 (Code Segment)[5]

Given two finite assessment sets A_i and A_0, the two sets S_i and S_0 of all possible state sets generated by A_i and A_0, respectively, and a many-one function f which maps S_i *onto* S_0, the ordered 5-tuple $T = \langle A_i, A_0, S_i, S_0, f \rangle$ is a *code segment* if and only if the following two conditions are satisfied:

5.1 (MAPPING)

For all state sets S_{ij} in S_i and S_{0k} in S_0, $f(S_{ij}) = S_{0k}$ if and only if when S_{ij} is a situation, then S_{0k} is a situation.

5.2 (MINIMAL DIFFERENCE)

For every assessment $\langle E_p, K_q \rangle$ in A_i, there exists some state $\langle E_p, k_{qr} \rangle$ of $\langle E_p, K_q \rangle$, two state sets S_{ij} and S_{ik} in S_i, and two state sets S_{0u} and S_{0v} in S_0 ($S_{0u} \neq S_{0v}$) such that (i) $S_{ij} \cap \sim (S_{ik}) = \{\langle E_p, k_{qr} \rangle\}$, (ii) $f(S_{ij}) = S_{0u}$, and (iii) $f(S_{ik}) = S_{0v}$.

We shall refer to the two assessment sets A_i and A_0 as the sets of *input assessments* and *output assessments*, respectively; and, similarly, we shall call the members of S_i and S_0 *input state sets* and *output state sets*.

Since a state set may be regarded as a potential situation, it follows that a code segment provides a mapping from one set of potential situations (the members of S_i) onto another set of potential situations (the members of S_0).[6] If a particular input state set is determined to be the actual situation after making the assessments indicated in A_i, then there is a unique output state set that also has the status of a situation. Although it would be possible (from one point of view) to interpret a code segment as one type of classification rule that people might actually carry around in their heads, the psychological evidence indicates that such an interpretation would be incorrect and that a code segment would better be conceptualized as a description of the *capability* of an individual to make inferences within a particular domain.

---

[5] A note on the selection of terminology might be appropriate before we go any further with this derivation. The term "code" will appear frequently throughout the discussion (as in the labels "code rule" and "code segment"); and, as might be expected, its use follows from several statements made by C. O. Frake (1964a: 132, 133; 1964b: 112), and from the notion of "recoding" discussed by Miller (1956). A "code segment," to illustrate, defines a mapping from one body of information to another, and therefore can be interpreted as describing the way in which elements of the first body are "recoded" (or "encoded") as elements of the second body. If the "cultural code" is to be considered the totality of recoding procedures, then it is apparent that a code segment gives a complete specification of the possible results of using one of these procedures—that is, a "segment" of the "cultural code." As we shall see within the space of a few definitions and theorems, and "ordered code rule" accounts for the mapping expressed in a code segment and gives a rule with which the coding task can be performed.

[6] There is some question as to whether or not it would be better to regard the output of a code segment as a situation or as a single correspondence. In the author's opinion, the latter alternative has the greater intuitive appeal, and thus far suffers from no contrary empirical evidence. Regarding the output as a situation, however, has the greater degree of generality, since we can always specify that A_0 has only one member and that the outputs are therefore potential situations containing only one correspondence apiece. For this reason, S_0 has been defined as a set of potential situations, rather than a set of potential correspondences generated by a single assessment. If this proves to be unsatisfactory, a few simple changes should suffice to correct the problem without altering the structure of the theory in any appreciable manner.

In order to facilitate further discussion of Definition 5, and to provide us with an illustration that we can enlarge upon throughout the remainder of this derivation, the following is offered as an example of a code segment.

EXAMPLE 1 (CODE SEGMENT)
We define a code segment

$$T = \langle A_i, A_0, S_i, S_0, f \rangle,$$

where

$$A_i = \{\langle E_1, K_1 \rangle, \langle E_2, K_2 \rangle\},$$
$$A_0 = \{\langle E_3, K_3 \rangle\},$$

and

$$K_1 = \{k_{11}, k_{12}\},$$
$$K_2 = \{k_{21}, k_{22}\},$$
$$K_3 = \{k_{31}, k_{32}, k_{33}\}.$$

The set S_i of all possible state sets generated by A_i is

$$S_i = \{S_{i1}, S_{i2}, S_{i3}, S_{i4}\},$$

where

$$S_{i1} = \{\langle E_1, k_{11} \rangle, \langle E_2, k_{21} \rangle\},$$
$$S_{i2} = \{\langle E_1, k_{11} \rangle, \langle E_2, k_{22} \rangle\},$$
$$S_{i3} = \{\langle E_1, k_{12} \rangle, \langle E_2, k_{21} \rangle\},$$
$$S_{i4} = \{\langle E_1, k_{12} \rangle, \langle E_2, k_{22} \rangle\}.$$

The set S_0 of all possible output state sets generated by A_0 is

$$S_0 = \{S_{01}, S_{02}, S_{03}\},$$

where

$$S_{01} = \{\langle E_3, k_{31} \rangle\},$$
$$S_{02} = \{\langle E_3, k_{32} \rangle\},$$
$$S_{03} = \{\langle E_3, k_{33} \rangle\}.$$

The mapping function f is specified as follows:

$$f(S_{i1}) = S_{01},$$
$$f(S_{i2}) = S_{02},$$
$$f(S_{i3}) = S_{01},$$
$$f(S_{i4}) = S_{03}.$$

For example, f indicates that if S_{i1} (the set $\{\langle E_1, k_{11} \rangle, \langle E_2, k_{21} \rangle\}$) is determined to be a situation, then S_{01} (the set $\{\langle E_3, k_{31} \rangle\}$) is the implied output situation.

We can now discuss the operation of the two conditions (5.1 and 5.2) specified in Definition 5 and their relevance for an interpretation of the theory.

Condition 5.1 describes the mapping function f, which relates the two sets of potential situations generated by A_i and A_0. Condition 5.2 performs a less obvious function. It requires for each assessment in A_i that there be two input state sets that differ from one another only in regard to one state of that assessment, and which map onto different outputs. In Example 1, S_{i2} and S_{i4} fulfill this condition for the assessment $\langle E_1, K_1 \rangle$; and S_{i1} and S_{i2} (or S_{i3} and S_{i4}) satisfy the requirement for $\langle E_2, K_2 \rangle$. Suppose, for example, that the definition lacked Condition 5.2. We could then construct a code segment that required an assessment in A_i for which there existed *no* pair of input state sets differing only in the result of this assessment and leading to different outputs. Such an assessment would not differentiate any pair of inputs with regard to their mapping, and hence would be totally irrelevant to the outcome in any application of the associated rule. We could construct an improper code segment of this type by altering K_3 (in Example 1) and S_0, and by changing the mapping function as follows:

$$f(S_{i1}) = S_{01} \quad (= \{\langle E_3, k_{31} \rangle\}),$$
$$f(S_{i2}) = S_{02} \quad (= \{\langle E_3, k_{32} \rangle\}),$$
$$f(S_{i3}) = S_{01} \quad (= \{\langle E_3, k_{31} \rangle\}),$$
$$f(S_{i4}) = S_{02} \quad (= \{\langle E_3, k_{32} \rangle\}).$$

(K_3 now contains only the members k_{31} and k_{32}.) Note that the result of the assessment $\langle E_1, K_1 \rangle$ is totally irrelevant to the outcome, which is now determined solely by the result of the assessment $\langle E_2, K_2 \rangle$. In summary, Condition 5.2 demands that every assessment called for by a code segment be relevant to the result of the information processing operations. For any interpretation of the theory which involves even a minimal notion of efficiency, a restriction of this type should be required.

Although a code segment has been defined as mapping *complete* descriptions of potential input situations onto potential outputs, it is often the case that full descriptions are not required to account for the mapping, and that if the members of a certain *subset* of states are known to be correspondences, then a unique output is automatically implied. This condition obtains when every potential input situation that contains that subset of states maps onto the same output. In Example 1, we note that this condition is fulfilled for the set of states $\{\langle E_2, k_{21} \rangle\}$, since the only two input state sets that contain this state (specifically, S_{i1} and S_{i3}) map onto the same output, S_{01}. Therefore, the knowledge that $\langle E_2, k_{21} \rangle$ is a correspondence is sufficient to imply that S_{01} is a situation; once this information is obtained, the assessment $\langle E_1, K_1 \rangle$ is irrelevant to the outcome. If such a subset of states is *minimal* (i.e., if it includes no smaller subset which fulfills the above condition), it is called a *simple path* to the particular output involved. The set $\{\langle E_2, k_{21} \rangle\}$, for example, is a simple path to S_{01}. We

Table 1. Simple Paths for Example 1.

Simple Path	To Output	Accounts for State Set(s)
$P_1 = \{\langle E_2, k_{21}\rangle\}$	S_{01}	S_{i1} and S_{i3}
$P_2 = \{\langle E_1, k_{11}\rangle, \langle E_2, k_{22}\rangle\}$	S_{02}	S_{i2}
$P_3 = \{\langle E_1, k_{12}\rangle, \langle E_2, k_{22}\rangle\}$	S_{03}	S_{i4}

say that a simple path *accounts for* the mapping of every state set of which it is a subset. This notion is formally presented in Definition 6.

Definition 6 (Simple Path)[7]

Given a code segment $T = \langle A_i, A_0, S_i, S_0, f\rangle$ and a state set S_{0j} in S_0, a set P_k of states of the assessments in A_i is a *simple path to S_{0j} generated by T* if and only if the following two conditions are satisfied:

6.1

For every S_{iq} in S_i such that $P_k \subseteq S_{iq}, f(S_{iq}) = S_{0j}$

6.2

There is no proper subset P_x of P_k $(P_x \subset P_k)$ such that for every S_{iq} in S_i where $P_x \subseteq S_{iq}, f(S_{iq}) = S_{0j}$.

The simple paths generated by the code segment in Example 1, and the state sets and mapping for which they account, are shown in Table 1.

The following theorem shows that for every input state set generated by A_i (in some given code segment T) there is at least one simple path that accounts for that state set.

Theorem 3 (Existence of Simple Paths)

Given a code segment $T = \langle A_i, A_0, S_i, S_0, f\rangle$, and given S_{ij} in S_i and S_{0q} in S_0 such that $f(S_{ij}) = S_{0q}$, there exists a simple path P_k to S_{0q} generated by T such that $P_k \subseteq S_{ij}$.

PROOF: Since the proof is intuitively fairly simple, though rather long in its complete form, we shall present only a sketch of the complete version. Assume that the theorem is false, and that there exists *no* set P_k of states of assessments in A_i such that Conditions 6.1 and 6.2 are fulfilled. Now, S_{ij} cannot be a simple path (by this assumption). Since Condition 6.1 is true for S_{ij}, Condition 6.2 must be false (if true, then S_{ij} would have to be a simple path). Therefore, there must exist some proper subset P_x of S_{ij} such that for every S_{ip} in S_i where $P_x \subseteq S_{ip}, f(S_{ip}) = S_{0q}$. Thus for P_x, Condition 6.1

---

[7] We can define "subset" and "proper subset" as follows: A set A is a subset of B $(A \subseteq B)$ if and only if for every a_i in A, a_i is also a member of B. A set A is a *proper subset* of B $(A \subset B)$ if and only if A is a subset of B *and* there is at least one b_j in B such that b_j is not a member of A.

must be true; and since P_z is not a simple path (by assumption), there must be some proper subset P_y of P_z such that Condition 6.1 is true for P_y. The same holds true for any $P_z \subseteq S_{ij}$ such that Condition 6.1 is true. By induction, therefore, we have an infinite series of smaller and smaller proper subsets of S_{ij} which meet Condition 6.1, but which fail Condition 6.2. Since S_{ij} must be finite in extension (Definition 5 and Axiom 2), such an infinite series of proper subsets cannot exist. Therefore, we must reject our initial assumption, and the theorem is proved. Q.E.D.

An important implication of Theorem 3 is that every code segment is capable of generating a set of simple paths which accounts for every potential input situation produced by the input assessments of that segment.

Definition 7 (Simple Code Rule)

Given a code segment $T = \langle A_i, A_0, S_i, S_0, f \rangle$, an ordered 5-tuple

$$R = \langle A_i, A_0, P, S_0, g \rangle,$$

where P is the set of all simple paths generated by T, and g is a function that maps P onto S_0, is a *simple code rule for* T if and only if the following condition is satisfied:
7.1 (MAPPING)
For every simple path P_k in P, and for every output state set S_{0j} in S_0, $g(P_k) = S_{0j}$ if and only if P_k is a simple path to S_{0j} generated by T.

Since a simple path is interpreted as a set of states minimally sufficient to imply a unique output (every state set that contains the path must go to the same output), we can think of a simple code rule as specifying the absolute minimum information a person would have to know about any given potential input situation in order to achieve the inferential capability described by the associated code segment. We can therefore extend the notion of accountability (mentioned in our discussion of simple paths) to say that if R is a simple code rule for T, then R *accounts for* T. As the next two theorems (4 and 5) will show, if we are given a code segment there is a unique simple code rule which accounts for that segment, and vice versa. It follows that the related problems of deriving a simple rule from a given code segment and deriving a code segment from a given simple rule both have determinate solutions: that is, a solution exists and it is unique. This property establishes the biuniqueness relationship that exists between these two elements of the theory.[8]

Theorem 4 (Existence and Uniqueness of Simple Code Rules)

Given a code segment $T = \langle A_i, A_0, S_q, S_0, f \rangle$, there exists one and only one simple code rule $R = \langle A_i, A_0, P, S_0, g \rangle$ such that R is a simple code rule for T.

---

[8] Probably the best example of a class of formal structures that have the properties of a simple rule comes from the area of componential analysis. The set of minimal componential definitions resulting from such an analysis—insofar as the analysis produces a true paradigm— and their mapping onto the members of a lexical set, can be expressed in a simple code rule.

PROOF: We shall first prove the existence portion of the theorem (that there is at least one such R), and then the uniqueness portion (that if an R exists, it is the only such R).

The only elements required by R which are not given in T are the set P and the mapping function g. We know that the set of simple paths generated by T exists (Theorem 3). Therefore, we have only to show that g is a function that maps P onto S_0. For this to be true, three conditions must be met:

(i) For every P_j in P, there exists an S_{0p} in S_0 such that $g(P_j) = S_{0p}$.

(ii) For every P_j in P, and S_{0p} and S_{0q} in S_0, $[g(P_j) = S_{0p}$ and $g(P_j) = S_{0q}]$ implies that $S_{0p} = S_{0q}$.

(iii) For every S_{0p} in S_0, there exists some P_j in P such that $g(P_j) = S_{0p}$.

Condition (i) is satisfied by Definition 7, since any P_j in P must be a simple path to some output. We now move to Condition (ii). Since P_j is a simple path generated by T, there must be some S_{ik} in S_i such that $P_j \subseteq S_{ik}$. (By Definition 5, S_i includes *all* possible combinations of states.) By Condition 7.1, if $g(P_j) = S_{0p}$ and $g(P_j) = S_{0q}$, then P_j must be a simple path to both S_{0p} and S_{0q}. And by Condition 6.1, it must be the case that $f(S_{ik}) = S_{0p}$ and $f(S_{ik}) = S_{0q}$. But according to Definition 5, f is a function, and therefore $S_{0p} = S_{0q}$. Hence, Condition (ii) is satisfied. With regard to Condition (iii), we know that for every S_{0p} in S_0 there must be some S_{ik} in S_i such that $f(S_{ik}) = S_{0p}$ (since f is a mapping *onto* S_0). And by Theorem 3 there must be some simple path P_j to S_{0p} generated by T. Since P is the set of all such simple paths by definition, P_j must be a member of P; and by Condition 7.1, we have $g(P_j) = S_{0p}$. Conditions (i), (ii), and (iii) are therefore satisfied, and there exists a simple code rule R for T.

We now move to the uniqueness problem. By the first part of this proof we know that there is at least one simple rule for T. Assume that R is such a simple rule. Let R' be another simple rule for T. If R is unique, then $R = R'$ and vice versa. Since P must be the same for both R and R' (it is the set of *all* simple paths generated by T), they can differ only in the mapping function. Let

$$R = \langle A_i, A_0, P, S_0, g \rangle$$

and let

$$R' = \langle A_i, A_0, P, S_0, g' \rangle.$$

Since the range and domain of g and g' are the same (P and S_0), they can differ only in the way they map P onto S_0. Now for some P_k in P and S_{0q} in S_0, $g(P_k) = S_{0q}$ if and only if P_k is a simple path to S_{0q} generated by T (Condition 7.1). Similarly, $g'(P_k) = S_{0q}$ if and only if P_k is a simple path to S_{0q} generated by T. Hence, $g(P_k) = S_{0q}$ if and only if $g'(P_k) = S_{0q}$. Therefore, $g = g'$, and it follows that $R = R'$. The simple code rule for T must consequently be unique. Q.E.D.

Theorem 5 (Uniqueness of a Code Segment for a Given Simple Code Rule)
Given a simple code rule $R = \langle A_i, A_0, P, S_0, g \rangle$, there exists one and only one code
segment $T = \langle A_i, A_0, S_i, S_0, f \rangle$ such that R is a simple code rule for T.

PROOF: The existence of T follows automatically from Definition 7, since R must be
derived from some code segment; and therefore, if R exists, T must exist.

We now move to the uniqueness problem. If there is only one code segment which
generates the simple code rule R, then for any pair of code segments T and T' such
that R is a simple code rule for both T and T', it must be the case that $T = T'$. This
is what we shall attempt to prove. Let R be a simple code rule for some pair of code
segments T and T'. Let

$$T = \langle A_i, A_0, S_i, S_0, f \rangle$$

and let

$$T' = \langle A_i, A_0, S_i, S_0, f' \rangle.$$

Since the range and domain of f are the same as those of f', the two functions can differ
only in the way they map S_i onto S_0. Now, for every S_{ij} in S_i and S_{0q} in S_0 such that
$f(S_{ij}) = S_{0q}$, there must be a P_k in P such that $g(P_k) = S_{0q}$ and $P_k \subseteq S_{ij}$ (Theorem 3
and Definition 7). And by Definition 6 we have $f'(S_{ij}) = S_{0q}$. Similarly, we can show
that if $f'(S_{ij}) = S_{0q}$, then $f(S_{ij}) = S_{0q}$. Therefore, we obtain $f(S_{ij}) = S_{0q}$ if and only if
$f'(S_{ij}) = S_{0q}$. Hence, $f = f'$, and it follows that $T = T'$. The code segment is therefore
unique. Q.E.D.

We now introduce two formal notions that will be required in subsequent definitions.

Definition 8 (State Sequence)[9]
A sequence $Q_i = \langle Q_{i1}, q_{i2}, \ldots, q_{in} \rangle$ of n states $\langle E_p, k_{qr} \rangle = q_{ij}$ is a *state sequence of
order n* if and only if for every pair of states q_{ij} and q_{ik} $(j \neq k)$ in Q_i, q_{ij} and q_{ik} are
states of different *assessments*.
A state sequence of order n is therefore a sequence of n states of different assessments.

Definition 9 (Initial Subsequence)
Given a sequence $X_i = \langle x_{i1}, x_{i2}, \ldots, x_{im} \rangle$ of m elements, a subsequence $X_i(n) =
\langle x_{i1}, x_{i2}, \ldots, x_{in} \rangle$ $(n \leq m)$ of the first n elements of X_i in order is the *nth initial sub-
sequence of X_i*.

For example, if we have a sequence $Z = \langle z_1, z_2, z_3, z_4 \rangle$, the sequence $Z(3) =
\langle z_1, z_2, z_3 \rangle$ is the third initial subsequence of Z: that is, the first three elements of
Z in order.

[9] For present purposes, we can regard a sequence of n elements as an ordered n-tuple.

Definition 10 introduces the notion of an ordered code rule ("ordered rule," for short). In many respects this is the most important element of the theory, and we shall devote the bulk of the remaining discussion to characterizing its role as the fundamental unit out of which information processing systems are constructed.

Definition 10 (Ordered Code Rule)[10]
Given a code segment $T = \langle A_i, A_0, S_i, S_0, f \rangle$ and the (unique) simple code rule $R = \langle A_i, A_0, P, S_0, g \rangle$ for T, an ordered 5-tuple $R^* = \langle A_i, A_0, P^*, S_0, g^* \rangle$, where P^* is a set of state sequences P_j^* consisting of states of assessments in A_i, and g^* is a mapping from P^* onto S_0, is an *ordered code rule for R and T* if and only if the following two conditions are satisfied:

10.1 (ACCOUNTABILITY)
For every P_j^* in P^* and every S_{0q} in S_0, $g^*(P_j^*) = S_{0q}$ if and only if there exists some simple path P_k in P such that $P_k \subseteq s(P_j^*)$ and $g(P_k) = S_{0q}$.

10.2 (ORDERING OF ASSESSMENTS)
For every P_j^* in P^* and for every nth initial subsequence $P_j^*(n)$ of P_j^*, if $P_{jn}^* = \langle E_p, k_{qr} \rangle$, then:

10.2.1
For every P_k^* in P^* such that $P_k^*(n-1) = P_j^*(n-1)$, P_{kn}^* is a state of $\langle E_p, K_q \rangle$,

10.2.2
For each state $\langle E_p, k_{qs} \rangle$ of $\langle E_p, K_q \rangle$, there is a P_k^* in P^* such that $P_k^*(n-1) = P_j^*(n-1)$ and $P_{kn}^* = \langle E_p, k_{qs} \rangle$, and

10.2.3
There exists some P_k^* in P^* and some state sequence Q_k such that $P_k^*(n-1) = P_j^*(n-1) = Q_k(n-1)$; and for all $i > n$, $Q_{k, i-1} = P_{ki}^*$, and for all P_q in P, $P_q \nsubseteq s(Q_k)$.

We shall refer to a state sequence P_k^* in P^* as an *ordered path in R^* to S_{0j}* (where S_{0j} is the output upon which the path is mapped), or, more simply, as an *ordered path*.

An ordered code rule differs from a code segment and a simple code rule in that it requires an ordering of assessments. We may interpret this ordering as a temporal one, and as indicating the step-by-step processing of needed information. The choice of each successive assessment depends only upon the results of preceding assessments; that is, upon correspondences already identified up to that point in the process. Suppose, for example, that in applying a hypothetical ordered rule, an individual has already made the assessments $\langle E_1, K_1 \rangle$ and $\langle E_2, K_2 \rangle$ and has determined that the states $\langle E_1, k_{11} \rangle$ and $\langle E_2, k_{23} \rangle$, respectively, are correspondences. At this point he knows that the next correspondence will have to be some state of the assessment $\langle E_4, K_5 \rangle$, for example; and this, consequently, is the next piece of information he processes (see Condition 10.2.2). When he has identified a complete sequence of

[10] We shall use the notation $s(X)$ to indicate the set of elements ordered by some sequence X.

such correspondences (that is, when he has decided which P_k^* in P^* accounts for the actual situation), the mapping indicates the output to be inferred. Such an inference can be made because each complete ordered path must contain all the elements of some simple path (Condition 10.1) which, as we have indicated, contains sufficient information to imply a unique output. It can also be shown, using Condition 10.2, that there must be a "unique beginner": that is, some assessment with which the process begins (see Theorem 6, below).

It should be stressed that while a code segment and its associated simple code rule exhibit the biuniqueness property, this relationship does not necessarily hold between a given code segment (or its simple code rule) and a particular ordered code rule. We can show that there always exists at least one ordered rule for any code segment (Theorem 7), and that for any ordered rule there exists a unique code segment and simple code rule (Theorem 10 and Corollary 10.1). But it can also be demonstrated that the problem of deriving an ordered code rule which accounts for some code segment does not always have a unique solution. In any but the most trivial cases (i.e., where the code segment involves only one input assessment) there is more than one possible ordering of the assessments. The problem of deciding between alternative orderings in empirical studies is an important one and will occupy us later in this paper.

We can exemplify the notion of an ordered code rule and illustrate the possibility of alternative orderings by continuing the development of Example 1. The two possible sets of ordered paths (P^* and $P^{*\prime}$) are given in Table 2, along with their respective mappings. A convenient and easy to read representation of ordered code rules utilizes

Table 2. Two Sets of Ordered Paths for Example 1.

P_j^* in P^* for Ordered Rule R^*	$g^*(P_j^*)$
$P_1^* = \langle\!\langle E_2, k_{21} \rangle\!\rangle$	S_{01}
$P_2^* = \langle\!\langle E_2, k_{22} \rangle, \langle E_1, k_{11} \rangle\!\rangle$	S_{02}
$P_3^* = \langle\!\langle E_2, k_{22} \rangle, \langle E_1, k_{12} \rangle\!\rangle$	S_{03}

P^* in $P^{*\prime}$ for Ordered Rule $R^{*\prime}$	$g^*(P_j^{*\prime})$
$P_1^{*\prime} = \langle\!\langle E_1, k_{11} \rangle, \langle E_2, k_{21} \rangle\!\rangle$	S_{01}
$P_2^{*\prime} = \langle\!\langle E_1, k_{11} \rangle, \langle E_2, k_{22} \rangle\!\rangle$	S_{02}
$P_3^{*\prime} = \langle\!\langle E_1, k_{12} \rangle, \langle E_2, k_{21} \rangle\!\rangle$	S_{01}
$P_4^{*\prime} = \langle\!\langle E_1, k_{12} \rangle, \langle E_2, k_{22} \rangle\!\rangle$	S_{03}

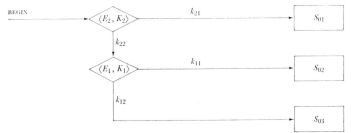

Figure 1. Rule R^*.

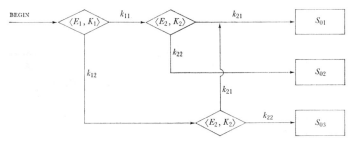

Figure 2. Rule R^{*1}.

some of the notational conventions of computer "flow diagrams."[11] Flow charts for the two ordered rules derived from Example 1 are shown in Figures 1 and 2. The diamond at each node of the diagram represents a single assessment (which is written inside), the labels on the arrows identify the possible correspondences (by indicating the categorization involved), and the rectangular terminating boxes display the potential output situations. Each ordered path is represented in the diagram by a chain of linked arrows originating at the first assessment (the "unique beginner," marked "Begin"), passing through a series of nodes, and terminating at some output. Figure 1, for example, can be read as follows: We start with the assessment marked "Begin" (that is, $\langle E_2, K_2 \rangle$). If E_2 corresponds to k_{22} (that is, if $\langle E_2, k_{22} \rangle$ is a correspondence), then the assessment $\langle E_1, K_1 \rangle$ is required. If E_1 corresponds to k_{11}, then we have completed the ordered path P_2^* (see Table 2), and the output situation S_{02} is indicated. Other ordered paths would be determined in the same manner.

We can use this notational scheme to simplify our discussion of the formal requirements expressed in Condition 10.2 of Definition 10. To begin with, an nth initial subsequence of some ordered path is represented by a connected chain of arrows originating at the first assessment and following the ordered path through the first n states. (It may, of course, be as long as the ordered path itself.) Suppose that we are

[11] Tree diagrams, which are structurally similar to flow charts, have been used from time to time by decision theorists and cognitive psychologists to represent several different kinds of information processing rules. See Luce and Raiffa (1957), Hunt (1962), and Hunt, Marin, and Stone (1966).

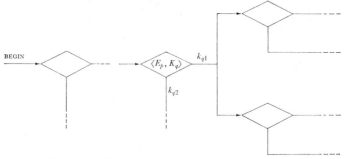

Figure 3. Violation of Condition 10. 2. 1.

given an ordered path P_j^* and some nth initial subsequence of this path, such that the nth arrow of this partial sequence represents a state of the assessment $\langle E_p, K_q \rangle$. The first part of Condition 10.2 requires that every other ordered path which follows the same route through the $(n-1)$th state have some state of $\langle E_p, K_q \rangle$ as its nth element. This must hold true for every nth initial subsequence of every ordered path. In other words, given a partial route through a flow diagram, every continuation of that route must begin with some state of a single given assessment. Condition 10.2 does not permit any ordered rule to have a set of ordered paths which could be partially represented by a diagram like the one in Figure 3. The second part (10.2.2) requires that for every assessment (node) in the diagram, and for each state of that assessment, there must be at least one ordered path that passes through the node and contains that state at the appropriate point in the sequence. If we had an ordered rule that specified the input assessment $\langle E_p, K_q \rangle$, for example, and the states of that assessment were $\langle E_p, k_{q1} \rangle$, $\langle E_p, k_{q2} \rangle$, and $\langle E_p, k_{q3} \rangle$, then no portion of the rule could be represented by a diagram such as the one in Figure 4 (since the state $\langle E_p, k_{q3} \rangle$ does not appear).

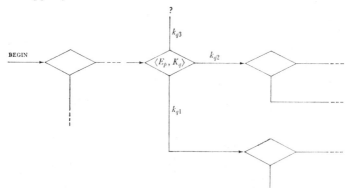

Figure 4. Violation of Condition 10. 2. 2.

The third part of Condition 10.2 demands that every assessment made in accordance with an information processing sequence specified in a given ordered code rule must be relevant to the outcome determined by that sequence. For purposes of illustration, we can temporarily delete this requirement and note the possible consequences. Suppose we are given an ordered path P^*_j in P^* and an nth initial subsequence of this path. We first take the set of all ordered paths that share the route of P^*_j through the $(n-1)$th state (including P^*_j in this set), and delete the nth state from each member. This forms the set of state sequences Q_j mentioned in 10.2.3. If each of these new sequences were to contain all of the states of some simple path given in the simple rule R (hence violating 10.2.3), then clearly the assessment whose states were deleted is irrelevant to deciding between the outputs which could still result following the nth assessment. (Recall that the information contained in a simple path is sufficient to imply a unique output.) The diagram in Figure 5a illustrates a potential ordered rule that violates Condition 10.2.3 at several points (specifically, in the placement of $\langle E_2, K_2 \rangle$ in the ordered paths stemming from $\langle E_1, k_{11} \rangle$, and in the placement of $\langle E_3, K_3 \rangle$ in the various paths extending from $\langle E_1, k_{12} \rangle$). The simple paths P_j (for the simple rule associated with the possible ordered rules incorrectly represented in Figure 5a) are as follows:

$$P_1 = \{\langle E_1, k_{11}\rangle, \langle E_3, k_{31}\rangle\} \quad \text{(to } S_{01}),$$
$$P_2 = \{\langle E_1, k_{11}\rangle, \langle E_3, k_{32}\rangle\} \quad \text{(to } S_{02}),$$
$$P_3 = \{\langle E_1, k_{12}\rangle, \langle E_2, k_{21}\rangle\} \quad \text{(to } S_{03}),$$
$$P_4 = \{\langle E_1, k_{12}\rangle, \langle E_2, k_{22}\rangle\} \quad \text{(to } S_{04}).$$

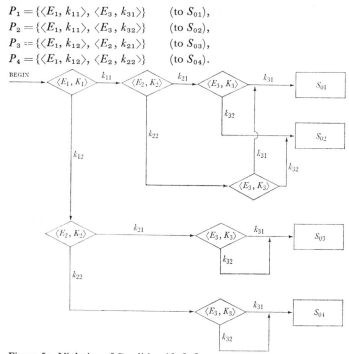

Figure 5a. Violation of Condition 10. 2. 3.

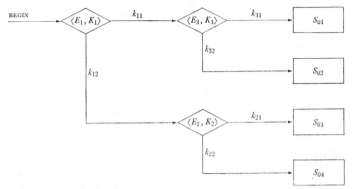

Figure 5b. Corrected to adhere to Condition 10. 2. 3.

If in all ordered paths starting with $\langle E_1, k_{11} \rangle$ in Figure 5a the states of $\langle E_2, K_2 \rangle$ are deleted, each of the resulting sequences contains the states of either P_1 or P_2. Although this assessment is relevant in all ordered paths starting with $\langle E_1, k_{12} \rangle$, it is not relevant once the correspondence $\langle E_1, k_{11} \rangle$ has been determined. A more obvious violation of Condition 10.2.3 concerns the placement of $\langle E_3, K_3 \rangle$ in the paths stemming from $\langle E_1, k_{12} \rangle$. This assessment contributes no information toward making a decision between S_{03} and S_{04}; this can be seen in the diagram or by studying the simple paths listed above. An ordered rule in which these violations are corrected is shown in Figure 5b.

We can now introduce several theorems relevant to the structure and existence of ordered code rules.

Theorem 6 (Unique Beginner)
Given an ordered code rule $R^* = \langle A_i, A_0, P^*, S_0, g^* \rangle$, there is an assessment $\langle E_p, K_q \rangle$ in A_i (the unique beginner) such that for every ordered path P_j^* in P^*, $P_{j_1}^*$ is some state of $\langle E_p, K_q \rangle$.

PROOF: The proof follows directly from Condition 10.2.1. For every pair of ordered paths P_j^* and P_k^* in P^*, $P_j^*(0) = P_k^*(0)$ (since this is the empty sequence). There must be some assessment $\langle E_p, K_q \rangle$ such that P_{j1}^* is one of its states. If P_{j1}^* is some state of $\langle E_p, K_q \rangle$, then by Condition 10.2.1, $P_{k_1}^*$ is also a state of this assessment. Since we have shown that this is true of any pair of ordered paths in P^*, it is true of all ordered paths in P^*. Q.E.D.

Theorem 7 (Existence of an Ordered Code Rule)
Given a code segment T and the (unique) simple code rule R for T, there exists at least one ordered code rule R^* such that R^* is an ordered code rule for R and T.

PROOF: To demonstrate the existence of such an ordered code rule, we need only show that it is possible to construct a set of ordered paths using the assessments in A_i, and to provide a mapping from this set to the members of S_0, such that the conditions of Definition 10 are satisfied. We shall sketch such a construction procedure here. First of all, we know that an ordered rule is derived from a given code segment and its associated simple code rule. To begin the construction, take all of the input state sets (the potential input situations) of the code segment and order their members in the same way, such that the first state of each sequence is a state of some assessment $\langle E_i, K_p \rangle$, the second state of every sequence is a state of another assessment $\langle E_j, K_q \rangle$, and so on. Map each of these sequences onto the output to which its corresponding input state set is mapped by the function f. Figure 5a, to which we referred earlier, represents such a set of sequences and shows that they produce a complete "tree" diagram or flow chart. Each sequence contains the elements of a simple path (Theorem 3) and hence fulfills Condition 10.1. They also fulfill Conditions 10.2.1 and 10.2.2 (which are needed to produce a complete tree of the type shown in Figure 5a). The set of sequences, however, may not adhere to Condition 10.2.3 (as we illustrated earlier). If this is the case, then irrelevant assessments are dropped from each path in which they contribute no relevant information. Such assessments must be deleted one at a time, and the modified structure should be checked for additional violations after each deletion. Since the set of potential ordered paths changes after each incorrect assessment is dropped, the mapping will have to be revised according to Condition 10.1. It should be clear, however, that this requirement (10.1) and the first two parts of 10.2 will still be fulfilled. When no additional deletions are required, then all of the conditions of Definition 10 will be met, and an ordered code rule for the given code segment will have been constructed. Figure 5b illustrates the result when this procedure is applied to the set of sequences shown in Figure 5a.

We now move on to the proof of several theorems that illustrate the accountability of a particular ordered code rule for its associated code segment and simple code rule.

Theorem 8 (Accountability of Ordered Paths for Situations)
Given a code segment $T = \langle A_i, A_0, S_i, S_0, f \rangle$, the (unique) simple code rule $R = \langle A_i, A_0, P, S_0, g \rangle$ for T, and $R^* = \langle A_i, A_0, P^*, S_0, g^* \rangle$ an ordered code rule for T and R: for every P_k^* in P^* and for every S_{ij} in S_i such that $s(P_k^*) \subseteq S_{ij}$, and for every S_{0q} in S_0, $g^*(P_k^*) = S_{0q}$ if and only if $f(S_{ij}) = S_{0q}$.

PROOF: If $g^*(P_k^*) = S_{0q}$, then by Condition 10.1 there must be some P_j in P such that $P_j \subseteq s(P_k^*)$ and $g(P_j) = S_{0q}$. Now if $s(P_k^*) \subseteq S_{ij}$, then $P_j \subseteq S_{ij}$. Since P_j is a simple path to S_{0q} generated by T (Condition 7.1) and $P_j \subseteq S_{ij}$, it must be true that $f(S_{ij}) = S_{0q}$ (Condition 6.1). Similarly, if P_k^* is an ordered path, there must be some P_u in P such that $P_u \subseteq s(P_k^*)$ (Condition 10.1). If $s(P_k^*) \subseteq S_{ij}$, then $P_u \subseteq S_{ij}$. Let $g(P_u) = S_{0z}$. By Condition 6.1, $f(S_{ij}) = S_{0z}$. But since we are given that $f(S_{ij}) = S_{0q}$, and since f is a function (Definition 5), we have $S_{0z} = S_{0q}$. Hence $g(P_u) = S_{0q}$ and $g^*(P_k^*) = S_{0q}$ (by Condition 10.1). Therefore, $g^*(P_k^*) = S_{0q}$ if and only if $f(S_{ij}) = S_{0q}$. Q.E.D.

Theorem 9 (Existence and Uniqueness of Ordered Paths)

Given a code segment $T = \langle A_i, A_0, S_i, S_0, f \rangle$ and an ordered code rule $R^* = \langle A_i, A_0, P^*, S_0, g^* \rangle$ for T: for every state set S_{ij} in S_i there exists one and only one ordered path P_k^* in P^* such that $s(P_k^*) \subseteq S_{ij}$.

PROOF: Since the proof of this theorem is long and overly tedious, it is not presented here. The proof is, however, very similar to the one used in Theorem 3; and the interested reader is referred there for a sketch of the procedure.

Theorem 8 shows that an ordered path accounts for the mapping of any potential situation of which its elements form a subset. Theorem 9 demonstrates that for any potential situation S_{ij} defined by a code segment T there exists exactly one ordered path P_k^*, specified by a given ordered code rule for T, such that the elements of P_k^* form a subset of S_{ij}. These two theorems jointly imply that all potential situations defined by some code segment T can be accounted for by an ordered code rule for T. Theorem 10 (following) shows that for any ordered code rule R^* there is one and only one code segment T such that R^* is an ordered code rule for T; and hence that the problem of determining the code segment accounted for by an ordered rule has a unique solution.

Theorem 10 (Uniqueness of a Code Segment for an Ordered Code Rule)

Given an ordered code rule $R^* = \langle A_i, A_0, P^*, S_0, g^* \rangle$, there is one and only one code segment $T = \langle A_i, A_0, S_i, S_0, f \rangle$ such that R^* is an ordered code rule for T.

PROOF: The proof is identical in form to the one presented for Theorem 5 and is not given here. The reader is referred to the earlier proof for an illustration of the procedure.

Corollary 10.1

Given an ordered code rule R^*, there is one and only one simple code rule R such that R^* is an ordered code rule for R.

PROOF: The proof follows directly from Theorems 4 and 10.

Although there exist a unique code segment and a unique simple rule for any given ordered rule (the subject of the last several theorems), the converse is not generally true. For any given code segment or simple code rule there will usually be more than one permissible ordered code rule. (Figures 1 and 2 illustrate a case in point.) Consequently, when we attempt to apply this theory to the description of a natural system, we are presented with the problem of choosing between alternative and equally valid (at least in the formal sense) analyses. We might want to ask, therefore, whether or not there exists an interesting subclass of ordered rules which has a greater likelihood of being represented in natural systems. In this connection we can enlarge upon an idea about human cognition that we alluded to earlier in the paper, and discuss its effects in generating such a subclass of ordered rules. The assumption involved can be stated as follows: *Human beings tend to process information in such a way as to minimize the long-run average number of items processed.* If we can interpret the processing of an item of information to be equivalent to making a single assessment, then the implication of this assumption is clear: individuals will tend to modify the internal structure of their ordered rules in such a way as to minimize the average number of assessments performed. This idea has been used so far to justify the "relevancy" condition in Definition 5 (Condition 5.2), which says that no code segment requires an assessment irrelevant to all decisions between outputs; and it can also be used in justifying Condition 10.2.3 in Definition 10, which states that at any stage of an information processing sequence the next assessment made must be relevant to the possible outcomes at that stage.

From the above assumption we can also derive the following proposition: *At any stage in an information processing sequence, the next assessment to be made minimizes the average number of subsequent assessments which must be made before an output can be determined.*[12] In terms of the tree diagram or flow chart representation of an ordered rule, this statement says in effect that the assessment at any given node is chosen so as to minimize the number of assessments in the branches that emanate from that point. We say that any ordered code rule that meets this requirement is an *efficiently ordered rule*. Without going into detail, an efficiently ordered rule can always be constructed for a given simple code rule by operating upon the set of simple paths contained in the latter. Construction proceeds in a step-by-step fashion by first selecting a unique beginner (the first assessment) and then, for each branch coming from this node, selecting a second assessment, and so on, such that each choice conforms to the efficiency requirement. The process is terminated in each branch as soon as the ordered set of states contains all the elements of a simple path and, therefore, is sufficient to indicate a single output.

Returning to Example 1 and the set of simple paths shown in Table 1, we note that if the assessment $\langle E_2, K_2 \rangle$ is chosen as the unique beginner, then one of its states $(\langle E_2, k_{21} \rangle)$ completes the simple path P_1 and leads directly to the output S_{01}. The other branch from this node must lead to the assessment $\langle E_1, K_1 \rangle$ before a simple path is accounted for. This produces the ordered rule shown in Figure 1. If, on the other hand, the assessment $\langle E_1, K_1 \rangle$ were taken as the unique beginner, then *both* branches which

---

[12] This proposition actually involves an additional simplifying assumption which states, in essence, that the potential input situations in a code segment have an equal "probability" of occurrence. In empirical cases this is obviously untrue, but the errors of analysis that it is capable of producing are relatively minor and occur only in very specific and limited circumstances. Since the potential errors are minimal, the fact that this assumption makes possible the detailed analysis of empirical cases is sufficient justification for its use.

emanate from this node must lead to $\langle E_2, K_2 \rangle$ before a simple path can be completed. The ordered rule that this generates is shown in Figure 2. The first process (producing rule R^*) obeys the efficiency requirement by picking a unique beginner that minimizes the number of subsequent assessments (only one additional assessment in one branch), while the second process does not (it requires an additional assessment in each of *two* branches). The former thus generates an efficiently ordered rule, as an inspection of Figures 1 and 2 should demonstrate. The algorithm that this procedure illustrates can be applied to simple rules of any degree of complexity to derive an efficiently ordered rule. In some cases more than one solution is possible, but it should be stressed that the range of alternative analyses is greatly reduced, usually to a set of ordered rules that differ from one another only in the relative sequencing of two adjacent assessments.

The notion of an efficiently ordered rule is an important one with regard to the theory's potential application in ethnographic description. If the efficiency assumption is justified—and available evidence indicates that it is—then we should expect to find that information processing routines actually in use by given individuals can be described in a valid manner by efficiently ordered rules. Since a simple code rule can be determined through elementary frame elicitation techniques, and since efficient rules can be derived in turn from simple rules, then it follows that we should have in hand a technique that requires data that are relatively easy to come by, and which produces descriptions showing a reasonable approximation to cognitive validity. Several tests performed in conjunction with the example presented in the Appendix to this paper indicate, though on a limited basis, that the approximation falls within quite acceptable limits.[13]

One other point deserves mention before we conclude this part of the discussion. It concerns a phenomenon we have called "recoding," following the usage of Miller (1956). In essence, recoding refers to information contained in the output of one ordered rule being used as part of the input information to a second rule. Since a given output is a set of states (a potential situation), and since the input of a rule is also a set of states, then the possibility of recoding is permitted by the formal structure of this theory. For example, in applying one ordered rule, there may be a required assessment for which the necessary information is not immediately available (i.e., it is not known which state of the assessment is a correspondence). If there exists a second rule that contains the states of this assessment in its output (if the assessment is a member of A_0), it can be employed to determine the actual correspondence. In such a case, we say that the input information to the second rule has been recoded in terms of a

---

[13] These tests consisted of sorting tasks in which the subject was asked to group terms on the basis of their similarity in use. After an initial partition was formed, the subject was asked whether or not any of the groups could be further partitioned into smaller subgroups, and then if any of the initial groups could be placed together in larger groupings. Since a set of ordered rules also generates partitions of a hierarchial type, the test could be used as evidence for the cognitive validity of the set of derived rules.

given output. Because of certain inherent limitations on the amount of information that an individual can process at any one time, some sort of recoding must take place in an information processing system of more than minimal complexity. This capability must also extend to any theory of human information processing which is to be used in the production of valid models for natural systems.

A Note on Cognitive Aspects Although this paper has been primarily concerned with a theory useful in the production of certain types of ethnographic statements, and is by no means a self-contained treatise on the psychology of thinking, we have already seen that our attempt to provide an interpretation for its formal notions depends heavily on a basic commitment to certain ideas about how people think and about their capabilities and limitations in organizing and processing specific kinds of information. This commitment involves such fundamental notions as the itemization of information (i.e., the cognitive representation of information as discrete units and not as continuously variable magnitudes), the sequential processing of information, the tendency toward efficient cognitive systems, limitations on the amount of information that can be processed at one time, recoding, contrast between the states of an assessment (Axiom 1), and so on. In several cases, these ideas have had to be modified or generalized to conform with the implications of well-founded ethnographic theory.

Unfortunately, limitations of space and the fact that this subject is outside the somewhat limited scope of the paper force us to postpone until a later time any detailed discussion of the relationship between this theory and cognitive psychology. We can say, however, and without any great reservations, that we have tried to keep the theory and its interpretation as thoroughly consistent as possible with relevant areas of cognitive and ethnographic theory. For the most part, the attempt has been successful; though there have certainly been cases in which simultaneous compatibility could not be maintained. These cases are interesting in themselves, since they ultimately reduce to conflicts between ethnography and cognitive psychology; but, again, they fall outside the scope of this paper and would be more appropriate to a general discussion devoted to the relationship between these two domains of study. We can only say that a discussion of this type is needed and, hopefully, will not be long in coming.

Appendix. Bisayan Terms of Personal Address

The set of efficiently ordered rules which appears in this Appendix is included solely for the purpose of exemplifying the theory developed in this paper. This example is not intended as a complete and/or valid ethnographic statement concerning the terms of personal address used by any group of Bisayan speakers.[14] It should be stressed that

---

[14] Bisayan (or Visayan) is a Philippine language in wide use among Christian Filipinos on Mindanao and the central group of islands known as the Visayas. Local dialects can vary widely within this area. The terminology analyzed here is most representative of the islands of Cebu and Leyte and their immediate environs.

the terminology and usage reported here is derived from interviews with a single informant under nonfield conditions, and should not be considered representative of any "typical" speaker of the informant's dialect, nor, perhaps, of the informant himself under more natural conditions.

Even with these reservations, however, the description is sufficiently adequate to indicate something of the complexity of naturally occurring information processing systems and their potential range of variation. In addition, there is some evidence (from the sorting task described in footnote 13) that the description does approximate a valid model of one portion of the informant's "cognitive map," and to this extent can be considered adequate.

The notation used in the following table and diagrams differs slightly from that presented in the body of the paper. Categorizations have been represented by capital letters which have as much mnemonic value as possible, and their member categories are symbolized by the same letters in lower case with identifying subscripts.

The entities and categorizations used in these rules are listed below in Table A1. The various assessments employed are shown in Figures A1 through A6.

Table A1. Entities and Categorizations for the Bisayan Example.

	Entities	Gloss
	E_1	"Alter," "addressee"
	E_2	"social occasion"
	E_3	"proname" (name or name substitute)
	E_4	"first name" (of Alter)
	E_5	"nickname" ("pet name") (of Alter)
	E_6	"social relationship with Alter"
	E_7	"personal background of Alter" (linguistic, "accultuative")
	E_8	"language" (appropriate)

Categorizations	Categories	Gloss
A		"relative age"
	a_1	"younger"
	a_2	"same"
	a_3	"older"
A'		"absolute age"
	a'_1	"young child"
	a'_2	other (contains several categories not differentiated in these rules)

Table A1 *continued*

Categorizations	Categories	Gloss
C		"membership in Ego's group of 'friends'"
	c_1	"member"
	c_2	"not a member"
E		(types of formal pronames)
	e_1	(Impossible to gloss; represents part of the proname
	e_2	classification scheme. Refer to Rule R_e^*.)
	e_3	
	e_4	
F		"permission of familiarity"
	f_1	"familiarity permitted"
	f_2	"familiarity not permitted"
K		"knowledge" (of some entity)
	k_1	"known"
	k_2	"unknown"
L		(Classification by language)
	l_1	"English"
	l_2	"Bisayan"
	l_3	"Spanish"
M		"marital status"
	m_1	"married"
	m_2	"unmarried," "single"
P		(Personal address classification scheme. Possible
	$p_1 - p_{19}$	correspondences are indicated in Rule R_p^*, P_1
		through P_{19}.)
Q		"request for intimacy" (involves a standard verbal
		formula)
	q_1	"request made"
	q_2	"request not made"
S		"relative status"
	s_1	"lower"
	s_2	"same"
	s_3	"higher"

Categorizations	Categories	Gloss
T		"possession of academic/professional title"
	t_1	"has title"
	t_2	"does not have title"
U		"degree of intimacy" (with Ego)
	u_1	"intimate friend"
	u_2	"casual acquaintance," "stranger"
V		"types of informal pronames"
	v_1	(See discussion of categorization E.)
	v_2	
	v_3	
W		"absolute social status," "wealth"
	w_1	"middle class," "poor"
	w_2	"high class," "wealthy"
X		"sex"
	x_1	"male"
	x_2	"female"

Note: The terms ʔ*ángga*ʔ, "nickname," "pet name," *pangalan*, "first name," and *titolo*, "academic/professional title," indicated in Rule R_p^* are not address terms *per se*, but refer to forms which will vary with the particular Alter involved.

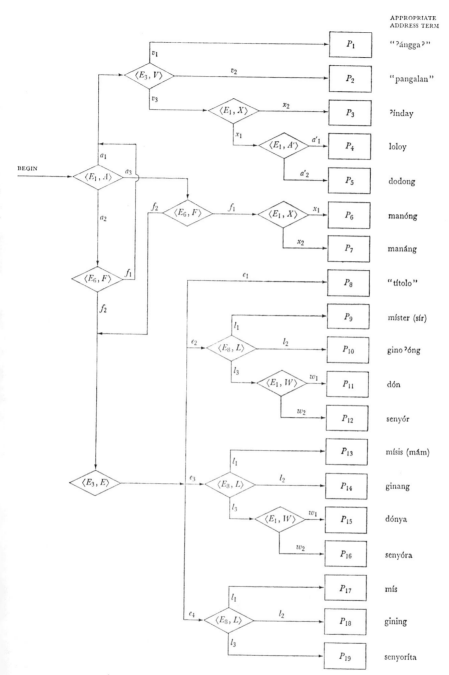

APPROPRIATE
ADDRESS TERM

P_1 "ʔángga ʔ"

P_2 "pangalan"

P_3 ʔínday

P_4 loloy

P_5 dodong

P_6 manóng

P_7 manáng

P_8 "títolo"

P_9 míster (sír)

P_{10} gino ʔóng

P_{11} dón

P_{12} senyór

P_{13} mísis (mám)

P_{14} ginang

P_{15} dónya

P_{16} senyóra

P_{17} mís

P_{18} gining

P_{19} senyoríta

Figure A1. Rule R_p^* for making assessment $\langle E_1, P \rangle$.

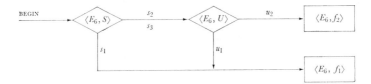

Figure A2. Rule R_f^* for making assessment $\langle E_6, F \rangle$.

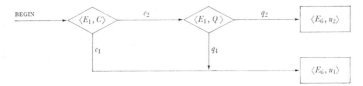

Figure A3. Rule R_u^* for making assessment $\langle E_6, U \rangle$.

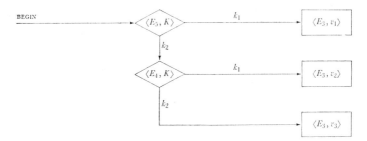

Figure A4. Rule R_v^* for making assessment $\langle E_3, V \rangle$.

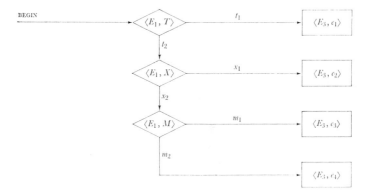

Figure A5. Rule R_e^* for making assessment $\langle E_3, E \rangle$.

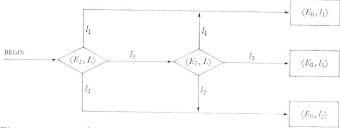

Figure A6. Rule R_i^* for making assessment $\langle E_8, L \rangle$.

References

Braithwaite, R. B.
1962 "Models in the Empirical Sciences," *in Logic, Methodology and Philosophy of Science*, Ernest Nagel, Patrick Suppes, and Alfred Tarski, eds (Stanford, Cal.: Stanford University Press), pp. 224–231.

Frake, Charles O.
1964a "Notes on Queries in Ethnography," *American Anthropologist*, 66, No. 3, Pt. 2: 132–145.
1964b "A Structural Description of Subanun 'religious behavior,'" in *Explorations in Cultural Anthropology*, Ward H. Goodenough, ed. (New York: McGraw-Hill Book Company), pp. 111–129.

Hunt, Earl B.
1962 *Concept Learning, an Information Processing Problem* (New York: John Wiley & Sons).

Hunt, Earl B., Janet Marin, and Philip J. Stone
1966 *Experiments in Induction* (New York: Academic Press).

Luce, R. Duncan, and Howard Raiffa
1957 *Games and Decisions: Introduction and Critical Survey* (New York: John Wiley & Sons).

Miller, George A.
1956 "The Magical Number Seven, Plus or Minus Two: Some Limits on our Capacity for Processing Information," *Psychological Review* 63 : 81–97.

Reitman, Walter R.
1965 *Cognition and Thought, an Information Processing Approach* (New York: John Wiley & Sons).

Suppes, Patrick
1957 *Introduction to Logic* (Princeton, N.J.: D. Van Nostrand Company).
1960 *Axiomatic Set Theory* (Princeton, N.J.: D. Van Nostrand Company).

Introduction

Keesing presents a further exemplification of Geoghegan's formal approach to ethnographic modeling. He uses this presentation of his original field data as a starting point for some observations on the implications of Geoghegan's approach for the general program of "ethnography as cultural grammar," enunciated for the past fifteen years or so by the new ethnographers, particularly by Ward Goodenough.

Keesing's application of the method constitutes an implicit extension of the domain of interpretation of the formalism. Whereas Geoghegan explicitly intends his formal structure to be restricted in interpretation to acts of classification within the minds of individual actors—having as outcomes acts of cognitive categorization—Keesing employs the formal structure to depict contingencies in social events leading to certain social outcomes. Keesing's use of Geoghegan's formalism is, in fact, restricted to the flow diagrams that Geoghegan has shown to be adequate for representing his (axiomatically developed) code rules. However, Keesing's applications are clearly not code rules in Geoghegan's intended interpretation but, more generally, any set of temporally or logically linked social events. This use raises some interesting mathematical problems that involve specification in purely formal terms of the types of structure that Keesing uses the flow diagrams to represent. The implicit message here, which is certainly worth the considerable effort that will be required to make it explicit, is that Geoghegan's formalism may be useful for a wider range of ethnographic and social anthropological tasks than those to whose solution it was originally addressed.

One especially interesting problem, which relates to Keesing's first four observations, is the following. We imagine a total ethnography expressed in terms of Geoghegan's code rules. In particular, we imagine that the long-recognized problem of linking or overlapping domains is solved by recoding, that is, by the fact that an assessment can itself be expressed as a code rule; in the flow-chart representation, a box in one flow chart can itself be expressed as another flow chart. A trivial example will serve as illustration.

Rule (2) is an assessment in rule (1). Let us say in such cases that rule (1) *dominates* rule (2), and let us also say that for any three distinct assessments (C_1, C_2, C_3) if C_1 dominates C_2 and C_2 dominates C_3, then C_1 dominates C_3. Consider a finite set S of code rules. We say S is a *simple sequence* only if its members can be arranged in a series $C_1, C_2, \ldots, C_n$ such that for any member C_i, there is no preceding member C_j (that is, $j < i$) such that C_j dominates C_i. Roughly, this means that a set of code rules may be arranged in a simple sequence just in case it does not contain any pair of mutually dependent assessments. We are now prepared to ask the empirical question:

2

Formalization and the Construction of Ethnographies
ROGER M. KEESING

Are ethnographies representable as simple sequences? This amounts to asking whether ethnographies are in some direct sense empirically decidable. That is, is culture in fact structured in such a way that "the empirical determination of its logical starting points" [Goodenough, W. H., 1951, *Property, Kin, and Community on Truk*, Yale University Publications in Anthropology, No. 46 (New Haven: Department of Anthropology, Yale University), pp. 11–12] is possible?

Keesing's sixth observation is also one which formally minded ethnographers may find challenging. Generally, the problem is to develop a well-defined and empirically motivated criterion of simplicity in enthnographic theory. The optimistic solver may note that the comparable problem is not solved in grammar, where the terrain is sometimes thought to be better charted.

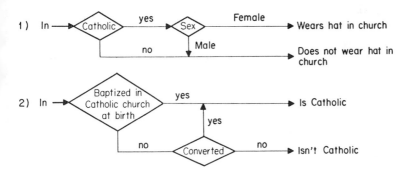

Nearly twenty years ago, Ward Goodenough boldly surveyed a path lying ahead for American anthropology (1951). In his analysis of Trukese social organization, he probed beneath the complexity of observed events to seek the underlying invariances —the principles whereby Trukese order and classify objects and events, and make decisions about appropriate social acts. His challenge, as I see it, was twofold. First, he showed how we could break small segments of a cultural code. His componential analysis of Trukese kin terms and his study of sexual distance showed strikingly how the internal order of small cultural subsystems could be laid bare by formal analysis.

A second challenge dealt with the overall structure or total architecture of an ethnography. A random collection of cultural recipes for classifying kin, transferring

Field work on Malaita, from November 1962 to November 1964 and in the summer of 1965, has been supported by the National Institutes of Health, U.S. Public Health Service. Analysis of the Kwaio data has been supported by the Social Service Research Council and by a Ford Foundation International-Comparative Grant. As in all my Kwaio research, I am indebted to my collaborator, Jonathan Fifi'i.

For useful suggestions on this paper, I am indebted to Harold Conklin, William Geoghegan, John Gilbert, Paul Kay, and Duane Metzger.

property, and residing postmaritally did not constitute a description of Trukese culture. Rather, Goodenough perceived that a large-scale ethnographic description requires a nonarbitrary ordering of subsystems, where one element must be defined in terms of another:

Characteristics by which one element of Trukese culture had to be defined were frequently other elements in the culture, which in turn required definition. . . . This experience led the writer to conclude that the empirical determination of logical starting points is a requisite for rigorous ethnographic description. (1951:11–12)

He called for "a method for isolating empirically what elements are functionally linked to a given set of initial definitions to form what may be called a structural system within the larger culture" (1951:12).

These two tasks laid out by Goodenough we might call the analysis of cultural iegments and the construction of ethnographies. American anthropology has met the first challenge with an outburst of enthusiasm. Methods for elegant analysis of domains, especially lexical ones, are being perfected, and we have been promised that they will lead to more rigorous and useful ethnographies. But the second challenge, it seems to me, has been largely ignored.[1] The proposition that the bits and pieces will cumulatively produce an adequate cultural description has not been demonstrated, and the problems of internal ordering that Goodenough perceived have not yet been squarely faced.

In this paper we will examine some problems in the internal ordering of large-scale cultural descriptions. We will suggest in particular that partial formalizations of data are useful not only in analyzing individual domains, but in linking them together into the larger structural systems glimpsed by Goodenough. We will draw for illustration on field data from the Kwaio of Malaita, British Solomon Islands (Keesing 1965, 1966b, 1967a, 1967b, 1969, 1970a, 1970b, 1970c).

We will begin by describing formally two contrasting Kwaio social categories. By then showing how this distinction operates in several domains, we will illustrate a number of points about the way domains fit together. In doing so, we will employ flow diagrams of the sort developed by William Geoghegan (Geoghegan 1970).

The two categories define degrees of social distance. To any Kwaio individual, any Alter—male or female—can be defined as *'ifi*, "closely related," or *kwaitaa*, "outsider." (*'ifi* usually denotes "dwelling house," but is frequently used to refer to Kwaio settlements, which are tiny clusters of one, two, or three households.) This classification entails two dimensions of meaning, one of genealogical distance (cf. Keesing 1967a, 1967b) and one of residential proximity. Their operation is diagramed in Figure 1. This semantic contrast could also, of course, be diagramed componentially.

This contrast between *'ifi* and *kwaitaa* is one of a set of dimensions that define rules for maintaining appropriate sexual distance. These are summarized in Table 1, in a

[1] With a few exceptions, notably work by Metzger and Williams. Anthropology research in Chiapas [the Chiapas Drinking Project and Harvard's continuing research in Zinacantan (Vogt 1965)] should provide more such useful exceptions.

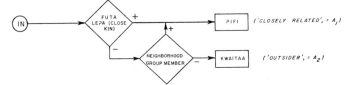

Figure 1. Distance of relationship.

Table 1. Sexual Distance Rules (Ordered on Guttman Scale).

Relationship of Male Ego to Female Alter	Scale Type	Behavioral Restrictions					
		I	II	III	IV	V	VI
ifa: *ifa geni*[a] (siblings-in-law)	1	X	X	X	X	X	X
fuŋo: *fuŋo geni* (parent–child-in-law)	2	—	X	X	X	X	X
$B_1C_{2,3}A_2$	3	—	—	X	X	X	X
$B_1C_2A_1$	4	—	—	—	X	X	X
$B_1C_3A_1$	5	—	—	—	—	X	X
B_2CA	6	—	—	—	—	—	X
B_1C_1A	7	—	—	—	- -	—	—

Restrictions	Key to Relationship
I: Male Ego subject to *suruŋa*[b]	A. Relationship of Alter to Ego
	A_1: Alter is *'ifi*
	A_2: Alter is *kwaitaa*
II: Should avoid participation in *doonŋa*, "ribald joking" with Alter	B. Sexuality
	B_1: Male Ego and female Alter sexually active
	B_2: Either male Ego or female Alter sexually
III: Cannot enter house when Alter is alone	inactive (defined in terms of maturation categories)
IV: Cannot step over Alter's legs	C. Marital Status of Female Alter
V: Cannot make *kwaisulafiŋaa*, "sexual reference," to Alter	C_1: Married to Ego
	C_2: Married to another
VI: Cannot have sexual intercourse with Alter	C_3: Not married

[a] For a formal analysis of Kwaio kin terms, see Keesing (1968).
[b] A curse a woman can use as an injunction against a real or classificatory brother-in-law, violation of which is a grave and expensive offense.

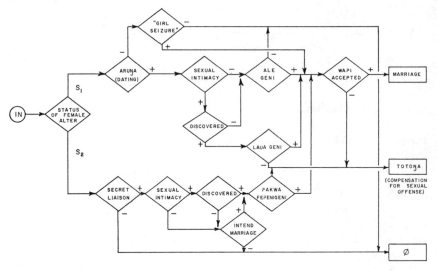

Figure 2. Sequence leading to marriage (for bachelor Ego).

Guttman scale (cf. Goodenough 1951: 117). Note that in a full ethnography we would have to include an analysis of maturation categories in order to apply dimension B at this point. (A componential analysis of maturation categories is set out in Keesing 1965.)

Another domain in which the 'ifi versus kwaitaa distinction operates is in marriage rules. In Figures 2 and 3 we map out in a flow diagram the possible sequences through which a bachelor can become married. Figure 2 shows two principal chains of events (with various permutations and alternative consequences) through which marriage can take place. Which one is followed depends on what category of girl is involved. We need not be concerned with the details of the sequences: they are set out in Keesing (1965). Here we need to note that the status of the girl (S_1 or S_2, which determines the type of affair and its possible consequences) is defined in part by the 'ifi versus kwaitaa distinction, and in part by whether the girl is sexually inexperienced or sexually experienced. This new distinction between two categories of unmarried women— laari'i, "virgins," and nao, "sexually experienced persons"—subdivides category C_3 (Table 1). Nao include widows, divorcees, and girls known publicly to have had sexual relations. This contrast between S_1 and S_2 is diagramed in Figure 3.

One of the possible outcomes of Figure 2 is a claim for totoŋa, "compensation for sexual offense." A number of other culturally possible sequences also lead to such claims—so that if we set them out in flow diagrams, totoŋa would appear as an outcome on several different diagrams. Somewhere in our ethnography, we must describe principles for deciding how much compensation can be legitimately

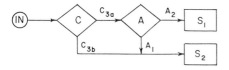

C_{3a}: laari'i, 'sexually inexperienced girl'

C_{3b}: nao, sexually experienced'

Figure 3. Status of female Alter.

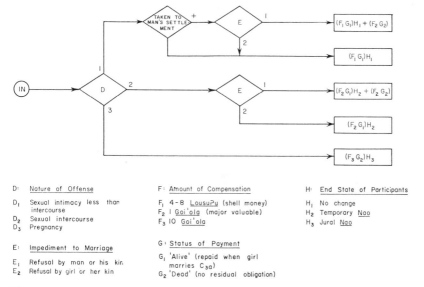

D:	Nature of Offense	F:	Amount of Compensation	H:	End State of Participants
D_1	Sexual intimacy less than intercourse	F_1	4-8 LousuꝬu (shell money)	H_1	No change
D_2	Sexual intercourse	F_2	1 Goi'ola (major valuable)	H_2	Temporary Nao
D_3	Pregnancy	F_3	10 Goi'ola	H_3	Jural Nao
		G:	Status of Payment		
E:	Impediment to Marriage	G_1	'Alive' (repaid when girl marries C_{3a})		
E_1	Refusal by man or his kin	G_2	'Dead' (no residual obligation)		
E_2	Refusal by girl or her kin				

Figure 4. Rules for *totoŋa*.

demanded, and the jural consequences of payments. These are set out here in another flow diagram, Figure 4.

Another outcome of the sequences in Figure 2 is marriage. Obviously a detailed description of principles for contracting and enacting marriages would take many pages. One of many sorts of information we must include is what sequences of gatherings and transactions take place in different kinds of marriages. Figure 5 illustrates the possible sequences, using a diagrammatic convention that makes clear our concern here with temporal, not logical, ordering. Such sequences could equally well be described algebraically or in symbolic logic. Note once more the operation of the *'ifi* versus *kwaitaa* distinction.

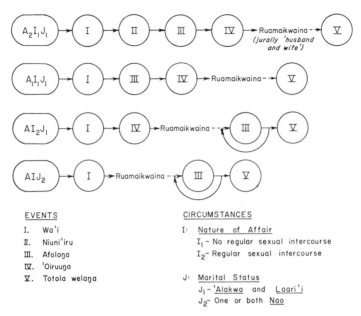

EVENTS

I.   Wa'i
II. Niuni'iru
III. Afoloŋa
IV. 'Oiruuŋa
V.   Totola welaŋa

CIRCUMSTANCES

I: Nature of Affair
I_1 – No regular sexual intercourse
I_2– Regular sexual intercourse

J: Marital Status
J_1 – 'Alakwa and Laari'i
J_2– One or both Nao

Figure 5. Event sequence in Kwaio marriage.

Let us pause now and draw some conclusions from these domains and their linkages. A first observation is that the "outputs" of one analysis frequently become "inputs," or important defining distinctions, in others. Thus, the 'ifi versus kwaitaa distinction applies to a number of domains; sexual distance rules are defined partly in terms of kinship and age categories, which we would have to define elsewhere.

A second observation is that it is often possible to construct general paradigms or models that specify the outcome of many different situations and sequences. If we use flow diagrams, this means that the outputs of a number of different diagrams can be "fed into" a single generalized model. This is illustrated by the rules for totoŋa compensation.

A third observation is that the ordering of domains is nonarbitrary. We must define categories of kinship distance (futa le'a, "closely related," versus futa laalala, "distantly related," and 'ame futa, "unrelated") before we can specify the 'ifi-kwaitaa distinction, and must define the latter, in addition to kin terms, before we can specify sexual distance rules. We must also have defined maturation categories, in terms of which "sexuality" is defined.

But a fourth observation is the warning that inevitably these domains do not string together in a simple order so that each successive element can be defined in terms of the preceding ones. Any large-scale description will have to confront seriously the problems of cross-referencing. For example, we cannot know how to classify individuals as '*ifi* and *kwaitaa* until we know what a neighborhood group is; that, however, must be described much later in the ethnography.

A fifth observation is that there is no simple, direct, and inevitable relation between the assignment to labeled social categories and principles for behaving in particular circumstances. The complexity of these relationships becomes obvious when we undertake seriously the ethnographic tasks I have illustrated. This suggests how overly simplistic many of us have been in assuming a direct relationship between kinship categories and behavior. In Kwaio culture, terms for affines turn out to be labels for social identities (Goodenough 1965), as in sexual distance rules; but terms for cognates do not. Behavioral principles for cognates turn out to depend on the *degree of kinship* distance, as in defining the '*ifi-kwaitaa* contrast, not on kinship terms (Keesing 1970a, 1970b, 1970c).

A sixth observation is that to produce a maximally economical ethnography, we cannot merely take each domain, devise the most parsimonious solution, and then put them all together. The briefest whole is not necessarily the sum of the briefest parts. The reasons for this can be simply illustrated. To do the most economical componential analysis of a domain, we might want to devise dimensions that would appear nowhere else in the ethnography. But if new ad hoc dimensions must be defined for each domain, the result can be much more complicated than use of a set of dimensions relevant in many domains. This is merely to say that in an ethnography, as in a grammar, economy is a long-run matter. Our search must be for analytical break-throughs that generalize and link domains together efficiently. Our preoccupation with little chunks of data in isolation has hampered advances here, and has led us to emphasize discovery procedures at the expense of the creativity, insight, and experimentation required to construct larger-scale ethnographies.

If we look, in these descriptive segments, at dimension C in Table 1, at its modification by subpartition in Figure 2, and finally at dimension J in Figure 5, we can perceive another aspect of the operation of dimensions in different domains. We could construct a formal paradigm of marital status that itself entails several dimensions and levels. To build a full paradigm here would require a digression beyond the scope of this paper. However, Table 2 illustrates the formal properties of such a paradigm, while introducing sufficient elements to account for the ethnographic segments we have described. Dimension C as here redefined operates in many domains, but assumes a greater number of possible values than before. Table 2 shows eight possible values on this dimension, themselves defined by the class-product intersection of distinctive features at a lower level; and in a full paradigm this would be complicated further. Describing the entire paradigm enables us to use values of C in a wide range of domains.

In Kwaio culture, the '*ifi-kwaitaa* contrast appears in several domains other than those we have discussed. For instance, the appropriate behavior when a nonresident visits a settlement falls into four paradigmatic subclasses, as indicated in Table 3, with

Table 2. A Complex Dimension of Contrast.

Dimension C—Sex–Marital Status

	Definition	Category, if Labeled
C_1	W_1	
C_2	W_2	
C_3	$W_1 X_1$	*luamaikwaina*
C_4	$W_1 X_2$	
C_5	$W_2 Y_1$	*nao*
C_6	$W_2 Y_2$	
C_7	$W_2 Y_2 Z_1$	*'alakwa*
C_8	$W_2 Y_2 Z_2$	*laali'i*
	etc.	

Subdimensions

W. General Marital Status

W_1: Married

W_2: Unmarried

X. Identity of Marriage Partner

X_1: Ego

X_2: Other

Y. Sexual Experience

Y_1: Experienced

Y_2: Inexperienced

Z. Sex (this of course a dimension that applies throughout Kwaio culture)

Z_1: Male

Z_2: Female

Table 3. Rules for Behavior in Social Identity Relationship Occupant of Settlement-Visitor to Settlement.

$A_1 K_1$ = Behavioral Rule Set 1 (Details not given)

$A_1 K_2$ = Behavioral Rule Set 2

$A_2 K_1$ = Behavioral Rule Set 3

$A_2 K_2$ = Behavioral Rule Set 4

K. Purpose of Visit

K_1: Destination

K_2: Passing Through

the *'ifi-kwaitaa* contrast providing one of the dimensions. Other distinctions that appear over and over again in Kwaio culture are "male" versus "female," "sacred" versus "secular," "patrilateral" versus "matrilateral," "live" versus "dead" (of transactions), "important" versus "unimportant," and so on.

A coded listing of these distinctions, such as we have hinted at in our notation, could contribute to long-range economy in using these distinctions of general relevance. We suggest also that formal treatment of such problems could provide a less impressionistic means of getting at symbolic oppositions than those used by Lévi-Strauss and Needham. At the same time this would help us to transcend the usual limitations of ethnoscience studies, in the direction of the broader sweep of *La Pensée sauvage*, by looking at the distribution of dimensions of meaning across different domains.

My efforts to put together Kwaio field data have turned up several other interesting problems of internal ordering. One is the way a very general principle can define, modify, or override principles for behavior in a number of contexts. For instance, the basic rule that the man is active instigator in sexual intercourse, and therefore jurally responsible, affects many domains in Kwaio culture: e.g., it operates to produce an asymmetry in the rules governing adultery.

Another very general principle defines appropriate behavior toward affines in the whole range of contexts in which persons are obligated to contribute shell valuables to their kin. Affines should contribute in the degree appropriate to the kinship position of the connecting spouse. This is diagramed, and the rule formally specified, in Keesing (1967a).

Another recurrent descriptive problem in linking domains is that some segment of behavior appears over and over again in different situations. This is true of *libaŋa*, a sacramental rite Kwaio undergo prior to many different sorts of contact with the sacred. If we can define sequences in a particular type of event in terms of formal segments, we can begin to deal effectively with the recurrence of the same segment in different strings in different parts of the ethnography.

Implied here is the problem I have raised elsewhere of finding better ways to describe *categories of situations* or contexts (Frake's "scenes" 1964; Keesing 1966a, 1970c). Having done so, we can study the distribution and interrelationships of situations, as in Figure 5 (cf. Metzger and Williams 1963; Frake 1964).

Another recurrent phenomenon is the occurrence of variant forms of a single general principle or distinction in complementary distribution in various situations. Goodenough himself noted this phenomenon with regard to Trukese property rules (1951: 64). A Kwaio example is the transaction *kwaeŋa*, "repayment for services rendered." Depending on the service and the context, repayment may be in shell money, various types of food, or services. This analytical problem recurs so often in the Kwaio data that it must be considered basic to the building of ethnographies; and we must devise economical ways to deal with it.

A related problem is the hierarchical ordering of principles for behavior in terms of levels of contrast. The social identity relationship between hosts and guests at various types of feasts is basically similar, with specific rules in complementary distribution according to the type of feast. But *some* rights and duties apply not only to host and guest at *any* feast, but in fact to the sponsor of *any type of gathering* and the persons who gather.

A further point concerns our usual emphasis on the semantics of folk taxonomies. This is one type of problem with which a larger ethnography must deal. Thus we must define a Kwaio category *osoŋa*, "feast," and then deal with the distinctive features that define each subtype of "feast" shown in Figure 6. This helps us to specify, say, the appropriate behavior of host and guest in each type of feast, and the principles entitling a person to *be* a guest. But is this all we need?

We also will want to specify what behavior is appropriate in a given set of circumstances. The antecedent conditions that lead a person to consider giving a *gumuŋa* feast in repayment for services rendered (say, for people who helped to build Ego's house) are unrelated to the circumstances that lead a person to consider giving a "mortuary feast" or a feast to repay a midwife. Decision models, using flow charts or other formal methods to show the alternatives and outcomes in a particular set of circumstances, can be effective here, as in Figure 7. Both this type of analysis and semantic analyses are required in a full cultural description; and our emphasis on folk taxonomies alone has been unfortunate.

Finally, we may make explicit a phenomenon implied in our formalizations. The diamonds on our flow diagrams indicate decisions to be made, or contingent circumstances that may or may not obtain. If they represent decisions to be made, we must somewhere else in the ethnography give principles for making them. This may require

OSOŊA, 'FEAST'

OMEA, 'MORTUARY FEAST'	TOLAŊA 'MARRIAGE FEAST'	BONI, 'WAKE'						
FONULANIWANE; FONULANIGENI; FONULANIPOIPOIŊA; ŊADAŊA; KEFE; etc. *(also categorized in at least three other contrast sets)*	AFOLOŊA; POIRUUŊA; KWAIPAIRIŊA	BONI, 'TEN-DAY WAKE'; PISILEPEBONI, 'FINAL WAKE'	GUMUŊA, 'LABOR-REWARDING FEAST'	FAŊANIMAE, 'FIRST DESACRALIZATION FEAST'	FAŊANIWANE, 'SECOND DESACRALIZATION FEAST'	FAŊANIGENI, 'FINAL DESACRALIZATION FEAST'	KWAEPOKOAPIŊA, 'MIDWIFE-REWARDING FEAST'	LALASIŊA, 'CURER-REWARDING FEAST'

Figure 6. Taxonomy of "feasts."

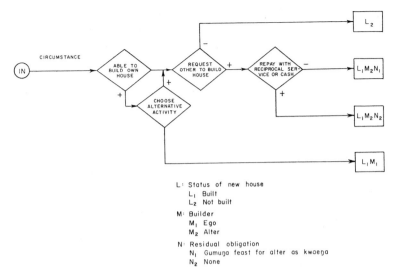

CIRCUMSTANCE

ABLE TO BUILD OWN HOUSE	
CHOOSE ALTERNATIVE ACTIVITY	
REQUEST OTHER TO BUILD HOUSE	
REPAY WITH RECIPROCAL SERVICE OR CASH	

L_2

$L_1 M_2 N_1$

$L_1 M_2 N_2$

$L_1 M_1$

L: Status of new house
   L_1 Built
   L_2 Not built
M: Builder
   M_1 Ego
   M_2 Alter
N: Residual obligation
   N_1 Gumuŋa feast for alter as kwaeŋa
   N_2 None

Figure 7. Alternatives when new house needed.

various methods of description, of which Figures 1 and 3 are illustrations. Note that this is formally similar to the operation of subroutines in computer programing. The complexity of these interlinked cultural principles, and the formidable problems of internal arrangement, emerge vividly if we attempt to account in detail for some aspect of social organization such as marriage payment or local group membership (cf. Keesing 1967a).

There seem to be two sources of the kinds of complexity we have described. One is the inherent intricacy of the cognitive ordering that must be involved in storing and manipulating cultural information. The second is imposed by the medium of ethnographic description: the serial order of the printed page. There seems no reason to assume that cognitive coding entails a similar linear constraint. This distinction could well be borne in mind as the "psychological reality" of structural descriptions is debated.

It should be emphasized that there are not neat "rules," amenable to formal description, that govern every possible decision and alternative. In many cases we we must deal discursively with alternative possibilities and strategies. At times, it will prove possible to assign statistical probabilities to various outcomes, though no "mechanical model" can be devised to specify the outcome in each possible set of circumstances.

We do not imply, then, that all of an ethnography can be reduced to formal "rules," semantic or behavioral; though we do believe that this could now be carried much further than has yet been demonstrated. Nor need we assume that a single set of decision-making principles or strategies is used by all actors in a society: the notions of cultural codes and their formal description need not imply uniformity. The point of such cultural description is not to reduce the richness and variability of human behavior to a set of "dehumanized" computer programs. Rather it is to discover, beneath that richness and variability, the invariances that make communication possible—the elements and structure of cultural codes. Kwaio cannot totally predict each other's actions; but they seldom surprise one another very much. We should, on principle, be able to replicate their expectations.

One reason human behavior is variable and not totally predictable is that cultural rules apply to "pure situations"—contexts of "pure kinship" or "pure litigation," etc. Actual behavioral situations are often mixed or ambiguous, so that two or more sets of cultural principles—often conflicting—can be applied. Another reason is that even where "rules" governing a situation are unambiguous, they seldom specify exact details of appropriate behavior. A Kwaio example will be instructive here. In *totoŋa* claims (see Figure 4) where ten *goi'ola* is the appropriate fine, this specifies the *number* of multiple-stringed valuables but not their denomination. This is determined through haggling, based on the details of the offense and the strength of the kin groups involved. In one recent case (recorded by my Kwaio field assistant after my return from the field, and thus a useful test of ethnographic theory), the guilty man's kin group was rather poor and weak, and could accumulate only seven *goi'ola* for the fine. The solution—to preserve appropriateness of form—was to divide one of the seven into four single-stringed pieces, so as to reach a total of ten.

The problems of internal ordering we have described apply to all segments of a cultural description, whether formalized or discursive. But where formalization has proven possible, it has brought these problems vividly to light and has offered hope of economically and systematically dealing with them. Putting segments together in effective fashion requires explicit and systematic description of each segment and its component elements.

I believe our attention to simple little domains one at a time has made the building of ethnographies look deceptively simple. But worse than that, it has prevented our examining systematically the problems entailed in linking domains together. Goodenough's second challenge still confronts us, and I feel we must meet it as squarely as we have met the first. My experience with the Kwaio data suggests that various sorts of formalization, notably flow diagrams, can help us immeasurably in systematically linking together the elements of a culture.

References
Frake, C. O.
1964 "A Structural Description of Subanun 'Religious Behavior,'" in *Explorations in Cultural Anthropology*, Ward H. Goodenough, ed. (New York: McGraw-Hill Book Company).

Geoghegan, W.
1970 "Information Processing Systems in Culture," in this volume, Chapter 10.

Goodenough, W. H.
1951 *Property, Kin, and Community on Truk*, Yale University Publications in Anthropology, No. 46 (New Haven: Department of Anthropology, Yale University).
1965 "Rethinking 'Status' and 'Role': Toward a General Model of the Cultural Organization of Social Relationships," in *The Relevance of Models for Social Anthropology*, M. Banton, ed. ASA Monographs 1, pp. 1–22.

Keesing, R. M.
1965 "Kwaio Marriage and Society," unpublished Ph.D. dissertation, Harvard University.
1966a Comment on B. H. Colby, "Ethnographic Semantics," *Current Anthropology* 7 : 3.
1966b "Kwaio Kindreds," *Southwestern Journal of Anthropology* 22 : 346–353.
1967a "Statistical and Decision Models of Social Structure: A Kwaio Case," *Ethnology* 6 : 1–16.
1967b "Christians and Pagans in Kwaio, Malaita," *Journal of the Polynesian Society* 76 : 82–100.
1969 "Kwaio Word Tabooing in its Cultural Context," *Journal of the Polynesian Society* (in press).
1970a "Shrines, Ancestors, and Cognatic Descent on Malaita," *American Anthropologist* (in press).
1970b "Kwaio Fosterage," *American Anthropologist* (in press).
1970c "Toward a Model of Role Analysis," in *A Handbook of Methods in Social Anthropology*, R. Cohen and R. Naroll, eds., Natural History Press, New York (in press).

Metzger, D., and G. Williams
1963 "A Formal Ethnographic Analysis of Tenejapa Ladino Weddings," *American Anthropologist* 65 : 1076–1101.

Vogt, E. Z.
1965 "Structural and Conceptual Replication in Zinacantan Culture," *American Anthropologist* 67 : 342–353.

Introduction

Boyd takes up Burling's (Burling, Robbin, 1964, "Cognition and Componential Analysis: God's Truth or Hocus Pocus?," *American Anthropologist* **66:20–28) challenge to furnish a formal criterion for choosing between alternative componential analyses. In order to establish this criterion he first develops a formal definition of dependence/independence between components. The major mathematical machinery employed involves a component's partitioning a set with operators in such a way that the partition possesses the substitution property.**

Having achieved a formal definition of pairwise dependence/independence between components, Boyd proposes a two-stage criterion for evaluating a componential analysis. First, an analysis is considered a solution only if the components form a partial order with respect to dependency. This is equivalent to saying that there are no mutual dependencies between components. Second, given two or more solutions to a componential analysis problem, that solution is preferred which has the smallest number of pairwise dependencies between components. The ideal solution, then, is one in which each component is independent of the other.

As Boyd points out, the formal solution he proposes to the problem of evaluating alternative componential analysis depends on the operators employed. He also cautions that the formal criterion proposed is not supposed to be a substitute for experimental validation of "psychological reality" but rather a stimulus and guide to such validation. These two suggestions together imply that one useful direction for further research might involve choosing a componential analysis on the combined grounds of linguistic motivation and psychological validation (via sorting tasks, etc.) and then searching for behavioral operators (e.g., "exercises authority over") which produce a high evaluation for the componential solution.

In any case, no future work in componential analysis should be undertaken without attention being paid to Boyd's approach to evaluation.

Several Australian marriage-class systems are discussed as well as the alternative analysis for American kinship of Wallace and Atkins (Wallace, A. F. C., and J. Atkins, 1960, "The Meaning of Kinship Terms," *American Anthropologist* **62:58–80) and of Romney and D'Andrade [Romney, A. K., and R. G. D'Andrade, 1964, "Cognitive Aspects of English Kin Terms," in** *Transcultural Studies in Cognition,* **A. K. Romney and R. G. D'Andrade (eds.),** *American Anthropologist* **66, No. 3, Pt. 2].**

This paper will try to answer Burling's challenge presented in his article "Componential Analysis: God's Truth or Hocus Pocus?" (1964). In this article, Burling correctly points out that the people doing componential analysis have given no

3
Componential Analysis and the Substitution Property
JOHN PAUL BOYD

formal criteria for distinguishing among the many possible ways of representing a set as the Cartesian product of smaller sets. The criterion suggested here is a fundamental concept in modern algebra and has proved useful in practical applications in physics and mathematical machine theory (automata theory). The point of this paper lies in the following principle: components should be as independent of each other as possible. The criterion for independence is the substitution property, which will be explained and illustrated below.

The formal objects to be studied are called *sets with operators*. A set E with operators Ω can be represented by means of a labeled directed graph with the property that from each point is defined at most one arrow with a given label from Ω. For example, the Kariera marriage class system has the following graph as

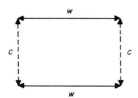

where the points represent marriage classes and the solid arrows labeled w represent the relation between a man and his wife. That is, an arrow of this kind between two classes means that men of the first class marry women in the second class. Similarly, the dotted arrows labeled c represent the relation of a man to his children. This notation follows White (1963).

Suppose we give the Kariera classes the following Cartesian representation, i.e., the componential analysis as illustrated by drawing (a). Notice that the components are *independent* of each other in the sense that we can operate on a point $F_i M_j$ with either c or w and find the value of, say, the F component of $(F_i M_j)c$ or $(F_i M_j)w$ without knowing M_j. This can be done since the F component is always the same for M_0 and M_1. For example, since $(F_0 M_0)w = F_1 M_1$ and $(F_0 M_1)w = F_1 M_0$, we know as soon as we see the F_0 and the w that the answer will have F_1 as its first value. The reader is advised to verify on the graph above that $(F_1 M_j)w$ has F_0 as its first coordinate for $j = 0,1$. Next check that F is independent of M under the c operation. Thus F is said to be independent of M under c and w. Similar remarks apply interchanging F and M, so that it is now verified that both components are independent of each other. This is clearly a desirable state of affairs. The next task is to show how to find componential analyses with independent components.

Now, if we forget about the M component, a partition is formed on the set E of points of the above graph. Recall that a partition of a set E is a collection of subsets of E, which we may call *blocks*, such that every point in E is a member of one and only one block. This partition, denoted by E/F, is formed by lumping together into one block those points that agree on F. Thus, if we circle the points that belong to the same block of E/F, the graph (a) looks as illustrated by graph (b):

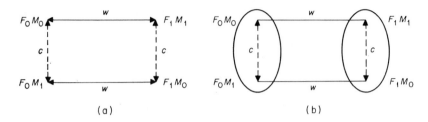

(a) (b)

We can now explain the notion of the substitution property that some partitions possess. If B is a block of a partition and α is an operator in Ω, then $B\alpha$ denotes the image of B under α, and $B\alpha$ is simply the set of points that can be reached from points in B by arrows labeled α. A partition has the *substitution property* if the image $B\alpha$ of every block B is a subset of some block B' for every operator α. In symbols, we must have $B\alpha \subseteq B'$. The above partition has the substitution property since w sends each block into the other and c sends each block into itself.

The fundamental importance of partitions with the substitution property lies in the fact that a new set with operators called the *quotient system* can be formed from the old *using the blocks of the partition as points*. Recalling that $B\alpha$ is the image of B under α, we wish to define $B^*\alpha$, the block of the partition that contains all the points in $B\alpha$. If B is a block, then the definition of $B^*\alpha$ in the quotient system is obvious and natural: $B^*\alpha = B'$ if and only if B' is a block and there exists an x in B such that $x\alpha$ is in B'. The substitution property ensures that this definition makes sense: that is, if $B^*\alpha$ is defined, then it is uniquely determined, so that the quotient system is again a set with operators. In the Kariera example, the quotient system E/F is shown in drawing (c). A quotient system in general is an algebraic approximation of the original system and gives partial information as to the structure of E.

Now, suppose we examine the quotient structure E/M formed by ignoring the F component. The induced partition is indicated as in drawing (d), and since it has the substitution property, the quotient can be formed as shown in drawing (e). Obviously E/F and E/M are patrilineal and matrilineal moiety systems.

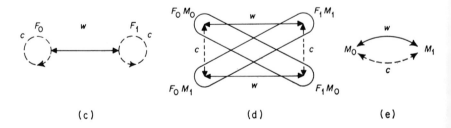

(c) (d) (e)

Incidentally, both E/F and E/M are examples of what sociologists call structural balance. A labeled digraph with two kinds of lines is said to be in *balance* if its points can be partitioned into two subsets such that lines between subsets are all of one kind and lines within subsets are all of the other kind. Since this theory originated from certain psychological notions of Heider (1946), the "within" lines are called "positive" and the "between" lines, "negative." But in the case of E/F, "within" lines are best interpreted as a "patrilineal line of descent," whereas the "between" lines represent the "marriage bond." That is, marriage is a negative relationship. Sociologists, however, deal with relatively unstructured phenomena, so they have had difficulty in finding real-life examples of structural balance, much less examples of simultaneous balance along two components, as in the Kariera case. Marriage class systems can be described by generalizations of the concept of structural balance.

It must be noted that the results of applying our principle are a little disappointing in the Kariera case. As one can easily verify, there are two other codings, or componential analyses, that are possible which involve a "generational" component. The generational quotient is formed by the partition shown by drawing (f) on E with the substitution property.

A further difficulty with the requirement that *all* components induce partitions with the substitution property is that it is impossible to make a componential analysis with this property in many interesting cases. For instance, the Ambrym marriage class system (Lane and Lane 1958), represented by drawing (g), has only the one nontrivial partition with the substitution property, but it is impossible to analyze into two or more components each having the substitution property since each new component induces a distinct partition. The solution to the problem is simply to accept the fact that not all components can be made independent of one another.

In order to define the notion of dependency between components, we first consider partitions induced by sets of components. We recall that given a set E and components $C_1, C_2, \ldots, C_n$, we say that the partition E/C_i induced by a component C_i is the finest partition such that, for each block B in E/C_i, every member of B agrees on C_i. We now define for any set of distinct components $C_{i_1}, C_{i_2}, \ldots, C_{i_k}$ the partition induced by C_{i_1} and C_{i_2} and $\cdots$ and C_{i_k}: $E/C_{i_1} C_{i_2} \cdots C_{i_k}$ is the smallest partition such that, for

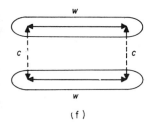

(f)

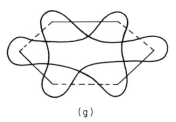

(g)

each block B in $E/C_{i_1} C_{i_2} \cdots C_{i_k}$, every member of B agrees on C_{i_1} and C_{i_2} and $\cdots$ and C_{i_k}.

Equipped with the notion of a partition induced by an arbitrary set of components, we define pairwise dependency between components as follows. Component Y *depends* upon component X if every set of components that includes Y and induces a partition with the substitution property must also include X. In the simple case of just two components, Y depends on X if and only if the partition E/Y does not have the substitution property.

We want as few pairs of components depending on each other as possible. In fact, this is the basis of the formal definition promised in the opening paragraph of the criterion for evaluating alternative componential solutions. It is also reasonable to require for purposes of a componential solution that the dependency relation be antisymmetric. That is, if X and Y are two different components and if Y depends on X, if we decree that X cannot depend on Y then the dependency operation becomes a partial ordering of the components, since dependency is easily seen to be reflexive and transitive. A componential analysis in which the dependency relation is a partial ordering is called a *loop-free* analysis since there are no dependency "loops" or cycles where X depends on Y and Y depends on X. If a componential analysis is loop-free we say it is a componential *solution*. A componential solution is preferable to a componential analysis that is not a solution. Given two or more solutions for a given corpus of data, the most highly valued is the one with the fewest pairwise dependencies between components.

The illustrated solution is given below for the Ambrym, where the T component depends upon M. E/T does not have the substitution property since, for example, $M_0 T_0$ and $M_1 T_0$ are in the same block of E/T but $(M_0 T_0)w = M_1 T_1$ and $(M_1 T_0)w = M_0 T_2$ are in different blocks of E/T because $T_1 \neq T_2$. On the other hand, the partition E/M does have the substitution property, so we can define the quotient system E/M, which is again the matrilineal moiety system. This suggests that the Ambrym system evolved from a system of matrilineal moieties. This interpretation is suggested also by the fact that the Ambrym have names for the matrilineal moieties and that these names are the same as those in the matrilineal areas to the north of Ambrym. (Obviously E/MT has the substitution property vacuously, since this partition assigns a distinct block to each point.)

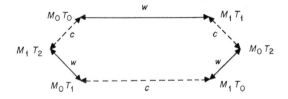

Table 1. Analysis by Wallace and Atkins (1960) of English (Yankee) kinship system. Linearity depends upon generation, but the other component pairs are independent. The values "l," "a," and "c" on the linearity component indicate "lineal," "ablineal," and "colineal," respectively.

Sex	Generation	Linearity	English kin terms
♂	+2	l	GF
♂	+2	a	U
♂	+2	c	Co
♂	+1	l	F
♂	+1	a	U
♂	+1	c	Co
♂	0	l	EGO
♂	0	a	B
♂	0	c	Co
♂	−1	l	S
♂	−1	a	Ne
♂	−1	c	Co
♂	−2	l	GS
♂	−2	a	Ne
♂	−2	c	Co
♀	+2	l	GM
.	.	.	.
.	.	.	.
.	.	.	.
etc.			

Another example of a componential solution is the componential analysis given by Wallace and Atkins (1960) of English. The three components they use are sex, generation, and linearity (see Tables 1, 2, and 3). It happens that their analysis has the substitution property for all components except that linearity depends upon generation. The reason that linearity is said to depend upon generation is that E/L does not have the substitution property but E/LG does, where L and G are the linearity and generational components, respectively, and where E/LG is the partition induced by putting points in the same block if they agree on the L *and* G components (Figures 1, 2, and 3).

Romney and D'Andrade (1964) also did a componential analysis of English, as shown in Table 4. This analysis has highly dependent components. For example, not one of the three partitions induced by lumping together terms that agree on

Table 2. **Graph of Wallace and Atkins, (1964) analysis of the Yankee kinship system restricted to males only. Arrows pointing up represent the "father" operator; horizontal arrows, the "brother" operator; and arrows pointing down (either horizontal or diagonal), the "son" operator.**

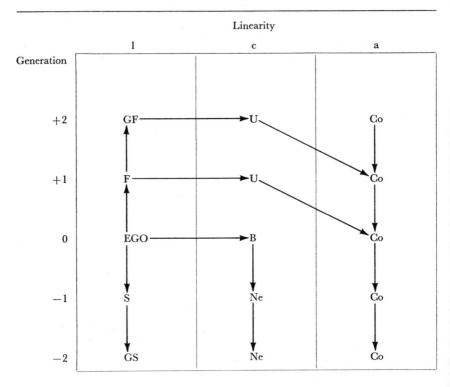

"linearity," "generation," or "distance" has the substitution property. E/linearity fails to have the substitution property because B and S agree on linearity (they are both "D" for "direct") but their respective sons disagree on this component: B's son = Ne is C (for "collateral") but S's son = GS is D again. Similarly, E/generation fails because while B and Co both occur on generation zero, their sons are in generation "$-$" and generation "0," respectively. Finally, E/distance fails because of B and Co again; this assumes that a cousin's son is a cousin.

It should be noted that with a different set of operators a different set of componential analyses would be favored. Since adding new operators can only destroy the substitution property, this means that to choose between two different componential analyses that both satisfy the criterion of independence of coordinates, new operators must be introduced. This is just saying that new empirical data must be sought.

Table 3. Graph of the quotient system E/G of the graph of Figure 2, formed by lumping terms that agree on generation. Again, females are excluded. The loops represent the "brother" operator.

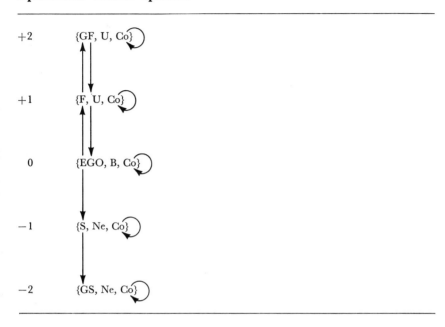

+2	{GF, U, Co}
+1	{F, U, Co}
0	{EGO, B, Co}
−1	{S, Ne, Co}
−2	{GS, Ne, Co}

Table 4. Romney and D'Andrade (1964) analysis of English (Yankee) kinship system.

Sex	Linearity	Generation	Distance	English kin term
♂	D	+	2	GF
♂	D	+	1	F
♂	D	0	0	B
♂	D	−	1	S
♂	D	−	2	GS
♂	C	+	2	U
♂	C	+	1	U
♂	C	0	0	Co
♂	C	−	1	Ne
♂	C	−	2	Ne
♀	D	+	2	GM
.	.	.	.	.
. etc.				

The next question is how does one choose a "good" set of operators. The operators chosen in this paper, such as "son of," "brother of," etc., were chosen merely because they are obvious and convenient; they can be read from kinship diagrams. Romney and D'Andrade (1964) have used other operators such as "can be modified by the word 'step.'" Their analysis does well with respect to the set of operators that they chose. The only comment on this problem that comes to mind is a lame exhortation for the use of as many "important" operators as possible.

It should be noted again that not all ambiguity is resolved using the criterion suggested here. In addition, the restriction to sets with operators excludes the "non-deterministic" type of labeled graph where there is more than one arrow of a given type from some points. Extending the analysis to cover this case can be shown to be equivalent to the problem of defining homomorphisms on relational systems, and this theory is still in the process of development (Thatcher 1964). Finally, it should be noted that the type of criterion suggested here is not intended to replace empirical tests as to the psychological reality of a given componential analysis. Rather, it is hoped that this criterion will inspire and direct such tests.

References

Burling, Robbins
1964 "Cognition and Componential Analysis: God's Truth or Hocus-Pocus?," *American Anthropologist* 66:20–28.

Heider, F.
1946 "Attitudes and Cognitive Organization," *Journal of Psychology* 21:107–112.

Lane, R. B., and B. S. Lane
1958 "A Reinterpretation of the 'Anamalous' Six Section Marriage System of Ambrym, New Hebrides," *Southwestern Journal of Anthropology* 12:406–416.

Romney, A. Kimball, and Roy Goodwin D'Andrade
1964 "Cognitive Aspects of English Kin Terms," *American Anthropologist* 66, No. 3, Pt. 2:146–170.

Thatcher, James W.
1964 "Homorphisms for Relational Systems," IBM Research Note NC-369, Thomas J. Watson Research Center, Yorktown Heights.

Wallace, Anthony F. C., and John Atkins
1960 "The Meaning of Kinship Terms," *American Anthropologist* 62:58–80.

White, Harrison
1963 *An Anatomy of Kinship* (Englewood Cliffs, N.J.: Prentice-Hall).

ADDITIONAL READING BIBLIOGRAPHY

Bourbaki, N.
1964 *Eléménts de Mathématique*, Vol. II, *Algèbre*, Chap. I, "Structures Algébriques," Deuxiéme Edition (Paris: Hermann et Cie), p. 1144.

Goodenough, Ward H.
1956 "Componential Analysis and the Study of Meaning," *Language*, 32:195–216.

Harary, Frank
1953 "On the Notion of Balance of a Signed Graph," *Michigan Mathematical Journal* 2:143–146.

Harrison, Michael A.
1965 *Introduction to Switching and Automata Theory* (New York: McGraw-Hill Book Company).

Lane, B. S., and R. B. Lane
1962 "Implicit Double Descent in South Australia and the North-Eastern New Hebrides," *Ethnology* 1:46–52.

Introduction

D'Andrade presents a model that predicts cultural features (semantic distinctions in kin terms) from social forces (descent and residence practices) via a mathematically explicit psychological theory of concept formation (stimulus sampling theory).

The approach is in the style of Murdock's classic treatise, with two important innovations. First, D'Andrade capitalizes on zero or non-zero table frequencies and interprets these as phenomena requiring explanation in themselves. This approach to tables—which might be phrased, "Look first for what never occurs and worry later about the relative frequencies of events that do occur"—is a useful one. It enables D'Andrade to derive theoretical propositions which then become part of the model used to predict the relative frequencies in the nonzero cells. In particular, D'Andrade notes that almost never does a semantic distinction occur in a language's cousin terms and not in its uncle terms. From this, it follows that a language not possessing a distinction must gain it, if at all, in its uncle terms before its cousin terms, and similarly that a language possessing a distinction in both uncle and cousin terms must lose it, if at all, in the cousin terms first. These propositions become part of the model used to predict accurately the proportions of uncle and cousin terminologies of various types cooccurring with various residence and descent practices.

The second innovation in studies of this type is that an explicit (stochastic) psychological model is employed which permits calculation of numerical distributions rather than mere statements of associational tendency.

D'Andrade's postscript, which indicates that his choice of the particular psychological model might now be different, does not vitiate the general methodology.

This paper presents an attempt to construct formal procedures for predicting certain aspects of kinship terminologies from features of social organization. Rather than listing a large number of associations between different features of social organization and types of kinship terminologies, this procedure operates directly on combinations of residence and descent categories to predict both uncle and cousin terms. In order to accomplish this, first a set of simple distinctions is defined which describes aspects of both kinship terminologies and social organization. A formula is then developed which, using these distinctions, generates with some accuracy distributions of types of kinship terminologies for combinations of features of social organization.

The usage for the term "formal" just given follows Lounsbury:

We may consider that a "formal account" of a collection of empirical data has been given when there have been specified (1) a set of primitive elements, and (2) a set of rules for operating on these, such that by application of the latter to the former, the

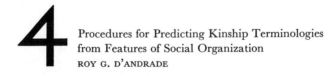

Procedures for Predicting Kinship Terminologies
from Features of Social Organization
ROY G. D'ANDRADE

elements of a "model" are generated; which model in turn comes satisfactorily close to being a facsimile or exact replica of the empirical data whose interrelatedness and systematic nature we are trying to understand (Lounsbury 1964:351).

The results of this attempt to construct formal procedures for predicting aspects of kinship terminologies add little new information to what is already known about how kin terms are associated with aspects of social organization (Murdock 1949). However, this procedure perhaps facilitates an understanding of how a number of social factors simultaneously affect terminological systems, and also reduces considerably the amount it is necessary for a person to remember in order to make such predictions. Other advantages of this procedure will be discussed in the concluding section of this paper.

The empirical data that have been used in this paper are taken from Murdock's World Ethnographic Atlas (1962). Not all of the 564 societies presented in the World Ethnographic Atlas have been used. No more than 8 societies were selected from each of the 60 different culture areas, and when "no information" was listed for any of the categories of social organization or kinship terminology, that society was also dropped from the sample.

The first step in constructing our predictive procedures is to discover how the various types of uncle terminology are related to types of cousin terminology. Unfortunately, Murdock lists a larger number of types of cousin terminology than it proves practical to utilize; for this reason societies with any one of five unusual types of cousin terminology have been dropped from the sample. However, these five unusual types accounted for a total of only seven societies.

Table 1 gives the association found between uncle and cousin terms for 339 societies. Murgin cousin terminology has been merged with Iroquois (five cases), and equivocal Eskimo cousin terminology has been merged with Eskimo (nine cases).

For each type of uncle and cousin terminology, a small kin-type chart has been drawn to clarify its definition when necessary.

The large number of zero or near-zero cells in Table 1 appears to indicate that a set of systematic relations may obtain between uncle and cousin terms. These relations can be shown more clearly by treating each type of uncle and cousin terminology as a product of the two distinctions that have been labeled lineal and cross on Table 1. The lineal distinction refers to the partitioning of kin types that contain at least one sibling link. For uncle terms, the lineal distinction distinguishes father and mother from their siblings, while for cousin terms the lineal distinction distinguishes the offspring of mother and father (i.e., brothers and sisters) from the offspring of the siblings of mother and father (i.e., father's brother's children, mother's brother's children, mother's sister's children, and father's sister's children).

The *cross* distinction refers to the partitioning of siblings of same sex (and their offspring) from the siblings of opposite sex (and their offspring). For uncle terms the cross distinction distinguishes father and father's brother from mother's brother (who

Table 1. Uncle and Cousin Terminologies from the World Ethnographic Sample

Cousin Terms	Uncle terms					(Total)	Graphic Definitions	Distinctions Cross	Distinctions Lineal
	Descriptive and Bifurcate Collateral	Bifurcate Merging	Derivative Bifurcate Merging	Lineal	Generational				
Descriptive	19	2	7	0	1	(29)		+	+
Crow	3	18	4	0	0	(25)		+	(−)
Omaha	6	16	8	0	0	(30)		+	(−)
Iroquois	33	34	24	0	0	(91)		+	−
Eskimo	18	0	2	36	1	(57)		−	+
Hawaiian	22	30	10	25	20	(107)		−	−
(Total)	(101)	(100)	(55)	(61)	(22)	(339)			
Graphic Definitions									
Distinctions Cross	+	+	+	−	−				
Distinctions Lineal	+	−	(+)	+	−				

Table 2. Relation between Uncle Terms and Cousin Terms for Cross Distinction.

	Uncle Terms	
Cousin Terms	Cross Distinction Made	Cross Distinction Not Made
Cross Distinction Made	174	1
Cross Distinction Not Made	82	82

is a cross-sex sibling of one of one's parents). For cousin terms the cross distinction distinguishes the offspring of mother's brother and father's sister from the offspring of mother's sister and father's brother.

If a society makes the lineal distinction in uncle terms, this means that parents will be terminologically differentiated from their siblings. These siblings may or may not be merged; if the society also makes the cross distinction, then father's brother is distinguished from mother's brother, and the system is described as *bifurcate collateral*; but if the society does not also make the cross distinction, then father's brother is terminologically merged with mother's brother, and the system is described as having *lineal uncle* terms. Thus a society may make use, as it were, of either or both of these types of distinctions, and the possible combinations of these two types of distinctions produce four logical types of uncle terminology, and four logical types of cousin terminology. Added distinctions or merging principles are needed to produce Crow, Omaha, and Murgin cousin terminology, and partial differentiation of the lineal distinction produces *derivative bifurcate merging* terminology, in which father's brother is called by a derivative of the term for father; for example, "little father."

The lineal and cross distinctions have been described at length because they are basic to the construction of further procedures. If we consider the relation between cousin and uncle terms according to these distinctions, certain effects become apparent.

Table 3. Relation between Uncle Terms and Cousin Terms for Lineal Distinction.

	Uncle Terms	
Cousin Terms	Lineal Distinction Made	Lineal Distinction Not Made
Lineal Distinction Made	82	4
Lineal Distinction Not Made	135	118

Table 2 presents the relation between uncle terms and cousin terms for the cross distinction, and Table 3 for the lineal distinction.

These tables indicate that, with very few exceptions, if a distinction is made for cousin terms, it will also be made for uncle terms. Also, if a distinction is not made for uncle terms, it will not be made for cousin terms. In a notational form, this state of affairs can be represented by saying that for any distinction D, in which the presence or absence of D for uncle terms is symbolized by a d or $\bar{d}$ in the initial position, and the presence or absence of D for cousin terms is symbolized by d or $\bar{d}$ in the final position, that the possible combinations of these symbols for uncle and cousin terms are dd, $d\bar{d}$, $\bar{d}d$, and $\bar{d}\bar{d}$. The combination $\bar{d}d$ rarely occurs, i.e., five times in 678 cases, or less than 1 percent of the time.

Assuming that changes in both uncle and cousin terms do not happen simultaneously, then it follows that

1. Given a system with some distinction completely absent, any change in the system for this distinction will first affect the uncle terms.

2. Once a distinction exists in the uncle terms, it may spread to the cousin terms, or it may disappear again out of the system.

3. Given a system with some distinction present in both uncle and cousin terms, any change in the system for this distinction will first affect the cousin terms.

Thus, the changes in a system which would result from continued application of a force that acts to create a distinction absent in the uncle and cousin terms may be graphed as shown in Figure 1. Changes in a system which would result from continued application of a force that acts to eliminate a distinction present in uncle and cousin terms may be graphed as in Figure 2.

Let us assume that in any society there are many sets of forces acting to create any distinction in the kin-term system, and also forces acting to eliminate any distinction. Typically these forces are not in balance, so that either the distinction is made or it is not made. These forces may be imagined to be composed of sets of stimuli which either are similar across kin-types partitioned by the distinction in question (and thereby through the mechanism of generalization tend to eliminate the distinction),

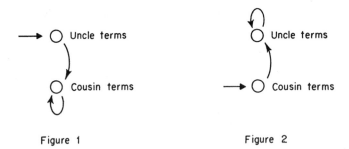

Figure 1   Figure 2

or are dissimilar across kin types partitioned by the relevant distinction (and through the psychological mechanism of discrimination tend to create the distinction) (Murdock 1949).

Further, let us assume that the distinctions that are present in any kin-term system are not the results of an averaging of these forces or sets of stimuli, since then only rarely would any distinction be either completely absent or completely present in any society. Instead, let us assume that each society becomes conditioned, with respect to any distinction, to only one set of stimuli out of the numerous sets that are actually present, and that this set is selected by a random sampling of those sets that are present. [See Atkinson, Bower, and Crothers (1965: Chap. 2) for a presentation of stimulus sampling theory with respect to concept learning.]

A society that has an equal number of sets of stimuli, or forces, acting both to create a distinction D and to eliminate that distinction D may be represented in a notational form as having (1 Sd: 1 $S\tilde{d}$), in which the S stands for a set of stimuli, and the d or $\tilde{d}$ for the effect of that set of stimuli as tending to create D (d) or eliminate $D(\tilde{d})$. A society that has twice as many forces or sets of stimuli making for a distinction as those acting to eliminate the distinction D may be represented as (2 Sd: 1 $S\tilde{d}$).

Suppose 99 societies, one-third of which has uncle and cousin terms of the form dd, one-third with uncle and cousin terms of the form $d\tilde{d}$, and the final third with uncle and cousin terms of the $\tilde{d}\tilde{d}$, were subjected uniformly to a condition in which there were twice as many forces acting to create some distinction as to eliminate it, i.e., (2 Sd: 1 $S\tilde{d}$). Since conditioning to each set of stimuli is random, there is twice as much chance that any given society will be affected by the Sd condition as the $S\tilde{d}$ condition. The results of such stimulus sampling on the 99 societies may be displayed in a simple matrix.

Original Number of Types of Uncle and Cousin Terminology	Stimulus Conditions		Outcome
	2 Sd	1 $S\tilde{d}$	
33 dd	22 dd	11 $d\tilde{d}$ ⎫	⎛ 44 dd
33 $d\tilde{d}$	22 dd	11 $\tilde{d}\tilde{d}$ ⎬	⎨ 33 $d\tilde{d}$
33 $\tilde{d}\tilde{d}$	22 $d\tilde{d}$	11 $\tilde{d}\tilde{d}$ ⎭	⎝ 22 $\tilde{d}\tilde{d}$

The outcome of 44 dd to 33 $d\tilde{d}$ to 22 $\tilde{d}\tilde{d}$ does not represent a stable situation, however, since if the social and cultural conditions remain the same, and the random sampling process continues, the 2:1 proportion of forces will continue to change the numbers for each type of system. The probable outcomes can again be represented by a simple matrix.

Second-Step Number of Types of Uncle and Cousin Terminology	Stimulus Conditions		
	2 Sd	:	1Sd̃
44 dd	29 dd[a]	15 dd̃ ⎞	⎛ 51 dd
33 dd̃	22 dd	11 d̃d̃ ⎬	⎨ 30 dd̃
22 d̃d̃	15 dd	7 d̃d̃ ⎠	⎝ 18 d̃d̃

[a] Figures rounded to nearest whole numbers

The outcome of 51 dd to 30 dd̃ to 18 d̃d̃ societies still does not represent a stable outcome. A third multiplication, using the same procedures, would result in 54 dd to 29 dd̃ to 16 d̃d̃. Thus, as the social and cultural conditions remain unchanged, stimulus conditions will continue to affect the number of types of kin-term systems until an equilibrium point is reached.

The equilibrium point for any proportion of Sd : Sd̃ conditions may be determined by the formula $p^2(dd):pq(dd̃):q^2(d̃d̃)$, in which p and q are the proportional figures for Sd and Sd̃. In the case above, in which the proportions are 2 Sd : 1 Sd̃, the equilibrium point is 4 dd : 2 dd̃ : 1 d̃d̃; or for 99 societies, the frequencies of 56.3 dd to 28.3 dd̃ to 14.1 d̃d̃. Given enough time, this equilibrium point will be reached no matter what the original frequencies of types of kin terms. In fact, any set of frequencies approach equilibrium rather rapidly; for example, it takes only five repeated multiplications of the 2 Sd : 1 Sd̃ stimulus conditions for a sample of societies beginning with only the d̃d̃ condition present to reach a close approximation of the 4 dd : 2 dd̃ : 1 d̃d̃ equilibrium point, i.e., (3.6 : 2 : 1).

In order to use this formula to predict kinship terminology, it is necessary to assign Sd values to various features of social organization. For this paper only residence and descent will be considered as features of social organization, although in theory any number of social variables may be used. Values for the lineal and cross distinctions for each type of residence and descent category are presented.

	Lineal	Cross
Bilateral Descent	1 Sl,	1 Sx̃
Patrilineal Descent	½ Sl̃,	1 Sx
Matrilineal Descent	1 Sl̃,	1 Sx
Neolocal Residence	1 Sl,	1 Sx̃
Bilocal Residence	1 Sl̃,	1 Sx̃
Patrilocal Residence	½ Sl̃,	1 Sx
Matrilocal Residence	1 Sl̃,	1 Sx
Avunculocal Residence	1 Sl̃,	1 Sx

The negative half-weight given to patrilineal descent and patrilocal residence with respect to the lineal distinction is based on the notion that "brothers can more easily be the foci for the process of segmentation in patrilineal descent groups than can either brothers or sisters in a matrilineal descent group" (Schneider 1961). The reasons for this are somewhat complex, but in the main related to the fact that authority is vested in males, so that a man and his wife can split away from a patrilineal descent group (or patrilocal residential group) without involving persons other than the wife, whereas in a matrilineal society, a man must bring his sister, and perhaps her spouse, in order to start a new matrilineal segment, making such fission more complex and difficult. Similarly, for fission of a matrilocal residential group to occur, it would be unlikely for a daughter without authority to found her own new residential group; rather it would be more likely that husbands would remove wives from their relatives, resulting in the weakening of matrilocal residence in general. This ease of patrilineal and patrilocal segmentation makes the lineal separation of parents from their siblings less unlikely than in matrilineal and matrilocal societies, and so was assigned a weight of only one-half.

All other categories have been given simple weights of one. The direction of the weight, toward either creating or eliminating a distinction, is determined by evaluating whether a category tends to place relevant kin types in similar situations or to place them in different situations. Bilocal residence, for example, in which both matrilocal and patrilocal residence occur with about equal frequency, is given the value of $1 \; S\bar{l}$, since the high frequency of joint residence means that one parent will be living with his or her siblings, placing them in an equivalent situation, and acting to eliminate the lineal distinction. Bilocal residence is given the value of $1 \; S\tilde{x}$, since the mixture of patrilocal and matrilocal residence means that same-sex siblings will not tend to live together, thus acting to eliminate a distinction between cross-sex siblings.

A weight of one is given for all categories of residence and descent (except patrilineality and patrilocality) simply because there appeared to be no known reasons for assigning a more differentiated set of weights. It would be possible to set weights so that the best possible approximation to the actual data could be obtained. However, at this stage of development in constructing a set of formal procedures, it appears less complex to assume every social condition produces as much effect as every other, and then observe where this assumption fails, rather than attempt exact replication and find ourselves at the mercy of any special effect unanticipated by our procedures.

In order to assign proportional stimulus condition values for any distinction to a particular society, we begin with the assumption that there already exists a set of stimuli acting to create the distinction, and an equivalent set of stimuli acting to eliminate the distinction. Thus every society begins with forces balanced at $1 \; Sd : 1 \; S\bar{d}$. Any features of social organization which would tend to create or eliminate the distinction are then added to this initial set of values. A society with matrilineal

Table 4. Association between Rules of Residence and Descent Groupings for 428 Societies Selected from the World Ethnographic Atlas. [a]

| Rules of Residence | Descent Groups | | | | |
	Patrilineal	Matrilineal	Both	None	Total
Patrilocal	*177*	9	*17*	*78*	281
Matrilocal	0	*32*	2	*30*	64
Avunculocal	0	*15*	1	1	17
Bilocal	3	1	1	*33*	38
Neolocal	1	1	0	*26*	28
	181	58	21	168	
					428

[a] Italic figures are included in the classification presented in the text.

descent and patrilocal residence, for example, would be given weights of 1 Sx for matrilineal descent, plus 1 Sx for patrilocal residence, which when added to the assumed initial situation of 1 Sx and 1 $S\bar{x}$, gives a sum of 3 Sx to 1 $S\bar{x}$.

The next step has been to combine residence and descent categories into a single classification. Table 4 presents the association observed between rules of residence and descent groupings for the World Ethnographic Atlas. Of the twenty cells produced by the intersection of five residence categories by four descent categories, eleven cells have observed frequencies of three or less. The combinations of residence and descent which have been selected for the final classification consist of those nine cells that contain more than three observations. These nine combinations conform closely to the theoretical expectations of what might be called "nontransitional" forms of social organization as analyzed by Murdock (1949), and include about 97 percent of the societies in the sample.

The nine combinations of residence and descent are presented in Table 5 along with the frequencies of uncle and cousin terminologies for each of these nine types of social organization. This table contains the basic data to be "predicted" by the procedures outlined earlier, except that the distinctions between Crow, Omaha, Murgin, and Iroquois terms will be ignored, and grouped together as a single class of cousin terms which makes the cross distinction but does not make the lineal distinction. The six cases of descriptive cousin terminology and bifurcate merging uncle terminology all occur in societies that actually have "derivative" bifurcate merging uncle terminology, and have been treated as if they made the lineal distinction both in the cousin terms and in the uncle terms.

Table 6 presents the data from Table 5 in altered form, along with the theoretical predictions made according to the procedures given in the foregoing. This table gives

Table 5. Association between Social Organization and Kinship Terminology for a Subsample of 286 Societies from the World Ethnographic Sample.

Descent Groups / Residence	None				Matrilineal			Patri- lineal	Both	Distinctions Made by Terms	
	Neo	Bi	Pat	Mat	Mat	Avunc	Pat	Pat	Pat	Cross	Lineal
Terms **Uncle** Cousin **Descriptive**											
and D	—	—	4	—	—	—	—	6	—	*xx*	*ll*
Bifurcate C	—	—	—	—	—	—	—	—	1	*xx*	*ll*
collateral O	—	1	—	—	—	—	—	2	—	*xx*	*ll*
M	—	—	—	—	—	—	—	1	—	*xx*	*ll*
I	—	1	4	1	2	—	1	16	1	*xx*	*ll*
E	2	1	9	—	—	—	—	5	—	*xx̃*	*ll*
H	1	3	7	3	—	1	1	6	—	*xx̃*	*ll*
Bifurcate **merging** D	—	—	—	—	—	—	—	6	—	*xx*	*ll*
C	—	—	—	1	5	2	2	2	2	*xx*	*l̃l*
O	—	—	—	1	—	—	—	16	1	*xx*	*ll*
M	—	—	—	—	—	—	—	—	2	*xx*	*ll*
I	3	—	6	3	4	7	1	18	8	*xx*	*ll*
H	—	4	7	4	4	2	1	12	1	*xx̃*	*ll*
Lineal E	11	5	12	4	1	—	—	4	—	*x̃x̃*	*ll*
H	2	3	14	4	—	—	—	2	—	*x̃x̃*	*ll*
Generation H	1	9	4	—	1	—	1	3	—	*x̃x̃*	*l̃l*

the frequency with which the lineal and cross distinctions are made for each of the nine residence and descent categories. The assigned Sd values are given for each category of residence and descent, and the proportions of Sd to $S\bar{d}$ for each combination of social categories. The theoretical predictions derived from these proportions are presented in parentheses immediately to the right of each frequency figure.

For some combinations of social organization, the theoretical predictions fit the data

Table 6. Observed and Theoretically Expected Frequencies for Lineal and Cross Distinctions in Uncle and Cousin Terms.[a]

Descent	Bilateral $Sl, S\tilde{x}$								Matrilineal Sl, Sx						Patrilineal $\frac{1}{2}Sl, Sx$		Both $1\frac{1}{2}Sl, 2Sx$	
Residence:	Neo $Sl, S\tilde{x}$		Bi $Sl, S\tilde{x}$		Pat $\frac{1}{2}Sl, Sx$		Mat $Sl, S\tilde{x}$		Mat Sl, Sx		Avunc Sl, Sx		Pat $\frac{1}{2}Sl, Sx$		Pat $\frac{1}{2}Sl, Sx$		Pat $\frac{1}{2}Sl, Sx$	
Total Stimulus Weights	$3Sl{:}1Sl$		$1Sl{:}1Sl$		$1\frac{1}{2}Sl{:}1Sl$		$1Sl{:}1Sl$		$1Sl{:}3Sl$		$1Sl{:}3Sl$		$1Sl{:}2\frac{1}{2}Sl$		$1Sl{:}2Sl$		$1Sl{:}3Sl$	
Lineal Uncle and Cousin Terms	O	E	O	E	O	E	O	E	O	E	O	E	O	E	O	E	O	E
ll	13	(19.9)	6	(9)	25	(31.8)	4	(7)	1	(1.3)	0	(0.9)	1	(0.7)	21	(14.4)	0	(1.1)
$l\tilde{l}$	3	(4.6)	8	(9)	25	(21)	8	(7)	2	(3.9)	1	(2.1)	2	(1.8)	27	(26.9)	2	(3.2)
$\tilde{l}\tilde{l}$	4	(1.5)	13	(9)	17	(14.1)	9	(7)	14	(11.8)	11	(9.3)	5	(4.5)	53	(57.8)	12	(9.7)
Total Stimulus Weights	$1Sx{:}3S\tilde{x}$		$1Sx{:}3S\tilde{x}$		$1Sx{:}1S\tilde{x}$		$1Sx{:}1S\tilde{x}$		$3Sx{:}1S\tilde{x}$		$3Sx{:}1S\tilde{x}$		$3Sx{:}1S\tilde{x}$		$3Sx{:}1S\tilde{x}$		$4Sx{:}1S\tilde{x}$	
Cross Uncle and Cousin Terms	O	E	O	E	O	E	O	E	O	E	O	E	O	E	O	E	O	E
xx	3	(1.5)	2	(2.1)	14	(22.3)	6	(7)	11	(11.8)	9	(8.3)	4	(4.5)	69	(69.9)	13	(10.7)
$x\tilde{x}$	3	(4.6)	8	(6.2)	23	(22.3)	7	(7)	4	(3.9)	3	(2.2)	2	(1.6)	23	(23.3)	1	(2.7)
$\tilde{x}\tilde{x}$	14	(13.9)	17	(18.7)	30	(22.3)	8	(7)	2	(1.3)	0	(0.92)	1	(0.5)	9	(7.8)	0	(0.7)

[a] O = observed, E = expected.

Table 7. Summary of Observed and Theoretically Expected Frequencies for Lineal Distinctions in Uncle and Cousin Terms.[a]

Sl to *Sĺ* proportions

Lineal	3:1		1⅓:1		1:1		1:1½		1:2⅓		1:3	
Distinctions	O	E	O	E	O	E	O	E	O	E	O	E
ll	13	(14)	25	(32)	10	(16)	21	(14)	0	(1)	1	(3)
lĺ	3	(5)	25	(21)	16	(16)	27	(30)	2	(2)	5	(10)
ĺĺ	4	(2)	17	(14)	22	(16)	53	(58)	5	(4)	37	(30)

[a] *O* = observed, *E* = expected.

very well. The best fits appear to occur with the cross distinction, especially in those conditions in which the expected proportions are a 3:1 ratio. Tables 7 and 8 present in summary form the data from Table 6, collapsing combinations of social features that have identical *Sd* proportions.

The poorer fits appear to occur with the lineal distinction, and also in cases that have proportions supposedly equally balanced. This discrepancy, which occurs for both distinctions, apparently results from a trend toward the absence of *any* distinctions in societies having combinations of social features that contain conflicting forces.

From Table 6, it can be seen that the half-weight for patrilineal and patrilocal conditions appears to be too strong still, since all combinations involving these two categories have expected frequencies that are more extreme than the observed frequencies, except for the double descent condition, which also includes the effect of matrilineal descent. The opposite effect on the lineal distinction appears to occur for the matrilineal and matrilocal cases, which for all combinations of social features have

Table 8. Summary of Observed and Theoretically Expected Frequencies for Cross Distinction in Uncle and Cousin Terms.[a]

Sx to *Sx̃* proportions

Cross	4:1		3:1		1:1		1:3	
Distinctions	O	E	O	E	O	E	O	E
xx	13	(11)	93	(88)	20	(30)	5	(4)
xx̃	1	(3)	32	(29)	30	(30)	11	(11)
x̃x̃	0	(1)	12	(10)	38	(30)	31	(34)

[a] *O* = observed, *E* = expected.

expected frequencies that are not as extreme as the observed data, although the discrepancy is not large.

The simple addition of "forces" or sets of stimuli for combinations of social categories assumes that there is no interaction between different types of categories. This assumption has not been badly damaged by the data. If we could also assume that there was no interaction for kin terms between lineal and cross distinctions, it would then be possible to compute the expected frequencies for each of the actual combinations of types of uncle and cousin terminologies on the basis of the frequencies of the cross and lineal distinctions (i.e., the row and column totals). However, the results of this test clearly show a strong interaction effect. This effect indicates that there are fewer cases than expected in which both uncle and cousin terms make *both* the lineal and cross distinction, and also fewer cases than expected in which uncle or cousin terms make *neither* distinction. In complementary fashion, there are more cases than expected in which one distinction is made in both uncle and cousin terms while the other distinction is not made at all. It is as if there were an optimal number of distinctions to be made, and a tendency for most of the distinctions to be on one dimension or on another.

This interaction between the lineal and cross distinction makes it difficult to predict from the theoretical procedures the actual combined types of uncle and cousin terminology. A special conversion table which would allow for interaction effects might be set up to transform the expected frequencies for the lineal and cross distinction to the proper distribution of actual uncle and cousin types of terminology, but at present this appears to be adding gilt to the already guilty. (See Table 9.)

By way of beginning a discussion, the sentence following the quotation from Lounsbury presented earlier raises an apt issue:

A formal account is thus an apparatus for predicting back the data at hand, thereby making them "understandable," i.e., showing them to be the lawful and expectable consequences of an underlying principle that may be presumed to be at work at their source. (Lounsbury 1964: 351)

The issue to be discussed concerns the nature of the "underlying principle that may be presumed to be at work" in the apparatus developed in this paper. Actually, there appear to be two general principles at work in our kin-term predictor. The first principle involves the relation between uncle and cousin terminologies, with the notion that a distinction must occur in uncle terms if that distinction also is to occur in cousin terms. From this generalization it follows that changes in uncle and cousin terminologies are restricted by certain rules: i.e., that distinctions occur in uncle terms before occurring in cousin terms and loss of a distinction occurs in cousin terms before occurring in uncle terms. This first set of principles attempts to make understandable some of the observed relations between uncle and cousin terminologies, and to direct the effects predicted by the stimulus sampling procedures into distributions of various distinctions.

Table 9. Interaction Effects between Lineal and Cross Distinctions for Uncle and Cousin Terms.[a]

	ll		$l\tilde{l}$		$\tilde{l}\tilde{l}$		Row
	O	E	O	E	O	E	Totals
Cross							
Distinctions	BC—D		BC—I, C, O, M		BM—I, C, O, M		
xx	16	(32.1)	31	(35.7)	84	(63.2)	131
	BC—E		BC—H		BM—H		
$x\tilde{x}$	17	(18.1)	22	(20.2)	35	(35.7)	74
	L— E		L— H		G	H	
$\tilde{x}\tilde{x}$	37	(19.8)	25	(22.1)	19	(39.1)	181
Column							Grand
Totals	70		78		138		Total
							286

[a] O = observed, E = expected.

The second set of principles involves the notion of stimulus sampling and equilibrium points. Assuming "that the extension or differentiation of kinship terms depends in every individual case upon the *total net effect* of all similarities and dissimilarities exhibited by the relatives in question" (Murdock 1949: 133), the problem then arises of determining just how the "total net effect" operates. The approach taken here rejects the stimulus averaging notion, and instead depends upon a random sampling procedure.

This approach contains many conceptual difficulties, some inherent in any attempt to relate psychological processes to cultural phenomena (such as the difficulty of independently defining stimuli without experimental manipulation, or of even relating denotative meaning at all to stimulus control of a response). The major advantage of using this theory, outside of the fact that it is of aid in predicting kin-term distinctions from social features, is that it presents a simple description of how change could occur and a mechanism to represent the way in which total net effects result from complex combinations of similarities and dissimilarities.

Postscript

I was originally attracted to stimulus sampling theory because it presented a simple model that could be applied to kinship terminologies. In a kinship terminological system, either a distinction is made or it is not. Stimulus sampling theory, I found could be used to predict from complex social situations to the simple yes-no selection of a distinction in a kinship sytem, and predict not just what would be found in the average case, but also the amount of variability that would be found across cases. The model, when applied to cross-cultural data concerning kinship terminologies and correlated features of social organization, gave reasonable results.

However, since 1964, when I first presented this paper to a meeting of the Anthropological section of the Mathematics in the Social Science Board, a number of modifications and alternative formulations have been made in this area of psychological theory. A recent study by Harris, for example, presents five different models for predicting from ratings of attractiveness to paired comparison choices, and finds that the stimulus sampling model does considerably less well than a majority response model, which assumes that the response to which the greater number of elements are conditioned will always be chosen over the response to which fewer elements are conditioned (Harris 1968) (Harris, R. J., 1968, "The Deterministic Nature of Probabalistic Choices among Identifiable Stimuli," *Journal of Experimental Psychology*, to be published).

In the light of such information, I now find my application of the stimulus sampling model less appealing. Perhaps societies do not sample just *one* out of all the relevant features of social organization. Instead, perhaps in each society there is an assessment based on almost all potentially relevant features, and a selection of the kinship distinction that is consonant with the majority of the features.

If this is true, then how could a stimulus sampling model have given such good results in predicting types of kinship terminology from features of social organization? The answer seems to be that the one-element stimulus sampling model would be predictive despite its literal inapplicability if the features of social organization used in this paper were only a small subset of the total number of social conditions which actually affect kinship terminologies, and if the larger set of features were only partially correlated with the smaller subset. The probabilistic nature of the predictions made here, then, would be a result not of the way society actually reacts but a result of the guesswork involved in extrapolating from a limited sample of features to the larger pool. The investigator's lack of knowledge, not the society's reaction, would be the source of indeterminacy.

It is likely that there are a number of other psychological models besides the majority response model and the stimulus sampling model, which, given various assumptions about the nature of the data, would also yield fairly good predictions. Perhaps none of these models will finally prove to be of general applicability. The theoretical structure of modern psychology seems to be in a period of rapid change. The best solution for anthropologists might be to use psychological models when such models work and are illuminating, but not to take the model as seriously as the empirical findings.

References

Atkinson, Richard C., Gordon H. Bower, and Edward J. Crothers
1965 *An Introduction to Mathematical Learning Theory* (New York: John Wiley and Sons).

Harris, R. J.
1968 "The Deterministic Nature of Probabalistic Choice among Identifiable Stimuli," *Journal of Experimental Psychology*, to be published.

Lounsbury, Floyd G.
1964 "The Formal Analysis of Crow- and Omaha-Type Kinship Terminologies," *Explorations in Cultural Anthropology*, Ward H. Goodenough, ed. (New York: McGraw-Hill Book Company).

Murdock, George Peter
1949 *Social Structure* (New York: Macmillan and Company).
1962 "World Ethnographic Atlas," *Ethnology* 1:113–136.

Schneider, D. M.
1961 "Introduction: the Distinctive Features of Matrilineal Descent Groups," in *Matrilineal Kinship*, D. M. Schneider, and K. Gough, eds. (Berkeley and Los Angeles: University of California Press).

COMPUTER METHODS 2

Introduction

Stefflre, Reich, and McClaran-Stefflre describe a number of computational procedures which, given a certain type of formally elicited data, produce classes of linguistic forms whose members are grammatically and/or semantically similar. The purpose is to discover the basic units of a "behavioral dictionary," which is conceived as a description of the structure of meaning, belief, and normatively associated behavior of a speech community.

The basic data employed are informants' judgments of acceptability (by various criteria) of utterances produced by systematic substitution of a finite list of m lexical items in a finite list of n utterance frames. The primary tool of analysis is the resulting $n \times m$ matrix, in which the entry a_{ij} is set equal to one if the informant judges as acceptable the utterance resulting from insertion of the ith lexical items in the jth potential utterance frame. Otherwise a_{ij} is set equal to zero. As one varies the criterion of acceptability from "grammatically" to "semantic acceptability" to "truth," one may speak of grammaticality matrices, semantic acceptability matrices, and belief matrices for a given list of lexemes.

The second stage of the analysis calculates a measure of similarity for each pair of rows and for each pair of columns in the matrix.

The third stage of analysis rearranges the rows and columns of the matrix so as to maximize similarity among neighbors. The result is a pictorial display of clumps of lexemes (and contexts) with similar distributional properties. The rearrangement program is described in an Appendix to the paper.

In addition, various reliability checks and shortcut procedures are described. The authors show that, given a 50-item lexeme list, two independent 50-item utterance frame lists produce similar classes of lexemes. They also show that informants who have been trained on the production of matrices learn to estimate in advance how the clumps will come out, whereas untrained informants cannot produce good estimates of this type.

It is the aim of this paper to present some eliciting and computational procedures for descriptive semantics. Specifically, we wish to (1) describe some techniques we have used to make estimates of distributional similarity and partial synonymity of forms, (2) describe some checks we made on our techniques to see if they measured what we wanted, (3) present some preliminary substantive results—e.g., some fine-grained word class structures in dialects of Spanish, Yucatec Maya, and Nahuatl, and (4) indicate how these techniques fit into our overall research program.

The goal of our efforts was to develop some simple mechanical devices that would let us put our informants' intuitive knowledge of the language studied to work for us.

Some Eliciting and Computational Procedures for Descriptive Semantics 5

VOLNEY STEFFLRE, PETER REICH, AND MARLYS MCCLARAN-STEFFLRE

We are interested in building a kind of dictionary–thesaurus–phrase structure device we call, for the moment, a *behavioral dictionary*—the point of which is to enable us to predict, for any new thing, event, or idea, the semantically appropriate descriptions members of the speech community studied can give it and, given each of the descriptions, what will be believed about the item and how it will be behaved toward.

The behavioral dictionary of a language consists of (1) lexical elements, (2) syntactic and semantic word class structures, (3) referential rules, (4) beliefs about and behavior toward members of each class, and (5) combinatorial rules.

The key component of a device like this is a description of the fine-grained word class structures in the language described. Word classes are bunches of elements that distribute alike across the indefinitely large set of sentence frames the language can produce without altering the informants' judgments of the acceptability of the utterances considered. The word class structures are the descriptions of the inter-relations of these bunches. By "fine-grained" word classes, we mean down to a level of detail on the order of 10,000 classes—about the level of detail it appears may be necessary to be adequate for a transformational grammar, or for fairly high-quality machine translation, or for a device of the type we envision.

We do not intend at this point to attempt to convince linguists or anthropologists that building a device like this is either feasible or interesting—within linguistics or anthropology. But we do feel that some of the techniques we have developed, and some of the results we have obtained, might be relevant to traditional problems in both these areas. The techniques described here include (1) informant-generated data matrices, (2) informants' ratings or rankings of the distributional similarity of forms for different kinds of matrices, and (3) informants' sortings of terms into piles that distribute alike in different kinds of matrices.

In producing data matrices, we first obtain from informants' lists of utterances and lists of forms, then substitute all forms in all frames and elicit from the informants' judgments regarding whether each item in this longer list of test utterances does or does not meet some criterion commonly used by speakers of the dialect in determining acceptability.

Table 1 is a matrix where the rows are utterances and the columns are contrast words, each, in this case, produced by the informant as a word that could substitute for the underlined word in the utterances. Thus contrast 1, *cambiar*, was given as a substitute for *apurar* in sentence 1, contrast 2, *castigar*, can substitute for *apurar* in sentence 2, and so on.

Then the informant substituted each contrast item in each frame and indicated acceptability of the sentence thus formed by a 1, unacceptability by a 0. For instance, the utterance formed by frame 1 with contrast 3, *El niño se debe alimentar para ir a la*

This research was partially supported by a National Science Foundation grant to Volney Stefflre for *Study of Some Relations between Language and Behavior* (NSF GS 688).

escuela is judged acceptable according to the criterion used, but the same frame with contrast 4, *El niño se debe cansar para ir a la escuela,* is judged unacceptable.

Tables 2 through 6 show how the data analysis takes place.

Table 2 calculates the similarity of each row to every other row in terms of the extent to which they exhibit the same pattern of ones and zeros. This measures the extent to which two frames allow the same form to be placed in them resulting in acceptable utterances. For example, rows 38 and 19 have similar patterns and their similarity is calculated to be 0.86. This means that of the 21 columns in which row 38 has a 1 and of the 21 columns in which row 19 has a 1, 18 columns, i.e., columns 15, 17, 18, etc., have 1's for both rows.

$$\frac{18 + 18}{21 + 21} = \frac{36}{42} = 0.86.$$

Table 3 takes the row-row similarity matrix of Table 1 and rearranges it so that rows similar to each other are placed near each other. Here, for example, rows 38 and 19 are next to each other. Table 4 then calculates the similarity of each column to every other column in terms of the distributional similarity of the forms that label the columns. For example, columns 21, *atento,* and 22, *loco,* can be seen to have similar patterns of distribution, and their distributional similarity is calculated to be 0.96.

$$\frac{24 + 24}{26 + 24} = 0.96$$

Table 5 rearranges the matrix, putting the columns like each other near each other. Here, columns 21 and 22 are next to each other, whereas 1, *cambiar,* and 22, *loco,* whose distributional similarity is 0.00 (see Table 4), are far apart.

Table 6 prints out the original data matrix with rows like each other near each other and columns like each other near each other. Columns between 11 and 34, with the labels *pensar, ver, atrasar, molestar, alimentar, llamar, hablar, castigar, visitar, cambiar, admirar,* form a cluster. The columns between 38 and 16 form another cluster, and columns 32 and 30 form a small cluster.

Tables 7 and 8 present more rearranged data matrices using the same frames and forms, but different criteria in making judgments. Our informants judged Spanish utterances for (1) *buena expresion,* which we have glossed "grammatical," (2) *tiene sentido,* which we equated roughly with "makes sense," and (3) *es cierto,* "true," which we took to indicate that the informants agreed with the utterance.

Tables 9 through 14 present a Yucatec Maya matrix run through the entire procedure.

For example, follow through the columns 10 *mehentak,*[1] "small," 16 *čičan,* "small," 19

---

[1] The language forms in the data are presented as produced by the informants. In the case of Yucatec and Nahuatl, the informants had learned a practical orthography.

sak, "white," 20 *ču̇l,* "wet," and 40 *saask̇ale'en,* "transparent." The distributional similarity of 10 and 16 is calculated (Table 12) to be 0.98; 10 and 19, 0.94; 10 and 20, 0.98; 10 and 40, 0.74. In the rearranged matrix (Table 14), columns 10, 16, 19 and 20 bunch together, and 40 is rather farther away.

Table 15 is a rearranged Yucatec matrix with distinct clusters.

Table 16 is a rearranged Nahuatl matrix, where, for example, columns 44 *Xochiketzal,* 39 *nantzin,* "grandmother," 37 *Petratzin,* 26 *Mariatzin,* 13 *tia* "aunt," 9 *notlazo,* "my loved one," 6 *nogonen,* "my son," 19 *tio,* "uncle," 20 *pale,* "father," 31 *tataseñor,* "grandfather," 36 *papan,* "daddy," and 40 *Juantzin,* all are seen to distribute alike.

It is perhaps worth commenting at this point that the criteria used in these matrices might differ from what a linguist would expect, and also differ for the different languages. In building data matrices of this kind, it seemed to us that the criteria used in a dialect should be ones the informant finds natural. Our Yucatec speakers pushed us into using *haču̇ʼ u tàan* versus *ma haču̇ʼ u tàan* judgments, which we have glossed as "grammatical" versus "ungrammatical" for their matrices. They wanted to use *ču̇imin tàan,* "talking like a horse" to indicate senseless utterances, and felt comfortable with *hah u tàan,* as in Table 9, which we have associated with agreement—i.e., the informant agrees with the utterance.

Our Spanish data were obtained from bilingual Mayans in Ticul, Yucatan, and the criteria our informants led us to use for Spanish may reflect Mayan influence. For example, *buena expresión* is offered by them as a translation for *haču̇ʼ u tàan,* "good talk." It is not certain that a speaker not coming from a Mayan background would find this criterion meaningful.

On the other hand, our Nahuatl informant from Hueyapan seems to prefer to use only one criterion in evaluating utterances: *cualle mota,* "can say," versus *amo mota,* "can't say." We cannot tell at this point if this is a stable difference between the two communities. In general, however, we expect to find that different speech communities may differ in terms of the number of criteria they use, in the criteria selected, and in the interrelations among the criteria.

It seems appropriate to explain briefly one kind of judgment we use—that of informant agreement with the utterance. Linguists, in general, have not bothered to obtain this kind of information, nor felt it to be an appropriate part of the description of a language. We obtained this information for two reasons.

First, we are interested in the grammar of agreement. The number of utterances about which an informant can make judgments of agreement and disagreement is as large as the number of utterances he can judge as grammatical. We have found more consensus among different English speaking informants in judgments of agreement than in judgments of grammaticality. Some shared set of rules must be acquired in the process of growing up that enables them to make judgments regarding whether they agree or disagree with novel utterances. A description of rules that generate all and only the utterances informants will believe and say they agree with is of some theoretical and practical interest, though not a matter likely to be of concern to linguists.

Second, a reasonable measure of the synonymity of pairs of forms is provided by the distributional similarity across frames of those pairs that do not alter informants' agreement responses to the whole utterance. To the extent to which data on partial synonymity are of interest to linguists engaged in such tasks as dictionary construction, distributional similarity of pairs of forms that do not alter truth values should also be of interest.

In testing to see how our techniques worked, we first checked to see if the patterns of distributional similarity of forms were stable across different sets of frames, with judgments given by different informants. This check was necessary because, in sampling an infinite population, a sample of 10,000 is more typical than a sample of 50. Here we have sets of 50 frames, and have calculated the distributional similarity of pairs of forms across these, rather than across a more reasonable but impractical 10,000 row matrix. It could be the case that different sets of 50 frames would give back very different patterns of distributional similarity for the same forms. It could also be the case that the use of different informants would give back very different patterns of distributional similarity of pairs of forms. To test this, we had different informants try the same forms using matrices containing different frames. The stability of the patterns of distributional similarity can be calculated by correlating the column-column similarity numbers from one matrix with the column-column similarity numbers from another matrix, using the same contrast words but different frames, and filled in by a different informant.

Table 17 presents correlations that suggest that using matrices containing only 50-sentence frames, we can obtain fairly stable estimates of the distributional similarity of pairs of forms.

We feel that our results using data matrices have met some of the criteria we wanted them to meet: (1) informants can learn to do the work fairly easily. We have prepared English, Japanese, Spanish, Yucatec, Nahuatl, and Tzeltal matrices, and have had little difficulty in training our informants to do the work. (2) Patterns of distributional similarity appear fairly stable across different sets of frames when judged by different informants using the same criterion.

The data matrices have several limitations. They are a slow, cumbersome procedure necessitating a fair amount of computer work, and the patterns of distributional similarity of forms sometimes chunk nicely into classes, and sometimes do not. For example, the matrix in Table 6 chunks nicely, while the matrix in Table 16 does not.

We felt that informants who were trained by having them construct matrices would become able to predict accurately the outcome of the word class computational procedures on new matrix data. In fact, informants' estimates compared favorably with the word class structures obtained from computation, both in terms of ease of collection of data and ease of interpretation. To train our informants, we first had them prepare cards containing pairs of forms and then rank order these cards from the pair whose members would distribute most alike in a particular type of matrix to the pair whose members would distribute least alike in that type of matrix. Informants were not instructed to think of any particular frames, but rather to imagine a 10,000 by 10,000 "matrix in the sky," and estimate the distributional similarity of the pair of forms across this great matrix in the sky from which our little 50×50 matrices were taken. We have no strong feeling about the use of this particular device for communicating to the informant the nature of the ranking task, but we found it worked fairly well, and communicated easily to the informants the notion of sampling.

Table 18a gives the correlations between the column-column similarity numbers for the word pairs, and the informant's estimate of the distributional similarity of the pair of forms in the great matrix in the sky. These estimates are, of course, done by informants who have not seen the data matrices they are estimating and do not themselves later do the data matrices. Informants who are familiar with matrices can be quickly trained to make accurate judgments. Table 18a shows such an example of the effects of training, where an informant's ranking improved from a correlation of 0.54 to 0.93. However, completely naïve speakers of a language who are unfamiliar with matrices find it difficult to make accurate estimates. Table 18a shows correlations for 20 naïve speakers of English which strongly suggest that their estimates of distributional similarity of forms in grammaticality matrices are heavily influenced by semantic considerations applicable to judgments of sense, but not to judgments of grammaticality.

We should sound a note of caution here—our Mexican informants had learned how column-column similarity was calculated, and had spent several months working with matrices. While they were trained in less than a week to make these judgments by having them compare their guesses of distributional similarity with the actual column-column similarity numbers, they had several months of relevant background experience to facilitate this process.

Tables 18b and 18c present data from informant rankings and distributional similarity in matrix 172 (see Tables 1–6) and matrix 129 (see Tables 9–14). Differences found here may be due to informant errors or to inadequacies in the matrices. Forms that do not fit in many of the frames in a matrix may exhibit bizarre patterns of similarity. Estimates of distributional similarity from matrices are more reliable for forms that fit a larger number of frames. Our informant estimates may correspond to the great matrix in the sky better than to a particular matrix in which a pair of terms are infrequently acceptable.

At this point we felt our informants understood what we meant when we asked them to judge the extent to which forms "distribute alike" in a particular matrix. So we moved over into a simpler procedure. The informants prepared cards containing single forms, and were told to "put together the forms that will distribute alike in an X matrix." In this task the informant makes piles of forms that he feels will distribute alike in a matrix formed using the criterion specified. If he feels that a form should go in several piles, he is allowed to "split" it, making up two cards for it if he feels the two piles represent different senses of the word. It should be noted here that paraphrase matrices have previously been done by informants to teach them about the "multiple meaning" of a single form.

For example, Table 19 presents an example of a paraphrase matrix. In a matrix of this kind, an informant is asked to give a list of utterances containing a particular word, and to attempt for each appearance of the word to produce a paraphrase appropriate for it in that context. The paraphrase obtained for the word in each frame is placed in all frames, and the informant asked to judge whether utterance i and frame i with paraphrase j replacing the original word mean roughly the same thing. For example, in Table 19, the rows are sentences built around the word *code*. The paraphrase for *code* in sentence 1, *try to break this code*, is *cipher*. When *cipher* is substituted for *code* in sentence 2, *he has a strong moral code*, the resulting sentence is judged unacceptable as a paraphrase for the original sentence. That is, the informant judges that *he has a strong moral code* and *he has a strong moral cipher* do not mean the same thing.

When run through the same type of analysis as the other matrix forms, the paraphrase matrix provides slightly different information. The measure of row-row similarity in this case indicates the extent to which the different appearances of the word allow the same paraphrases without alteration in the meaning of the utterance. The column-column similarity numbers indicate the extent to which the two words labeling the columns can serve as paraphrases for the same appearances of the term. A "clump" of 1's indicates, in this case, a group of appearances of the term that allow similar paraphrases, and a set of paraphrases that are appropriate for that particular group of appearances of the term.

During the word class sorting task, we have found it useful to be able to give the informant the following additional instructions: (1) "are there any other forms that should go in that pile?"; (2) "are there any other forms that should go between those piles?"; (3) "put together the piles that will distribute more similarly"; and (4) "subdivide that pile putting together the forms that will distribute alike."

Tables 20b, 21b, and 22 represent some data we obtained through the sorting procedures for word classes in Spanish and Yucatec.

To check if our informants still remember what they are supposed to be doing, we can take forms our informants have sorted and use these as column headings in matrices to be filled out by other naïve informants who know nothing of the sorting procedure. If the forms our trained informants pile together distribute alike in these matrices, and the rearrangement of the matrix puts the forms sorted together near each other, then we know our techniques are functioning. The matrix procedure, then, can be used in training informants and for quality control of other faster and simpler procedures for pulling out word class structures.

Tables 8, 20a, and 21a show the matrices that check the sortings. For example, in the Spanish sorting according to the criterion of *cierto* (Table 20b), it can be seen that the members of "Clase B" represented in the checking matrix in Table 20a are next to each other in the columns between 81 and 88. The matrix in Table 21a agrees to a certain extent with the sorting presented in Table 21b. For instance, the first five columns of the matrix with labels *ʔoƙot*, "dance," *hanah*, "eat," *ʔawat*, "shout," *t'àan*, "speak," *ƙay*, "sing," correspond to a sorted pile (Table 21b, lower right) with members *ȼikbal*, "converse," *ƙay*, "sing," *ʔoƙot*, "dance," *čeʔeh*, "laugh," *ʔawat*, "shout," *t'àan* "speak," *papaška?t'àan*, "applauded."

A more precise quantitative test of the adequacy of our informants' sorting is possible through (1) comparing the within-pile distributional similarity numbers with the between-pile distributional similarity numbers, and (2) comparing the structural nearness of a pair of terms in informants' sorting with the distributional similarity of the terms in the checking matrices.

Our conclusions can be briefly stated: (1) informants can be trained to do matrices; (2) patterns of distributional similarity of pairs of forms are fairly stable across different haphazardly selected sets of 50 frames; (3) informants can be trained quite quickly to predict fairly accurately the patterns of distributional similarity of pairs of forms, and (4) informants can be easily trained to sort forms in a manner that corresponds to properties of their distribution in that language.

To do the kind of descriptive semantics our interest in behavioral dictionaries demands, it appears necessary to describe: (1) word class structures, (2) the combinatorial rules that determine which classes combine acceptably in forming short simple utterances, (3) the combinatorial rules that determine the manner in which the meaning of elements in the classes interact when they are placed in combination, and (4) the referential rules of use of forms and the productive rules for inclusion of new forms in old classes.[2]

The work presented here is a preliminary study trying to test some techniques for pulling out word classes. It presents only preliminary results.

Appendix

This Appendix describes the computer program that was developed to perform the analysis described in this paper. The program is called MAPS (*MA*trix *P*rocessing *S*ystem) and is composed of a basic input/output program plus a set of subroutines which is called on to perform the various options as they are requested.

MAPS accepts as data any matrix up to a maximum of 94 × 94. The matrix can be either square or rectangular, but, whatever the size, there must be the same number of data columns on each card of input for any given matrix, or an error comment is printed and the data set is skipped. A set of Boolean control cards (each beginning with an asterisk in column 1) determines which features of the program will be in

[2] The type of dictionary discussed here is described more fully in Stefflre's book *Language and Behavior* (see References).

effect for any given data set. If no options are requested by means of these control cards, the input matrix is read in and then printed out with row and column totals and the grand total (see Tables 1, 7, and 9), but no further analysis is performed. The options include the rest of what has been discussed in the paper plus other minor program features.

The program can do the following:

1. Read in a data matrix and print it out with labels and row and column totals.
2. Compute and print out row-row and column-column similarity matrices.
3. Compute and print out a number that is an indication of the amount of structure in the matrix.
4. Rearrange the matrices (input, row-row, column-column) so that the groupings become more apparent.
5. Produce a scatter plot of row-row and/or column-column similarities of two matrices.
6. Allow for variations in input and output:
a. The format can be changed to allow input of frequency type data—numbers other than zeros and ones, floating point (decimal) data instead of integer data—and input of rows that are more than one card long.
b. Output (print) parameters can be changed to allow for variations in column width, page size, and the number of decimal places to be printed in the floating point matrices.

The Similarity Measure This is a number which ranges from 0.00 to 1.00, and is an indication of the "alikeness" or similarity of two rows or two columns. The following represents the computation that is done to calculate this number (e.g., for columns):

$$A2_{ij} = \frac{\frac{1}{2}(a_{ki} + a_{kj} - |a_{ki} - a_{kj}|)}{\frac{1}{2}(\text{Tot col } i + \text{Tot col } j)}$$

This means, in essence, that the number of "matches" (nonzero) between every two rows is found, multiplied by 2, and then divided by the combined row totals for each pair. This gives the similarity number for each pair of columns in the matrix.

The Rearrangement (sorting) Procedure The rearrangement of the similarity matrices is accomplished by making successive passes through the matrix, applying an increasingly weaker criterion of equivalence on each pass. Numbers that fall within the range of equivalence for any particular pass (e.g., first pass, between 1.0 and 0.9; second pass, between 1.0 and 0.8, etc.) are "attached" to one end or the other of a "linear equivalence chain," depending on the number (there being a similarity number "available" for attachment at each end of the chain) to which it is most similar.

The parameter used to define the equivalence groups is preset at 0.1 (which means 10 passes through the matrix to "link" all the numbers), but can be redefined to any size desired by means of a parameter control card. A larger parameter means fewer passes and less computer time, but also less precision in the rearrangement of the numbers. The opposite is true for a smaller parameter.

The Program The program was written in the MAD language (*M*ichigan *A*lgorithmic *D*ecoder), and for a computer of the IBM 7090-7094 size and has been rewritten for IBM's 1130 and the 360 series. At present, it has been run only at the University of Michigan, but should work on any 7090-7094 size installation which will handle the Michigan Executive System (which can be obtained through SHARE).

References

Stefflre, V.

In preparation (1970). *Language and Behavior* (Reading, Mass.: Addison-Wesley).

Table 1

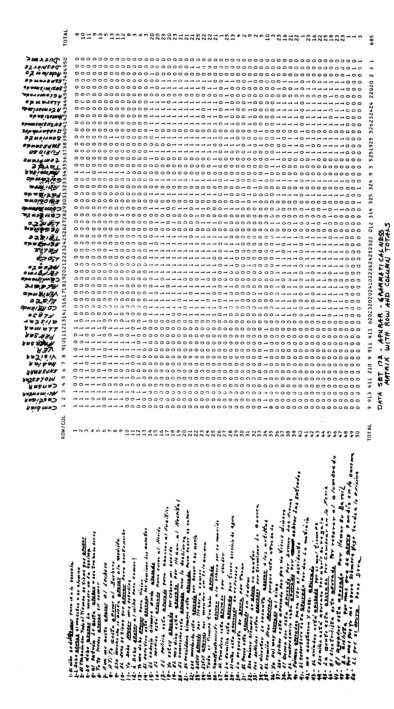

Table 2

DATA SET 172***APURAR***GRAMMATICALNESS (JM)

SIMILARITY MATRIX - ROW

ROW/ROW	1	2	3	4	5	6	7	8	9	10	11	12	13	14	15	16	17	18	19	20	21	22	23	24
1	1.00	.78	.74	.71	.76	.31	.67	.67	.70	.50	.00	.57	.36	.00	.00	.00	.00	.00	.00	.00	.00	.00	.00	.00
2	.78	1.00	.67	.63	.87	.40	.78	.87	.82	.56	.31	.75	.15	.00	.00	.00	.00	.00	.00	.00	.00	.00	.00	.00
3	.74	.67	1.00	.80	.83	.63	.67	.67	.70	.63	.14	.47	.43	.00	.00	.00	.00	.00	.00	.00	.00	.00	.00	.00
4	.71	.63	.80	1.00	.82	.43	.64	.64	.67	.82	.17	.53	.50	.00	.00	.00	.00	.00	.00	.00	.00	.00	.00	.00
5	.76	.87	.83	.82	1.00	.44	.77	.85	.80	.76	.38	.63	.38	.00	.00	.00	.00	.00	.00	.00	.00	.00	.00	.00
6	.31	.40	.63	.43	.44	1.00	.44	.44	.47	.46	.25	.36	.50	.00	.00	.00	.00	.00	.00	.00	.00	.00	.00	.00
7	.67	.78	.67	.64	.77	.44	1.00	.85	.88	.57	.25	.63	.25	.06	.18	.17	.12	.17	.18	.18	.18	.16	.17	.17
8	.67	.87	.67	.64	.85	.44	.85	1.00	.80	.57	.38	.63	.25	.06	.12	.11	.12	.06	.06	.12	.12	.11	.11	.11
9	.70	.82	.70	.67	.80	.47	.88	.80	1.00	.60	.27	.67	.27	.00	.06	.06	.00	.06	.06	.06	.06	.11	.06	.06
10	.50	.56	.63	.82	.76	.46	.57	.57	.60	1.00	.36	.71	.55	.00	.00	.00	.00	.00	.00	.00	.00	.00	.00	.00
11	.00	.31	.14	.17	.38	.25	.25	.38	.27	.36	1.00	.22	.33	.00	.00	.00	.00	.00	.00	.00	.00	.00	.00	.00
12	.57	.75	.47	.53	.63	.36	.63	.63	.67	.71	.22	1.00	.22	.00	.00	.00	.00	.00	.00	.00	.00	.00	.00	.00
13	.36	.15	.43	.50	.38	.50	.25	.25	.27	.55	.33	.22	1.00	.00	.00	.00	.00	.00	.00	.00	.00	.00	.00	.00
14	.00	.00	.00	.00	.00	.00	.06	.06	.00	.00	.00	.00	.00	1.00	.70	.79	.75	.70	.73	.78	.73	.76	.67	.71
15	.00	.00	.00	.00	.00	.00	.18	.12	.06	.00	.00	.00	.00	.70	1.00	.88	.80	.84	.83	.78	.78	.80	.86	.81
16	.00	.00	.00	.00	.00	.00	.17	.11	.06	.00	.00	.00	.00	.79	.88	1.00	.88	.91	.86	.91	.86	.92	.89	.93
17	.00	.00	.00	.00	.00	.00	.12	.12	.00	.00	.00	.00	.00	.75	.80	.88	1.00	.88	.83	.83	.83	.84	.81	.86
18	.00	.00	.00	.00	.00	.00	.17	.06	.06	.00	.00	.00	.00	.70	.84	.91	.88	1.00	.91	.86	.86	.88	.89	.93
19	.00	.00	.00	.00	.00	.00	.18	.06	.06	.00	.00	.00	.00	.73	.83	.86	.83	.91	1.00	.86	.81	.87	.84	.88
20	.00	.00	.00	.00	.00	.00	.18	.12	.06	.00	.00	.00	.00	.78	.78	.91	.83	.86	.86	1.00	.86	.91	.84	.88
21	.00	.00	.00	.00	.00	.00	.18	.12	.06	.00	.00	.00	.00	.73	.78	.86	.83	.86	.81	.86	1.00	.91	.79	.88
22	.00	.00	.00	.00	.00	.00	.16	.11	.11	.00	.00	.00	.00	.76	.80	.92	.84	.88	.87	.91	.91	1.00	.85	.89
23	.00	.00	.00	.00	.00	.00	.17	.11	.06	.00	.00	.00	.00	.67	.86	.89	.81	.89	.84	.84	.79	.85	1.00	.86
24	.00	.00	.00	.00	.00	.00	.17	.11	.06	.00	.00	.00	.00	.71	.81	.93	.86	.93	.88	.88	.88	.89	.86	1.00
25	.00	.00	.00	.00	.00	.00	.18	.12	.06	.00	.00	.00	.00	.73	.83	.86	.78	.82	.76	.76	.81	.78	.74	.84
26	.00	.00	.00	.00	.00	.00	.00	.00	.00	.00	.00	.00	.00	.00	.10	.08	.10	.08	.09	.09	.00	.08	.09	.09
27	.00	.00	.00	.00	.00	.00	.16	.11	.05	.00	.00	.00	.00	.76	.84	.96	.84	.92	.87	.91	.87	.92	.89	.94
28	.00	.00	.00	.00	.00	.00	.23	.08	.08	.00	.00	.00	.00	.48	.61	.67	.61	.67	.65	.71	.71	.68	.69	.63
29	.00	.00	.00	.00	.00	.00	.00	.00	.00	.00	.00	.00	.00	.25	.17	.22	.17	.22	.24	.32	.24	.28	.31	.15
30	.00	.00	.00	.00	.00	.00	.00	.00	.00	.00	.00	.00	.00	.00	.00	.00	.00	.00	.00	.00	.00	.00	.00	.00
31	.00	.00	.00	.00	.00	.00	.00	.00	.00	.00	.00	.00	.00	.48	.48	.50	.48	.56	.53	.60	.60	.53	.45	.58
32	.00	.00	.00	.00	.00	.00	.00	.00	.00	.00	.00	.00	.00	.00	.00	.00	.00	.00	.00	.00	.00	.00	.00	.00
33	.00	.00	.00	.00	.00	.00	.00	.00	.00	.00	.00	.00	.00	.24	.16	.21	.24	.29	.31	.15	.23	.27	.30	.30
34	.78	.90	.76	.74	.87	.53	.87	.87	.91	.67	.31	.75	.31	.00	.00	.00	.00	.00	.00	.00	.00	.00	.00	.00
35	.00	.00	.00	.00	.00	.00	.00	.00	.00	.00	.00	.00	.00	.09	.09	.08	.00	.08	.00	.00	.00	.00	.08	.08
36	.00	.00	.00	.00	.00	.00	.17	.11	.06	.00	.00	.00	.00	.74	.88	.87	.84	.87	.82	.77	.82	.79	.80	.84
37	.00	.00	.00	.00	.00	.00	.00	.07	.00	.00	.00	.00	.00	.72	.78	.82	.83	.77	.70	.76	.76	.78	.74	.79
38	.00	.00	.00	.00	.00	.00	.18	.12	.06	.00	.00	.00	.00	.73	.83	.91	.88	.91	.86	.90	.90	.91	.88	.93
39	.00	.00	.00	.00	.00	.00	.17	.06	.06	.00	.00	.00	.00	.67	.81	.89	.86	.98	.93	.84	.84	.85	.86	.95
40	.00	.00	.00	.00	.00	.00	.00	.00	.00	.00	.00	.00	.00	.10	.00	.00	.00	.00	.00	.00	.00	.00	.00	.00
41	.00	.00	.00	.00	.00	.00	.17	.11	.06	.00	.00	.00	.00	.74	.84	.91	.88	.91	.95	.91	.86	.92	.89	.93
42	.00	.00	.00	.00	.00	.00	.21	.07	.07	.00	.00	.00	.00	.61	.78	.77	.67	.77	.76	.70	.70	.68	.63	.79
43	.00	.00	.00	.00	.00	.00	.17	.11	.06	.00	.00	.00	.00	.76	.86	.93	.95	.93	.88	.88	.88	.89	.86	.91
44	.00	.00	.00	.00	.00	.00	.16	.11	.05	.00	.00	.00	.00	.76	.89	.96	.89	.96	.91	.91	.87	.92	.94	.94
45	.00	.00	.00	.00	.00	.00	.19	.06	.13	.00	.00	.00	.00	.58	.58	.73	.68	.78	.77	.72	.77	.79	.75	.80
46	.00	.00	.00	.00	.00	.00	.17	.11	.06	.00	.00	.00	.00	.79	.84	.96	.88	.91	.91	.95	.91	.96	.89	.93
47	.00	.00	.00	.00	.00	.00	.17	.11	.06	.00	.00	.00	.00	.79	.84	.96	.88	.91	.91	.95	.91	.96	.89	.93
48	.00	.00	.00	.00	.00	.00	.00	.00	.00	.00	.00	.00	.00	.10	.00	.00	.00	.00	.00	.00	.00	.00	.00	.00
49	.00	.00	.00	.00	.00	.00	.00	.00	.00	.00	.00	.00	.00	.00	.00	.00	.00	.00	.00	.00	.09	.08	.00	.00
50	.00	.00	.00	.00	.00	.00	.00	.00	.00	.00	.00	.00	.00	.00	.00	.00	.00	.00	.00	.00	.00	.00	.00	.00

Table 3

DATA SET 172***APURAR***GRAMMATICALNESS (JM)

SIMILARITY MATRIX - ROW

ROW/ROW	49	48	26	35	11	13	6	12	10	4	3	5	2	8	34	9	7	1	31	14	37	21	39	19
49	1.00	.00	.00	.00	.00	.00	.00	.00	.00	.00	.00	.00	.00	.00	.00	.00	.00	.00	.00	.00	.00	.09	.00	.00
48	.00	1.00	.00	.00	.00	.00	.00	.00	.00	.00	.00	.00	.00	.00	.00	.00	.00	.00	.00	.10	.00	.00	.00	.00
26	.00	.00	1.00	.00	.00	.00	.00	.00	.00	.00	.00	.00	.00	.00	.00	.00	.00	.00	.00	.00	.12	.00	.09	.09
35	.00	.00	.00	1.00	.00	.00	.00	.00	.00	.00	.00	.00	.00	.00	.00	.00	.00	.00	.00	.09	.00	.00	.08	.00
11	.00	.00	.00	.00	1.00	.33	.25	.22	.36	.17	.14	.38	.31	.38	.31	.27	.25	.00	.00	.00	.00	.00	.00	.00
13	.00	.00	.00	.00	.33	1.00	.50	.22	.55	.50	.43	.38	.15	.25	.31	.27	.25	.36	.00	.00	.00	.00	.00	.00
6	.00	.00	.00	.00	.25	.50	1.00	.36	.45	.43	.63	.44	.40	.44	.53	.47	.44	.31	.00	.00	.00	.00	.00	.00
12	.00	.00	.00	.00	.22	.22	.36	1.00	.71	.53	.47	.63	.75	.63	.75	.67	.63	.57	.00	.00	.00	.00	.00	.00
10	.00	.00	.00	.00	.36	.55	.46	.71	1.00	.82	.63	.76	.56	.57	.67	.60	.57	.50	.00	.00	.00	.00	.00	.00
4	.00	.00	.00	.00	.17	.50	.43	.53	.82	1.00	.80	.82	.63	.64	.74	.67	.64	.71	.00	.00	.00	.00	.00	.00
3	.00	.00	.00	.00	.14	.43	.63	.47	.63	.80	1.00	.83	.67	.67	.76	.70	.67	.74	.00	.00	.00	.00	.00	.00
5	.00	.00	.00	.00	.38	.38	.44	.63	.76	.82	.83	1.00	.87	.85	.87	.80	.77	.76	.00	.00	.00	.00	.00	.00
2	.00	.00	.00	.00	.31	.15	.40	.75	.56	.63	.67	.87	1.00	.87	.90	.82	.78	.78	.00	.00	.00	.00	.00	.00
8	.00	.00	.00	.00	.38	.25	.44	.63	.57	.64	.67	.85	.87	1.00	.87	.80	.85	.67	.00	.06	.07	.12	.06	.06
34	.00	.00	.00	.00	.31	.31	.53	.75	.67	.74	.76	.87	.90	.87	1.00	.91	.87	.78	.00	.00	.00	.00	.00	.00
9	.00	.00	.00	.00	.27	.27	.47	.67	.60	.67	.70	.80	.82	.80	.91	1.00	.88	.70	.00	.00	.00	.06	.06	.06
7	.00	.00	.00	.00	.25	.25	.44	.63	.57	.64	.67	.77	.78	.85	.87	.88	1.00	.67	.00	.06	.00	.18	.17	.18
1	.00	.00	.00	.00	.00	.36	.31	.57	.50	.71	.74	.76	.78	.67	.78	.70	.67	1.00	.00	.00	.00	.00	.00	.00
31	.00	.00	.00	.00	.00	.00	.00	.00	.00	.00	.00	.00	.00	.00	.00	.00	.00	.00	1.00	.48	.64	.60	.58	.53
14	.00	.10	.00	.09	.00	.00	.00	.00	.00	.00	.00	.00	.00	.06	.00	.00	.06	.00	.48	1.00	.72	.73	.67	.73
37	.00	.00	.12	.00	.00	.00	.00	.00	.00	.00	.00	.00	.00	.07	.00	.00	.00	.00	.64	.72	1.00	.76	.74	.70
21	.09	.00	.00	.00	.00	.00	.00	.00	.00	.00	.00	.00	.00	.12	.00	.06	.18	.00	.60	.73	.76	1.00	.84	.81
39	.00	.00	.09	.08	.00	.00	.00	.00	.00	.00	.00	.00	.00	.06	.00	.06	.17	.00	.58	.67	.74	.84	1.00	.93
19	.00	.00	.09	.00	.00	.00	.00	.00	.00	.00	.00	.00	.00	.06	.00	.06	.18	.00	.53	.73	.70	.81	.93	1.00
38	.00	.00	.09	.00	.00	.00	.00	.00	.00	.00	.00	.00	.00	.12	.00	.06	.18	.00	.60	.73	.86	.90	.88	.86
27	.00	.00	.08	.07	.00	.00	.00	.00	.00	.00	.00	.00	.00	.11	.00	.05	.16	.00	.53	.76	.78	.87	.89	.87
24	.00	.00	.09	.08	.00	.00	.00	.00	.00	.00	.00	.00	.00	.11	.00	.06	.17	.00	.58	.71	.79	.88	.95	.88
18	.00	.00	.08	.08	.00	.00	.00	.00	.00	.00	.00	.00	.00	.06	.00	.06	.17	.00	.56	.70	.77	.86	.98	.91
16	.00	.00	.08	.08	.00	.00	.00	.00	.00	.00	.00	.00	.00	.11	.00	.06	.17	.00	.50	.79	.82	.86	.89	.86
20	.00	.00	.09	.00	.00	.00	.00	.00	.00	.00	.00	.00	.00	.12	.00	.06	.18	.00	.60	.78	.76	.86	.84	.86
22	.08	.00	.08	.00	.00	.00	.00	.00	.00	.00	.00	.00	.00	.11	.00	.11	.16	.00	.53	.76	.78	.91	.85	.87
41	.00	.00	.08	.00	.00	.00	.00	.00	.00	.00	.00	.00	.00	.11	.00	.06	.17	.00	.56	.74	.77	.86	.93	.95
43	.00	.00	.09	.00	.00	.00	.00	.00	.00	.00	.00	.00	.00	.11	.00	.06	.17	.00	.52	.76	.84	.88	.91	.88
44	.00	.00	.08	.07	.00	.00	.00	.00	.00	.00	.00	.00	.00	.11	.00	.05	.16	.00	.53	.76	.78	.87	.94	.91
46	.00	.00	.08	.00	.00	.00	.00	.00	.00	.00	.00	.00	.00	.11	.00	.06	.17	.00	.56	.79	.82	.91	.89	.91
47	.00	.00	.08	.00	.00	.00	.00	.00	.00	.00	.00	.00	.00	.11	.00	.06	.17	.00	.56	.79	.82	.91	.89	.91
17	.00	.00	.10	.00	.00	.00	.00	.00	.00	.00	.00	.00	.00	.12	.00	.00	.12	.00	.48	.75	.83	.83	.86	.83
23	.00	.00	.09	.08	.00	.00	.00	.00	.00	.00	.00	.00	.00	.11	.00	.06	.17	.00	.45	.67	.74	.79	.86	.84
15	.00	.00	.10	.09	.00	.00	.00	.00	.00	.00	.00	.00	.00	.12	.00	.06	.18	.00	.48	.70	.78	.78	.81	.83
36	.00	.00	.08	.23	.00	.00	.00	.00	.00	.00	.00	.00	.00	.11	.00	.06	.17	.00	.44	.74	.72	.82	.84	.82
25	.00	.00	.09	.25	.00	.00	.00	.00	.00	.00	.00	.00	.00	.12	.00	.06	.18	.00	.47	.73	.70	.81	.79	.76
42	.00	.00	.12	.21	.00	.00	.00	.00	.00	.00	.00	.00	.00	.07	.00	.07	.21	.00	.56	.61	.63	.70	.79	.76
45	.00	.00	.00	.00	.00	.00	.00	.00	.00	.00	.00	.00	.00	.06	.00	.13	.19	.00	.52	.58	.59	.77	.80	.77
28	.00	.00	.00	.00	.00	.00	.00	.00	.00	.00	.00	.00	.00	.08	.00	.08	.23	.00	.45	.48	.48	.71	.63	.65
29	.00	.00	.00	.00	.00	.00	.00	.00	.00	.00	.00	.00	.00	.00	.00	.00	.00	.00	.15	.25	.10	.24	.15	.24
33	.00	.00	.00	.00	.00	.00	.00	.00	.00	.00	.00	.00	.00	.00	.00	.00	.00	.00	.14	.24	.29	.23	.30	.31
40	.00	.00	.00	.00	.00	.00	.00	.00	.00	.00	.00	.00	.00	.00	.00	.00	.00	.00	.00	.10	.00	.00	.00	.00
50	.00	.00	.00	.00	.00	.00	.00	.00	.00	.00	.00	.00	.00	.00	.00	.00	.00	.00	.00	.00	.00	.00	.00	.00
32	.00	.00	.00	.00	.00	.00	.00	.00	.00	.00	.00	.00	.00	.00	.00	.00	.00	.00	.00	.00	.00	.00	.00	.00
30	.00	.00	.00	.00	.00	.00	.00	.00	.00	.00	.00	.00	.00	.00	.00	.00	.00	.00	.00	.00	.00	.00	.00	.00

DATA SET 172***APURAR***GRAMMATICALNESS (JM)

SIMILARITY MATRIX - ROW

25	26	27	28	29	30	31	32	33	34	35	36	37	38	39	40	41	42	43	44	45	46	47	48	49	50
.00	.00	.00	.00	.00	.00	.00	.00	.00	.78	.00	.00	.00	.00	.00	.00	.00	.00	.00	.00	.00	.00	.00	.00	.00	.00
.00	.00	.00	.00	.00	.00	.00	.00	.00	.90	.00	.00	.00	.00	.00	.00	.00	.00	.00	.00	.00	.00	.00	.00	.00	.00
.00	.00	.00	.00	.00	.00	.00	.00	.00	.76	.00	.00	.00	.00	.00	.00	.00	.00	.00	.00	.00	.00	.00	.00	.00	.00
.00	.00	.00	.00	.00	.00	.00	.00	.00	.74	.00	.00	.00	.00	.00	.00	.00	.00	.00	.00	.00	.00	.00	.00	.00	.00
.00	.00	.00	.00	.00	.00	.00	.00	.00	.87	.00	.00	.00	.00	.00	.00	.00	.00	.00	.00	.00	.00	.00	.00	.00	.00
.00	.00	.00	.00	.00	.00	.00	.00	.00	.53	.00	.00	.00	.00	.00	.00	.00	.00	.00	.00	.00	.00	.00	.00	.00	.00
.18	.00	.16	.23	.00	.00	.00	.00	.00	.87	.00	.17	.00	.18	.17	.00	.17	.21	.17	.16	.19	.17	.17	.00	.00	.00
.12	.00	.11	.08	.00	.00	.00	.00	.00	.87	.00	.11	.07	.12	.06	.00	.11	.07	.11	.11	.06	.11	.11	.00	.00	.00
.06	.00	.05	.08	.00	.00	.00	.00	.00	.91	.00	.06	.00	.06	.06	.00	.06	.07	.06	.05	.13	.06	.06	.00	.00	.00
.00	.00	.00	.00	.00	.00	.00	.00	.00	.67	.00	.00	.00	.00	.00	.00	.00	.00	.00	.00	.00	.00	.00	.00	.00	.00
.00	.00	.00	.00	.00	.00	.00	.00	.00	.31	.00	.00	.00	.00	.00	.00	.00	.00	.00	.00	.00	.00	.00	.00	.00	.00
.00	.00	.00	.00	.00	.00	.00	.00	.00	.75	.00	.00	.00	.00	.00	.00	.00	.00	.00	.00	.00	.00	.00	.00	.00	.00
.00	.00	.00	.00	.00	.00	.00	.00	.00	.31	.00	.00	.00	.00	.00	.00	.00	.00	.00	.00	.00	.00	.00	.00	.00	.00
.73	.00	.76	.48	.25	.00	.48	.00	.24	.00	.09	.74	.72	.73	.67	.10	.74	.61	.76	.76	.58	.79	.79	.10	.00	.00
.83	.10	.84	.61	.17	.00	.48	.00	.16	.00	.09	.88	.78	.83	.81	.00	.84	.78	.86	.89	.58	.84	.84	.00	.00	.00
.86	.08	.96	.67	.22	.00	.50	.00	.21	.00	.08	.87	.82	.91	.89	.00	.91	.77	.93	96	.73	.96	.96	.00	.00	.00
.78	.10	.84	.61	.17	.00	.48	.00	.24	.00	.00	.84	.83	.88	.86	.00	.88	.67	.91	.79	.68	.88	.88	.00	.00	.00
.82	.08	.92	.67	.22	.00	.56	.00	.29	.00	.08	.87	.77	.91	.98	.00	.91	.77	.93	.96	.78	.91	.91	.00	.00	.00
.76	.09	.87	.65	.24	.00	.53	.00	.31	.00	.00	.82	.70	.86	.93	.00	.95	.76	.88	.91	.77	.91	.91	.00	.00	.00
.76	.09	.91	.71	.32	.00	.60	.00	.15	.00	.00	.77	.76	.90	.84	.00	.91	.70	.88	.91	.72	.95	.95	.00	.00	.00
.81	.00	.87	.71	.24	.00	.60	.00	.23	.00	.00	.82	.76	.90	.84	.00	.86	.70	.88	.87	.77	.91	.91	.00	.09	.00
.78	.08	.92	.68	.28	.00	.53	.00	.27	.00	.00	.79	.78	.91	.85	.00	.92	.68	.89	.92	.79	.96	.96	.00	.08	.00
.74	.09	.89	.69	.31	.00	.45	.00	.30	.00	.08	.80	.74	.88	.86	.00	.89	.63	.86	.94	.75	.89	.89	.00	.00	.00
.84	.09	.94	.63	.15	.00	.58	.00	.30	.00	.08	.84	.79	.93	.95	.00	.93	.79	.91	.94	.80	.93	.93	.00	.00	.00
1.00	.09	.83	.53	.16	.00	.47	.00	.15	.00	.25	.95	.70	.81	.79	.00	.77	.81	.84	.83	.62	.82	.82	.00	.00	.00
.09	1.00	.08	.00	.00	.00	.00	.00	.00	.00	.00	.08	.12	.09	.09	.00	.08	.12	.09	.08	.00	.08	.08	.00	.00	.00
.83	.08	1.00	.68	.28	.00	.53	.00	.27	.00	.07	.83	.78	.91	.89	.00	.92	.73	.89	.96	.79	.96	.96	.00	.00	.00
.53	.00	.68	1.00	.47	.00	.45	.00	.22	.00	.00	.56	.48	.71	.63	.00	.67	.55	.63	.68	.65	.72	.72	.00	.00	.00
.16	.00	.28	.47	1.00	.00	.15	.00	.22	.00	.00	.15	.10	.24	.15	.00	.22	.00	.15	.28	.18	.30	.30	.00	.00	.00
.00	.00	.00	.00	.00	1.00	.00	1.00	.00	.00	.00	.00	.00	.00	.00	.00	.00	.00	.00	.00	.00	.00	.00	.00	.00	.80
.47	.00	.53	.45	.15	.00	1.00	.00	.14	.00	.00	.44	.64	.60	.58	.00	.56	.56	.52	.53	.52	.56	.56	.00	.00	.00
.00	.00	.00	.00	.00	1.00	.00	1.00	.00	.00	.00	.00	.00	.00	.00	.00	.00	.00	.00	.00	.00	.00	.00	.00	.00	.80
.15	.00	.27	.22	.22	.00	.14	.00	1.00	.00	.00	.14	.29	.31	.30	.33	.29	.10	.22	.27	.35	.29	.29	.00	.00	.00
.00	.00	.00	.00	.00	.00	.00	.00	.00	1.00	.00	.00	.00	.00	.00	.00	.00	.00	.00	.00	.00	.00	.00	.00	.00	.00
.25	.00	.07	.00	.00	.00	.00	.00	.00	.00	1.00	.23	.00	.00	.08	.00	.00	.21	.00	.07	.00	.00	.00	.00	.00	.00
.95	.08	.83	.56	.15	.00	.44	.00	.14	.00	.23	1.00	.72	.82	.84	.00	.83	.82	.89	.88	.63	.83	.83	.00	.00	.00
.70	.12	.78	.48	.10	.00	.64	.00	.29	.00	.00	.72	1.00	.86	.74	.00	.77	.63	.84	.78	.59	.82	.82	.00	.00	.00
.81	.09	.91	.71	.24	.00	.60	.00	.31	.00	.00	.82	.86	1.00	.88	.00	.91	.70	.93	.91	.77	.95	.95	.00	.00	.00
.79	.09	.89	.63	.15	.00	.58	.00	.30	.00	.08	.84	.74	.88	1.00	.00	.93	.79	.91	.94	.80	.89	.89	.00	.00	.00
.00	.00	.00	.00	.00	.00	.00	.00	.33	.00	.00	.00	.00	.00	.00	1.00	.00	.00	.00	.00	.00	.00	.00	.00	.00	.00
.77	.08	.92	.67	.22	.00	.56	.00	.29	.00	.00	.83	.77	.91	.93	.00	1.00	.72	.93	.96	.78	.96	.96	.00	.00	.00
.81	.12	.73	.55	.00	.00	.56	.00	.10	.00	.21	.82	.63	.70	.79	.00	.72	1.00	.74	.73	.65	.72	.72	.00	.00	.00
.84	.09	.89	.63	.15	.00	.52	.00	.22	.00	.00	.89	.84	.93	.91	.00	.93	.74	1.00	.94	.75	.93	.93	.00	.00	.00
.83	.08	.96	.68	.28	.00	.53	.00	.27	.00	.07	.88	.78	.91	.94	.00	.96	.73	.94	1.00	.74	.96	.96	.00	.00	.00
.62	.00	.79	.65	.18	.00	.52	.00	.35	.00	.00	.63	.59	.77	.80	.00	.78	.65	.75	.74	1.00	.78	.78	.00	.00	.00
.82	.08	.96	.72	.30	.00	.56	.00	.29	.00	.00	.83	.82	.95	.89	.00	.96	.72	.93	.96	.78	1.00	1.00	.00	.00	.00
.82	.08	.96	.72	.30	.00	.56	.00	.29	.00	.00	.83	.82	.95	.89	.00	.96	.72	.93	.96	.78	1.00	1.00	.00	.00	.00
.00	.00	.00	.00	.00	.00	.00	.00	.00	.00	.00	.00	.00	.00	.00	.00	.00	.00	.00	.00	.00	.00	.00	1.00	.00	.00
.00	.00	.00	.00	.00	.00	.00	.00	.00	.00	.00	.00	.00	.00	.00	.00	.00	.00	.00	.00	.00	.00	.00	.00	1.00	.00
.00	.00	.00	.00	.00	.80	.00	.80	.00	.00	.00	.00	.00	.00	.00	.00	.00	.00	.00	.00	.00	.00	.00	.00	.00	1.00

STRUCTURE VALUE =

DATA SET 172***APURAR***GRAMMATICALNESS (JM)

SIMILARITY MATRIX - ROW

38	27	24	18	16	20	22	41	43	44	46	47	17	23	15	36	25	42	45	28	29	33	40	50	32	30
.00	.00	.00	.00	.00	.00	.08	.00	.00	.00	.00	.00	.00	.00	.00	.00	.00	.00	.00	.00	.00	.00	.00	.00	.00	.00
.00	.00	.00	.00	.00	.00	.00	.00	.00	.00	.00	.00	.00	.00	.00	.00	.00	.00	.00	.00	.00	.00	.00	.00	.00	.00
.09	.08	.09	.08	.08	.09	.08	.08	.09	.08	.08	.08	.10	.09	.10	.08	.09	.12	.00	.00	.00	.00	.00	.00	.00	.00
.00	.07	.08	.08	.08	.00	.00	.00	.00	.07	.00	.00	.00	.08	.09	.23	.25	.21	.00	.00	.00	.00	.00	.00	.00	.00
.00	.00	.00	.00	.00	.00	.00	.00	.00	.00	.00	.00	.00	.00	.00	.00	.00	.00	.00	.00	.00	.00	.00	.00	.00	.00
.00	.00	.00	.00	.00	.00	.00	.00	.00	.00	.00	.00	.00	.00	.00	.00	.00	.00	.00	.00	.00	.00	.00	.00	.00	.00
.00	.00	.00	.00	.00	.00	.00	.00	.00	.00	.00	.00	.00	.00	.00	.00	.00	.00	.00	.00	.00	.00	.00	.00	.00	.00
.00	.00	.00	.00	.00	.00	.00	.00	.00	.00	.00	.00	.00	.00	.00	.00	.00	.00	.00	.00	.00	.00	.00	.00	.00	.00
.00	.00	.00	.00	.00	.00	.00	.00	.00	.00	.00	.00	.00	.00	.00	.00	.00	.00	.00	.00	.00	.00	.00	.00	.00	.00
.00	.00	.00	.00	.00	.00	.00	.00	.00	.00	.00	.00	.00	.00	.00	.00	.00	.00	.00	.00	.00	.00	.00	.00	.00	.00
.00	.00	.00	.00	.00	.00	.00	.00	.00	.00	.00	.00	.00	.00	.00	.00	.00	.00	.00	.00	.00	.00	.00	.00	.00	.00
.00	.00	.00	.00	.00	.00	.00	.00	.00	.00	.00	.00	.00	.00	.00	.00	.00	.00	.00	.00	.00	.00	.00	.00	.00	.00
.00	.00	.00	.00	.00	.00	.00	.00	.00	.00	.00	.00	.00	.00	.00	.00	.00	.00	.00	.00	.00	.00	.00	.00	.00	.00
.12	.11	.11	.06	.11	.12	.11	.11	.11	.11	.11	.11	.12	.11	.12	.11	.12	.07	.06	.08	.00	.00	.00	.00	.00	.00
.00	.00	.00	.00	.00	.00	.00	.00	.00	.00	.00	.00	.00	.00	.00	.00	.00	.00	.00	.00	.00	.00	.00	.00	.00	.00
.06	.05	.06	.06	.06	.06	.11	.06	.06	.05	.06	.06	.00	.06	.06	.06	.06	.07	.13	.08	.00	.00	.00	.00	.00	.00
.18	.16	.17	.17	.17	.18	.16	.17	.17	.16	.17	.17	.12	.17	.18	.17	.18	.21	.19	.23	.00	.00	.00	.00	.00	.00
.00	.00	.00	.00	.00	.00	.00	.00	.00	.00	.00	.00	.00	.00	.00	.00	.00	.00	.00	.00	.00	.00	.00	.00	.00	.00
.60	.53	.58	.56	.50	.60	.53	.56	.52	.53	.56	.56	.48	.45	.48	.44	.47	.56	.52	.45	.15	.14	.00	.00	.00	.00
.73	.76	.71	.70	.79	.78	.76	.74	.76	.76	.79	.79	.75	.67	.70	.74	.73	.61	.58	.48	.25	.24	.10	.00	.00	.00
.86	.78	.79	.77	.82	.76	.78	.77	.84	.78	.82	.82	.83	.74	.78	.72	.70	.63	.59	.48	.10	.29	.00	.00	.00	.00
.90	.87	.88	.86	.86	.86	.91	.86	.88	.87	.91	.91	.83	.79	.78	.82	.81	.70	.77	.71	.24	.23	.00	.00	.00	.00
.88	.89	.95	.98	.89	.84	.85	.93	.91	.94	.89	.89	.86	.86	.81	.84	.79	.79	.80	.63	.15	.30	.00	.00	.00	.00
.86	.87	.88	.91	.86	.86	.87	.95	.88	.91	.91	.91	.83	.84	.83	.82	.76	.76	.77	.65	.24	.31	.00	.00	.00	.00
1.00	.91	.93	.91	.91	.90	.91	.91	.93	.91	.95	.95	.88	.88	.83	.82	.81	.70	.77	.71	.24	.31	.00	.00	.00	.00
.91	1.00	.94	.92	.96	.91	.92	.92	.89	.95	.96	.96	.84	.89	.84	.83	.83	.73	.79	.68	.28	.27	.00	.00	.00	.00
.93	.94	1.00	.93	.93	.88	.89	.93	.91	.94	.93	.93	.86	.86	.81	.84	.84	.79	.80	.63	.15	.30	.00	.00	.00	.00
.91	.92	.93	1.00	.91	.86	.88	.91	.93	.96	.91	.91	.88	.89	.84	.87	.82	.77	.78	.67	.22	.29	.00	.00	.00	.00
.91	.96	.93	.91	1.00	.91	.92	.91	.93	.95	.96	.96	.88	.89	.88	.87	.86	.77	.73	.67	.22	.21	.00	.00	.00	.00
.90	.91	.88	.86	.91	1.00	.91	.91	.88	.91	.95	.95	.83	.84	.78	.77	.76	.70	.72	.71	.32	.15	.00	.00	.00	.00
.91	.92	.89	.88	.92	.91	1.00	.92	.89	.92	.96	.96	.84	.85	.80	.79	.78	.68	.79	.68	.28	.27	.00	.00	.00	.00
.91	.92	.93	.91	.91	.91	.92	1.00	.93	.96	.96	.96	.88	.89	.84	.83	.77	.72	.78	.67	.22	.29	.00	.00	.00	.00
.93	.89	.91	.93	.93	.88	.89	.93	1.00	.94	.93	.93	.95	.86	.86	.89	.84	.74	.75	.63	.15	.22	.00	.00	.00	.00
.91	.96	.94	.96	.96	.91	.92	.96	.94	1.00	.96	.96	.89	.94	.89	.88	.83	.73	.74	.68	.28	.27	.00	.00	.00	.00
.95	.96	.93	.91	.96	.95	.96	.96	.93	.96	1.00	1.00	.88	.89	.84	.83	.82	.72	.78	.72	.30	.29	.00	.00	.00	.00
.95	.96	.93	.91	.96	.95	.96	.96	.93	.96	1.00	1.00	.88	.89	.84	.83	.82	.72	.78	.72	.30	.29	.00	.00	.00	.00
.88	.84	.86	.88	.88	.83	.84	.88	.95	.89	.88	.88	1.00	.81	.80	.84	.78	.67	.68	.61	.17	.24	.00	.00	.00	.00
.88	.89	.86	.89	.89	.84	.85	.89	.86	.94	.89	.89	.81	1.00	.86	.80	.74	.63	.75	.69	.31	.30	.00	.00	.00	.00
.83	.84	.81	.84	.88	.78	.80	.84	.86	.89	.84	.84	.80	.86	1.00	.88	.83	.78	.58	.61	.17	.16	.00	.00	.00	.00
.82	.83	.84	.87	.87	.77	.79	.83	.89	.88	.83	.83	.84	.80	.88	1.00	.95	.82	.63	.56	.15	.14	.00	.00	.00	.00
.81	.83	.84	.82	.86	.76	.78	.77	.84	.83	.82	.82	.78	.74	.83	.95	1.00	.81	.62	.53	.16	.15	.00	.00	.00	.00
.70	.73	.79	.77	.77	.70	.68	.72	.74	.73	.72	.72	.67	.63	.78	.82	.81	1.00	.65	.55	.00	.10	.00	.00	.00	.00
.77	.79	.80	.78	.73	.72	.79	.78	.75	.74	.78	.78	.68	.75	.58	.63	.62	.65	1.00	.65	.18	.35	.00	.00	.00	.00
.71	.68	.63	.67	.67	.71	.68	.67	.63	.68	.72	.72	.61	.69	.61	.56	.53	.55	.65	1.00	.47	.22	.00	.00	.00	.00
.24	.28	.15	.22	.22	.32	.28	.22	.15	.28	.30	.30	.17	.31	.17	.15	.16	.00	.18	.47	1.00	.22	.00	.00	.00	.00
.31	.27	.30	.29	.21	.15	.27	.29	.22	.27	.29	.29	.24	.30	.16	.14	.15	.10	.35	.22	.22	1.00	.33	.00	.00	.00
.00	.00	.00	.00	.00	.00	.00	.00	.00	.00	.00	.00	.00	.00	.00	.00	.00	.00	.00	.00	.00	.33	1.00	.00	.00	.00
.00	.00	.00	.00	.00	.00	.00	.00	.00	.00	.00	.00	.00	.00	.00	.00	.00	.00	.00	.00	.00	.00	.00	1.00	.80	.80
.00	.00	.00	.00	.00	.00	.00	.00	.00	.00	.00	.00	.00	.00	.00	.00	.00	.00	.00	.00	.00	.00	.00	.80	1.00	1.00
.00	.00	.00	.00	.00	.00	.00	.00	.00	.00	.00	.00	.00	.00	.00	.00	.00	.00	.00	.00	.00	.00	.00	.80	1.00	1.00

Table 4

DATA SET 172***APURAR***GRAMMATICALNESS (JM)

SIMILARITY MATRIX - COLUMN

COL/COL	1	2	3	4	5	6	7	8	9	10	11	12	13	14	15	16	17	18	19	20	21	22	23	24
1	1.00	.89	.82	.46	.80	.18	.84	1.00	.67	.70	.46	.90	.53	.07	.00	.00	.00	.12	.00	.00	.00	.00	.06	.00
2	.89	1.00	.82	.31	.80	.18	.84	.89	.78	.60	.46	.90	.40	.07	.00	.00	.00	.12	.00	.00	.00	.00	.06	.00
3	.82	.82	1.00	.47	.92	.27	.87	.82	.73	.83	.35	.92	.63	.06	.00	.00	.00	.11	.00	.00	.00	.00	.05	.00
4	.46	.31	.47	1.00	.53	.33	.43	.46	.31	.53	.25	.53	.80	.00	.00	.00	.00	.00	.00	.00	.00	.00	.00	.00
5	.80	.80	.92	.53	1.00	.31	.86	.80	.80	.82	.40	.91	.47	.06	.00	.00	.00	.11	.00	.00	.00	.00	.06	.00
6	.18	.18	.27	.33	.31	1.00	.00	.18	.00	.31	.00	.15	.25	.00	.00	.00	.00	.00	.00	.00	.00	.00	.00	.00
7	.84	.84	.87	.43	.86	.00	1.00	.84	.84	.67	.43	.95	.50	.07	.00	.00	.00	.12	.00	.00	.00	.00	.06	.00
8	1.00	.89	.82	.46	.80	.18	.84	1.00	.67	.70	.46	.90	.53	.07	.00	.00	.00	.12	.00	.00	.00	.00	.06	.00
9	.67	.78	.73	.31	.80	.00	.84	.67	1.00	.70	.62	.80	.27	.07	.00	.00	.00	.12	.00	.00	.00	.00	.06	.00
10	.70	.60	.83	.53	.82	.31	.67	.70	.70	1.00	.40	.73	.59	.06	.00	.00	.00	.11	.00	.00	.00	.00	.06	.00
11	.46	.46	.35	.25	.40	.00	.43	.46	.62	.40	1.00	.40	.20	.08	.00	.00	.00	.00	.00	.00	.00	.00	.00	.00
12	.90	.90	.92	.53	.91	.15	.95	.90	.80	.73	.40	1.00	.59	.06	.00	.00	.00	.11	.00	.00	.00	.00	.06	.00
13	.53	.40	.63	.80	.47	.25	.50	.53	.27	.59	.20	.59	1.00	.00	.00	.00	.00	.00	.00	.00	.00	.00	.00	.00
14	.07	.07	.06	.00	.06	.00	.07	.07	.07	.06	.08	.06	.00	1.00	.84	.85	.75	.73	.47	.90	.83	.82	.80	.79
15	.00	.00	.00	.00	.00	.00	.00	.00	.00	.00	.00	.00	.00	.84	1.00	.79	.88	.81	.61	.93	.90	.89	.88	.87
16	.00	.00	.00	.00	.00	.00	.00	.00	.00	.00	.00	.00	.00	.85	.79	1.00	.70	.73	.47	.86	.83	.82	.80	.84
17	.00	.00	.00	.00	.00	.00	.00	.00	.00	.00	.00	.00	.00	.75	.88	.70	1.00	.73	.53	.86	.83	.86	.80	.84
18	.12	.12	.11	.00	.11	.00	.12	.12	.12	.11	.00	.11	.00	.73	.81	.73	.73	1.00	.53	.83	.88	.88	.94	.85
19	.00	.00	.00	.00	.00	.00	.00	.00	.00	.00	.00	.00	.00	.47	.61	.47	.53	.53	1.00	.63	.56	.59	.57	.55
20	.00	.00	.00	.00	.00	.00	.00	.00	.00	.00	.00	.00	.00	.90	.93	.86	.86	.83	.63	1.00	.92	.91	.89	.89
21	.00	.00	.00	.00	.00	.00	.00	.00	.00	.00	.00	.00	.00	.83	.90	.83	.83	.88	.56	.92	1.00	.96	.94	.90
22	.00	.00	.00	.00	.00	.00	.00	.00	.00	.00	.00	.00	.00	.82	.89	.82	.86	.88	.59	.91	.96	1.00	.94	.89
23	.06	.06	.05	.00	.06	.00	.06	.06	.06	.06	.00	.06	.00	.80	.88	.80	.80	.94	.57	.89	.94	.94	1.00	.92
24	.00	.00	.00	.00	.00	.00	.00	.00	.00	.00	.00	.00	.00	.79	.87	.84	.84	.85	.55	.89	.90	.89	.92	1.00
25	.00	.00	.00	.00	.00	.00	.00	.00	.00	.00	.00	.00	.00	.81	.84	.76	.81	.83	.63	.91	.88	.87	.85	.80
26	.00	.00	.00	.00	.00	.00	.00	.00	.00	.00	.00	.00	.00	.00	.00	.00	.00	.00	.00	.00	.00	.00	.00	.00
27	.00	.00	.00	.00	.00	.00	.00	.00	.00	.00	.00	.00	.00	.50	.57	.50	.44	.61	.55	.59	.58	.56	.59	.51
28	.17	.17	.13	.00	.14	.00	.15	.17	.17	.14	.00	.14	.00	.09	.15	.09	.17	.22	.00	.08	.14	.15	.14	.15
29	.00	.00	.00	.00	.00	.00	.00	.00	.00	.00	.00	.00	.00	.65	.59	.71	.65	.63	.42	.67	.65	.68	.67	.70
30	.00	.00	.00	.00	.00	.00	.00	.00	.00	.00	.00	.00	.00	.00	.00	.00	.00	.00	.00	.00	.00	.00	.00	.00
31	.00	.00	.00	.00	.00	.00	.00	.00	.00	.00	.00	.00	.00	.84	.92	.80	.84	.86	.57	.94	.98	.94	.92	.88
32	.00	.00	.00	.00	.00	.00	.00	.00	.00	.00	.00	.00	.00	.00	.00	.00	.00	.00	.00	.00	.00	.00	.00	.00
33	.00	.00	.00	.00	.00	.00	.00	.00	.00	.00	.00	.00	.00	.77	.94	.77	.82	.88	.59	.87	.92	.92	.90	.85
34	.89	.89	.82	.31	.80	.36	.74	.89	.67	.70	.46	.80	.40	.07	.00	.00	.00	.12	.00	.00	.00	.00	.06	.00
35	.00	.00	.00	.00	.00	.00	.00	.00	.00	.00	.00	.00	.00	.17	.15	.17	.00	.15	.15	.16	.14	.07	.14	.15
36	.00	.00	.00	.00	.00	.00	.00	.00	.00	.00	.00	.00	.00	.24	.21	.24	.08	.21	.13	.22	.26	.21	.27	.21
37	.00	.00	.00	.00	.00	.00	.00	.00	.00	.00	.00	.00	.00	.84	.92	.80	.84	.86	.57	.94	.98	.94	.92	.88
38	.00	.00	.00	.00	.00	.00	.00	.00	.00	.00	.00	.00	.00	.56	.71	.62	.77	.74	.41	.68	.76	.74	.73	.81
39	.12	.12	.11	.00	.11	.00	.11	.12	.12	.11	.07	.11	.00	.80	.83	.76	.76	.94	.57	.85	.90	.90	.96	.88
40	.00	.00	.00	.00	.00	.00	.00	.00	.00	.00	.00	.00	.00	.09	.15	.09	.17	.00	.00	.08	.07	.07	.07	.08
41	.00	.00	.00	.00	.00	.00	.00	.00	.00	.00	.00	.00	.00	.83	.90	.83	.83	.88	.56	.92	1.00	.96	.94	.90
42	.00	.00	.00	.00	.00	.00	.00	.00	.00	.00	.00	.00	.00	.84	.87	.79	.79	.81	.55	.93	.94	.89	.88	.83
43	.00	.00	.00	.00	.00	.00	.00	.00	.00	.00	.00	.00	.00	.82	.85	.82	.77	.83	.53	.91	.96	.92	.90	.85
44	.00	.00	.00	.00	.00	.00	.00	.00	.00	.00	.00	.00	.00	.82	.89	.77	.82	.88	.53	.91	.96	.92	.90	.85
45	.00	.00	.00	.00	.00	.00	.00	.00	.00	.00	.00	.00	.00	.09	.16	.09	.18	.15	.00	.08	.14	.15	.15	.16
46	.00	.00	.00	.00	.00	.00	.00	.00	.00	.00	.00	.00	.00	.75	.84	.70	.80	.82	.53	.86	.87	.86	.89	.88
47	.00	.00	.00	.00	.00	.00	.00	.00	.00	.00	.00	.00	.00	.75	.79	.75	.85	.77	.47	.81	.87	.86	.80	.84
48	.00	.00	.00	.00	.00	.00	.00	.00	.00	.00	.00	.00	.00	.09	.08	.09	.09	.00	.00	.08	.07	.08	.07	.08
49	.00	.00	.00	.00	.00	.00	.00	.00	.00	.00	.00	.00	.00	.17	.15	.17	.09	.15	.00	.16	.14	.15	.14	.15
50	.00	.00	.00	.00	.00	.00	.00	.00	.00	.00	.00	.00	.00	.00	.00	.00	.00	.00	.00	.00	.00	.00	.00	.00

Table 5

DATA SET 172***APURAR***GRAMMATICALNESS (JM)

SIMILARITY MATRIX - COLUMN

COL/COL	26	11	9	10	5	3	12	7	2	8	1	34	13	4	6	49	28	45	38	47	46	17	24	39
26	.00	.00	.00	.00	.00	.00	.00	.00	.00	.00	.00	.00	.00	.00	.00	.00	.00	.00	.00	.00	.00	.00	.00	.00
11	.00	1.00	.62	.40	.40	.35	.40	.43	.46	.46	.46	.46	.20	.25	.00	.00	.00	.00	.00	.00	.00	.00	.00	.07
9	.00	.62	1.00	.70	.80	.73	.80	.84	.78	.67	.67	.67	.27	.31	.00	.00	.17	.00	.00	.00	.00	.00	.00	.12
10	.00	.40	.70	1.00	.82	.83	.73	.67	.60	.70	.70	.70	.59	.53	.31	.00	.14	.00	.00	.00	.00	.00	.00	.11
5	.00	.40	.80	.82	1.00	.92	.91	.86	.80	.80	.80	.80	.47	.53	.31	.00	.14	.00	.00	.00	.00	.00	.00	.11
3	.00	.35	.73	.83	.92	1.00	.92	.87	.82	.82	.82	.82	.63	.47	.27	.00	.13	.00	.00	.00	.00	.00	.00	.11
12	.00	.40	.80	.73	.91	.92	1.00	.95	.90	.90	.90	.80	.59	.53	.15	.00	.14	.00	.00	.00	.00	.00	.00	.11
7	.00	.43	.84	.67	.86	.87	.95	1.00	.84	.84	.84	.74	.50	.43	.00	.00	.15	.00	.00	.00	.00	.00	.00	.11
2	.00	.46	.78	.60	.80	.82	.90	.84	1.00	.89	.89	.89	.40	.31	.18	.00	.17	.00	.00	.00	.00	.00	.00	.12
8	.00	.46	.67	.70	.80	.82	.90	.84	.89	1.00	1.00	.89	.53	.46	.18	.00	.17	.00	.00	.00	.00	.00	.00	.12
1	.00	.46	.67	.70	.80	.82	.90	.84	.89	1.00	1.00	.89	.53	.46	.18	.00	.17	.00	.00	.00	.00	.00	.00	.12
34	.00	.46	.67	.70	.80	.82	.80	.74	.89	.89	.89	1.00	.40	.31	.36	.00	.17	.00	.00	.00	.00	.00	.00	.12
13	.00	.20	.27	.59	.47	.63	.59	.50	.40	.53	.53	.40	1.00	.80	.25	.00	.00	.00	.00	.00	.00	.00	.00	.00
4	.00	.25	.31	.53	.53	.47	.53	.43	.31	.46	.46	.31	.80	1.00	.33	.00	.00	.00	.00	.00	.00	.00	.00	.00
6	.00	.00	.00	.31	.31	.27	.15	.00	.18	.18	.18	.36	.25	.33	1.00	.00	.00	.00	.00	.00	.00	.00	.00	.00
49	.00	.00	.00	.00	.00	.00	.00	.00	.00	.00	.00	.00	.00	.00	.00	1.00	.33	.00	.18	.17	.17	.09	.15	.14
28	.00	.00	.17	.14	.14	.13	.14	.15	.17	.17	.17	.17	.00	.00	.00	.33	1.00	.40	.18	.17	.17	.17	.15	.14
45	.00	.00	.00	.00	.00	.00	.00	.00	.00	.00	.00	.00	.00	.00	.00	.00	.40	1.00	.19	.18	.18	.18	.16	.15
38	.00	.00	.00	.00	.00	.00	.00	.00	.00	.00	.00	.00	.00	.00	.00	.18	.18	.19	1.00	.82	.67	.77	.81	.73
47	.00	.00	.00	.00	.00	.00	.00	.00	.00	.00	.00	.00	.00	.00	.00	.17	.17	.18	.82	1.00	.75	.85	.84	.80
46	.00	.00	.00	.00	.00	.00	.00	.00	.00	.00	.00	.00	.00	.00	.00	.17	.17	.18	.67	.75	1.00	.80	.88	.84
17	.00	.00	.00	.00	.00	.00	.00	.00	.00	.00	.00	.00	.00	.00	.00	.09	.17	.18	.77	.85	.80	1.00	.84	.76
24	.00	.00	.00	.00	.00	.00	.00	.00	.00	.00	.00	.00	.00	.00	.00	.15	.15	.16	.81	.84	.88	.84	1.00	.88
39	.00	.07	.12	.11	.11	.11	.11	.11	.12	.12	.12	.12	.00	.00	.00	.14	.14	.15	.73	.80	.84	.76	.88	1.00
23	.00	.00	.06	.06	.06	.05	.06	.06	.06	.06	.06	.06	.00	.00	.00	.14	.14	.15	.73	.80	.89	.80	.92	.96
18	.00	.00	.12	.11	.11	.11	.11	.12	.12	.12	.12	.12	.00	.00	.00	.15	.22	.15	.74	.77	.82	.73	.85	.94
44	.00	.00	.00	.00	.00	.00	.00	.00	.00	.00	.00	.00	.00	.00	.00	.15	.15	.15	.74	.82	.86	.82	.85	.86
43	.00	.00	.00	.00	.00	.00	.00	.00	.00	.00	.00	.00	.00	.00	.00	.15	.07	.08	.70	.82	.86	.77	.85	.86
42	.00	.00	.00	.00	.00	.00	.00	.00	.00	.00	.00	.00	.00	.00	.00	.15	.08	.08	.67	.79	.88	.79	.83	.83
41	.00	.00	.00	.00	.00	.00	.00	.00	.00	.00	.00	.00	.00	.00	.00	.14	.14	.14	.76	.87	.87	.83	.90	.90
25	.00	.00	.00	.00	.00	.00	.00	.00	.00	.00	.00	.00	.00	.00	.00	.08	.08	.08	.63	.76	.81	.81	.80	.85
22	.00	.00	.00	.00	.00	.00	.00	.00	.00	.00	.00	.00	.00	.00	.00	.15	.15	.15	.74	.86	.86	.86	.89	.90
21	.00	.00	.00	.00	.00	.00	.00	.00	.00	.00	.00	.00	.00	.00	.00	.14	.14	.14	.76	.87	.87	.83	.90	.90
37	.00	.00	.00	.00	.00	.00	.00	.00	.00	.00	.00	.00	.00	.00	.00	.14	.14	.15	.73	.84	.89	.84	.88	.88
33	.00	.00	.00	.00	.00	.00	.00	.00	.00	.00	.00	.00	.00	.00	.00	.15	.15	.15	.74	.82	.82	.82	.85	.90
31	.00	.00	.00	.00	.00	.00	.00	.00	.00	.00	.00	.00	.00	.00	.00	.14	.14	.15	.73	.84	.89	.84	.88	.88
15	.00	.00	.00	.00	.00	.00	.00	.00	.00	.00	.00	.00	.00	.00	.00	.15	.15	.16	.71	.79	.84	.88	.87	.83
20	.00	.00	.00	.00	.00	.00	.00	.00	.00	.00	.00	.00	.00	.00	.00	.16	.08	.08	.68	.81	.86	.86	.89	.85
14	.00	.08	.07	.06	.06	.06	.06	.07	.07	.07	.07	.07	.00	.00	.00	.17	.09	.09	.56	.75	.75	.75	.79	.80
16	.00	.00	.00	.00	.00	.00	.00	.00	.00	.00	.00	.00	.00	.00	.00	.17	.09	.09	.62	.75	.70	.70	.84	.76
29	.00	.00	.00	.00	.00	.00	.00	.00	.00	.00	.00	.00	.00	.00	.00	.12	.12	.13	.67	.59	.59	.65	.70	.62
19	.00	.00	.00	.00	.00	.00	.00	.00	.00	.00	.00	.00	.00	.00	.00	.00	.00	.00	.41	.47	.53	.53	.55	.57
27	.00	.00	.00	.00	.00	.00	.00	.00	.00	.00	.00	.00	.00	.00	.00	.00	.00	.14	.39	.44	.56	.44	.51	.59
36	.00	.00	.00	.00	.00	.00	.00	.00	.00	.00	.00	.00	.00	.00	.00	.00	.00	.00	.00	.00	.32	.08	.21	.20
35	.00	.00	.00	.00	.00	.00	.00	.00	.00	.00	.00	.00	.00	.00	.00	.00	.00	.00	.00	.00	.17	.00	.15	.14
48	.00	.00	.00	.00	.00	.00	.00	.00	.00	.00	.00	.00	.00	.00	.00	.00	.00	.00	.00	.00	.09	.09	.08	.00
40	.00	.00	.00	.00	.00	.00	.00	.00	.00	.00	.00	.00	.00	.00	.00	.00	.00	.00	.09	.00	.09	.17	.08	.00
50	.00	.00	.00	.00	.00	.00	.00	.00	.00	.00	.00	.00	.00	.00	.00	.00	.00	.00	.00	.00	.00	.00	.00	.00
32	.00	.00	.00	.00	.00	.00	.00	.00	.00	.00	.00	.00	.00	.00	.00	.00	.00	.00	.00	.00	.00	.00	.00	.00
30	.00	.00	.00	.00	.00	.00	.00	.00	.00	.00	.00	.00	.00	.00	.00	.00	.00	.00	.00	.00	.00	.00	.00	.00

DATA SET 172•••APURAR•••GRAMMATICALNESS (JM)

SIMILARITY MATRIX - COLUMN

25	26	27	28	29	30	31	32	33	34	35	36	37	38	39	40	41	42	43	44	45	46	47	48	49	50
.00	.00	.00	.17	.00	.00	.00	.00	.00	.89	.00	.00	.00	.00	.12	.00	.00	.00	.00	.00	.00	.00	.00	.00	.00	.00
.00	.00	.00	.17	.00	.00	.00	.00	.00	.89	.00	.00	.00	.00	.12	.00	.00	.00	.00	.00	.00	.00	.00	.00	.00	.00
.00	.00	.00	.13	.00	.00	.00	.00	.00	.82	.00	.00	.00	.00	.11	.00	.00	.00	.00	.00	.00	.00	.00	.00	.00	.00
.00	.00	.00	.00	.00	.00	.00	.00	.00	.31	.00	.00	.00	.00	.00	.00	.00	.00	.00	.00	.00	.00	.00	.00	.00	.00
.00	.00	.00	.14	.00	.00	.00	.00	.00	.80	.00	.00	.00	.00	.11	.00	.00	.00	.00	.00	.00	.00	.00	.00	.00	.00
.00	.00	.00	.00	.00	.00	.00	.00	.00	.36	.00	.00	.00	.00	.00	.00	.00	.00	.00	.00	.00	.00	.00	.00	.00	.00
.00	.00	.00	.15	.00	.00	.00	.00	.00	.74	.00	.00	.00	.00	.11	.00	.00	.00	.00	.00	.00	.00	.00	.00	.00	.00
.00	.00	.00	.17	.00	.00	.00	.00	.00	.89	.00	.00	.00	.00	.12	.00	.00	.00	.00	.00	.00	.00	.00	.00	.00	.00
.00	.00	.00	.17	.00	.00	.00	.00	.00	.67	.00	.00	.00	.00	.12	.00	.00	.00	.00	.00	.00	.00	.00	.00	.00	.00
.00	.00	.00	.14	.00	.00	.00	.00	.00	.70	.00	.00	.00	.00	.11	.00	.00	.00	.00	.00	.00	.00	.00	.00	.00	.00
.00	.00	.00	.00	.00	.00	.00	.00	.00	.46	.00	.00	.00	.00	.07	.00	.00	.00	.00	.00	.00	.00	.00	.00	.00	.00
.00	.00	.00	.14	.00	.00	.00	.00	.00	.80	.00	.00	.00	.00	.11	.00	.00	.00	.00	.00	.00	.00	.00	.00	.00	.00
.00	.00	.00	.00	.00	.00	.00	.00	.00	.40	.00	.00	.00	.00	.00	.00	.00	.00	.00	.00	.00	.00	.00	.00	.00	.00
.81	.00	.53	.09	.65	.00	.84	.00	.77	.07	.17	.24	.84	.56	.80	.09	.83	.84	.82	.82	.09	.75	.75	.09	.17	.00
.84	.00	.57	.15	.59	.00	.92	.00	.94	.00	.15	.21	.92	.71	.83	.15	.90	.87	.85	.89	.16	.84	.79	.08	.15	.00
.76	.00	.50	.09	.71	.00	.80	.00	.77	.00	.17	.24	.80	.62	.76	.09	.83	.79	.82	.77	.09	.70	.75	.09	.17	.00
.81	.00	.44	.17	.65	.00	.84	.00	.82	.00	.00	.08	.84	.77	.76	.17	.83	.79	.77	.82	.18	.80	.85	.09	.09	.00
.83	.00	.61	.22	.63	.00	.86	.00	.88	.12	.15	.21	.86	.74	.94	.00	.88	.81	.83	.88	.15	.82	.77	.00	.15	.00
.63	.00	.55	.00	.42	.00	.57	.00	.59	.00	.15	.13	.57	.41	.57	.00	.56	.55	.53	.53	.00	.53	.47	.00	.00	.00
.91	.00	.59	.08	.67	.00	.94	.00	.87	.00	.16	.22	.94	.68	.85	.08	.92	.93	.91	.91	.08	.86	.81	.08	.16	.00
.88	.00	.58	.14	.65	.00	.98	.00	.92	.00	.14	.26	.98	.76	.90	.07	1.00	.94	.96	.96	.14	.87	.87	.07	.14	.00
.87	.00	.56	.15	.68	.00	.94	.00	.92	.00	.07	.21	.94	.74	.90	.07	.96	.89	.92	.92	.15	.86	.86	.08	.15	.00
.85	.00	.59	.14	.67	.00	.92	.00	.90	.06	.14	.27	.92	.73	.96	.07	.94	.88	.90	.90	.15	.89	.80	.07	.14	.00
.80	.00	.51	.15	.70	.00	.88	.00	.85	.00	.15	.21	.88	.81	.88	.08	.90	.83	.85	.85	.16	.88	.84	.08	.15	.00
1.00	.00	.65	.08	.61	.00	.89	.00	.87	.00	.16	.22	.89	.63	.85	.00	.88	.89	.87	.87	.08	.81	.76	.00	.08	.00
.00	.00	.00	.00	.00	.00	.00	.00	.00	.00	.00	.00	.00	.00	.00	.00	.00	.00	.00	.00	.00	.00	.00	.00	.00	.00
.65	.00	1.00	.00	.38	.00	.59	.00	.61	.00	.40	.47	.59	.39	.59	.00	.58	.57	.56	.61	.14	.56	.44	.00	.00	.00
.08	.00	.00	1.00	.12	.00	.14	.00	.15	.17	.00	.00	.14	.18	.14	.00	.14	.08	.07	.15	.40	.17	.17	.00	.33	.00
.61	.00	.38	.12	1.00	.00	.62	.00	.58	.00	.00	.11	.62	.67	.62	.12	.65	.59	.63	.63	.13	.59	.59	.13	.12	.00
.00	.00	.00	.00	.00	1.00	.00	1.00	.00	.00	.00	.00	.00	.00	.00	.00	.00	.00	.00	.00	.00	.00	.00	.00	.00	.50
.89	.00	.59	.14	.62	.00	1.00	.00	.90	.00	.14	.27	1.00	.73	.88	.07	.98	.96	.94	.98	.15	.89	.84	.07	.14	.00
.00	.00	.00	.00	.00	1.00	.00	1.00	.00	.00	.00	.00	.00	.00	.00	.00	.00	.00	.00	.00	.00	.00	.00	.00	.00	.50
.87	.00	.61	.15	.58	.00	.90	.00	1.00	.00	.15	.21	.90	.74	.90	.07	.92	.85	.88	.88	.15	.82	.82	.00	.15	.00
.00	.00	.00	.17	.00	.00	.00	.00	.00	1.00	.00	.00	.00	.00	.12	.00	.00	.00	.00	.00	.00	.00	.00	.00	.00	.00
.16	.00	.40	.00	.00	.00	.14	.00	.15	.00	1.00	.75	.14	.00	.14	.00	.14	.15	.15	.15	.00	.17	.00	.00	.00	.00
.22	.00	.47	.00	.11	.00	.27	.00	.21	.00	.75	1.00	.27	.00	.20	.25	.26	.29	.28	.28	.00	.32	.00	.29	.00	.00
.89	.00	.59	.14	.62	.00	1.00	.00	.90	.00	.14	.27	1.00	.73	.88	.07	.98	.96	.94	.98	.15	.89	.84	.07	.14	.00
.63	.00	.39	.18	.67	.00	.73	.00	.74	.00	.00	.00	.73	1.00	.73	.09	.76	.67	.70	.74	.19	.67	.82	.00	.18	.00
.85	.00	.59	.14	.62	.00	.88	.00	.90	.12	.14	.20	.88	.73	1.00	.00	.90	.83	.86	.86	.15	.84	.80	.00	.14	.00
.00	.00	.00	.00	.12	.00	.07	.00	.07	.00	.00	.25	.07	.09	.00	1.00	.07	.08	.07	.07	.00	.09	.00	.40	.00	.00
.88	.00	.58	.14	.65	.00	.98	.00	.92	.00	.14	.26	.98	.76	.90	.07	1.00	.94	.96	.96	.14	.87	.87	.07	.14	.00
.89	.00	.57	.08	.59	.00	.96	.00	.85	.00	.15	.29	.96	.67	.83	.08	.94	1.00	.98	.94	.08	.88	.79	.08	.15	.00
.87	.00	.56	.07	.63	.00	.94	.00	.88	.00	.15	.28	.94	.70	.86	.07	.96	.98	1.00	.92	.08	.86	.82	.08	.15	.00
.87	.00	.61	.15	.63	.00	.98	.00	.88	.00	.15	.28	.98	.74	.86	.07	.96	.94	.92	1.00	.15	.86	.82	.08	.15	.00
.08	.00	.14	.40	.13	.00	.15	.00	.15	.00	.00	.00	.15	.19	.15	.00	.14	.08	.08	.15	1.00	.18	.18	.00	.00	.00
.81	.00	.56	.17	.59	.00	.89	.00	.82	.00	.17	.32	.89	.67	.84	.09	.87	.88	.86	.86	.18	1.00	.75	.09	.17	.00
.76	.00	.44	.17	.59	.00	.84	.00	.82	.00	.00	.00	.84	.82	.80	.00	.87	.79	.82	.82	.18	.75	1.00	.00	.17	.00
.00	.00	.00	.00	.13	.00	.07	.00	.00	.00	.00	.29	.07	.00	.00	.40	.07	.08	.08	.08	.00	.09	.00	1.00	.00	.00
.08	.00	.00	.33	.12	.00	.14	.00	.15	.00	.00	.00	.14	.18	.14	.00	.14	.15	.15	.15	.00	.17	.17	.00	1.00	.00
.00	.00	.00	.00	.00	.50	.00	.50	.00	.00	.00	.00	.00	.00	.00	.00	.00	.00	.00	.00	.00	.00	.00	.00	.00	1.00

STRUCTURE VALUE = .8095

DATA SET 172•••APURAR•••GRAMMATICALNESS (JM)

SIMILARITY MATRIX - COLUMN

23	18	44	43	42	41	25	22	21	37	33	31	15	20	14	16	29	19	27	36	35	48	40	50	32	30
.00	.00	.00	.00	.00	.00	.00	.00	.00	.00	.00	.00	.00	.00	.00	.00	.00	.00	.00	.00	.00	.00	.00	.00	.00	.00
.00	.00	.00	.00	.00	.00	.00	.00	.00	.00	.00	.00	.00	.00	.08	.00	.00	.00	.00	.00	.00	.00	.00	.00	.00	.00
.06	.12	.00	.00	.00	.00	.00	.00	.00	.00	.00	.00	.00	.00	.07	.00	.00	.00	.00	.00	.00	.00	.00	.00	.00	.00
.06	.11	.00	.00	.00	.00	.00	.00	.00	.00	.00	.00	.00	.00	.06	.00	.00	.00	.00	.00	.00	.00	.00	.00	.00	.00
.06	.11	.00	.00	.00	.00	.00	.00	.00	.00	.00	.00	.00	.00	.06	.00	.00	.00	.00	.00	.00	.00	.00	.00	.00	.00
.05	.11	.00	.00	.00	.00	.00	.00	.00	.00	.00	.00	.00	.00	.06	.00	.00	.00	.00	.00	.00	.00	.00	.00	.00	.00
.06	.11	.00	.00	.00	.00	.00	.00	.00	.00	.00	.00	.00	.00	.06	.00	.00	.00	.00	.00	.00	.00	.00	.00	.00	.00
.06	.12	.00	.00	.00	.00	.00	.00	.00	.00	.00	.00	.00	.00	.07	.00	.00	.00	.00	.00	.00	.00	.00	.00	.00	.00
.06	.12	.00	.00	.00	.00	.00	.00	.00	.00	.00	.00	.00	.00	.07	.00	.00	.00	.00	.00	.00	.00	.00	.00	.00	.00
.06	.12	.00	.00	.00	.00	.00	.00	.00	.00	.00	.00	.00	.00	.07	.00	.00	.00	.00	.00	.00	.00	.00	.00	.00	.00
.06	.12	.00	.00	.00	.00	.00	.00	.00	.00	.00	.00	.00	.00	.07	.00	.00	.00	.00	.00	.00	.00	.00	.00	.00	.00
.06	.12	.00	.00	.00	.00	.00	.00	.00	.00	.00	.00	.00	.00	.07	.00	.00	.00	.00	.00	.00	.00	.00	.00	.00	.00
.00	.00	.00	.00	.00	.00	.00	.00	.00	.00	.00	.00	.00	.00	.00	.00	.00	.00	.00	.00	.00	.00	.00	.00	.00	.00
.00	.00	.00	.00	.00	.00	.00	.00	.00	.00	.00	.00	.00	.00	.00	.00	.00	.00	.00	.00	.00	.00	.00	.00	.00	.00
.00	.00	.00	.00	.00	.00	.00	.00	.00	.00	.00	.00	.00	.00	.00	.00	.00	.00	.00	.00	.00	.00	.00	.00	.00	.00
.14	.15	.15	.15	.15	.14	.08	.15	.14	.14	.15	.14	.15	.16	.17	.17	.12	.00	.00	.00	.00	.00	.00	.00	.00	.00
.14	.22	.15	.07	.08	.14	.08	.15	.14	.14	.15	.14	.15	.08	.09	.09	.12	.00	.00	.00	.00	.00	.00	.00	.00	.00
.15	.15	.15	.08	.08	.14	.08	.15	.14	.15	.15	.15	.16	.08	.09	.09	.13	.00	.14	.00	.00	.00	.00	.00	.00	.00
.73	.74	.74	.70	.67	.76	.63	.74	.76	.73	.74	.73	.71	.68	.56	.62	.67	.41	.39	.00	.00	.00	.09	.00	.00	.00
.80	.77	.82	.82	.79	.87	.76	.86	.87	.84	.82	.84	.79	.81	.75	.75	.59	.47	.44	.00	.00	.00	.00	.00	.00	.00
.89	.82	.86	.86	.88	.87	.81	.86	.87	.89	.82	.89	.84	.86	.75	.70	.59	.53	.56	.32	.17	.09	.09	.00	.00	.00
.80	.73	.82	.77	.79	.83	.81	.86	.83	.84	.82	.84	.88	.86	.75	.70	.65	.53	.44	.08	.00	.09	.17	.00	.00	.00
.92	.85	.85	.85	.83	.90	.80	.89	.90	.88	.85	.88	.87	.89	.79	.84	.70	.55	.51	.21	.15	.08	.08	.00	.00	.00
.96	.94	.86	.86	.83	.90	.85	.90	.90	.88	.90	.88	.83	.85	.80	.76	.62	.57	.59	.20	.14	.00	.00	.00	.00	.00
1.00	.94	.90	.90	.88	.94	.85	.94	.94	.92	.90	.92	.88	.89	.80	.80	.67	.57	.59	.27	.14	.07	.07	.00	.00	.00
.94	1.00	.88	.83	.81	.88	.83	.88	.88	.86	.88	.86	.81	.83	.73	.73	.63	.53	.61	.21	.15	.00	.00	.00	.00	.00
.90	.88	1.00	.92	.94	.96	.87	.92	.96	.98	.88	.98	.89	.91	.82	.77	.63	.53	.61	.28	.15	.08	.07	.00	.00	.00
.90	.83	.92	1.00	.98	.96	.87	.92	.96	.94	.88	.94	.85	.91	.82	.82	.63	.53	.56	.28	.15	.08	.07	.00	.00	.00
.88	.81	.94	.98	1.00	.94	.89	.89	.94	.96	.85	.96	.87	.93	.84	.79	.59	.55	.57	.29	.15	.08	.08	.00	.00	.00
.94	.88	.96	.96	.94	1.00	.88	.96	1.00	.98	.92	.98	.90	.92	.83	.83	.65	.56	.58	.26	.14	.07	.07	.00	.00	.00
.85	.83	.87	.87	.89	.88	1.00	.87	.88	.89	.87	.89	.84	.91	.81	.76	.61	.63	.65	.22	.16	.00	.00	.00	.00	.00
.94	.88	.92	.92	.89	.96	.87	1.00	.96	.94	.92	.94	.89	.91	.82	.82	.68	.59	.56	.21	.07	.08	.07	.00	.00	.00
.94	.88	.96	.96	.94	1.00	.88	.96	1.00	.98	.92	.98	.90	.92	.83	.83	.65	.56	.58	.26	.14	.07	.07	.00	.00	.00
.92	.86	.98	.94	.96	.98	.89	.94	.98	1.00	.90	1.00	.92	.94	.84	.80	.62	.57	.59	.27	.14	.07	.07	.00	.00	.00
.90	.88	.88	.88	.85	.92	.87	.92	.92	.90	1.00	.90	.94	.87	.77	.77	.58	.59	.61	.21	.15	.00	.07	.00	.00	.00
.92	.86	.98	.94	.96	.98	.89	.94	.98	1.00	.90	1.00	.92	.94	.84	.80	.62	.57	.59	.27	.14	.07	.07	.00	.00	.00
.88	.81	.89	.85	.87	.90	.84	.89	.90	.92	.94	.92	1.00	.93	.84	.79	.59	.61	.57	.21	.15	.08	.15	.00	.00	.00
.89	.83	.91	.91	.93	.92	.91	.91	.92	.94	.87	.94	.93	1.00	.90	.86	.67	.63	.59	.22	.16	.08	.08	.00	.00	.00
.80	.73	.82	.82	.84	.83	.81	.82	.83	.84	.77	.84	.84	.90	1.00	.85	.65	.47	.50	.24	.17	.09	.09	.00	.00	.00
.80	.73	.77	.82	.79	.83	.76	.82	.83	.80	.77	.80	.79	.86	.85	1.00	.71	.47	.50	.24	.17	.09	.09	.00	.00	.00
.67	.63	.63	.63	.59	.65	.61	.68	.65	.62	.58	.62	.59	.67	.65	.71	1.00	.42	.38	.11	.00	.13	.12	.00	.00	.00
.57	.53	.53	.53	.55	.56	.63	.59	.56	.57	.59	.57	.61	.63	.47	.47	.42	1.00	.55	.13	.15	.00	.00	.00	.00	.00
.59	.61	.61	.56	.57	.58	.65	.56	.58	.59	.61	.59	.57	.59	.50	.50	.38	.55	1.00	.47	.40	.00	.00	.00	.00	.00
.27	.21	.28	.28	.29	.26	.22	.21	.26	.27	.21	.27	.21	.22	.24	.24	.11	.13	.47	1.00	.75	.29	.25	.00	.00	.00
.14	.15	.15	.15	.15	.14	.16	.07	.14	.14	.15	.14	.15	.16	.17	.17	.00	.15	.40	.75	1.00	.00	.00	.00	.00	.00
.07	.00	.08	.08	.08	.07	.00	.08	.07	.07	.00	.07	.08	.08	.09	.09	.13	.00	.00	.29	.00	1.00	.40	.00	.00	.00
.07	.00	.07	.07	.08	.07	.00	.07	.07	.07	.07	.07	.15	.08	.09	.09	.12	.00	.00	.25	.00	.40	1.00	.00	.00	.00
.00	.00	.00	.00	.00	.00	.00	.00	.00	.00	.00	.00	.00	.00	.00	.00	.00	.00	.00	.00	.00	.00	.00	1.00	.50	.50
.00	.00	.00	.00	.00	.00	.00	.00	.00	.00	.00	.00	.00	.00	.00	.00	.00	.00	.00	.00	.00	.00	.00	.50	1.00	1.00
.00	.00	.00	.00	.00	.00	.00	.00	.00	.00	.00	.00	.00	.00	.00	.00	.00	.00	.00	.00	.00	.00	.00	.50	1.00	1.00

Table 6

ROW/COL	REGAÑAN 26	PENSAR 11	VER 9	ATRASAR 10	MOLESTAR 5	ALIMENTAR 3	LLAMAR 12	HABLAR 7	CASTIGAR 2	VISITAR 8	CAMBIAR 1	ADMIRAR 34	ALISTAR 13	CANSAR 4	ENFERMAR 6	DESPIERTE 49	CONTENTA 28	ACLOMERADA 45	EMPEZANDO 38	ESPERANDO 47	ENSIMISMADO 46	VENIENDO 17	ATRASADO 24	SONRIENTE 39	FELIZ 23	ALEGRE 18	LLORANDO 44	ATEMORIZADO 43	HORRORISADO 42	ENTUSIASMADO 41	TRISTE 25	LOCO 22	ATENTO 21	FURIOSO 37	GRITANDO 33	FATIGADO 31	CORRIENDO 15	EMFERMO 20	FLOJO 14	LISTO 16	COMPRANDO 29	CAMINANDO 19	LENTO 27	TEMPRANO 36	TARDE 35	ADELANTO 48	ACOBARDADOS 40	DUERME 50	ANIMA 32	EMOCIONA 30	TOTAL
49	0	0	0	0	0	0	0	0	0	0	0	0	0	0	0	1	0	0	0	0	0	0	0	0	0	0	0	0	0	0	0	0	0	0	0	0	0	0	0	0	0	0	0	0	0	0	0	0	0	0	1
48	0	0	0	0	0	0	0	0	0	0	0	0	0	0	0	0	0	0	0	0	0	0	0	0	0	0	0	0	0	0	0	0	0	0	0	0	0	0	0	0	0	0	0	0	0	1	0	0	0	0	1
26	0	0	0	0	0	0	0	0	0	0	0	0	0	0	0	0	0	0	0	0	0	0	0	0	0	0	0	0	0	0	1	0	0	0	0	0	0	0	0	0	0	0	0	0	0	0	0	0	0	0	1
35	0	0	0	0	0	0	0	0	0	0	0	0	0	0	0	0	0	0	0	0	0	0	0	0	0	0	0	0	0	0	0	0	0	0	0	0	0	0	0	0	0	0	1	1	1	0	0	0	0	0	3
11	0	1	1	1	0	0	0	0	0	0	0	0	0	0	0	0	0	0	0	0	0	0	0	0	0	0	0	0	0	0	0	0	0	0	0	0	0	0	0	0	0	0	0	0	0	0	0	0	0	0	3
13	0	0	0	1	0	1	0	0	0	0	0	0	1	0	0	0	0	0	0	0	0	0	0	0	0	0	0	0	0	0	0	0	0	0	0	0	0	0	0	0	0	0	0	0	0	0	0	0	0	0	3
6	0	0	0	1	1	1	0	0	0	0	0	1	0	0	1	0	0	0	0	0	0	0	0	0	0	0	0	0	0	0	0	0	0	0	0	0	0	0	0	0	0	0	0	0	0	0	0	0	0	0	5
12	0	0	1	0	1	1	1	1	1	0	0	0	0	0	0	0	0	0	0	0	0	0	0	0	0	0	0	0	0	0	0	0	0	0	0	0	0	0	0	0	0	0	0	0	0	0	0	0	0	0	6
10	0	0	1	1	1	1	1	1	0	0	0	0	1	1	0	0	0	0	0	0	0	0	0	0	0	0	0	0	0	0	0	0	0	0	0	0	0	0	0	0	0	0	0	0	0	0	0	0	0	0	8
4	0	0	0	1	1	1	1	1	0	1	1	0	1	1	0	0	0	0	0	0	0	0	0	0	0	0	0	0	0	0	0	0	0	0	0	0	0	0	0	0	0	0	0	0	0	0	0	0	0	0	9
3	0	0	0	1	1	1	1	0	1	1	1	1	1	1	1	0	0	0	0	0	0	0	0	0	0	0	0	0	0	0	0	0	0	0	0	0	0	0	0	0	0	0	0	0	0	0	0	0	0	0	11
5	0	1	1	1	1	1	1	1	1	1	1	1	1	1	0	0	0	0	0	0	0	0	0	0	0	0	0	0	0	0	0	0	0	0	0	0	0	0	0	0	0	0	0	0	0	0	0	0	0	0	13
2	0	1	1	0	1	1	1	1	1	1	1	1	0	0	0	0	0	0	0	0	0	0	0	0	0	0	0	0	0	0	0	0	0	0	0	0	0	0	0	0	0	0	0	0	0	0	0	0	0	0	10
8	0	1	1	1	1	1	1	1	1	1	1	1	0	0	0	0	0	0	0	0	0	0	0	1	0	0	0	0	0	0	0	0	0	0	0	0	0	0	1	0	0	0	0	0	0	0	0	0	0	0	13
34	0	0	1	1	1	1	1	1	1	1	1	1	0	0	0	0	0	0	0	0	0	0	0	0	0	0	0	0	0	0	0	0	0	0	0	0	0	0	0	0	0	0	0	0	0	0	0	0	0	0	10
9	0	0	1	1	1	1	1	1	1	1	1	1	0	0	0	0	1	0	0	0	0	0	0	0	0	1	0	0	0	0	0	0	0	0	0	0	0	0	0	0	0	0	0	0	0	0	0	0	0	0	12
7	0	0	1	1	1	1	1	1	1	1	1	1	0	0	0	0	0	0	0	0	0	0	0	1	1	1	0	0	0	0	0	0	0	0	0	0	0	0	0	0	0	0	0	0	0	0	0	0	0	0	13
1	0	0	0	0	0	1	1	1	1	1	1	1	1	0	0	0	0	0	0	0	0	0	0	0	0	0	0	0	0	0	0	0	0	0	0	0	0	0	0	0	0	0	0	0	0	0	0	0	0	0	8
31	0	0	0	0	0	0	0	0	0	0	0	0	0	0	0	0	0	0	1	1	0	0	0	0	0	0	1	1	1	1	0	0	1	1	0	1	0	0	0	0	0	0	0	0	0	0	0	0	0	0	9
14	0	0	0	0	0	0	0	0	0	0	0	0	0	0	0	0	0	0	0	0	1	1	1	0	1	0	1	1	1	1	0	1	1	1	0	1	1	1	1	1	1	0	0	1	0	1	1	0	0	0	20
37	0	0	0	0	0	0	0	0	0	0	0	0	0	0	0	0	0	0	0	1	0	1	0	0	0	0	1	1	1	1	1	1	1	1	1	1	1	1	1	1	0	0	0	0	0	0	0	0	0	0	16
21	0	0	0	0	0	0	0	0	0	0	0	0	0	0	0	1	0	0	1	1	1	0	1	1	1	1	1	1	1	1	0	1	1	1	1	1	1	1	1	1	0	0	0	0	0	0	0	0	0	0	21
39	0	0	0	0	0	0	0	0	0	0	0	0	0	0	0	0	0	0	1	1	1	1	1	1	1	1	1	1	1	1	1	1	1	1	1	1	1	1	0	0	0	1	1	0	0	0	0	0	0	0	22
19	0	0	0	0	0	0	0	0	0	0	0	0	0	0	0	0	0	0	1	0	1	1	1	1	1	1	1	1	1	1	1	1	1	1	1	1	1	1	0	0	1	1	0	0	0	0	0	0	0	0	21
38	0	0	0	0	0	0	0	0	0	0	0	0	0	0	0	0	0	0	1	1	0	1	1	1	1	1	1	1	1	1	1	1	1	1	1	1	1	1	1	1	0	0	0	0	0	0	0	0	0	0	21
27	0	0	0	0	0	0	0	0	0	0	0	0	0	0	0	0	0	1	1	1	1	1	1	1	1	1	1	1	1	1	1	1	1	1	1	1	1	1	1	1	1	0	1	0	0	0	0	0	0	0	25
24	0	0	0	0	0	0	0	0	0	0	0	0	0	0	0	0	0	0	1	1	1	1	1	1	1	1	1	1	1	1	1	1	1	1	1	1	1	1	1	0	0	0	1	0	0	0	0	0	0	0	22
18	0	0	0	0	0	0	0	0	0	0	0	0	0	0	0	0	0	0	1	1	1	1	1	1	1	1	1	1	1	1	1	1	1	1	1	1	1	1	0	1	0	1	1	0	0	0	0	0	0	0	23
16	0	0	0	0	0	0	0	0	0	0	0	0	0	0	0	0	0	0	0	1	1	1	1	1	1	1	1	1	1	1	1	1	1	1	1	1	1	1	1	1	1	0	1	0	0	0	0	0	0	0	23
20	0	0	0	0	0	0	0	0	0	0	0	0	0	0	0	0	0	0	1	1	1	1	1	1	1	1	1	1	1	1	1	1	1	1	0	1	0	1	1	1	1	0	0	0	0	0	0	0	0	0	21
22	0	0	0	0	0	0	0	0	0	0	0	0	0	0	0	1	1	0	1	1	1	1	1	1	1	1	1	1	1	1	1	1	1	1	1	1	1	1	1	1	1	0	0	0	0	0	0	0	0	0	25
41	0	0	0	0	0	0	0	0	0	0	0	0	0	0	0	0	0	0	1	1	1	1	1	1	1	1	1	1	1	1	1	1	1	1	1	1	1	1	1	0	1	1	0	0	0	0	0	0	0	0	23
43	0	0	0	0	0	0	0	0	0	0	0	0	0	0	0	0	0	0	0	1	1	1	1	1	1	1	1	1	1	1	1	1	1	1	1	1	1	1	1	1	0	1	0	0	0	0	0	0	0	0	22
44	0	0	0	0	0	0	0	0	0	0	0	0	0	0	0	0	0	0	1	1	1	1	1	1	1	1	1	1	1	1	1	1	1	1	1	1	1	1	1	1	1	1	1	0	0	0	0	0	0	0	25
46	0	0	0	0	0	0	0	0	0	0	0	0	0	0	0	0	0	0	1	1	1	1	1	1	1	1	1	1	1	1	1	1	1	1	1	1	1	1	1	1	1	0	0	0	0	0	0	0	0	0	23
47	0	0	0	0	0	0	0	0	0	0	0	0	0	0	0	0	0	0	1	1	1	1	1	1	1	1	1	1	1	1	1	1	1	1	1	1	1	1	1	1	1	0	0	0	0	0	0	0	0	0	23
17	0	0	0	0	0	0	0	0	0	0	0	0	0	0	0	0	0	0	0	1	1	1	1	1	1	0	0	1	1	1	1	1	1	1	1	1	1	1	1	1	0	1	0	0	0	0	0	0	0	0	20
23	0	0	0	0	0	0	0	0	0	0	0	0	0	0	0	0	0	0	1	1	0	1	1	1	1	1	1	0	0	1	1	1	1	1	1	1	1	1	1	1	1	1	1	0	0	0	0	0	0	0	22
15	0	0	0	0	0	0	0	0	0	0	0	0	0	0	0	0	0	0	0	0	0	0	0	1	1	1	1	1	1	1	1	1	1	1	1	1	1	1	1	1	1	1	1	0	0	0	0	0	0	0	20
36	0	0	0	0	0	0	0	0	0	0	0	0	0	0	0	0	0	0	0	0	1	0	1	1	1	1	1	1	1	1	1	1	1	1	1	1	1	1	1	1	0	1	1	1	1	0	0	0	0	0	23
25	0	0	0	0	0	0	0	0	0	0	0	0	0	0	0	0	0	0	0	0	1	0	1	1	1	1	1	1	1	1	0	1	1	1	1	1	1	1	1	1	0	0	1	1	1	0	0	0	0	0	21
42	0	0	0	0	0	0	0	0	0	0	0	0	0	0	0	0	0	0	0	0	1	0	0	1	1	1	1	1	1	1	1	1	1	1	1	1	0	0	0	0	0	0	1	1	0	0	0	0	0	0	16
45	0	0	0	0	0	0	0	0	0	0	0	0	0	0	0	0	1	1	1	1	1	1	1	1	1	1	1	0	0	1	0	1	1	1	1	1	1	0	0	0	0	0	0	0	0	0	0	0	0	0	18
28	0	0	0	0	0	0	0	0	0	0	0	0	0	0	0	0	0	0	1	1	0	0	1	1	1	1	0	1	0	1	0	1	1	0	1	0	0	0	0	1	1	0	0	0	0	0	0	0	0	0	13
29	0	0	0	0	0	0	0	0	0	0	0	0	0	0	0	0	0	0	1	0	0	0	1	0	0	0	0	0	0	0	0	0	0	0	0	0	0	0	0	1	1	0	0	0	0	0	0	0	0	0	4
33	0	0	0	0	0	0	0	0	0	0	0	0	0	0	0	0	0	0	1	0	0	1	0	0	0	0	0	0	0	0	0	0	0	0	1	0	1	0	0	0	0	0	0	0	0	0	1	0	0	0	5
40	0	0	0	0	0	0	0	0	0	0	0	0	0	0	0	0	0	0	0	0	0	0	0	0	0	0	0	0	0	0	0	0	0	0	0	0	0	0	0	0	0	0	0	0	0	0	1	0	0	0	1
50	0	0	0	0	0	0	0	0	0	0	0	0	0	0	0	0	0	0	0	0	0	0	0	0	0	0	0	0	0	0	0	0	0	0	0	0	0	0	0	0	0	0	0	0	0	0	0	1	1	1	3
32	0	0	0	0	0	0	0	0	0	0	0	0	0	0	0	0	0	0	0	0	0	0	0	0	0	0	0	0	0	0	0	0	0	0	0	0	0	0	0	0	0	0	0	0	0	0	0	0	1	1	2
30	0	0	0	0	0	0	0	0	0	0	0	0	0	0	0	0	0	0	0	0	0	0	0	0	0	0	0	0	0	0	0	0	0	0	0	0	0	0	0	0	0	0	0	0	0	0	0	0	1	1	2
TOTAL	0	4	9	11	11	13	11	10	9	9	9	9	6	4	2	3	3	2	19	20	20	20	23	25	25	24	24	24	23	26	22	24	26	25	24	25	23	22	20	20	14	10	12	5	3	2	3	1	3	3	685

DATA SET 173 - APURAR - SENSE (FM)
SORTED MATRIX WITH ROW AND COLUMN TOTALS

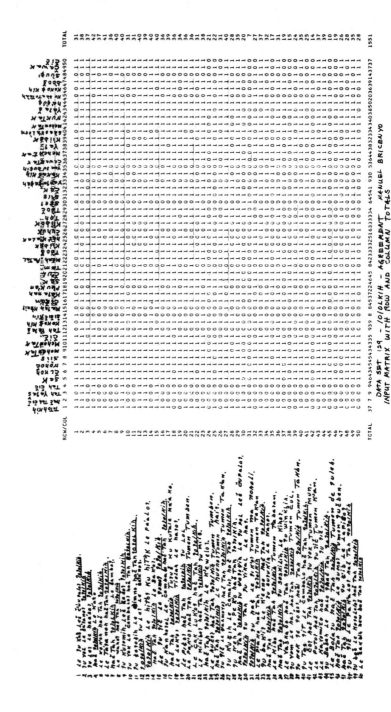

Table 8

Table 9

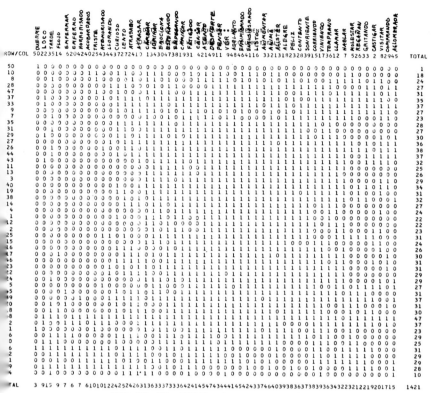

DATA SET 174 —APURAR— AGREEMENT (JM)
SORTED MATRIX WITH ROW AND COLUMN TOTALS

Table 10

DATA SET NO. 129 /C/OLKIH***AGREEMENT MANUEL BRICENYO (

SIMILARITY MATRIX - ROW

ROW/ROW	1	2	3	4	5	6	7	8	9	10	11	12	13	14	15	16	17	18	19	20	21	22	23	24
1	1.00	.75	.74	.77	.79	.75	.78	.76	.82	.94	.77	.73	.74	.82	.79	.81	.80	.72	.74	.81	.81	.74	.84	.50
2	.75	1.00	.91	.88	.88	.84	.89	.87	.95	.72	.90	.97	.99	.82	.85	.89	.86	.84	.81	.86	.84	.84	.87	.54
3	.74	.91	1.00	.89	.92	.87	.90	.91	.94	.76	.85	.88	.89	.86	.83	.93	.89	.90	.85	.90	.88	.79	.91	.62
4	.77	.88	.89	1.00	.89	.92	.87	.93	.93	.77	.82	.88	.86	.90	.90	.90	.86	.90	.84	.92	.92	.79	.88	.63
5	.79	.88	.92	.89	1.00	.92	.96	.96	.91	.82	.91	.86	.87	.91	.83	.96	.92	.88	.87	.96	.93	.88	.93	.66
6	.75	.84	.87	.92	.92	1.00	.91	.96	.86	.78	.86	.84	.82	.94	.86	.91	.92	.88	.85	.91	.94	.83	.89	.68
7	.78	.89	.90	.87	.96	.91	1.00	.92	.89	.81	.93	.89	.88	.87	.79	.94	.93	.86	.86	.92	.92	.87	.92	.60
8	.76	.87	.91	.93	.96	.96	.92	1.00	.90	.79	.87	.85	.86	.95	.88	.95	.91	.87	.89	.95	.92	.85	.92	.69
9	.82	.95	.94	.93	.91	.86	.89	.90	1.00	.79	.87	.92	.94	.85	.88	.95	.89	.89	.86	.92	.89	.82	.92	.59
10	.94	.72	.76	.77	.82	.78	.81	.79	.79	1.00	.81	.73	.71	.85	.79	.84	.83	.75	.80	.84	.84	.77	.87	.54
11	.77	.90	.85	.82	.91	.86	.93	.87	.87	.81	1.00	.87	.89	.85	.76	.93	.86	.84	.83	.90	.90	.94	.90	.54
12	.73	.97	.88	.88	.86	.84	.89	.85	.92	.73	.87	1.00	.96	.80	.85	.87	.86	.84	.81	.84	.84	.82	.85	.52
13	.74	.99	.89	.86	.87	.82	.88	.86	.94	.71	.89	.96	1.00	.81	.84	.88	.85	.83	.79	.85	.83	.86	.86	.53
14	.82	.82	.86	.90	.91	.94	.87	.95	.85	.85	.85	.80	.81	1.00	.88	.89	.89	.84	.84	.92	.92	.82	.92	.69
15	.79	.85	.83	.90	.83	.86	.79	.88	.88	.79	.76	.85	.84	.88	1.00	.82	.78	.82	.81	.84	.84	.76	.79	.62
16	.81	.89	.93	.90	.96	.91	.94	.95	.95	.84	.93	.87	.88	.89	.82	1.00	.93	.89	.91	.97	.94	.87	.97	.63
17	.80	.86	.89	.86	.92	.92	.93	.91	.89	.83	.86	.86	.85	.89	.78	.93	1.00	.85	.85	.91	.91	.80	.94	.60
18	.72	.84	.90	.90	.88	.88	.86	.87	.89	.75	.84	.84	.83	.84	.82	.89	.85	1.00	.83	.89	.92	.84	.86	.63
19	.74	.81	.85	.84	.87	.85	.86	.89	.86	.80	.83	.81	.79	.84	.81	.91	.85	.83	1.00	.89	.86	.80	.89	.62
20	.81	.86	.90	.92	.96	.91	.92	.95	.92	.84	.90	.84	.85	.92	.84	.97	.91	.89	.89	1.00	.97	.87	.95	.67
21	.81	.84	.88	.92	.93	.94	.92	.92	.89	.84	.90	.84	.83	.92	.84	.94	.91	.92	.86	.97	1.00	.87	.92	.67
22	.74	.84	.79	.79	.88	.83	.87	.85	.82	.77	.94	.82	.86	.82	.76	.87	.80	.84	.80	.87	.87	1.00	.84	.50
23	.84	.87	.91	.88	.93	.89	.92	.92	.92	.87	.90	.85	.86	.92	.79	.97	.94	.86	.89	.95	.92	.84	1.00	.61
24	.50	.54	.62	.63	.66	.68	.60	.69	.59	.54	.54	.52	.53	.69	.62	.63	.60	.63	.62	.67	.67	.50	.61	1.00
25	.57	.70	.71	.66	.75	.67	.72	.71	.68	.57	.75	.68	.69	.65	.58	.72	.66	.69	.64	.72	.69	.75	.70	.42
26	.61	.72	.79	.82	.82	.83	.78	.87	.76	.65	.71	.70	.71	.85	.79	.81	.77	.78	.80	.84	.81	.68	.78	.81
27	.76	.85	.88	.88	.91	.94	.89	.95	.88	.82	.85	.85	.84	.90	.85	.92	.91	.82	.89	.89	.87	.79	.90	.66
28	.75	.79	.74	.71	.80	.75	.81	.76	.76	.78	.88	.76	.78	.79	.65	.81	.81	.72	.71	.78	.78	.81	.85	.53
29	.82	.88	.92	.88	.94	.92	.93	.93	.93	.85	.94	.85	.86	.91	.83	.99	.92	.90	.90	.96	.96	.88	.96	.64
30	.63	.66	.56	.55	.60	.56	.61	.57	.63	.55	.67	.63	.68	.53	.57	.61	.54	.50	.56	.57	.57	.67	.59	.29
31	.21	.27	.27	.20	.27	.25	.28	.26	.26	.21	.32	.26	.30	.21	.21	.28	.26	.19	.20	.23	.23	.32	.27	.14
32	.62	.65	.72	.75	.78	.76	.73	.81	.69	.62	.66	.63	.64	.78	.72	.73	.70	.70	.75	.76	.73	.62	.71	.75
33	.82	.80	.84	.84	.86	.90	.85	.91	.83	.82	.82	.78	.79	.94	.81	.88	.87	.79	.85	.85	.85	.76	.91	.66
34	.73	.91	.87	.84	.90	.85	.91	.89	.89	.76	.95	.89	.90	.83	.75	.94	.87	.82	.88	.91	.88	.89	.91	.53
35	.58	.55	.52	.54	.56	.59	.53	.56	.53	.58	.58	.53	.54	.56	.56	.57	.57	.53	.51	.60	.60	.58	.55	.53
36	.77	.90	.85	.82	.91	.86	.93	.87	.87	.81	1.00	.87	.89	.85	.76	.93	.86	.84	.83	.90	.90	.94	.90	.54
37	.52	.63	.64	.56	.64	.57	.65	.61	.61	.56	.68	.61	.62	.58	.47	.65	.66	.55	.57	.62	.58	.60	.67	.45
38	.26	.49	.50	.49	.54	.54	.55	.51	.47	.30	.57	.51	.48	.47	.40	.51	.48	.59	.49	.51	.55	.57	.49	.61
39	.69	.61	.69	.73	.72	.74	.70	.75	.69	.69	.69	.59	.60	.75	.75	.73	.67	.70	.76	.73	.73	.65	.71	.67
40	.82	.88	.92	.88	.94	.89	.93	.93	.93	.85	.91	.85	.86	.88	.80	.99	.95	.87	.90	.96	.93	.85	.96	.61
41	.71	.60	.68	.63	.68	.64	.66	.68	.68	.75	.61	.62	.59	.68	.62	.72	.72	.62	.71	.69	.66	.54	.76	.61
42	.31	.31	.39	.50	.43	.51	.36	.52	.41	.31	.31	.30	.30	.52	.44	.44	.42	.48	.46	.48	.48	.31	.42	.63
43	.76	.80	.81	.89	.84	.85	.79	.86	.83	.79	.76	.81	.79	.86	.94	.79	.76	.82	.85	.82	.82	.76	.77	.62
44	.77	.88	.92	.86	.95	.92	.93	.94	.91	.80	.89	.86	.90	.89	.81	.96	.95	.85	.88	.93	.91	.86	.94	.63
45	.34	.38	.38	.27	.38	.35	.39	.36	.32	.34	.39	.36	.37	.36	.32	.35	.37	.30	.36	.30	.30	.34	.38	.45
46	.52	.67	.64	.59	.68	.60	.69	.64	.64	.56	.72	.64	.66	.58	.51	.69	.66	.65	.64	.65	.62	.68	.67	.55
47	.63	.75	.70	.74	.76	.75	.74	.76	.73	.67	.81	.73	.77	.76	.73	.77	.71	.74	.70	.81	.81	.88	.75	.47
48	.64	.64	.71	.74	.77	.78	.72	.79	.68	.71	.68	.65	.63	.79	.82	.72	.69	.69	.81	.75	.75	.68	.70	.65
49	.79	.85	.89	.88	.97	.89	.93	.93	.91	.82	.91	.83	.84	.88	.80	.96	.89	.87	.90	.96	.93	.88	.93	.64
50	.71	.67	.74	.80	.77	.81	.72	.82	.74	.71	.71	.65	.66	.82	.79	.78	.72	.75	.81	.81	.81	.71	.76	.69

Table 11

DATA SET NO. 129 /C/OLKIH***AGREEMENT MANUEL BRICENYO (

SIMILARITY MATRIX ROW

ROW/ROW	42	38	30	41	39	24	48	47	50	32	26	22	33	49	36	27	17	11	21	18	16	8	7	5
42	1.00	.41	.18	.46	.53	.63	.48	.35	.52	.59	.62	.31	.47	.45	.31	.44	.42	.31	.48	.48	.44	.52	.36	.43
38	.41	1.00	.40	.40	.46	.61	.51	.44	.47	.52	.57	.57	.42	.56	.57	.44	.48	.57	.55	.59	.51	.51	.55	.54
30	.18	.40	1.00	.31	.36	.29	.42	.48	.42	.30	.31	.67	.53	.58	.67	.53	.54	.67	.57	.50	.61	.57	.61	.60
41	.46	.40	.31	1.00	.69	.61	.64	.47	.64	.73	.71	.54	.74	.70	.61	.71	.72	.61	.66	.62	.72	.68	.66	.68
39	.53	.46	.36	.69	1.00	.67	.85	.60	.85	.86	.87	.65	.75	.75	.69	.72	.67	.69	.73	.70	.73	.75	.70	.72
24	.63	.61	.29	.61	.67	1.00	.65	.47	.69	.75	.81	.50	.66	.64	.54	.66	.60	.54	.67	.63	.63	.69	.60	.66
48	.48	.51	.42	.64	.85	.65	1.00	.63	.86	.84	.85	.68	.74	.76	.68	.76	.69	.68	.75	.69	.72	.79	.72	.77
47	.35	.44	.48	.47	.60	.47	.63	1.00	.70	.57	.67	.88	.67	.75	.81	.70	.71	.81	.81	.74	.77	.76	.74	.76
50	.52	.47	.42	.64	.85	.69	.86	.70	1.00	.84	.85	.71	.83	.79	.71	.79	.72	.71	.81	.75	.78	.82	.72	.77
32	.59	.52	.30	.73	.86	.75	.84	.57	.84	1.00	.93	.62	.78	.77	.66	.78	.70	.66	.73	.70	.73	.81	.73	.78
26	.62	.57	.31	.71	.87	.81	.85	.67	.85	.93	1.00	.68	.79	.82	.71	.82	.77	.71	.81	.78	.81	.87	.78	.82
22	.31	.57	.67	.54	.65	.50	.68	.88	.71	.62	.68	1.00	.76	.88	.94	.79	.80	.94	.87	.84	.87	.85	.87	.88
33	.47	.42	.53	.74	.75	.66	.74	.67	.83	.78	.79	.76	1.00	.86	.82	.91	.87	.82	.85	.79	.88	.91	.85	.86
49	.45	.56	.58	.70	.75	.64	.76	.75	.79	.77	.82	.88	.86	1.00	.91	.88	.89	.91	.93	.87	.96	.93	.93	.97
36	.31	.57	.67	.61	.69	.54	.68	.81	.71	.66	.71	.94	.82	.91	1.00	.85	.86	1.00	.90	.84	.93	.87	.93	.91
27	.44	.44	.53	.71	.72	.66	.76	.70	.79	.78	.82	.79	.91	.88	.85	1.00	.91	.85	.87	.82	.92	.95	.89	.91
17	.42	.48	.54	.72	.67	.60	.69	.71	.72	.70	.77	.80	.87	.89	.86	.91	1.00	.86	.91	.85	.93	.91	.93	.92
11	.31	.57	.67	.61	.69	.54	.68	.81	.71	.66	.71	.94	.82	.91	1.00	.85	.86	1.00	.90	.84	.93	.87	.93	.91
21	.48	.55	.57	.66	.73	.67	.75	.81	.81	.73	.81	.87	.85	.93	.90	.87	.91	.90	1.00	.92	.94	.92	.92	.93
18	.48	.59	.50	.62	.70	.63	.69	.74	.75	.70	.78	.84	.79	.87	.84	.82	.85	.84	.92	1.00	.89	.87	.86	.88
16	.44	.51	.61	.72	.73	.63	.72	.77	.78	.73	.81	.87	.88	.96	.93	.92	.93	.93	.94	.89	1.00	.95	.94	.96
8	.52	.51	.57	.68	.75	.69	.79	.76	.82	.81	.87	.85	.91	.93	.87	.95	.91	.87	.92	.87	.95	1.00	.92	.96
7	.36	.55	.61	.66	.70	.60	.72	.74	.72	.73	.78	.87	.85	.93	.93	.89	.93	.93	.92	.86	.94	.92	1.00	.96
5	.43	.54	.60	.68	.72	.66	.77	.76	.77	.78	.82	.88	.86	.97	.91	.91	.92	.91	.93	.88	.96	.96	.96	1.00
3	.39	.50	.56	.68	.69	.62	.71	.70	.74	.72	.79	.79	.84	.89	.85	.88	.89	.85	.88	.90	.93	.91	.90	.92
2	.31	.49	.66	.60	.61	.54	.64	.75	.67	.65	.72	.84	.80	.85	.90	.85	.86	.90	.84	.84	.89	.87	.89	.88
9	.41	.47	.63	.68	.69	.59	.68	.73	.74	.69	.76	.82	.83	.91	.87	.88	.89	.87	.89	.89	.95	.90	.89	.91
12	.30	.51	.63	.62	.59	.52	.65	.73	.65	.63	.70	.82	.78	.83	.87	.85	.86	.87	.84	.84	.87	.85	.89	.86
13	.30	.48	.68	.59	.60	.53	.63	.77	.66	.64	.71	.86	.79	.84	.89	.84	.85	.89	.83	.83	.88	.86	.88	.87
34	.35	.55	.65	.67	.64	.53	.67	.79	.70	.68	.73	.89	.81	.90	.95	.86	.87	.95	.88	.82	.94	.89	.91	.90
20	.48	.51	.57	.69	.73	.67	.75	.81	.81	.76	.84	.87	.85	.96	.90	.89	.91	.90	.97	.89	.97	.95	.92	.96
23	.42	.49	.59	.76	.71	.61	.70	.75	.76	.71	.78	.84	.91	.93	.90	.90	.94	.90	.92	.86	.97	.92	.92	.93
29	.45	.52	.62	.70	.75	.64	.73	.79	.79	.71	.79	.88	.89	.94	.94	.91	.92	.94	.96	.90	.99	.93	.93	.94
40	.45	.48	.58	.73	.71	.61	.70	.75	.76	.71	.79	.85	.86	.94	.91	.91	.95	.91	.93	.87	.99	.93	.93	.94
44	.42	.48	.61	.69	.70	.63	.72	.77	.75	.73	.80	.86	.87	.92	.89	.94	.95	.89	.91	.85	.96	.94	.93	.95
6	.51	.54	.56	.64	.74	.68	.78	.75	.81	.76	.83	.83	.90	.89	.86	.94	.92	.86	.94	.88	.91	.96	.91	.92
4	.50	.49	.55	.63	.73	.63	.74	.74	.80	.75	.82	.79	.84	.88	.82	.88	.86	.82	.92	.90	.90	.93	.87	.89
14	.52	.47	.53	.68	.75	.69	.79	.76	.82	.78	.85	.82	.94	.88	.85	.90	.89	.85	.92	.84	.89	.95	.87	.91
15	.44	.40	.57	.62	.75	.62	.82	.73	.79	.72	.79	.76	.81	.80	.76	.85	.78	.76	.84	.82	.82	.88	.79	.83
43	.43	.42	.53	.58	.79	.62	.86	.67	.80	.75	.79	.76	.81	.83	.76	.83	.76	.76	.82	.82	.79	.86	.79	.84
19	.46	.49	.56	.71	.76	.62	.81	.70	.81	.75	.80	.80	.85	.90	.83	.89	.85	.83	.86	.83	.91	.89	.86	.87
10	.31	.30	.55	.75	.69	.54	.71	.67	.71	.62	.65	.77	.82	.82	.81	.82	.83	.81	.84	.75	.84	.79	.81	.82
1	.31	.26	.63	.71	.69	.50	.64	.63	.71	.62	.61	.74	.82	.79	.77	.76	.80	.77	.81	.72	.81	.76	.78	.79
28	.33	.56	.63	.60	.54	.53	.54	.67	.57	.51	.58	.81	.77	.79	.88	.74	.81	.88	.78	.72	.81	.76	.81	.80
25	.33	.54	.43	.60	.57	.42	.56	.75	.64	.69	.64	.75	.64	.74	.75	.68	.66	.75	.69	.69	.72	.71	.72	.75
46	.30	.59	.21	.68	.65	.55	.55	.62	.60	.70	.72	.68	.61	.70	.72	.64	.66	.72	.62	.65	.69	.64	.69	.68
37	.24	.47	.31	.68	.56	.45	.51	.53	.55	.61	.64	.60	.61	.67	.68	.61	.66	.68	.58	.55	.65	.61	.65	.64
35	.39	.31	.22	.67	.63	.53	.53	.65	.62	.59	.63	.58	.56	.58	.58	.56	.57	.58	.60	.53	.57	.56	.53	.56
31	.19	.27	.52	.25	.19	.14	.17	.30	.11	.12	.16	.32	.18	.24	.32	.21	.26	.32	.23	.19	.28	.26	.28	.27
45	.08	.56	.33	.46	.41	.45	.42	.22	.37	.43	.39	.34	.43	.36	.39	.36	.37	.39	.30	.30	.35	.36	.39	.38

DATA SET NO. 129 /O/OLKIH***AGREEMENT MANUEL BRICENYO (

SIMILARITY MATRIX - ROW

25	26	27	28	29	30	31	32	33	34	35	36	37	38	39	40	41	42	43	44	45	46	47	48	49	50
.57	.61	.76	.75	.82	.63	.21	.62	.82	.73	.58	.77	.52	.26	.69	.82	.71	.31	.76	.77	.34	.52	.63	.64	.79	.71
.70	.72	.85	.79	.88	.66	.27	.65	.80	.91	.55	.90	.63	.49	.61	.88	.60	.31	.80	.88	.38	.67	.75	.64	.85	.67
.71	.79	.88	.74	.92	.56	.27	.72	.84	.87	.52	.85	.64	.50	.69	.92	.68	.39	.81	.92	.38	.64	.70	.71	.89	.74
.66	.82	.88	.71	.88	.55	.20	.75	.84	.84	.54	.82	.56	.49	.73	.88	.63	.50	.89	.86	.27	.59	.74	.74	.88	.80
.75	.82	.91	.60	.94	.60	.27	.78	.86	.90	.56	.91	.64	.54	.72	.94	.68	.43	.84	.95	.38	.68	.76	.77	.97	.77
.67	.83	.94	.75	.92	.56	.25	.76	.90	.85	.59	.86	.57	.54	.74	.89	.64	.51	.85	.92	.35	.60	.75	.78	.89	.81
.72	.78	.89	.81	.93	.61	.28	.73	.85	.91	.53	.93	.65	.55	.70	.93	.66	.36	.79	.93	.39	.69	.74	.72	.93	.72
.71	.87	.95	.76	.93	.57	.26	.81	.91	.89	.56	.87	.61	.51	.75	.93	.68	.52	.86	.94	.36	.64	.76	.79	.93	.82
.68	.76	.88	.76	.93	.63	.26	.69	.83	.89	.53	.87	.61	.47	.69	.93	.68	.41	.83	.91	.32	.64	.73	.68	.91	.74
.57	.65	.82	.78	.85	.55	.21	.62	.82	.76	.58	.81	.56	.30	.69	.85	.75	.31	.79	.80	.34	.56	.67	.71	.82	.71
.75	.71	.85	.68	.94	.67	.32	.66	.82	.95	.58	1.00	.68	.57	.69	.91	.61	.31	.76	.89	.39	.72	.81	.68	.91	.71
.68	.70	.85	.76	.85	.63	.26	.63	.78	.89	.53	.87	.61	.51	.59	.85	.62	.30	.81	.86	.36	.64	.73	.65	.83	.65
.69	.71	.84	.78	.86	.68	.30	.64	.79	.90	.54	.89	.62	.48	.60	.86	.59	.30	.79	.90	.37	.66	.77	.63	.84	.66
.65	.85	.90	.79	.91	.53	.21	.78	.94	.83	.56	.85	.58	.47	.75	.88	.68	.52	.86	.89	.36	.58	.76	.79	.88	.82
.58	.79	.85	.65	.83	.57	.21	.72	.81	.75	.56	.76	.47	.40	.75	.80	.62	.44	.94	.81	.32	.51	.73	.82	.80	.79
.72	.81	.92	.81	.99	.61	.28	.73	.88	.94	.57	.93	.65	.51	.73	.99	.72	.44	.79	.96	.35	.69	.77	.72	.96	.78
.66	.77	.91	.81	.92	.54	.26	.70	.87	.87	.57	.86	.66	.48	.67	.95	.72	.42	.76	.95	.37	.66	.71	.69	.89	.72
.69	.78	.82	.72	.90	.50	.19	.70	.79	.82	.53	.84	.55	.59	.70	.87	.62	.48	.82	.85	.30	.65	.74	.69	.87	.75
.64	.80	.89	.71	.90	.56	.20	.75	.85	.88	.51	.83	.57	.49	.76	.90	.71	.46	.85	.88	.36	.64	.70	.81	.90	.81
.72	.84	.89	.78	.96	.57	.23	.76	.85	.91	.60	.90	.62	.51	.73	.96	.69	.48	.82	.93	.30	.65	.81	.75	.96	.81
.69	.81	.87	.78	.96	.57	.23	.73	.85	.88	.60	.90	.58	.55	.73	.93	.66	.48	.82	.91	.30	.62	.81	.75	.93	.81
.75	.68	.79	.81	.88	.67	.32	.62	.76	.89	.58	.94	.60	.57	.65	.85	.54	.31	.76	.86	.34	.68	.88	.68	.88	.71
.70	.78	.90	.85	.96	.59	.27	.71	.91	.91	.55	.90	.67	.49	.71	.96	.76	.42	.77	.94	.38	.67	.75	.70	.93	.76
.42	.81	.66	.53	.64	.29	.14	.75	.66	.53	.53	.54	.45	.61	.67	.61	.61	.63	.62	.63	.45	.55	.47	.65	.64	.69
1.00	.64	.68	.60	.70	.43	.28	.69	.64	.78	.62	.75	.63	.54	.57	.70	.60	.33	.54	.69	.31	.68	.75	.56	.74	.64
.64	1.00	.82	.58	.79	.31	.16	.93	.79	.73	.63	.71	.64	.57	.87	.79	.71	.62	.79	.80	.39	.72	.67	.85	.82	.85
.68	.82	1.00	.74	.91	.53	.21	.78	.91	.86	.56	.85	.61	.44	.72	.91	.71	.44	.83	.94	.36	.64	.70	.76	.88	.79
.60	.58	.74	1.00	.83	.63	.34	.51	.77	.83	.49	.88	.64	.56	.54	.83	.60	.33	.65	.78	.47	.64	.67	.54	.79	.57
.70	.79	.91	.83	1.00	.62	.29	.71	.89	.93	.58	.94	.63	.52	.75	.97	.70	.45	.81	.95	.36	.67	.79	.73	.94	.79
.43	.31	.53	.63	.62	1.00	.52	.30	.53	.65	.22	.67	.31	.40	.36	.58	.31	.18	.53	.61	.33	.21	.48	.42	.58	.42
.28	.16	.21	.34	.29	.52	1.00	.12	.18	.31	.25	.32	.31	.27	.19	.29	.25	.19	.14	.30	.35	.15	.30	.17	.24	.11
.69	.93	.78	.51	.71	.30	.12	1.00	.78	.68	.59	.66	.61	.52	.86	.71	.73	.59	.75	.73	.43	.70	.57	.84	.77	.84
.64	.79	.91	.77	.89	.53	.18	.78	1.00	.81	.56	.82	.61	.42	.75	.86	.74	.47	.81	.87	.43	.61	.67	.74	.86	.83
.78	.73	.86	.83	.93	.65	.31	.68	.81	1.00	.57	.95	.67	.55	.64	.93	.67	.35	.72	.90	.38	.71	.79	.67	.90	.70
.62	.63	.56	.49	.58	.22	.25	.59	.56	.57	1.00	.58	.56	.31	.63	.58	.67	.39	.52	.57	.30	.61	.65	.53	.58	.62
.75	.71	.85	.88	.94	.67	.32	.66	.82	.95	.58	1.00	.68	.57	.69	.91	.61	.31	.76	.89	.39	.72	.81	.68	.91	.71
.63	.64	.61	.64	.63	.31	.31	.61	.61	.67	.56	.68	1.00	.47	.56	.67	.68	.24	.46	.62	.41	.84	.53	.51	.67	.55
.54	.57	.44	.56	.52	.40	.27	.52	.42	.55	.31	.57	.47	1.00	.46	.48	.40	.41	.42	.48	.56	.59	.44	.51	.56	.47
.57	.87	.72	.54	.75	.36	.19	.86	.75	.64	.63	.69	.56	.46	1.00	.71	.69	.53	.79	.70	.41	.65	.60	.85	.75	.85
.70	.79	.91	.83	.97	.58	.29	.71	.86	.93	.58	.91	.67	.48	.71	1.00	.73	.45	.78	.95	.36	.70	.75	.70	.94	.76
.60	.71	.71	.60	.70	.31	.25	.73	.74	.67	.67	.61	.68	.40	.69	.73	1.00	.46	.58	.69	.46	.68	.47	.64	.70	.64
.33	.62	.44	.33	.45	.18	.19	.59	.47	.35	.39	.31	.24	.41	.53	.45	.46	1.00	.43	.42	.08	.30	.35	.48	.45	.52
.54	.79	.83	.65	.81	.53	.14	.75	.81	.72	.52	.76	.46	.42	.79	.78	.58	.43	1.00	.79	.34	.54	.67	.86	.83	.80
.69	.80	.94	.78	.95	.61	.30	.73	.87	.90	.57	.89	.62	.48	.70	.95	.69	.42	.79	1.00	.37	.66	.77	.72	.92	.75
.31	.39	.36	.47	.36	.33	.35	.43	.43	.38	.30	.39	.41	.56	.41	.36	.46	.08	.34	.37	1.00	.48	.22	.42	.36	.37
.68	.72	.64	.64	.67	.21	.15	.70	.61	.71	.61	.72	.84	.59	.65	.70	.68	.30	.54	.66	.48	1.00	.62	.55	.70	.60
.75	.67	.70	.67	.79	.48	.30	.57	.67	.79	.65	.81	.53	.44	.60	.75	.47	.35	.67	.77	.22	.62	1.00	.63	.75	.70
.56	.85	.76	.54	.73	.42	.17	.84	.74	.67	.53	.68	.51	.51	.85	.70	.64	.48	.86	.72	.42	.55	.63	1.00	.76	.86
.74	.82	.88	.79	.94	.58	.24	.77	.86	.90	.58	.91	.67	.56	.75	.94	.70	.45	.83	.92	.36	.70	.75	.76	1.00	.79
.64	.85	.79	.57	.79	.42	.11	.84	.83	.70	.62	.71	.55	.47	.85	.76	.64	.52	.80	.75	.37	.60	.70	.86	.79	1.00

STRUCTURE VALUE = .4982

DATA SET NO. 129 /C/OLKIH***AGREEMENT MANUEL BRICENYO (

SIMILARITY MATRIX - ROW

3	2	9	12	13	34	20	23	29	40	44	6	4	14	15	43	19	10	1	28	25	46	37	35	31	45
.39	.31	.41	.30	.30	.35	.48	.42	.45	.45	.42	.51	.50	.52	.44	.43	.46	.31	.31	.33	.33	.30	.24	.39	.19	.08
.50	.49	.47	.51	.48	.55	.51	.49	.52	.48	.48	.54	.49	.47	.40	.42	.49	.30	.26	.56	.54	.59	.47	.31	.27	.56
.56	.66	.63	.63	.68	.65	.57	.59	.62	.58	.61	.56	.55	.53	.57	.53	.56	.55	.63	.63	.43	.21	.31	.22	.52	.33
.68	.60	.68	.62	.59	.67	.69	.76	.70	.73	.69	.64	.63	.68	.62	.58	.71	.75	.71	.60	.60	.68	.68	.67	.25	.46
.69	.61	.69	.59	.60	.64	.73	.71	.75	.71	.70	.74	.73	.75	.75	.79	.76	.69	.69	.54	.57	.65	.56	.63	.19	.41
.62	.54	.59	.52	.53	.53	.67	.61	.64	.61	.63	.68	.63	.69	.62	.62	.62	.54	.50	.53	.42	.55	.45	.53	.14	.45
.71	.64	.68	.65	.63	.67	.75	.70	.73	.70	.72	.78	.74	.79	.82	.86	.81	.71	.64	.54	.56	.55	.51	.53	.17	.42
.70	.75	.73	.73	.77	.79	.81	.75	.79	.75	.77	.75	.74	.76	.73	.67	.70	.67	.63	.67	.75	.62	.53	.65	.30	.22
.74	.67	.74	.65	.66	.70	.81	.76	.79	.76	.75	.81	.80	.82	.79	.80	.81	.71	.71	.57	.64	.60	.55	.62	.11	.37
.72	.65	.69	.63	.64	.68	.76	.71	.71	.71	.73	.76	.75	.78	.72	.75	.75	.62	.62	.51	.69	.70	.61	.59	.12	.43
.79	.72	.76	.70	.71	.73	.84	.78	.79	.79	.80	.83	.82	.85	.79	.79	.80	.65	.61	.58	.64	.72	.64	.63	.16	.39
.79	.84	.82	.82	.86	.89	.87	.84	.88	.85	.86	.83	.79	.82	.76	.76	.80	.77	.74	.81	.75	.68	.60	.58	.32	.34
.84	.80	.83	.78	.79	.81	.85	.91	.89	.86	.87	.90	.84	.94	.81	.81	.85	.82	.82	.77	.64	.61	.61	.56	.18	.43
.89	.85	.91	.83	.84	.90	.96	.93	.94	.94	.92	.89	.88	.88	.80	.83	.90	.82	.79	.79	.74	.70	.67	.58	.24	.36
.85	.90	.87	.87	.89	.95	.90	.90	.94	.91	.89	.86	.82	.85	.76	.76	.83	.81	.77	.88	.75	.72	.68	.58	.32	.39
.88	.85	.88	.85	.84	.86	.89	.90	.91	.91	.94	.94	.88	.90	.85	.83	.89	.82	.76	.74	.68	.64	.61	.56	.21	.36
.89	.86	.89	.86	.85	.87	.91	.94	.92	.95	.95	.92	.86	.89	.78	.76	.85	.83	.80	.81	.66	.66	.66	.57	.26	.37
.85	.90	.87	.87	.89	.95	.90	.90	.94	.91	.89	.86	.82	.85	.76	.76	.83	.81	.77	.88	.75	.72	.68	.58	.32	.39
.88	.84	.89	.84	.83	.88	.97	.92	.96	.93	.91	.94	.92	.92	.84	.82	.86	.84	.81	.78	.69	.62	.58	.60	.23	.30
.90	.84	.89	.84	.83	.82	.89	.86	.90	.87	.85	.88	.90	.84	.82	.82	.83	.75	.72	.72	.69	.65	.55	.53	.19	.30
.93	.89	.95	.87	.88	.94	.97	.97	.99	.99	.96	.91	.90	.89	.82	.79	.91	.84	.81	.81	.72	.69	.65	.57	.28	.35
.91	.87	.90	.85	.86	.89	.95	.92	.93	.93	.94	.96	.93	.95	.88	.86	.89	.79	.76	.76	.71	.64	.61	.56	.26	.36
.90	.89	.89	.89	.88	.91	.92	.92	.93	.93	.93	.91	.87	.87	.79	.79	.86	.81	.78	.81	.72	.69	.65	.53	.28	.39
.92	.88	.91	.86	.87	.90	.96	.93	.94	.94	.95	.92	.89	.91	.83	.84	.87	.82	.79	.80	.75	.68	.64	.56	.27	.38
1.00	.91	.94	.88	.89	.87	.90	.91	.92	.92	.92	.87	.89	.86	.83	.81	.85	.76	.74	.74	.71	.64	.64	.52	.27	.38
.91	1.00	.95	.97	.99	.91	.86	.87	.88	.88	.88	.84	.88	.82	.85	.80	.81	.72	.75	.79	.70	.67	.63	.55	.27	.38
.94	.95	1.00	.92	.94	.89	.92	.92	.93	.93	.91	.86	.93	.85	.88	.83	.86	.79	.82	.76	.68	.64	.61	.53	.26	.32
.88	.97	.92	1.00	.96	.89	.84	.85	.85	.85	.86	.84	.88	.80	.85	.81	.81	.73	.73	.76	.68	.64	.61	.53	.26	.36
.89	.99	.94	.96	1.00	.90	.85	.86	.86	.86	.90	.82	.86	.81	.84	.79	.79	.71	.74	.78	.69	.66	.62	.54	.30	.37
.87	.91	.89	.89	.90	1.00	.91	.91	.93	.93	.90	.85	.84	.83	.75	.72	.88	.76	.73	.83	.78	.71	.67	.57	.31	.38
.90	.86	.92	.84	.85	.91	1.00	.95	.96	.96	.93	.91	.92	.92	.84	.82	.89	.84	.81	.78	.72	.65	.62	.60	.23	.30
.91	.87	.92	.85	.86	.91	.95	1.00	.96	.96	.94	.89	.88	.92	.79	.77	.89	.87	.84	.85	.70	.67	.67	.55	.27	.38
.92	.88	.93	.85	.86	.93	.96	.96	1.00	.97	.95	.92	.88	.91	.83	.81	.90	.85	.82	.83	.70	.67	.63	.58	.29	.36
.92	.88	.93	.85	.86	.93	.96	.96	.97	1.00	.95	.89	.88	.88	.80	.78	.90	.85	.82	.83	.70	.70	.67	.58	.29	.36
.92	.88	.91	.86	.90	.90	.93	.94	.95	.95	1.00	.92	.86	.89	.81	.79	.88	.80	.77	.78	.69	.66	.62	.57	.30	.37
.87	.84	.86	.84	.82	.85	.91	.89	.92	.89	.92	1.00	.92	.94	.86	.85	.85	.78	.75	.75	.67	.60	.57	.59	.25	.35
.89	.88	.93	.88	.86	.84	.92	.88	.88	.88	.86	.92	1.00	.90	.90	.89	.84	.77	.77	.71	.66	.59	.56	.54	.20	.27
.86	.82	.85	.80	.81	.83	.92	.92	.91	.88	.89	.94	.90	1.00	.88	.86	.84	.85	.82	.79	.65	.58	.58	.56	.21	.36
.83	.85	.88	.85	.84	.75	.84	.79	.83	.80	.81	.86	.90	.88	1.00	.94	.81	.79	.79	.65	.58	.51	.47	.56	.21	.32
.81	.80	.83	.81	.79	.72	.82	.77	.81	.78	.79	.85	.89	.86	.94	1.00	.85	.79	.76	.65	.54	.54	.46	.52	.14	.34
.85	.81	.86	.81	.79	.88	.89	.89	.90	.90	.88	.85	.84	.84	.81	.85	1.00	.80	.74	.71	.64	.64	.57	.51	.20	.36
.76	.72	.79	.73	.71	.76	.84	.87	.85	.85	.80	.78	.77	.85	.79	.79	.80	1.00	.94	.78	.57	.56	.56	.58	.21	.34
.74	.75	.82	.73	.74	.73	.81	.84	.82	.82	.77	.75	.77	.82	.79	.76	.74	.94	1.00	.75	.57	.52	.52	.58	.21	.34
.74	.79	.76	.76	.78	.83	.78	.85	.83	.83	.78	.75	.71	.79	.65	.65	.71	.78	.75	1.00	.60	.64	.64	.49	.34	.47
.71	.70	.68	.68	.69	.78	.72	.70	.70	.70	.69	.67	.66	.65	.58	.54	.64	.57	.57	.60	1.00	.68	.63	.62	.28	.31
.64	.67	.64	.64	.66	.71	.65	.67	.67	.70	.66	.60	.59	.58	.51	.54	.64	.56	.52	.64	.68	1.00	.84	.61	.15	.48
.64	.63	.61	.61	.62	.67	.62	.67	.63	.67	.62	.57	.56	.58	.47	.46	.57	.56	.52	.64	.63	.84	1.00	.56	.31	.41
.52	.55	.53	.53	.54	.57	.60	.55	.58	.58	.57	.59	.54	.56	.56	.52	.51	.58	.58	.49	.62	.61	.56	1.00	.25	.30
.27	.27	.26	.26	.30	.31	.23	.27	.29	.29	.30	.25	.20	.21	.21	.14	.20	.21	.21	.34	.28	.15	.31	.25	1.00	.35
.38	.38	.32	.36	.37	.38	.30	.38	.36	.36	.37	.35	.27	.36	.32	.34	.36	.34	.34	.47	.31	.48	.41	.30	.35	1.00

Table 12

DATA SET NO. 129 /O/OLKIH***AGREEMENT MANUEL BRICENYO (

SIMILARITY MATRIX - COLUMN

COL/COL	1	2	3	4	5	6	7	8	9	10	11	12	13	14	15	16	17	18	19	20	21	22	23	24
1	1.00	.32	.30	.35	.82	.85	.83	.80	.85	.85	.86	.30	.79	.31	.22	.85	.78	.44	.82	.85	.27	.78	.86	.66
2	.32	1.00	.63	.88	.23	.28	.27	.27	.24	.24	.33	.63	.17	.13	.27	.23	.27	.07	.23	.23	.13	.20	.30	.15
3	.30	.63	1.00	.78	.33	.31	.33	.33	.35	.35	.32	1.00	.29	.00	.35	.33	.39	.26	.33	.33	.35	.35	.38	.29
4	.35	.88	.78	1.00	.29	.35	.33	.33	.31	.31	.41	.78	.21	.12	.35	.30	.35	.19	.29	.30	.24	.27	.38	.24
5	.82	.23	.33	.29	1.00	.90	.95	.95	.94	.94	.84	.33	.87	.30	.30	.95	.82	.62	1.00	.97	.30	.93	.81	.81
6	.85	.28	.31	.35	.90	1.00	.91	.93	.88	.88	.85	.31	.78	.31	.31	.89	.80	.49	.90	.91	.24	.85	.82	.82
7	.83	.27	.33	.33	.95	.91	1.00	.93	.91	.91	.85	.33	.86	.26	.30	.93	.85	.63	.95	.93	.30	.87	.85	.85
8	.80	.27	.33	.33	.95	.93	.93	1.00	.91	.91	.85	.33	.86	.30	.30	.91	.83	.54	.95	.93	.30	.92	.85	.82
9	.85	.24	.35	.31	.94	.88	.91	.91	1.00	1.00	.85	.35	.85	.24	.31	.98	.80	.58	.94	.98	.27	.92	.82	.82
10	.85	.24	.35	.31	.94	.88	.91	.91	1.00	1.00	.85	.35	.85	.24	.31	.98	.80	.58	.94	.98	.27	.92	.82	.82
11	.86	.33	.32	.41	.84	.85	.85	.85	.85	.85	1.00	.32	.78	.28	.33	.85	.83	.49	.84	.85	.28	.83	.91	.74
12	.30	.63	1.00	.78	.33	.31	.33	.33	.35	.35	.32	1.00	.29	.00	.35	.33	.39	.26	.33	.33	.35	.35	.38	.29
13	.79	.17	.29	.21	.87	.78	.86	.86	.85	.85	.78	.29	1.00	.17	.13	.88	.82	.59	.87	.88	.34	.91	.81	.72
14	.31	.13	.00	.12	.30	.31	.26	.30	.24	.24	.28	.00	.17	1.00	.25	.26	.13	.07	.30	.26	.00	.20	.29	.29
15	.22	.27	.35	.35	.30	.31	.30	.30	.31	.31	.33	.35	.13	.25	1.00	.30	.22	.20	.30	.30	.13	.24	.24	.34
16	.85	.23	.33	.30	.95	.89	.93	.91	.98	.98	.85	.33	.88	.26	.30	1.00	.83	.60	.95	.98	.26	.92	.82	.82
17	.78	.27	.39	.35	.82	.80	.85	.83	.80	.80	.83	.39	.82	.13	.22	.83	1.00	.58	.82	.80	.36	.86	.83	.71
18	.44	.07	.26	.19	.62	.49	.63	.54	.58	.58	.49	.26	.59	.07	.20	.60	.58	1.00	.62	.60	.33	.59	.40	.62
19	.82	.23	.33	.29	1.00	.90	.95	.95	.94	.94	.84	.33	.87	.30	.30	.95	.82	.62	1.00	.97	.30	.93	.81	.81
20	.85	.23	.33	.30	.97	.91	.93	.93	.98	.98	.85	.33	.88	.26	.30	.98	.80	.60	.97	1.00	.26	.92	.82	.82
21	.27	.13	.35	.24	.30	.24	.30	.30	.27	.27	.28	.35	.34	.00	.13	.26	.36	.33	.30	.26	1.00	.32	.34	.29
22	.78	.20	.35	.27	.93	.85	.87	.92	.92	.92	.83	.35	.91	.20	.24	.92	.86	.59	.93	.92	.32	1.00	.80	.75
23	.86	.30	.38	.38	.81	.82	.85	.85	.82	.82	.91	.38	.81	.29	.24	.82	.83	.40	.81	.82	.34	.80	1.00	.73
24	.66	.15	.29	.24	.81	.82	.85	.82	.82	.82	.74	.29	.72	.29	.34	.82	.71	.62	.81	.82	.29	.75	.73	1.00
25	.68	.25	.35	.29	.68	.68	.66	.69	.74	.74	.60	.35	.75	.12	.24	.71	.61	.34	.68	.71	.24	.72	.66	.62
26	.26	.09	.24	.24	.48	.51	.52	.49	.47	.47	.43	.24	.44	.17	.42	.49	.42	.63	.48	.49	.17	.48	.33	.65
27	.66	.15	.29	.24	.81	.82	.85	.82	.82	.82	.74	.29	.72	.29	.34	.82	.71	.62	.81	.82	.29	.75	.73	1.00
28	.91	.35	.38	.38	.78	.76	.79	.77	.79	.79	.85	.38	.78	.24	.20	.79	.83	.44	.78	.79	.34	.77	.88	.64
29	.87	.34	.42	.42	.82	.83	.86	.86	.83	.83	.93	.42	.79	.29	.29	.84	.85	.43	.82	.84	.33	.82	.99	.75
30	.28	.31	.13	.27	.15	.16	.16	.16	.16	.16	.24	.13	.18	.00	.00	.16	.28	.14	.15	.16	.00	.17	.21	.05
31	.80	.27	.33	.33	.95	.93	.93	1.00	.91	.91	.85	.33	.86	.30	.30	.91	.83	.54	.95	.93	.30	.92	.85	.82
32	.82	.25	.32	.32	.92	.86	.91	.88	.90	.90	.84	.32	.85	.29	.29	.93	.82	.57	.92	.93	.29	.84	.84	.81
33	.39	.13	.00	.11	.29	.35	.30	.33	.31	.31	.32	.00	.25	.82	.24	.33	.17	.06	.29	.33	.12	.24	.33	.33
34	.72	.27	.41	.31	.76	.74	.77	.72	.77	.77	.71	.41	.78	.21	.26	.77	.72	.54	.76	.77	.32	.72	.70	.76
35	.24	.00	.00	.00	.20	.21	.20	.16	.21	.21	.20	.00	.18	.00	.15	.20	.14	.15	.20	.20	.31	.17	.21	.21
36	.90	.33	.40	.40	.85	.81	.86	.84	.86	.86	.93	.40	.83	.27	.27	.86	.85	.48	.85	.86	.32	.85	.96	.72
37	.86	.24	.34	.30	.96	.90	.92	.92	.99	.99	.86	.34	.87	.27	.31	.99	.81	.58	.96	.99	.27	.93	.83	.81
38	.75	.27	.38	.34	.88	.81	.89	.87	.86	.86	.82	.38	.86	.13	.26	.84	.85	.67	.88	.87	.30	.90	.79	.76
39	.64	.15	.29	.24	.79	.80	.83	.81	.80	.80	.72	.29	.70	.30	.35	.81	.70	.63	.79	.81	.25	.73	.71	.98
40	.80	.25	.29	.24	.76	.74	.74	.79	.74	.74	.71	.29	.81	.24	.20	.74	.74	.29	.76	.74	.29	.80	.79	.55
41	.85	.24	.35	.31	.94	.88	.91	.91	1.00	1.00	.85	.35	.85	.24	.31	.98	.80	.58	.94	.98	.27	.92	.82	.82
42	.83	.30	.37	.37	.91	.87	.92	.89	.94	.94	.91	.37	.84	.21	.29	.92	.86	.58	.91	.92	.29	.90	.88	.82
43	.80	.22	.38	.30	.88	.81	.84	.89	.86	.86	.85	.38	.88	.17	.30	.87	.88	.57	.88	.89	.35	.90	.85	.73
44	.85	.25	.31	.31	.96	.92	.95	.95	.92	.92	.82	.31	.88	.28	.28	.95	.85	.61	.96	.95	.28	.91	.80	.80
45	.49	.30	.41	.34	.61	.63	.58	.62	.57	.57	.55	.41	.54	.21	.36	.55	.53	.48	.61	.58	.29	.61	.53	.60
46	.79	.19	.31	.22	.83	.78	.84	.84	.81	.81	.70	.31	.93	.23	.14	.84	.77	.52	.83	.84	.36	.85	.78	.72
47	.84	.26	.38	.33	.89	.85	.86	.88	.90	.90	.84	.38	.85	.26	.21	.90	.79	.56	.89	.93	.30	.86	.83	.78
48	.27	.10	.26	.26	.43	.46	.47	.44	.46	.46	.41	.26	.38	.18	.36	.47	.39	.61	.43	.44	.18	.46	.30	.60
49	.89	.32	.39	.39	.87	.82	.88	.85	.88	.88	.94	.39	.84	.27	.27	.88	.84	.51	.87	.88	.31	.86	.94	.74
50	.86	.32	.39	.39	.87	.85	.88	.88	.88	.88	.97	.39	.82	.27	.31	.88	.86	.51	.87	.88	.31	.86	.94	.77

Table 13

DATA SET NO. 129 /C/OLKIH***AGREEMENT MANUEL BRICENYO (

SIMILARITY MATRIX - COLUMN

COL/COL	35	21	33	14	15	48	26	18	34	39	27	24	46	13	47	42	41	37	22	20	19	16	10	9
35	1.00	.31	.14	.00	.15	.21	.19	.15	.29	.22	.21	.21	.20	.18	.23	.18	.21	.20	.17	.20	.20	.20	.21	.21
21	.31	1.00	.12	.00	.13	.18	.17	.33	.32	.25	.29	.29	.36	.34	.30	.29	.27	.27	.32	.26	.30	.26	.27	.27
33	.14	.12	1.00	.82	.24	.17	.16	.06	.26	.34	.33	.33	.31	.25	.33	.24	.31	.34	.24	.33	.29	.33	.31	.31
14	.00	.00	.82	1.00	.25	.18	.17	.07	.21	.30	.29	.29	.23	.17	.26	.21	.24	.27	.20	.26	.30	.26	.24	.24
15	.15	.13	.24	.25	1.00	.36	.42	.20	.26	.35	.34	.34	.14	.13	.21	.29	.31	.31	.24	.30	.30	.30	.31	.31
48	.21	.18	.17	.18	.36	1.00	.93	.61	.45	.61	.60	.60	.36	.38	.42	.48	.46	.45	.46	.44	.43	.47	.46	.46
26	.19	.17	.16	.17	.42	.93	1.00	.63	.52	.67	.65	.65	.38	.44	.44	.50	.47	.47	.48	.49	.48	.49	.47	.47
18	.15	.33	.06	.07	.20	.61	.63	1.00	.54	.63	.62	.62	.52	.59	.56	.58	.58	.58	.59	.60	.62	.60	.58	.58
34	.29	.32	.26	.21	.26	.45	.52	.54	1.00	.77	.76	.76	.76	.78	.75	.74	.77	.76	.72	.77	.76	.77	.77	.77
39	.22	.25	.34	.30	.35	.61	.67	.63	.77	1.00	.98	.98	.71	.70	.76	.81	.80	.79	.73	.81	.79	.81	.80	.80
27	.21	.29	.33	.29	.34	.60	.65	.62	.76	.98	1.00	1.00	.72	.72	.78	.82	.82	.81	.75	.82	.81	.82	.82	.82
24	.21	.29	.33	.29	.34	.60	.65	.62	.76	.98	1.00	1.00	.72	.72	.78	.82	.82	.81	.75	.82	.81	.82	.82	.82
46	.20	.36	.31	.23	.14	.36	.38	.52	.76	.71	.72	.72	1.00	.93	.80	.76	.81	.82	.85	.84	.83	.84	.81	.81
13	.18	.34	.25	.17	.13	.38	.44	.59	.78	.70	.72	.72	.93	1.00	.85	.84	.85	.87	.91	.88	.87	.88	.85	.85
47	.23	.30	.33	.26	.21	.42	.44	.56	.75	.76	.78	.78	.80	.85	1.00	.86	.90	.92	.86	.93	.89	.90	.90	.90
42	.18	.29	.24	.21	.29	.48	.50	.58	.74	.81	.82	.82	.76	.84	.86	1.00	.94	.93	.90	.92	.91	.92	.94	.94
41	.21	.27	.31	.24	.31	.46	.47	.58	.77	.80	.82	.82	.81	.85	.90	.94	1.00	.99	.92	.98	.94	.98	1.00	1.00
37	.20	.27	.34	.27	.31	.45	.47	.58	.76	.79	.81	.61	.82	.87	.92	.93	.99	1.00	.93	.99	.96	.99	.99	.99
22	.17	.32	.24	.20	.24	.46	.48	.59	.72	.73	.75	.75	.85	.91	.86	.90	.92	.93	1.00	.92	.93	.92	.92	.92
20	.20	.26	.33	.26	.30	.44	.49	.60	.77	.81	.82	.82	.84	.88	.93	.92	.98	.99	.92	1.00	.97	.98	.98	.98
19	.20	.30	.29	.30	.30	.43	.48	.62	.76	.79	.81	.81	.83	.87	.89	.91	.94	.96	.93	.97	1.00	.95	.94	.94
16	.20	.26	.33	.26	.30	.47	.49	.60	.77	.81	.82	.82	.84	.88	.90	.92	.98	.99	.92	.98	.95	1.00	.98	.98
10	.21	.27	.31	.24	.31	.46	.47	.58	.77	.80	.82	.82	.81	.85	.90	.94	1.00	.99	.92	.98	.94	.98	1.00	1.00
9	.21	.27	.31	.24	.31	.46	.47	.58	.77	.80	.82	.82	.81	.85	.90	.94	1.00	.99	.92	.98	.94	.98	1.00	1.00
7	.20	.30	.30	.26	.30	.47	.52	.63	.77	.83	.85	.85	.84	.86	.86	.92	.91	.92	.87	.93	.95	.93	.91	.91
5	.20	.30	.29	.30	.30	.43	.48	.62	.76	.79	.81	.81	.83	.87	.89	.91	.94	.96	.93	.97	1.00	.95	.94	.94
8	.16	.30	.33	.30	.30	.44	.49	.54	.72	.81	.82	.82	.84	.86	.88	.89	.91	.92	.92	.93	.95	.91	.91	.91
31	.16	.30	.33	.30	.30	.44	.49	.54	.72	.81	.82	.82	.84	.86	.88	.89	.91	.92	.92	.93	.95	.91	.91	.91
32	.22	.29	.32	.29	.29	.44	.49	.57	.79	.79	.81	.81	.83	.85	.90	.86	.90	.92	.84	.93	.92	.93	.90	.90
44	.18	.28	.31	.28	.28	.44	.48	.61	.75	.78	.80	.80	.84	.88	.88	.89	.92	.94	.91	.95	.96	.95	.92	.92
6	.21	.24	.35	.31	.31	.46	.51	.49	.74	.80	.82	.82	.78	.78	.85	.87	.88	.90	.85	.91	.90	.89	.88	.88
1	.24	.27	.39	.31	.22	.27	.26	.44	.72	.64	.66	.66	.79	.79	.84	.83	.85	.86	.78	.85	.82	.85	.85	.85
28	.21	.34	.29	.24	.20	.26	.24	.44	.70	.62	.64	.64	.75	.78	.81	.85	.79	.81	.77	.79	.78	.79	.79	.79
36	.20	.32	.31	.27	.27	.32	.35	.48	.73	.71	.72	.72	.78	.83	.85	.92	.86	.88	.85	.86	.85	.86	.86	.86
29	.21	.33	.33	.29	.29	.33	.36	.43	.72	.73	.75	.75	.77	.79	.85	.89	.83	.85	.82	.84	.82	.84	.83	.83
23	.21	.34	.33	.29	.24	.30	.33	.40	.70	.71	.73	.73	.78	.81	.83	.88	.82	.83	.80	.82	.81	.82	.82	.82
11	.20	.28	.32	.28	.33	.41	.43	.49	.71	.72	.74	.74	.70	.78	.84	.91	.85	.86	.83	.85	.84	.85	.85	.85
49	.19	.31	.30	.27	.27	.35	.38	.51	.75	.72	.74	.74	.77	.84	.87	.94	.88	.89	.86	.88	.87	.88	.88	.88
50	.19	.31	.30	.27	.31	.39	.42	.51	.75	.75	.77	.77	.74	.82	.87	.94	.88	.89	.86	.88	.87	.88	.88	.88
38	.14	.30	.13	.13	.26	.50	.56	.67	.74	.74	.76	.76	.78	.86	.81	.92	.86	.85	.90	.87	.88	.84	.86	.86
17	.14	.36	.17	.13	.22	.39	.42	.58	.72	.70	.71	.71	.77	.82	.79	.86	.80	.81	.86	.80	.82	.83	.80	.80
43	.19	.35	.26	.17	.30	.35	.41	.57	.74	.71	.73	.73	.84	.88	.88	.85	.86	.88	.90	.89	.88	.87	.86	.86
40	.21	.29	.29	.24	.20	.17	.20	.29	.60	.52	.55	.55	.81	.81	.69	.71	.74	.75	.80	.74	.76	.74	.74	.74
25	.20	.24	.24	.12	.24	.26	.29	.34	.65	.60	.62	.62	.79	.75	.63	.68	.74	.72	.72	.71	.68	.71	.74	.74
45	.32	.29	.21	.21	.36	.59	.61	.48	.56	.58	.60	.60	.57	.54	.58	.60	.57	.56	.61	.58	.61	.55	.57	.57
12	.00	.35	.00	.00	.35	.26	.24	.26	.41	.29	.29	.29	.31	.29	.38	.37	.35	.34	.35	.33	.33	.33	.35	.35
3	.00	.35	.30	.00	.35	.26	.24	.26	.41	.29	.29	.29	.31	.29	.38	.37	.35	.34	.35	.33	.33	.33	.35	.35
4	.00	.24	.11	.12	.35	.26	.24	.19	.31	.24	.24	.24	.22	.21	.33	.37	.31	.30	.27	.30	.29	.30	.31	.31
2	.00	.13	.13	.13	.27	.10	.09	.07	.27	.15	.15	.15	.19	.17	.26	.30	.24	.24	.20	.23	.23	.23	.24	.24
30	.18	.00	.00	.00	.00	.00	.00	.14	.17	.05	.05	.05	.10	.18	.18	.22	.16	.16	.17	.16	.15	.16	.16	.16

DATA SET NO. 129 /O/OLKIH***AGREEMENT MANUEL BRICENYO (

SIMILARITY MATRIX - COLUMN

25	26	27	28	29	30	31	32	33	34	35	36	37	38	39	40	41	42	43	44	45	46	47	48	49	50
.68	.26	.66	.91	.87	.28	.80	.82	.39	.72	.24	.90	.86	.75	.64	.80	.85	.83	.80	.85	.49	.79	.84	.27	.89	.86
.25	.09	.15	.35	.34	.31	.27	.25	.13	.27	.00	.33	.24	.27	.15	.25	.24	.30	.22	.25	.30	.19	.26	.10	.32	.32
.35	.24	.29	.38	.42	.13	.33	.32	.00	.41	.00	.40	.34	.38	.29	.29	.35	.37	.38	.31	.41	.31	.38	.26	.39	.39
.29	.24	.24	.38	.42	.27	.33	.32	.11	.31	.00	.40	.30	.34	.24	.24	.31	.37	.30	.31	.34	.22	.33	.26	.39	.39
.68	.48	.81	.78	.82	.15	.95	.92	.29	.76	.20	.85	.96	.88	.79	.76	.94	.91	.88	.96	.61	.83	.89	.43	.87	.87
.68	.51	.82	.76	.83	.16	.93	.86	.35	.74	.21	.81	.90	.81	.80	.74	.88	.87	.81	.92	.63	.78	.85	.46	.82	.85
.66	.52	.85	.79	.86	.16	.93	.91	.30	.77	.20	.86	.92	.89	.83	.74	.91	.92	.84	.95	.58	.84	.86	.47	.88	.88
.69	.49	.82	.77	.86	.16	1.00	.88	.33	.72	.16	.84	.92	.87	.81	.79	.91	.89	.89	.95	.62	.84	.88	.44	.85	.88
.74	.47	.82	.79	.83	.16	.91	.90	.31	.77	.21	.86	.99	.86	.80	.74	1.00	.94	.86	.92	.57	.81	.90	.46	.88	.88
.74	.47	.82	.79	.83	.16	.91	.90	.31	.77	.21	.86	.99	.86	.80	.74	1.00	.94	.86	.92	.57	.81	.90	.46	.88	.88
.60	.43	.74	.85	.93	.24	.85	.84	.32	.71	.20	.93	.86	.82	.72	.71	.85	.91	.85	.82	.55	.70	.84	.41	.94	.97
.35	.24	.29	.38	.42	.13	.33	.32	.00	.41	.00	.40	.34	.38	.29	.29	.35	.37	.38	.31	.41	.31	.38	.26	.39	.39
.75	.44	.72	.78	.79	.18	.86	.85	.25	.78	.18	.83	.87	.86	.70	.81	.85	.84	.88	.88	.54	.93	.85	.38	.84	.82
.12	.17	.29	.24	.29	.00	.30	.29	.82	.21	.00	.27	.27	.13	.30	.24	.24	.21	.17	.28	.21	.23	.26	.18	.27	.27
.24	.42	.34	.20	.29	.00	.30	.29	.24	.26	.15	.27	.31	.26	.35	.20	.31	.29	.30	.28	.36	.14	.21	.36	.27	.31
.71	.49	.82	.79	.84	.16	.91	.93	.33	.77	.20	.86	.99	.84	.81	.74	.98	.92	.87	.95	.55	.84	.90	.47	.88	.88
.61	.42	.71	.83	.85	.28	.83	.82	.17	.72	.14	.85	.81	.85	.70	.74	.80	.86	.88	.85	.53	.77	.79	.39	.84	.86
.34	.63	.62	.44	.43	.14	.54	.57	.06	.54	.15	.48	.58	.67	.63	.29	.58	.58	.57	.61	.48	.52	.56	.61	.51	.51
.68	.48	.81	.78	.82	.15	.95	.92	.29	.76	.20	.85	.96	.88	.79	.76	.94	.91	.88	.96	.61	.83	.89	.43	.87	.87
.71	.49	.82	.79	.84	.16	.93	.93	.33	.77	.20	.86	.99	.87	.81	.74	.98	.92	.89	.95	.58	.84	.93	.44	.88	.88
.24	.17	.29	.34	.33	.00	.30	.29	.12	.32	.31	.32	.27	.30	.25	.29	.27	.29	.35	.28	.29	.36	.30	.18	.31	.31
.72	.48	.75	.77	.82	.17	.92	.84	.24	.72	.17	.85	.93	.90	.73	.80	.92	.90	.90	.91	.61	.85	.86	.46	.86	.86
.66	.33	.73	.88	.99	.21	.85	.84	.33	.70	.21	.96	.83	.79	.71	.79	.82	.88	.85	.80	.53	.78	.83	.30	.94	.94
.62	.65	1.00	.64	.75	.05	.82	.81	.33	.76	.21	.72	.81	.76	.98	.55	.82	.82	.73	.80	.60	.72	.78	.60	.74	.77
1.00	.29	.62	.62	.64	.13	.69	.67	.24	.65	.20	.66	.72	.63	.60	.72	.74	.68	.70	.67	.53	.79	.63	.26	.65	.61
.29	1.00	.65	.24	.36	.00	.49	.49	.16	.52	.19	.35	.47	.56	.67	.20	.47	.50	.41	.48	.61	.38	.44	.93	.38	.42
.62	.65	1.00	.64	.75	.05	.82	.81	.33	.76	.21	.72	.81	.76	.98	.55	.82	.82	.73	.80	.60	.72	.78	.60	.74	.77
.62	.24	.64	1.00	.90	.31	.77	.78	.29	.70	.21	.93	.81	.76	.62	.76	.79	.85	.82	.80	.49	.75	.81	.26	.91	.89
.64	.36	.75	.90	1.00	.20	.86	.85	.33	.72	.21	.97	.85	.81	.73	.78	.83	.89	.86	.81	.56	.77	.85	.33	.96	.96
.13	.00	.05	.31	.20	1.00	.16	.17	.00	.17	.18	.24	.16	.23	.05	.26	.16	.22	.18	.21	.15	.10	.18	.00	.23	.23
.69	.49	.82	.77	.86	.16	1.00	.88	.33	.72	.16	.84	.92	.87	.81	.79	.91	.89	.89	.95	.62	.84	.88	.44	.85	.88
.67	.49	.81	.78	.85	.17	.88	1.00	.32	.79	.22	.86	.92	.81	.79	.70	.90	.86	.86	.90	.56	.83	.90	.44	.85	.85
.24	.16	.33	.29	.33	.00	.33	.32	1.00	.26	.14	.31	.34	.13	.34	.29	.31	.24	.26	.31	.21	.31	.33	.17	.30	.30
.65	.52	.76	.70	.72	.17	.72	.79	.26	1.00	.29	.73	.76	.74	.77	.60	.77	.74	.74	.75	.56	.76	.75	.45	.75	.75
.20	.19	.21	.21	.21	.18	.16	.22	.14	.29	1.00	.20	.20	.14	.22	.21	.21	.18	.19	.18	.32	.20	.23	.21	.19	.19
.66	.35	.72	.93	.97	.24	.84	.86	.31	.73	.20	1.00	.88	.84	.71	.78	.86	.92	.86	.84	.54	.78	.85	.32	.99	.96
.72	.47	.81	.81	.85	.16	.92	.92	.34	.76	.20	.88	1.00	.85	.79	.75	.99	.93	.88	.94	.56	.82	.92	.45	.89	.89
.63	.56	.76	.76	.81	.23	.87	.81	.13	.74	.14	.84	.85	1.00	.74	.70	.86	.92	.84	.86	.62	.78	.81	.50	.85	.85
.60	.67	.98	.62	.73	.05	.81	.79	.34	.77	.22	.71	.79	.74	1.00	.52	.80	.81	.71	.78	.58	.71	.76	.61	.72	.75
.72	.20	.55	.76	.78	.26	.79	.70	.29	.60	.21	.78	.75	.70	.52	1.00	.74	.71	.76	.80	.49	.81	.69	.17	.77	.74
.74	.47	.82	.79	.83	.16	.91	.90	.31	.77	.21	.86	.99	.86	.80	.74	1.00	.94	.86	.92	.57	.81	.90	.46	.88	.88
.68	.50	.82	.85	.89	.22	.89	.86	.24	.74	.18	.92	.93	.92	.81	.71	.94	1.00	.85	.89	.60	.76	.86	.48	.94	.94
.70	.41	.73	.82	.86	.18	.89	.86	.26	.74	.19	.86	.88	.84	.71	.76	.86	.85	1.00	.86	.59	.84	.88	.35	.85	.88
.67	.48	.80	.80	.81	.21	.95	.90	.31	.75	.18	.84	.94	.86	.78	.80	.92	.89	.86	1.00	.57	.84	.88	.44	.85	.85
.53	.61	.60	.49	.56	.15	.62	.56	.21	.56	.32	.54	.56	.62	.58	.49	.57	.60	.59	.57	1.00	.57	.58	.59	.53	.56
.79	.38	.72	.75	.77	.10	.84	.83	.31	.76	.20	.78	.82	.78	.71	.81	.81	.76	.84	.84	.57	1.00	.80	.36	.77	.74
.63	.44	.78	.81	.85	.18	.88	.90	.33	.75	.23	.85	.92	.81	.76	.69	.90	.86	.88	.88	.58	.80	1.00	.42	.87	.87
.26	.93	.60	.26	.33	.00	.44	.44	.17	.45	.21	.32	.45	.50	.61	.17	.46	.48	.35	.44	.59	.36	.42	1.00	.35	.39
.65	.38	.74	.91	.96	.23	.85	.85	.30	.75	.19	.99	.89	.85	.72	.77	.88	.94	.85	.85	.53	.77	.87	.35	1.00	.97
.61	.42	.77	.89	.96	.23	.88	.85	.30	.75	.19	.96	.89	.85	.75	.74	.88	.94	.88	.85	.56	.74	.87	.39	.97	1.00

STRUCTURE VALUE = .5384

DATA SET NO. 129 /O/OLKIH***AGREEMENT MANUEL BRICENYO (

SIMILARITY MATRIX - COLUMN

7	5	8	31	32	44	6	1	28	36	29	23	11	49	50	38	17	43	40	25	45	12	3	4	2	30
.20	.20	.16	.16	.22	.18	.21	.24	.21	.20	.21	.21	.20	.19	.19	.14	.14	.19	.21	.20	.32	.00	.00	.00	.00	.18
.30	.30	.30	.30	.29	.28	.24	.27	.34	.32	.33	.34	.28	.31	.31	.30	.36	.35	.29	.24	.29	.35	.35	.24	.13	.00
.30	.29	.33	.33	.32	.31	.35	.39	.29	.31	.33	.33	.32	.30	.30	.13	.17	.26	.29	.24	.21	.00	.00	.11	.13	.00
.26	.30	.30	.30	.29	.28	.31	.31	.24	.27	.29	.29	.28	.27	.27	.13	.13	.17	.24	.12	.21	.00	.00	.12	.13	.00
.30	.30	.30	.30	.29	.28	.31	.22	.20	.27	.29	.24	.33	.27	.31	.26	.22	.30	.20	.24	.36	.35	.35	.35	.27	.00
.47	.43	.44	.44	.44	.44	.46	.27	.26	.32	.33	.30	.41	.35	.39	.50	.39	.35	.17	.26	.59	.26	.26	.26	.10	.00
.52	.48	.49	.49	.49	.48	.51	.26	.24	.35	.36	.33	.43	.38	.42	.56	.42	.41	.20	.29	.61	.24	.24	.24	.09	.00
.63	.62	.54	.54	.57	.61	.49	.44	.44	.48	.43	.40	.49	.51	.51	.67	.58	.57	.29	.34	.48	.26	.26	.19	.07	.14
.77	.76	.72	.72	.79	.75	.74	.72	.70	.73	.72	.70	.71	.75	.75	.74	.72	.74	.60	.65	.56	.41	.41	.31	.27	.17
.83	.79	.81	.81	.79	.78	.80	.64	.62	.71	.73	.71	.72	.72	.75	.74	.70	.71	.52	.60	.58	.29	.29	.24	.15	.05
.85	.81	.82	.82	.81	.80	.82	.66	.64	.72	.75	.73	.74	.74	.77	.76	.71	.73	.55	.62	.60	.29	.29	.24	.15	.05
.85	.81	.82	.82	.81	.80	.82	.66	.64	.72	.75	.73	.74	.74	.77	.76	.71	.73	.55	.62	.60	.29	.29	.24	.15	.05
.84	.83	.84	.84	.83	.84	.78	.79	.75	.78	.77	.78	.70	.77	.74	.78	.77	.84	.81	.79	.57	.31	.31	.22	.19	.10
.86	.87	.86	.86	.85	.88	.78	.79	.78	.83	.79	.81	.78	.84	.82	.86	.82	.88	.81	.75	.54	.29	.29	.21	.17	.18
.86	.89	.88	.88	.90	.88	.85	.84	.81	.85	.85	.83	.84	.87	.87	.81	.79	.88	.69	.63	.58	.38	.38	.33	.26	.18
.92	.91	.89	.89	.86	.89	.87	.83	.85	.92	.89	.88	.91	.94	.94	.92	.86	.85	.71	.68	.60	.37	.37	.37	.30	.22
.91	.94	.91	.91	.90	.92	.88	.85	.79	.86	.83	.82	.85	.88	.88	.86	.80	.86	.74	.74	.57	.35	.35	.31	.24	.16
.92	.96	.92	.92	.92	.94	.90	.86	.81	.88	.85	.83	.86	.89	.89	.85	.81	.88	.75	.72	.56	.34	.34	.30	.24	.16
.87	.93	.92	.92	.84	.91	.85	.78	.77	.85	.82	.80	.83	.86	.86	.90	.86	.90	.80	.72	.61	.35	.35	.27	.20	.17
.93	.97	.93	.93	.93	.95	.91	.85	.79	.86	.84	.82	.85	.88	.88	.87	.80	.89	.74	.71	.58	.33	.33	.30	.23	.16
.95	1.00	.95	.95	.92	.96	.90	.82	.78	.85	.82	.81	.84	.87	.87	.88	.82	.88	.76	.68	.61	.33	.33	.29	.23	.15
.93	.95	.91	.91	.93	.95	.89	.85	.79	.86	.84	.82	.85	.88	.88	.84	.83	.87	.74	.71	.55	.33	.33	.30	.23	.16
.91	.94	.91	.91	.90	.92	.88	.85	.79	.86	.83	.82	.85	.88	.88	.86	.80	.86	.74	.74	.57	.35	.35	.31	.24	.16
.91	.94	.91	.91	.90	.92	.88	.85	.79	.86	.83	.82	.85	.88	.88	.86	.80	.86	.74	.74	.57	.35	.35	.31	.24	.16
1.00	.95	.93	.93	.91	.95	.91	.83	.79	.86	.86	.85	.85	.88	.88	.89	.85	.84	.74	.66	.58	.33	.33	.33	.27	.16
.95	1.00	.95	.95	.92	.96	.90	.82	.78	.85	.82	.81	.84	.87	.87	.88	.82	.88	.76	.68	.61	.33	.33	.29	.23	.15
.93	.95	1.00	1.00	.88	.95	.93	.80	.77	.84	.86	.85	.85	.85	.88	.87	.83	.89	.79	.69	.62	.33	.33	.33	.27	.16
.93	.95	1.00	1.00	.88	.95	.93	.80	.77	.84	.86	.85	.85	.85	.88	.87	.83	.89	.79	.69	.62	.33	.33	.33	.27	.16
.91	.92	.88	.88	1.00	.90	.86	.82	.78	.86	.85	.84	.84	.85	.85	.81	.82	.86	.70	.67	.56	.32	.32	.32	.25	.17
.95	.96	.95	.95	.90	1.00	.92	.85	.80	.84	.81	.80	.82	.85	.85	.86	.85	.86	.80	.67	.57	.31	.31	.31	.25	.21
.91	.90	.93	.93	.86	.92	1.00	.85	.76	.81	.83	.82	.85	.82	.85	.81	.80	.81	.74	.68	.63	.31	.31	.35	.28	.16
.83	.82	.80	.80	.82	.85	.85	1.00	.91	.90	.87	.86	.86	.89	.86	.75	.78	.80	.80	.68	.49	.30	.30	.35	.32	.28
.79	.78	.77	.77	.78	.80	.76	.91	1.00	.93	.90	.88	.85	.91	.89	.76	.83	.82	.76	.62	.49	.38	.38	.38	.35	.31
.86	.85	.84	.84	.86	.84	.81	.90	.93	1.00	.97	.96	.93	.99	.96	.84	.85	.86	.78	.66	.54	.40	.40	.40	.33	.24
.86	.82	.86	.86	.85	.81	.83	.87	.90	.97	1.00	.99	.93	.96	.96	.81	.85	.86	.78	.64	.56	.42	.42	.42	.34	.20
.85	.81	.85	.85	.84	.80	.82	.86	.88	.96	.99	1.00	.91	.94	.94	.79	.83	.85	.79	.66	.53	.38	.38	.38	.30	.21
.85	.84	.85	.85	.84	.82	.85	.86	.85	.93	.93	.91	1.00	.94	.97	.82	.83	.85	.71	.60	.55	.32	.32	.41	.33	.24
.88	.87	.85	.85	.85	.85	.82	.89	.91	.99	.96	.94	.94	1.00	.97	.85	.84	.85	.77	.65	.53	.39	.39	.39	.32	.23
.88	.87	.88	.88	.85	.85	.85	.86	.89	.96	.96	.94	.97	.97	1.00	.85	.86	.88	.74	.61	.56	.39	.39	.39	.32	.23
.89	.88	.87	.87	.81	.86	.81	.75	.76	.84	.81	.79	.82	.85	.85	1.00	.85	.84	.70	.63	.62	.38	.38	.34	.27	.23
.85	.82	.83	.83	.82	.85	.80	.78	.83	.85	.85	.83	.83	.84	.86	.85	1.00	.88	.74	.61	.53	.39	.39	.35	.27	.28
.84	.88	.89	.89	.86	.86	.81	.80	.82	.86	.86	.85	.85	.85	.88	.84	.88	1.00	.76	.70	.59	.38	.38	.30	.22	.18
.74	.76	.79	.79	.70	.80	.74	.80	.76	.78	.78	.79	.71	.77	.74	.70	.74	.76	1.00	.72	.49	.29	.29	.24	.25	.26
.66	.68	.69	.69	.67	.67	.68	.68	.62	.66	.64	.66	.60	.65	.61	.63	.61	.70	.72	1.00	.53	.35	.35	.29	.25	.13
.58	.61	.62	.62	.56	.57	.63	.49	.49	.54	.56	.53	.55	.53	.56	.62	.53	.59	.49	.53	1.00	.41	.41	.34	.30	.15
.33	.33	.33	.33	.32	.31	.31	.30	.38	.40	.42	.38	.32	.39	.39	.38	.39	.38	.29	.35	.41	1.00	1.00	.78	.63	.13
.33	.33	.33	.33	.32	.31	.31	.30	.38	.40	.42	.38	.32	.39	.39	.38	.39	.38	.29	.35	.41	1.00	1.00	.78	.63	.13
.33	.29	.33	.33	.32	.31	.35	.35	.38	.40	.42	.38	.41	.39	.39	.34	.35	.30	.24	.29	.34	.78	.78	1.00	.88	.27
.27	.23	.27	.27	.25	.25	.28	.32	.35	.33	.34	.30	.33	.32	.32	.27	.27	.22	.25	.25	.30	.63	.63	.88	1.00	.31
.16	.15	.16	.16	.17	.21	.16	.28	.31	.24	.20	.21	.24	.23	.23	.23	.28	.18	.26	.13	.15	.13	.13	.27	.31	1.00

Table 14

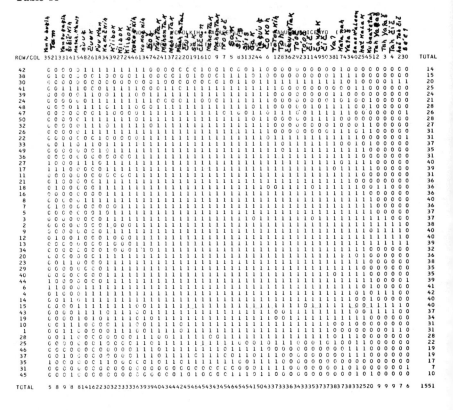

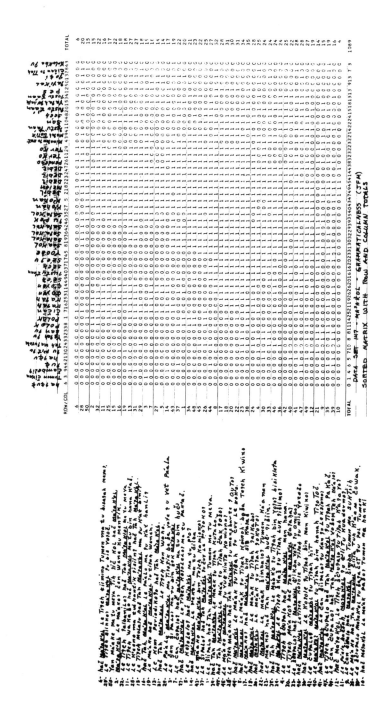

Table 15

Table 16

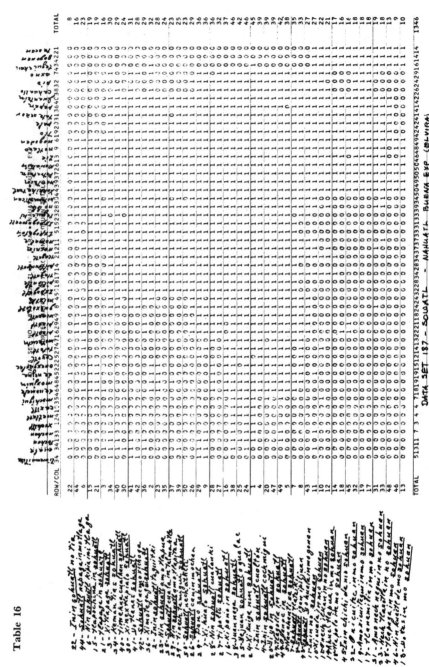

DATA SET 187 — SQUATL — NAHUATL — BUENA EXP (ELVIRA)
SORTED MATRIX WITH ROW AND COLUMN TOTALS

Table 17. Cross-Frame Cross-Informant Reliability Checks.

The correlations between the 1,225 form-pairs distributional similarity in an X-type matrix done by informant A with frames 1–50, and their distributional similarity in another X-type matrix done by informant B with frames 51–100.

English, *laundry*, aggrement matrix. Informants CP and LB	0.79
Japanese, *Gimu*, Criterion 1, SS & HS	0.89
Japanese, *Gimu*, Criterion 1, HS & SS	0.77
Japanese, *Gimu*, Criterion 3, SS & HS	0.78
Japanese, *Gimu*, Criterion 3, HS & SS	0.83

Table 18a. Informants' Ability to Estimate Form-Pair Distributional Similarity.

Matrix 174—*apurar*, "cierto"	0.79 (95 pairs)
Matrix 102—*ʔistikyah*, "maʔaloʔo u ťàan"	0.86 (96 pairs)

Example of Effects of Training

Informant A.V.—First Yucatec Matrix 104—*ʔistikyah*, "hah u ťàan"	0.54 (101 pairs)
Informant A.V.—Second Yucatec Matrix 129—*ʔoʔolkih*, "hah u ťàan"	0.93 (97 pairs)

Naïve Speakers of English

Estimated D.S.		Observed Distributional Similarity	
		Sense	Grammaticalness
	Sense	0.38	0.08
	Grammaticalness	0.57	0.56

Table 18b. Informant Estimates and Observed Distributional Similarity (Matrix 172).

Word	Word	Informant Ranking	Observed Dist. Sim.	Word	Word	Informant Ranking	Observed Dist. Sim.
01	07	01	84	01	30	51	00
01	10	02	70	01	20	52	00
01	08	03	100	01	18	53	12
01	11	04	46	01	49	54	00
01	72	05	90	01	22	55	00
01	06	06	16	01	25	56	00
01	04	07	46	01	33	57	00
01	34	08	89	05	15	58	00
01	02	09	89	10	20	59	00
01	03	10	82	01	36	60	00
01	05	11	80	01	46	61	00
01	09	12	67	01	19	62	00
01	73	13	53	01	15	63	00
50	09	14	00	01	17	64	00
50	23	15	00	01	28	65	17
50	25	16	00	01	32	66	00
50	18	17	00	01	45	67	00
50	39	18	00	01	42	68	00
50	34	19	00	01	26	69	00
50	35	20	00	50	05	70	00
50	49	21	00	50	20	71	00
50	07	22	00	50	45	72	00
50	11	23	00	50	32	73	00
50	08	24	00	50	28	74	00
50	02	25	00	50	14	75	00
50	12	26	00	50	24	76	00
50	14	27	00	50	15	77	00
50	73	28	00	50	37	78	00
50	10	29	00	50	17	79	00
50	06	30	00	50	31	80	00
50	13	31	00	50	33	81	00
01	41	32	00	50	47	82	00
01	47	33	00	50	29	83	00
01	29	34	00	50	27	84	00
01	35	35	00	30	40	85	00
01	39	36	12	50	26	86	00
01	33	37	06	50	48	87	00
01	24	38	00	50	46	88	00
01	44	39	00	50	43	89	00
01	38	40	00	50	22	90	00
01	43	41	00	50	30	91	50
01	48	42	00	50	42	92	00
01	74	43	07	50	41	93	00
01	27	44	00	50	44	94	00
01	37	45	00	50	16	95	00
01	76	46	00	50	36	96	00
01	27	47	00	50	19	97	00
01	50	48	00	50	21	98	00
01	40	49	00	50	38	99	00
01	37	50	00	50	40	100	00

Table 18c. Informant Estimates and Observed Distributional Similarity (Matrix 129).

Word	Word	Informant Ranking	Observed Dist. Sim.	Word	Word	Informant Ranking	Observed Dist. Sim.
21	30	01	00	18	20	50	60
12	14	02	00	05	47	51	89
18	33	03	06	16	18	52	60
15	17	04	22	06	45	53	63
14	38	05	13	11	40	54	71
17	35	06	14	24	28	55	64
21	31	07	30	06	46	56	78
14	15	08	25	23	24	57	73
04	48	09	26	17	34	58	72
03	48	10	26	13	39	59	70
13	15	11	13	22	24	60	75
22	30	12	17	11	13	61	78
16	35	13	20	24	27	62	100
13	14	14	17	22	29	63	88
12	40	15	29	17	19	64	82
12	39	16	29	07	49	65	89
15	37	17	31	16	17	66	83
15	36	18	27	10	11	67	85
25	26	19	29	11	41	68	85
15	16	20	30	22	23	69	80
20	21	21	26	07	45	70	58
14	16	22	26	13	38	71	80
14	37	23	37	09	11	72	100
11	12	24	32	08	43	73	89
19	21	25	30	02	03	74	63
03	50	26	39	23	29	75	99
04	05	27	29	05	46	76	83
19	33	28	29	10	42	77	94
21	23	29	34	09	43	78	85
21	22	30	32	10	41	79	100
12	13	31	29	20	22	80	92
04	47	32	33	23	28	81	88
04	49	33	39	16	36	82	86
04	06	34	35	09	42	83	94
03	49	35	39	08	10	84	91
02	04	36	88	05	06	85	90
02	50	37	32	20	31	86	93
02	49	38	32	20	32	87	93
01	02	39	32	07	09	88	91
05	07	40	95	09	10	89	100
03	05	41	33	08	09	90	91
10	12	42	35	19	32	91	92
18	34	43	54	19	20	92	97
24	26	44	65	06	07	93	91
17	18	45	58	08	44	94	95
25	27	46	62	07	08	95	93
23	25	47	66	07	44	96	95
24	25	48	62	06	08	97	93
18	19	49	62				

Table 19

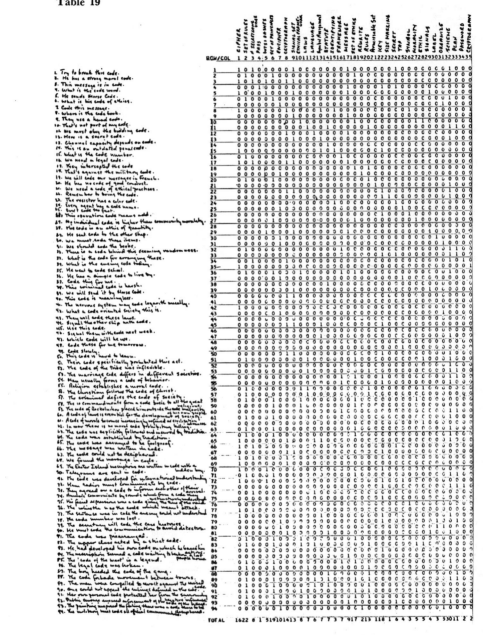

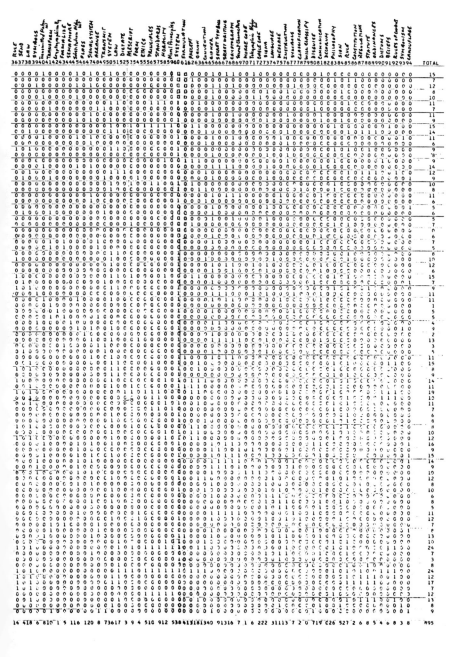

Table 20a

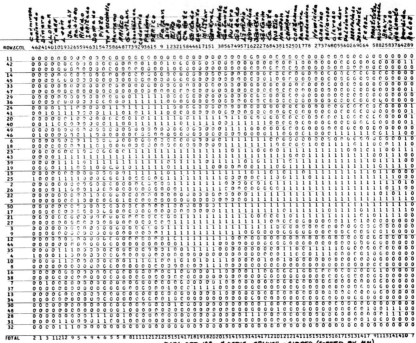

DATA SET 185 - M. ORTIS - SPANISH - CIERTO (SORTED BY MM)

SORTED MATRIX WITH ROW AND COLUMN TOTALS

```
...ISH**CIERTO(SORTED BY MM)
...ND COLUMN TOTALS

24471218 67069456314353113038 866 73784341379728720825 62835   TOTAL
```

The following is a binary data matrix followed by handwritten Spanish sentences:

1	La luz se reforma en un fenomeno de la Naturaleza
9	Amo a Dios sobre todas las cosas
10	Amo a Dios sobre todas las cosas
12	Señor hazme su voluntad o primera tierra como en el cielo
7	El que esta cansado debe descansar
5	El cielo esta muy azul
3	alquilar una bicicleta Resulta caro
5	Los huevos de la caverna son muy chicos
6	La paloma vuela por el zocalo
16	El ticiclo que me regalas los ya lo perdi
17	Con el dinero me comprare un automovil
38	Todos nosotros tenemos un alma
35	A mi hijo le gusta llorar mucho
5	Hay que ser muy atento para causar buena impresion
15	Jose se sintio airado cuando supo que le ofendieron
15	Julian estaba aislado cuando le dijeron que se saco la loteria
26	Mi amigo siempre estaba sentado en la esquina
44	que limpio esta aquel niño
54	A Enrique le llamon el rustico en la escuela
51	Mi tio mato una chachalaca anoche
38	se escapo el leon del circo
35	en el maufraio solo el perro se salvo
33	Mataron un toro brave en el rastro
29	se escapo de la prision el homicida
28	Hay que tenerle miedo a Victor porque es amelaldado
24	Si eres tu mismo nadie te va a respetar
27	el dia que se casa Maria la acusaron como prostituta
31	Ante la sociedad ella fue una sandaganera
27	el cabo que da la instruccion esta borracho
18	Luis se considera un buen saltarin
16	El presidente actual esta feliz
16	Yucatan es la tierra del faizan y el venado
10	no hay nada mejor que el libro que enseña la verdad
6	El buen soldado muere con dignidad en los campos de batalla
17	Murio pelaando en el campo del honor
10	cuando mi hijo la palabra carnivoro se me crispan los nervios
14	Luis por ser muy vivaracho le apodan el tigre
4	Durante los dias de examenes el jurado me reprendio
10	El dormilon siempre se mantiene ileso anoche verde
6	Fue consignado al tribunal para menores
8	se necesita una plama para lavar tu libertad
12	El que no respeta la leyes un infractor
13	La geografia se llama nuevo mundo
9	En mi nacion reina la paz
8	Tu tienes derecha a ser un buen Mexicano
6	Un caballo chicao es dificil de domar
12	ya quedo manso mi caballo
6	El tigre del circo fue domado con facilidad
3	El jabali es un animal muy peligroso

```
5 7 8 6 7 7 5 6 5 7 4 2 4 5 4 8 4 3 5 6 4 3 2 2 3 3 5 6 6 2    857
```

Mapa del Sorteo de Clases de Palabras efectuado en el criterio de "Cierta"

Clase "A" Y sus divisiones	Clase "B" Y sus divisiones	CLASE "C" y sus divisiones	Clase "D" Y SUS DIVISIONES	CLASE "E" Y SUS DIVISIONES	CLASE "F" Y SUS DIVISIONES	CLASE "F" DIVISION N° 22
Division N° 1 en pena imp MORIBUNDO PACIENTE APOCADO HOMOSEXUAL	Division N° 1 MAFFIA MALEANTE FICHADO Pandillero Contrabandista TRAFICANTE HAMPON	DIVISIÓN N° 1 COMUNISTA IZQUIERDISTA AGITADOR IZQUIERDISTA TERRORISTA	DIVISIÓN N° 1 CABO SOLDADO TENIENTE GENDARME GENERAL SARGENTO MILITAR CADETE	DIVISION N° 1 DEUDOR MOROSO MALINTENCIONADO DESPREOCUPADO DESVIRTUADO SINVERGÜENZA	DIVISION N° 1 NATIVO MAYA INDÍGENA SALVAJE	PROGRESISTA PRÓSPERO DESTACADO CONQUISTADO
Division N° 2 Pálido DÉBIL Raquítico amarillento Desgarbado disminuido	Division N° 2 LADRÓN DICTADOR MAÑOSO ASESINO ATRACADOR DELINCUENTE	división N° 2 LIBERAL DICTADOR MANDÓN AUTORITARIO DOMINANTE	DIVISIÓN N° 2 PILOTO AVIADOR VOLADOR RAUDO VELOZ VIAJAL	DIVISION N° 2 ORIÓN IRREVERENTE TRICADOR	DIVISION N° 2 PROVINCIANO HUASTECO NAHUATL VAROSO	DIVISION N° 23 OPACADO RADIOLOGADO ACOMODADO
Division N° 3 Tuberculoso Diabético Hemolítico Canceroso acatarrado	Division N° 3 Delincuente maliviviente Picaro Falsificador Tramposo	división N° 3 ROGADOR REGRESO INJUSTO	DIVISIÓN N° 3	DIVISION N° 3 GROSERO MALCRIADO MALEDUCADO MALEDUCADO	DIVISION N° 3 P. MAYA CHAPARRO DIMINUTO CHICO BAJO	DIVISION N° 24 FASTIDIADO ESPERANZADO
Division N° 4 Operado COJO TUERTO MOCHO manco Lisiado Dañado Como frecuente	Division N° 4 Sativo Violador Secuestrador Repulsivo	DIVISIÓN N° 4 CORRIENTE OPONENTE COMBATIVO GUERRERO	DIVISION N° 4	DIVISION N° 4 ODIOSO FASTIDIOSO ENOJOSO	DIVISION N° 4 CRIOLLO LATINO LATINO	DIVISION N° 25 CARIÑADO ZAPATERO
Division N° 5 Melancólico Ensimismado Crumi apesadumbrado	Division N° 5 ajusticiado enjuiciado Encerrado Guayavado Recluso Reo	DIVISIÓN N° 5 COMANDANTE AGENTE VIGILANTE VELADOR	DIVISION N° 5 COMANDANTE AGENTE VIGILANTE VELADOR	DIVISION N° 5 RUIDOSO ESCANDALOSO BULLANGUERO ALBOROTADO DIABLO	DIVISION N° 5 CAPITALINO METROPOLITANO AZTECA	
Division N° 6 Hechizado embrujado	Division N° 6 Ladrón Ratero Hurtador Rapaz Raptor	DIVISIÓN N° 6 OFICIAL DETECTIVE GUARDIÁN MAESTRANZO TORPO	DIVISION N° 6	DIVISION N° 6 OLGAZAN VAGO FLOJO	DIVISION N° 6 FUERTE SALUDABLE ROBUSTO FORNIDO FORZUDO	
Division N° 7 Preocupado pendenciero afligido	Division N° 7 TAHUR JUGADOR aDOCADOR Raguetero	DIVISIÓN N° 7 Secretaria Tesorera Oficinista Escribiente Contador Empleado Burócrata	DIVISION N° 7 VALIENTE SEÑOR ARTICULADO RESPETO	DIVISION N° 7 INDIGNO IGNORANTE BRUTO	DIVISION N° 7 ASIÁTICO ORIENTAL	
Division N° 8 Bilioso Receloso Posesivo	Division N° 8 Prostituta Ramera Meretriz Prelua Mula Nudista	DIVISIÓN N° 9	DIVISION N° 8 PEQUEÑO CALISTO VANIDOSO ORNITO	DIVISION N° 8 PRESUMIDO PAISITO EJECUTIVO PACHOTO	DIVISION N° 8 SERVIDOR LABORIOSO APLICADO TRABAJADOR ATICADO	
Division N° 9 LOCO Obnocido TURULATO baboso Distraído Desquiciado embebecido extrasado	Division N° 9 VICIOSO ALCOHÓLICO BORRACHO Beliodo Acostumbrado abstemio marihuano Fumador drogadicto		DIVISION N° 9 VIOLENTO RUDO VIRIL APAYA	DIVISION N° 9 ALTANERO MEZQUINADO PRESUMIDO DISGUSTANTE TERROR	DIVISION N° 9 CAMPESINO PUEBLERINO PARRICERO BRASERO MANTECOSO	
Division N° 10 deslenguado Golpeado apachurrado Magullado adolorido	Division N° 10 CHAMPADO INQUIETO Parrandero aventurado		DIVISION N° 10	DIVISION N° 10 SERVICIADO ESPECTACULAR	DIVISION N° 10 SASTRE MODISTA BORDADORA COSTURERA	
Division N° 11 Tirado Posado Caído Sentado acostado echado dormido	Division N° 11 MAÑOSO peligroso escurridizo FERIL LUCHADO		DIVISION N° 11 BRAVO EGOÍSTA IMPARCIAL	DIVISION N° 11 RÚSTICO CREOLLO GRINGO NACO	DIVISION N° 11 LAVANDERA PLANCHADORA	
Division N° 12 Viejo anciano veterano cansado	Division N° 12 fugado Escondido guarauido escapado		DIVISION N° 12 FURIOSO IRRITADO MOLESTO MALHUMORADO	DIVISION N° 12 MISERABLE DESGRACIADO IMPÍO	DIVISION N° 12 BARRENDERA TRASNOCHADA CAMASTRERA HOTELERA	
Division N° 13 entumida acurrucada ciática	Division N° 13 Sancionado infractor acusado amenazado buscado			DIVISION N° 13 MANCHADO AFECTOSO	DIVISION N° 13 COSTURERA TRABAJADA TEXTILERA	
Division N° 14 GOLOSO GORDO ayagoso Comelón Barrigón	Division N° 14 Escubidor complice			DIVISION N° 14 NAUSEADO AFECTOSO SUSIA PULGOSO PUERCO	DIVISION N° 14 REFRESQUERA REFRESQUERA DULCERA	
Division N° 15 Sediento Hambriento	Division N° 15 Molestoso SISTEMA perliscran limosnera				DIVISION N° 15 CUIDADORA NODRIZA NIÑERA NOVELISA MADRINA	
					DIVISION N° 16 FLORIDOR ELECTRICISTA MECÁNICO TÉCNICO	
					DIVISION N° 17 ACOPLADO ORGANIZADOR EMPRENDEDOR	
					DIVISION N° 18 CALZADO CONFIADO TRANQUILO SATISFECHO CONTENTO CONFIADO	
					DIVISION N° 19 CONOCIDO APRECIADO LEAL DECENTE HONRADO	
					DIVISION N° 20 POBRE HUMILDE ANCLADO ENCLAVADO AMOLADO	
					DIVISION N° 21 AFECTUOSO BUENO ATENTO	

Por Manuel Medina

CLASE "G"	CLASE "H"	CLASE "I"	CLASE "J"	CLASE "K"	CLASE "L"	CLASE "L'"
Y SUS DIVISIONES	Y SUS DIVISIONES	Y SUS DIVISIONES	Y SUS DIVISIONES	Y SUS DIVISIONES	Y SUS DIVISIONES	Y SUS DIVISIONES

CLASE "G" — Y SUS DIVISIONES

DIVISION No 1 — AMERICANO, GRINGO, YANQUI
DIVISION No 2 — EXTRANJERO, FORANEO
DIVISION No 3 — PELIROJO, GUERO, BLANCO
DIVISION No 4 — NEGRO, MORENO, MULATO, PRIETO
DIVISION No 5 — PELADO, GRANDE, INMENSO, GIGANTE
DIVISION No 6 — ALTO, LARGO, DELGADO, FLACO, HUESUDO
DIVISION No 7 — PASADOR, VAGABON, TURISTA, VISITANTE
DIVISION No 8 — CAMINANTE, ANDANTE, ERRANTE, AMBULANTE, PASEABLE
DIVISION No 9 — MIEDOSO, GALLON, OSIOSO, COBARDE, INTREMETIDO
DIVISION No 10 — ENTUSIASMADO, MORIFICADO

CLASE "H" — Y SUS DIVISIONES

DIVISION No 1 — EXTRAVAGANTE, FAGUEOSO, CAPITALISTO, ALGODOLADO, RICO
DIVISION No 2 — HEREDERO, APODERADO, ACCIONISTA, HACMATE, BANQUERO
DIVISION No 3 — AHORCADOR, NEGOCIANTE, COMERCIANTE
DIVISION No 4 — COMPRADOR, VENDEDOR, ALMACENISTA, VENDEDOR, BECAMBIENTE, TENDERO
DIVISION No 5 — PRESTAMISTA, EMBARGADOR, AGIOTISTA, HIPOTECARIO
DIVISION No 6 — ENVIDIOSO, LUCRATIVO, AMBICIOSO, AVARO
DIVISION No 7 — APROVECHADO, EXPLOTADOR, VIVIDOR, VENTAJISTA, ESTRUMIDOR
DIVISION No 8 — AMPARADO, MIEDOSO, AFRONTADO, MALTRACIO, IMPREVISTENTE

CLASE "I" — Y SUS DIVISIONES

DIVISION No 1 — SALTARIN, TRAVESISTA, CANTANTE, MAGO, ARTISTA
DIVISION No 2 — RESITADOR, RECITADOR, RESEÑADOR, DECLAMADOR, POETA
DIVISION No 3 — NUARANCERO, SILBADOR, RUMBERO, BAILADOR, DANZANTE
DIVISION No 4 — MELODIOSO, CANTADISTA, GUITARRISTA, FILARMONICO, MUSICO
DIVISION No 5 — ORADOR, FLOROLISTA
DIVISION No 5 — PIANISTA, VIOLINISTA, ORQUESTA, BANDA
DIVISION No 6 — ESCRITOR, GRABISTA, DIBUMISTA, HUMORISTA, ESCULTOR, PAYASO
DIVISION No 7 — DRIOSO, INFAMOSO, BONITO, GUAPO, BELLA, LINDO, SIMPATICO
DIVISION No 8 — FELIZ, RISUEÑO, CONTENTO, ALEGRE, DIVERTIDO
DIVISION No 9 — PRESTADO, ACASANADO, DICHOSO
DIVISION No 10 — UGENSISTA, ROMANTICA, AGOMANTICA, CASADERA

CLASE "J" — Y SUS DIVISIONES

DIVISION No 1 — MEXICO, BOLIVIA, PANTERA, ENSEÑANZA, DENTISTA
DIVISION No 2 — CATEDRATICO, MAESTRO, ACADEMICO, APARTADOR, GRADUADO, IMPARTIVO
DIVISION No 3 — ALUMNO, INTERNO, INTELIGENTE, TOMADOR
DIVISION No 4 — ESTUDIOSO, APLICADO, APICADO, APLICADO, ESTUDIA
DIVISION No 4 — DEMOTISTA
DIVISION No 5 — BELIGISTA, NAGADOR, DANLISTA, TENISTA, AUTOMOVILISTA
DIVISION No 6 — PUEBLO, POPULAR, BANANA, ASCASO
DIVISION No 7 — MODELO, PEINADA, PROCEDADA, VESTIDA
DIVISION No 8 — AMISTADO, AMISTABLE, SOCIABLE, AMABLE, GENTIL, CORTES
DIVISION No 9 — PATETICO, DIFERENTE, TERIO, PRUDENTE
DIVISION No 10 — CASADA, HOGAREÑA, ACOMPAÑADO, INMOBLE, ARRIMONADA
DIVISION No 11 — PERICO, LENTO, CALMOSO, PASMOSO
DIVISION No 12 — ABUSADO, ABICIONADO, ESPECTADOR

CLASE "K" — Y SUS DIVISIONES

DIVISION No 1 — CATOLICO, RELIGIOSO, SABADITA, PROTESTANTE, ORTODOXO, PRESBITERIANO
DIVISION No 2 — PADRE, CURA, SACERDOTE, CARAS MAL, MONJE, SCMPRIPITO, MINISTRO, PRESBITERO
DIVISION No 3 — LOABLE, VICIOSO, JUSTIFICANTE, ARRODILLADO, PIADOSO, DEVOTO
DIVISION No 4 — BENEFACTOR, BONDADOSO, CARITATIVO
DIVISION No 5 — AMOROSO, CELOSO, COMPLACIDO
DIVISION No 6 — INOCENTE, AYUDADO, DISTINGUIDO, AGRADABLE

CLASE "L" — Y SUS DIVISIONES

DIVISION No 1 — CARNIBORO, LEON, TIGRE, MAMIFERO
DIVISION No 2 — BURRO, CUADRUPEDO
DIVISION No 3 — MARRANO, TERESQUINTLE, TABORI, O
DIVISION No 4 — FRISCO, FEROZ, RABIOSO
DIVISION No 5 — FEO, LUGUBRE, HORRENDO, HORRIFILANTE
DIVISION No 6 — MORADO, MONTES, PERJUDICIAL
DIVISION No 7 — LOBARTIJA, CAMALEON, LAGARTO
DIVISION No 8 — MOTADO, SUMERGIDO, HUMEDO, MOJADO, SCUATICO
DIVISION No 9 — FATO, DAMSO
DIVISION No 10 — HICHON, PALOMA, ASVILLA
DIVISION No 11 — PAVO, PLUMIFERO, GUAJOLOTE, FAISAN
DIVISION No 12 — GALLINA, CODORNIS, CHACLASISCA
DIVISION No 13 — CRUDA, SABROSO, SANCOCHADO, ASADO, COMESTIBLE
DIVISION No 14 — CRIADO, CEBADO, ALCANZADO, CAZADO, MAMSO
DIVISION No 15 — DESPLUMADO, DESFELLEJADO, DESHABRIDA, MALTRATADO
DIVISION No 16 — PONZOÑOSO, RASTRERO, VENENOSO, REPTIL, CULEBRA
DIVISION No 17 — CILINDRICO, REDONDO, ENROSCADO
DIVISION No 17 — TRABADO, PREMIDA
DIVISION No 18 — PICADOR, CHUPADOR
DIVISION No 20 — PELUDO, VELLUDO
DIVISION No 21 — BLANDO, SUAVE
DIVISION No 22 — ASOLEADO, SECO
DIVISION No 23 — POROSO, ESCAMOSO, ESPINOSO, ASPERO
DIVISION No 24 — AGUSTADO, ASOMBRADO

CLASE "L'" — Y SUS DIVISIONES

DIVISION No 1 — PINTO, BICOLOR, RAYADO
DIVISION No 16 — ROTO, COBRADO, ESCARLATO
DIVISION No 17 — LLORON, CHILLON, CHOCHON, LAGRIMOSO
DIVISION No 18 — MOTADO, ALOGADO, FLITEJADA, ENVEJENADA, ASFIXIADO
DIVISION No 19 — SUELTO, LIBRE

Table 21a

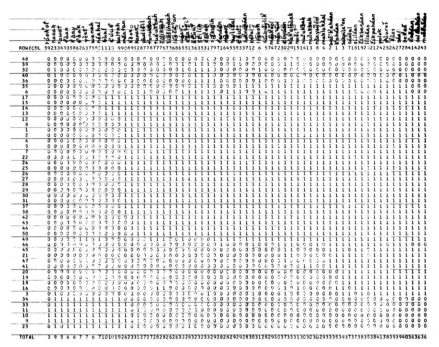

DATA SET 181 - F.MOO - MAYAN - BUBNA EXP (SORTED BY MB)
SORTED MATRIX WITH ROW AND COLUMN TOTALS

```
                                    ***BUENA EXP.(SORTED BY MB)
                                    ROW AND COLUMN TOTALS

444547545657606166667828384858616172238466970814849503243988   TOTAL

0 0 0 0 0 0 0 0 0 2 0 0 0 0 0 0 0 0 0 0 0 0 0 0 0 0 0 1 1 0 0 0 0 0
0 0 0 0 0 0 0 0 0 0 1 1 0 0 0 0 0 0 0 0 0 0 0 0 0 0 1 1 0
0 0 0 0 0 0 0 0 0 0 0 0 0 0 0 0 0 0 0 0 0 0 0 0 1 1 1 0
0 0 0 0 0 0 0 0 0 0 0 0 0 0 0 0 0 0 0 0 0 0 0 0 1 1 1 0
0 0 0 0 0 0 0 0 0 0 1 0 0 0 0 0 1 0 0 0 0 0 0 0 0 1 1 0
0 0 0 1 0 0 0 0 0 0 0 0 0 1 1 1 1 1 1 0 0 0 1 0 0 0
0 0 0 0 1 0 0 0 0 0 1 0 0 0 1 0 0 0 0 1 0 0 1 1 1 1
1 1 1 1 1 1 1 1 1 1 1 1 1 1 1 1 1 1 1 1 1 1 0 0 0 0
1 1 1 1 1 1 1 1 1 1 1 1 1 1 1 1 1 1 1 1 1 1 1 0 0 0 0
1 1 1 1 1 1 1 1 1 1 1 1 1 1 1 1 1 1 1 1 1 1 1 0 0 0 0
1 1 1 1 1 1 1 1 1 1 1 1 1 1 1 1 1 1 1 1 1 1 0 0 0 0
1 1 1 1 1 1 1 1 1 1 1 1 1 1 1 1 1 1 1 1 1 1 0 0 0
1 1 1 1 1 1 1 1 1 1 1 1 1 1 1 1 1 1 1 1 1 1 0 0 0
1 1 1 1 1 1 1 1 1 1 1 1 1 1 1 1 1 1 1 1 1 1 0 0 0
1 1 1 1 1 1 1 1 1 1 1 1 1 1 1 1 1 1 1 1 1 0 0 0
1 1 1 1 1 1 1 1 1 1 1 1 1 1 1 1 1 1 1 1 1 0 0 0
1 1 1 1 1 1 1 1 1 1 1 1 1 1 1 1 1 1 1 1 0 0 0
1 1 1 1 1 1 1 1 1 1 1 1 1 1 1 1 1 1 1 1 0 0 0
1 1 1 1 1 1 1 1 1 1 1 1 1 1 1 1 1 1 1 0 0 0
1 1 1 1 1 1 1 1 1 1 1 1 1 1 1 1 1 1 1 0 0 0
1 1 1 1 1 1 1 1 1 1 1 1 1 1 1 1 1 1 0 0 0
1 1 1 1 1 1 1 1 1 1 1 1 1 1 1 1 1 1 0 0 0
1 1 1 1 1 1 1 1 1 1 1 1 1 1 1 1 1 0 0 0
1 1 1 1 1 1 1 1 1 1 1 1 1 1 1 1 1 0 0 0
1 1 1 1 1 1 1 1 1 1 1 1 1 1 1 1 0 0 0
1 1 1 1 1 1 1 1 1 1 1 1 1 1 1 0 0 0
1 1 1 1 1 1 1 1 1 1 1 1 1 1 1 0 0 0
1 1 1 1 1 1 1 1 1 1 1 1 1 1 0 0 0
1 1 1 1 1 1 1 1 1 0 1 1 1 1 1 0 0 0
1 1 1 1 1 1 1 1 1 1 1 1 1 0 0 0
1 1 1 1 1 1 1 1 1 1 2 1 1 1 1 0 0 0
1 1 1 1 1 1 1 1 1 1 1 1 1 0 0 0
0 1 1 1 1 1 1 1 1 1 0 1 1 1 0 0 0
0 1 1 1 1 1 1 1 1 1 1 0 1 1 0 0 0
1 1 1 1 1 1 1 1 1 1 1 1 0 0 0
1 1 0 1 1 1 1 1 1 1 1 0 0 0
1 1 1 1 1 1 1 1 1 1 0 0 0
1 1 1 1 1 1 1 1 1 1 0 0 0
1 1 1 1 1 1 1 1 1 1 1 0 0 0
1 1 1 1 1 1 1 1 1 0 0 0
1 1 1 1 1 1 1 1 1 0 0 0
0 0 0 0 0 0 0 0 0 0 0 0 0
0 0 0 0 0 0 0 0 0 0 0 0 0
0 0 0 0 0 0 0 0 0 0 0 0 0
0 0 0 0 0 0 0 0 0 0 0 0 0
0 0 0 0 0 0 0 0 0 0 0 0 0

363736363836353637374038737363737373734343532333231313011 6 6 1   2563
```

3 su²lak le šišpah tši ²u klík ²u ²šamigós
11 behla²y tin hantah ²untu kúuš
9 <u>kitan</u> ²u k²aba² ²u k²enih k²daš
9 le señoráa tu kon ²uulun
14 ²untuh ši²áaš tin manah
36 le ší²lli² yan tin wilmalo? ydaš
41 ²dogik ²untah <u>lóokoh</u>
77 <u>ší hdan</u> le ²oši señdorko
77 nuší² ²u tšatah le páalo?
77 ²untuh báalše? šišaneh nušukbah
77 <u>nuší ukbak</u> le mdak ku kdonolo?
74 le šan ššúupal wáalakbalo? <u>ké?el</u>
74 <u>náayayáal</u> le mdak ku šdano?
75 <u>kohdan</u> ²u tšatah le ššúupalo?
75 ²in šan ²li š?neh <u>wáš²k²ahdan</u>
75 ²untuh mdak yan šsen ti? lošii²ah <u>maklukšal</u>
75 le máak ku bisdaloh <u>táubulyli²?</u>
74 <u>tšatal</u> ²in wala? mlis
74 le wakaš ku bisdalo? <u>²ál</u>
74 <u>paloš</u> ²in wala? škaš
74 ²in besine?y haš p²úuruš
74 haš <u>kdas</u> le báalše? yan ²u k²daki yišo?
74 le šydáš kašo? haš <u>sšal</u>
74 ²umpeh š²ilbe? haš <u>sek²eš</u>
74 le máak ku š²áaklo? <u>k²ak²albkak</u>
74 ²untu š²imin k²ime? <u>š²oydan</u>
77 le báalše? k²ašdano? <u>k²ek²en</u>
74 <u>šak²nahdan</u> le ²ulun k²šin²šdabo?
74 le tšak²in lišdaneh <u>²okolšden</u>
71 le p²eak? páuš²o? šan <u>sšlk²ak²an</u>
71 ²untuh ²ôokol bisdabe? <u>mošk²ašan</u>
71 le wakaš kun paybilo? <u>wšlk²ahdan</u>
71 <u>hak²áanyôšl</u> ²in wala? š²imin
63 le kooh yan k²ašo? sahak tu k²donoh
11 <u>šešp²dan</u> yiš le ššúupalo?
32 ²u šelek le mdak ku bin ²lš kôolo? <u>léaušan</u>
34 <u>šikpahšan</u> ²u sakih yiš le p²eak²o?
36 ²u hdanih le wšahah hatšan
37 <u>kašdan</u> ²u šš o oe ²u pôol le k²úupalo?
43 ²u ndakaš le šši palo? <u>lišdan</u>
43 <u>šilšan</u> ²u ndo²e le k²úupalo?
35 <u>sakpildeo</u> bondanih le ndaho?
11 ²untuh kdonolah k²en <u>?awaš</u> ku yšušbiš
12 le páal yan ?eškindo šan <u>p²dan</u> ku m²entik
14 teše? k²an báuš ku m²entik
14 ²in weaš me²yahe? tu <u>š²úu²š</u>?
14 ²u yšumih le kantina?o k²on <u>kulšah</u> ku m²entik
13 <u>tenes tšak²in</u> hanš

Table 21b

Kinsahmak.	ča waK	KuuȻ	haȼa'an	Me'e K'aan
go'oKoL	Ka'angh	S'uuȻ	Lo'oȼa'an	Lo'oȼa'an
Kasatach	Kohoč	SKiLi?	henča'eTaan	Kučaan
daatetch	PoLoK	KiTan	Kokha'eTa'an	TePaon
Saaaooh	Goolosoh	Kolun	Kaa T'a'an	Leataan
Ta Kaanyupo'oL	honah	Siimik	SeeP'aan	Lo'pan
K'uu$	POUNUS	SuLa?	Cičaan	Pela'an
P$u$uuL	Cič Muuk	Sakal	Paȼga'aTaan	K'iinTaan
Pek'a'an	?aȼ	SaY	Puȼa'an	ča Kaan
	Saal,	K'eK'en	Pa ȼan	MoRo?ȼahan
PolitiKooh	ȼ'oYaan	ȼ'iimin	Yača'an	Lonȼe Taan
$ouT	$eK'eč	buKoh	hilča?Taan	SoTaan,
AYiiKaL	Kaas		Moča?Taan	WaLKa'saan
Konoh	K'eKkl bak		MimPehaan	Noȼ K'a'saan
			MURUȼTunTaan	SaLKa'saan
Ka'aLtah	9 indioh		faa ča'an	Ka'saan
$'uuc	WiiT		SiKhaȼ Kubah	Peika?PaȼTaan
$ouL	Wiinik		Lubaan	hoo'saan
TuubuL YiiK	Mea'sewaal		Kimbe'saan	TohooȼinTaan
Ka'aya Yool	hod Ka hih			PalKahčinTan
KuukT'aan	KuuLih	Weneh	
Maal Keniadoh	Ken	KiKi?anKih	PonPon čaK
Keyah	Waay	MuuČukbah	SouSuTKubah
Saa loybaah	PeLYa?ah	motoK'bah	go KoH
Poo'cih		PokoKbah	MuuYah
Maa K'ooL		ȼinikbah	Paasa?Ka?
$iñiKTa'an	Pee$	KuLuKbah	Ka$ Ku ba?
	Krabah	Komokbah	Kambal
Ko'haan	ȼoKo$	Satmubah	P?Kalak
$uue	SuuLun	KoKoKbah	$ii? Kalak
$uuL	Cičan	Čilibah	ininbah
TuubuL Yik	AK?o'oK	$eleKbah	halK'eLaK
Ka'ayaYool		TuȼuKbah	
KuukTaan	Ka'adreh	haya?nahaan	Komboh
Senahaan	YunKiin	Pisčan	Puus.
BaKPieten	KaaTooLiKoh		SuuSioh
Wa$ Ka'han	YoaKooliTooh	ȼ'entaan	PaaPaY
Poo$'oKoh	Sa'aKKisTo'en	Luk na hahan	K'ooK'oL
Koo'oc	P'uuL	PoLohKinTo?an	Tu.?
MaaKLuKaaL		han Taa'n	Siis
$o'op	Polisiah	Kabaa'n	Kohel
$eTe	Kanan	Cu Kaan	
Saatal	KKaTčI?	Kat?a'an	ȼiK ba'al
LooKoh	KNU $I?	Di Sa a'n	K'aay
$aah	guȼben	TohoLTa'an	?ooK'oT
Ton$an	Ci ha a'n	Pa KaLTaa'n	Ce?eh
MaTooL		YaKunTaan	$awat
KilkaTaha'an	ȼeel	ȼi?KPa ha'an	T'a'an
	Limpioh	PuuSa?an	PapaS Ke?Taan
MeeYhil	Sak	SoKolTaan	
$ieKeLih	ha?uut	Ka Laan	
Kaa Kal	Kii eKelen	Liisaan	YaTioL
Sa'a poL	K'iiboK	Kombesaan	Ko?
K'oo$	ȼieKiinahan	KahLolTaan	ȼ'iib
Smiis	Ka'ni PoL	Lomaan	Kaat
PaaLi$'iL	Ča KPoL	Sii Laan,	?u$
Kom?MUUK		Cik besaan	Kii'mak YooL
		ȼ'a'an	KonTenToh

SORT OF WORDS CHECKED
IN MATRIX 181 (see table #22A)

Table 22

HABLAR	PENSAR	FELIZ	CAMINAR	ADELANTO	ENFERMO	COMPRANDO
LLAMAR	VER	ALEGRE	CORRIENDO	DESPIERTE	ENFERMAR	AGLOMERADA
MOLESTAR	ADMIRAR	ENTUSIASMADO	ATRASAR	ESPERANDO	LLORANDO	ACOSTUMBRADOS
CASTIGAR	VISITAR	SONRIENDO	VINIENDO	TARDE	TRISTE	ENSIMISMADO
REGAÑAR	CONTEMPLAR	CONTENTO	ALIMENTAR	TEMPRANO	DUERME	CAMBIAR
CANSAR	APURAR	LISTO		EMPESANDO	FLOJO	ALISTAR
GRITANDO		ANIMA		COMENSANDO	LENTO	FIAR
		CURIOSO		APURAR	FATIGADO	JUNTADA
		LOCO			HORRORISADO	
		ATENTO				
		EMOCIONA				

Introduction

Colby describes an application of Philip Stone's General Inquirer family of computer programs to thematic analysis of Japanese folktales.

The General Inquirer system is a program for counting frequencies of previously defined classes of words, or other segments, in running texts. The investigator creates equivalence classes of words (or stems or roots) for some specific purpose (e.g., words felt to be indicative of achievement motivation). He then inserts a *dictionary* where the words defined to be equivalent are listed. The classes of words are called *tags*. The program then tabulates tag frequencies. The system also has provisions for subtags, for concordance retrieval of tag members, and various other convenient accoutrements.

Colby has created a General Inquirer dictionary specifically for Japanese folktales. Working with a sample of 63 tales, he splits each tale into nine segments. He counts tags by segment, pooling all of the 63 tales in each of the nine segment counts. He then selects those tags showing the greatest variation in frequency across segments for the pooled tales. These frequencies are graphed showing a profile of the rise and fall of emphasis on particular themes (tags) in the course of the tales generally.

The improvement in computers and computer languages for handling alphameric data brings new possibilities to the anthropological study of texts. With the increase in storage capacity, flexibility, and speech for counting, classifying, and mapping word occurrences, one can now use methods that can reveal theme patterns in folktales and other narratives. These patterns were found with the General Inquirer system developed at the Harvard Laboratory of Social Relations by Philip J. Stone and his colleagues. The main part of this system is a dictionary of entry words grouped into conceptual units called tags. The entry words of the dictionary are compared to the words of a text. Every time a specific word is found in the text a tally is made for the tag to which the word belongs. The resulting tag tally is printed. Additional features of the system include a text and tag list that displays the sentences of the text on the left and the appropriate tags on the right; a retrieval program that can retrieve sentences containing the words of a specific tag; and a graphing program that can graph tag frequencies of different texts for visual comparison. The system has been more fully described elsewhere (Stone *et al.*: 1966).

The most attractive feature of the General Inquirer system is a flexibility that allows the use of different dictionaries according to the purpose of the analysis. Existing dictionaries include a general psychosociological dictionary which has been used in distinguishing real from simulated suicide notes (Stone *et al.* 1963), in studying small group discussions of Harvard students (Dunphy 1964), and in analyzing presidential nomination acceptance speeches (Smith *et al.* 1966). There is a Stanford political

The Shape of Narrative Concern in Japanese Folktales **6**

BENJAMIN N. COLBY

dictionary developed for studying content pertaining to international relations (Holsti 1966), a dictionary at Yale for analyzing editorial comment (Namenwirth and Brewer 1966) and various specialized dictionaries at Harvard for counting such things as achievement imagery and words relating to an Icarus theme. Finally, there is an anthropological dictionary for analyzing folktales and other narratives which I have developed during the last three years at the Museum of New Mexico in Santa Fe. The Santa Fe Dictionary in its present version contains 74 independent or "first-order" tags consisting of words that appear only in one tag and no other; and 7 "second-order" tags which contain words that have also been used in defining some of the first-order tags. Because the second-order tags are not independent they have not been used in statistical tests of correlation. Most of the 74 first-order tags are subdivided into two or three subcategories each. Counting the subcategories and those first-order tags that do not have subdivisions there are 195 independent word groups representing different conceptual themes in the Santa Fe Dictionary plus seven second-order tags totaling 202 conceptual categories in all.

In some cases, tags or their subcategories are defined by only one or a very few high-frequency words. Other times a tag can have more than 300 entry words. The first subcategory of the DOMINANCE tag consists of just two words, "let" and "may." The second and third subcategories of the DOMINANCE tag have 60 and 52 entry words, respectively. The entire dictionary contains 4,331 entry words. Many of these entry words are in a root form so that different grammatical forms of the word will be counted. For example, the entry word "talk" will not only cause talk to be counted whenever it appears in a text but also talks, talked, and talking.

The entry words have been especially selected for analyzing English translations of folktales. While the meaning of a given entry word may vary considerably in the context of a folktale, broadly speaking there is usually one meaning that occurs more frequently than others, and this is the meaning intended in the dictionary. When a tag consists of enough entry words, deviations from the intended concept for any one word form do not greatly affect the overall pattern of the tag frequencies. Nevertheless, some tags will measure enough "deviant" usages to necessitate an inspection of sentence retrievals from the text to delete them. The greatest difference in usage exists between the literary style of translated folktales and some types of colloquial speech. Since the Santa Fe Dictionary was designed to be "culture free" in order to analyze effectively translated texts of other cultures, it cannot be sensitive to some of the special usages in the conversational idiom of American college students or teenagers, for example.

The dictionary currently in use is the third in a series of dictionaries I have developed for studying folktales. The revisions in this third Santa Fe Dictionary are based on experience in counting words of folktales from more than 21 cultures. While a fourth revision is contemplated, it will first be necessary to develop new procedures and work on folktales in the original language. This will provide a better understanding of translation problems and idiosyncratic variations in thematic structure. Such an understanding will make the substantial effort of revising or constructing another dictionary more productive.

Some of the theoretical assumptions underlying the third Santa Fe Dictionary can be seen in the way it has been organized in the outline shown in Table 1. All subcategories followed by an (e) consist of the entry word or words in the title of the subcategory. The number in parenthesis is the number of the tag. The tags are listed alphabetically and numbered consecutively in printouts by the computer rather than in the order of the outline, since the outline may be changed from time to time according to the type of analysis undertaken. All tags are indicated by capital letters, subcategories of tags by italics.

At first this dictionary was used for standard tag tallies in the usual manner. But recently a new technique was tried in order to discover basic patterns of narrative concern. Each tale in a set of 63 Japanese folktales (Seki 1963) was divided into nine sections of equal length. All the first sections of the folktales were pooled for one tag tally, all the second sections for another, and so on through the ninth section. The results were analyzed with statistical test programs to winnow the patterns and select those with the most distinct frequency differences.

Counting all subcategories and those tags without subcategories, 45 out of 195 independent conceptual units showed patterns that were statistically significant at the 0.01 level, using a χ^2 test.[1] The use of a significance level was solely for selecting the most obvious or definite patterns. Not enough is understood about the interdependencies of themes and concepts, about contextual influence, or about semantic information in narrative to place any further interpretation on a significance level for patterns such as these.

The frequency patterns of conceptual units are determined by the topic with which a given part of the folktale may be concerned. It would thus not be surprising to find patterns in a single folktale. But it is surprising to find patterns when nine parts of 63 folktales are tallied. This does not mean, however, that every one of the 63 folktales instances the patterns. The major part of any one pattern is often supplied by only a handful of the longer stories. Future work will require a careful study of the degree to which a particular story contributes to the summary pattern. The simplest procedure is to subtract the folktale with the highest frequency and see if the pattern remains unchanged.

One constellation of patterns that has been especially illuminating in analyzing the Japanese folktales has to do with the interplay between dominance, obedience, loyalty and strategy. This interplay is shown to a certain extent in the frequencies for subcategories of the DOMINANCE tag. There are three phases of emphasis in the progression of the stories from beginning to end which can be seen in Figure 1. The

---

[1] I am indebted to Chien-pai Han for running the statistical tests and to Marshall Smith for suggesting the use of his statistical programs.

Table 1.   Organization of Tags in the Third Santa Fe Dictionary.

I. Plot Structure

A. Characters

1. Family

KIN AFFINAL (39)

Husband

Wife

In-laws

KIN CONSANGUINEAL (40)

Lineal-Nuclear Family

Siblings

Nonnuclear

2. Persons

PERSON SELF (50)

I (e)

Me (e)

My-Mine-Myself (e)

PERSON SELVES (51)

We (e)

Us (e)

Our-Ourselves (e)

PERSON OTHER (52)

You, Your

They, Their

SEX FEMALE (63)

She (e)

Her (e)

Woman

SEX MALE (64)

He-Him (e)

His (e)

Man

CHILDREN (12)

Boy

Girl

Child

B. Setting and Plot Movement

1. Basic Orientation and Movement

(a) Time

ASPECT (04)

Again (e)

Continuation

Begin-End

TIME (69)

When-Then-Now (e)

Time Units

Time References

BEING (09)

Present and Future Tenses of To Be

Past Tense of To Be

DOING (21)

Present Tense of To Do

Past Tense of To Do

(b) Space

ATTITUDE (07)

Remain

Posture

POSITION (55)

Sequence

Position-Determining Action

Location

(c) Movement in Time and Space

MOVE (43)

Intransitive

Transitive

Speed

GO (32)

Go-Went

Come-Came

Leave-Arrive

TRAVEL (72)

Fly-Flew

Mode of Travel

Journey

2. Description

GENERAL (29)

Specified

Unspecified

QUANTITY-GENERAL (57)

Some (e)

Very (e)

Quantity

QUANTITY-SPECIFIC (58)

Two-Half-Second (e)

Three-Third (e)

Number

SIZE (65)

Large

Small

Dimensions

FORM (26)

3. Actions and Problem Situations

(a) Actions

COMMUNICATE (15)

Conversation

Paracommunication

Communication

WORK (74)

Hunt-Fish-Gather

Agriculture-Herding

Make-Use

MARRIAGE (42)

Marry

Wedding

RETAIN (59)

Ownership-Retention

Acquisition

Collection-Dispersion

GET (30)

Get-Got

Procure

Table 1.   Organization of Tags in the Third Santa Fe Dictionary (*Contd.*)

Want	SKY-WEATHER (66)	*Try*
DESTRUCTION (19)	*Sky*	*Fear*
Destruction-Disintegration	*Weather*	NEGATIVE (44)
Penetration-Cutting	*Moisture Concern*	*No-Not* (e)
Destructive-Action	DIFFICULTY (20)	*Oppose*
(b) Problem Situations	*Difficulty*	
II. Behavior	TIRED (70)	*How* (e)
A. Personality and the	*Tired*	*Why*
Individual	*Sleep*	COGNITIVE (14)
1. Body and Physiology	*Awake*	*If* (e)
FREUDIAN AO (27)	DEATH (18)	*Verification*
Anal	*Death*	*Thought and Learning*
Oral	*Death-Related*	CONNECTIVES (17)
FREUDIAN SEX (28)	2. Emotions	*But* (e)
Male	PLEASURE (54)	*Both-Also* (e)
Female	*Play-Game-Ceremony*	*Or-Unless* (e)
Intersexual	*Pleasure*	4. Perception
EAT-DRINK (23)	*Expressive of Happiness*	OBSERVE (49)
Eat	SAD (61)	*See, saw*
Drink	*Expressions of Sorrow*	*Look* (e)
Food Preparation	*Sorrow*	*Search, Appear, Watch*
BODY PART (10)	ANGER (02)	SENSORY (62)
Head Parts	*Anger*	*Taste, Smell, Sensory Enjoy-*
Interior Parts	*Dislike*	*ment*
Exterior Parts	*Provocation*	*Color*
KINESTHETIC (41)	AFFECTION (01)	*Touch*
Run-Ran (e)	*Empathy*	SOUND (67)
Dance	*Love*	*Hear*
Carry-Climb-Jump	*Bodily Contact*	*Music*
HEALTH-SICKNESS (35)	STATUS-REACTION (68)	*Noise*
State of Health	*Status-Ascend*	5. Abilities
State of Sickness	*Status-Descend*	POWER (56)
Curing Process	3. Cognition	*Magical-Monetary Power*
GROWTH AND AGE STATUS	CAUSE (11)	*Strength*
(34)	*Because* (e)	*Fortitude*
Growth	*Thus*	EFFICACY (24)
Birth	INTERROGATIVE (38)	*Can* (e)
Age	*What* (e)	*Preparation-Protection*

Table 1. Organization of Tags in the Third Santa Fe Dictionary (*Contd.*)

Success-Efficacy	2. Control	TRANSFORM (71)
B. Social Interaction	DOMINATE (22)	*Become-Became* (e)
1. Cooperation and Com-	*Let-May* (e)	*Change*
petition	*Mild Domination*	ROLE (60)
ASK (03)	*Strong Domination*	*Supernatural Role*
Ask (e)	C. Culture and Environ-	*Nonsupernatural Role*
Request	ment	CLOTHING (13)
GIVE (31)	1. Values	*Clothe* (e)
Gave-Give-Given	EVALUATION (25)	*Attire*
ASSIST (05)	*Positive Evaluation*	OBJECT-NATURAL (46)
Cooperation	*Negative Evaluation*	*Animals*
Dependence	BEAUTY (08)	*Plants*
COMMUNITY (16)	*Beauty* (e)	*Inanimate*
People	*Attractive*	OBJECT-GENERAL (47)
Community	NORM-HABIT (45)	*It* (e)
Alone	*Way* (e)	*Thing*
ATTACK (06)	*Right* (e)	*Whatever*
Kill	*Law-Custom-Manner*	OBJECT-CULTURAL (48)
Fight	2. Particulars	GREEK ELEMENTS (33)
WITHDRAW (73)	IDENTIFY (37)	*Earth-Air*
Hid-Hidden (e)	*Name Demonstratives*	*Fire*
Avoid	*Comparatives*	*Water*

III. Second-Order Tags	STATUS-HIGHER (77)	SYMBOL-FEMALE (80)
SIGN-ACCEPT (75)	STATUS-LOWER (78)	SYMBOL-MALE (81)
SIGN-REJECT (76)	STATUS-PEER (79)	

first concerns requests for permission, routine acknowledgments of established patterns of dominance, and attempts at persuasion. This is most noticeable in the *Mild Domination* subcategory and is very likely the main substance of the *Let & May* subcategory (I have not yet been able to examine retrieved sentences of the latter category) and to a much smaller extent in the *Strong Domination* subcategory. In Figure 1 it can be seen how all three of these subcategories follow initially the same relative frequency patterns. However, in the middle and end, the *Mild Domination* and *Strong Domination* subcategories are diametrically opposed to the *Let & May* subcategory. They reflect a shift away from persuasion and routine dominance to a strong concern with obedience which reaches a peak in section 8 and accounts for a few instances in section 9. Cases of obedience or disobedience in this section are more

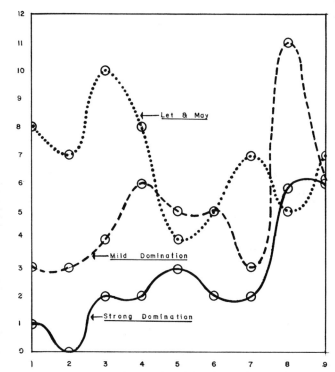

Figure 1. The relative frequencies of the three subcategories of the DOMINANCE tag for the combined first to ninth parts (from left to right on the horizontal line) of 63 Japanese folktales. The frequency scale (the vertical line) is half the actual frequency.

often focal to the plot while earlier cases are not. In this section there are changes in tactics and strategy, tests of loyalty, a choice between two loyalties, and disobedience of crucial instructions. The third phase occurs in the ninth section. Most instances of dominance in this last section deal with victory, defeat, and punishment.

Figure 2 shows the patterns for PLACE, *Home, Magic & Wealth,* and PLEASURE. The high initial frequency of the PLACE tag represents the use of PLACE words to describe the setting of the stories. The *Home* subcategory shows two high regions, one at section 3 and a broader one around sections 5 and 6. This reflects the tendency of the "Supernatural Husbands and Wives" folktales (a classification made by the editor of these folktales[2]) to have a structure of dual location: the original home of the protagonist and a second home. Seven out of the eight stories in this classification have this pattern, as do some of the stories elsewhere in the collection.

Magic & Wealth and PLEASURE first reach their highest value at section 7. Though in

[2] Computer pattern studies of folktales may eventually lead to a "natural" classification of folktales. This possibility is now being explored in conjunction with factor analysis.

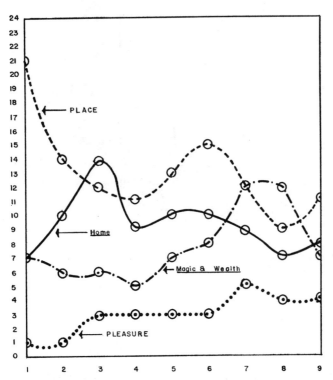

Figure 2. The relative frequencies of PLACE, *Home*, *Magic & Wealth*, and PLEASURE for the combined first to ninth parts (from left to right on the horizontal line) of 63 Japanese folktales. The frequency scale (the vertical line) is half the actual frequency.

the first case the subcategory title includes magic, what is measured in the Japanese folktales is predominantly a concern with wealth. Wealth and pleasure as themes in the folktales might be called preliminary goals, because they are reached relatively early toward the end of the tales, and because they soon give way to concern with dominance (and obedience), as shown in Figure 1, and then finally to a concern with kinship and prestige as the final goal, as shown in the graphs for KINSHIP-CONSANGUINEAL and STATUS-HIGH (a second-order tag) in Figure 3. The high end frequency for KINSHIP-CONSANGUINEAL reflects an interest in establishing security and happiness for consanguineal kinfolks, especially parents and grandparents, along with security and happiness for the main protagonists. The high frequency in the ninth part for STATUS-HIGH reflects an interest in attaining higher social status. Figure 3 shows how these final goals contrast with COMMUNICATION, which is highest during the middle of the folktales, when the difficulties and complications of the plots require communication for the perception, understanding, and solution of the difficulties.

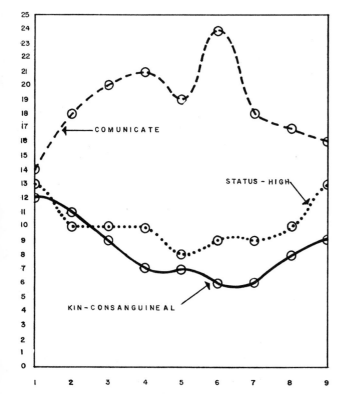

Figure 3. The relative frequencies of COMMUNICATE, STATUS-HIGH, and KIN-CONSANGUINEAL for the combined first to ninth parts (from left to right on the horizontal line) of 63 Japanese folktales. The frequency scale (the vertical line) is half the actual frequency.

We are just at the threshold in this new area of culture pattern study. One of the most interesting and difficult problems ahead is the designing of experiments to test the proposition that those areas with the most marked or definite patterns are culturally important. Before doing this, however, we must understand how patterns relate to each other at various levels, how different patterns emerge for different groups of stories, and how these relate to larger ones that may hold for virtually all the folktales of a social group. Further, we will have to investigate different versions of the same folktale and different folktales told by the same person. We are now attempting some of these studies by working directly in the original language, in this case, Ixil Maya.[3]

After completing these studies we hope to further develop the theory of cultural

[3] For a discussion of translation distortion in the computer analysis of folktales, see Colby (1966b).

templates (Colby 1966a). This theory describes the telling of folktales as a cognitive process involving mental schemata and cognitive templates or pattern parts, the end result being a folktale with patterns such as those we are attempting to measure.

References

Colby, Benjamin N.
1966a "Cultural Patterns in Narrative," *Science* 151: 793–798.
1966b "The Analysis of Culture Content and the Patterning of Narrative Concern in Texts," *American Anthropologist* 68, No. 2, Pt. 1: 374–388.

Dunphy, D. C.
1964 "Social Change in Self-Analytic Groups," unpublished Ph.D. dissertation, Harvard University.

Holsti, Ole R.
1966 "East-West Conflict and Sino-Soviet Relations," in *The General Inquirer: A Computer Approach to Content Analysis*, Philip J. Stone *et al.*, eds. (Cambridge, Mass.: M.I.T. Press), pp. 343–358.

Namenwirth, J. Zvi, and Thomas L. Brewer
1966 "Elite Editorial Comment on the European and Atlantic Communities in Four Countries," in *The General Inquirer: A Computer Approach to Content Analysis*, Philip J. Stone *et al.*, eds. (Cambridge, Mass.: M.I.T. Press), pp. 401–427.

Seki, Keigo, (ed.)
1963 *Folktales of Japan* (London: Routledge & Kegan Paul).

Smith, Marshall S., Philip J. Stone, and Evelyn Glenn
1966 "A Content Analysis of Twenty Presidential Nomination Acceptance Speeches," in *The General Inquirer: A Computer Approach to Content Analysis*, Philip J. Stone *et al.*, eds. (Cambridge, Mass.: M.I.T. Press), pp. 359–400.

Stone, P. J., D. M. Ogilvie, and D. C. Dunphy
1963: "Distinguishing Real from Simulated Suicide Notes using General Inquirer Procedures," Paper read at the Joint Annual Meeting of the American College of Neuropsychopharmacology.

Stone, P. J., *et al.*, eds.
1966 *The General Inquirer: A Computer Approach to Content Analysis* (Cambridge, Mass.: M.I.T. Press).

Introduction

Gilbert's paper presents both an operational computer system for analysis of genealogical data and a general discussion of possible computer applications in kinship and related areas.

The paper presupposes no prior familiarity with computers on the part of the reader. The explanation of how Gilbert's system operates is phrased in terms available to the general anthropological reader. The paper may thus serve as an introduction for anthropologists to the kinds of things computers can do for them. A simple description is presented of how a particular genealogical program operates, what it does, and how nongenealogical information may be included and nongenealogical questions answered. This provides the basis for a discussion of some of the kinds of questions computers may be expected to answer for anthropologists in the future.

Gilbert touches on one area that will probably become of increasing interest: the utilization of computers by anthropologists while still in the field. It is a commonplace of the "new" ethnography (and much of the best "old" ethnography) that analysis and data gathering proceed apace in the field, that one always tries to ask the next question on the basis of full analysis of the questions and answers one already has. Gilbert suggests quite reasonably that computer analysis should be no exception to this rule. The logistics are, of course, difficult, prohibitively so in technologically remote areas at present. Communication with the computer center by ordinary mail proved too slow in the first and only (as far as I am aware) ethnographic project that attempted to use computer analysis to guide further data collection while still in the field: the Chiapas Drinking Project of D. G. Metzer and G. Williams in 1964.

There is, however, with the increasing use of time sharing and scope viewing (in contrast to printouts), every reason to believe that effective use of the computer during the field stay is now or will very soon be feasible in areas such as the American Southwest. As Gilbert also points out, such utilization will require that anthropologists pay increasing attention to the format in which they receive data from their informants.

In discussing the application of computers to any subject one runs two risks. The first of these is that everything will be outdated before it gets into print. The second is

Part of the work reported in this article was done while the author was statistical consultant at the Center for Advanced Study in the Behavioral Sciences, and was supported by NSF Grant No. GS-289. The article was written while the author was L. L. Thurstone Distinguished Fellow at the Psychometric Laboratory, University of North Carolina at Chapel Hill. This fellowship was partially supported by a PHS research grant, M-10006, from the National Institute of Mental Health, Public Health Service.

7

Computer Methods in Kinship Studies

JOHN P. GILBERT

that one will get so carried away with what could be done (as opposed to what has been done), that the reader thinks that a great deal more has been accomplished than is in fact the case.

In the first part of this paper I will discuss a program that is operational, and hence trivial. This program is a building block that can be utilized by anyone wishing to study kinship problems on the computer. The program organizes kinship data within the computer so that the information contained in the data is readily available for further analysis.

A rather detailed discussion of the underlying ideas is given in the hope that it will serve several functions. It discusses the problem in enough detail so that the anthropologist who would like to write a similar program for his own use can do so. However, it is written in general enough terms so he can incorporate modifications and use his favorite programing language. For the reader who has had little, or no, experience with computers, it is hoped that this discussion will give him a superficial view of how it is possible to attack such problems on the computer, and also how some quite general principles have led to specific decisions in the program. The computer expert will see that several rather standard techniques have been applied to a specific problem, and there is not much news for him in this section.

In the second part of the paper I discuss programs that could be developed in the future. The question is not whether a useful program could be written to analyze some aspect of kinship data, but rather can a whole battery of useful programs be written. This discussion is given in the hope that it will be of use to anthropologists in deciding what resources are to be allocated to the use of computers in anthropology. Since such a discussion must contain implicit judgments about what anthropology is about, I warn the reader that I am not an anthropologist and that he should read with caution. The limitation to kinship-type programs is not because of any feeling that this is the only field of anthropology to which computers can be applied, but rather because it is the part of the subject with which I have had the most experience. For this reason, the discussion can contribute to only part of the overall picture. For an idea of the variety of computer applications to anthropology, see Hymes (1965).

1. Organization of Data

I now turn to the consideration of how the data should be organized. At first blush this might seem to be the most trivial of the problems facing the would-be programer of an anthropological problem. This is not the case, however, as it is hoped the following discussion will demonstrate by indicating what factors are involved.

Although it is possible to be interested in analyzing kinship data that have been generated within the computer itself (Gilbert and Hammel 1966) the typical application will be oriented toward data collected in the field. For such data there are two problems. Not only must we decide the format within the machine, but we must also devise a method of transferring the data from field notes to a suitable input medium for the computer. This input medium will usually be punched cards, but in many places paper tape could be used, and it is to be hoped that in the near future optical readers will be available. With any of these media there will always be a translation problem, since the way the data are represented in the field notes is not the way in which we will represent them inside the machine. Indeed, we will be lucky if the field notes do not have to be "hand coded" before they can be transcribed to the input media. One of the goals of data organization is to minimize that part of the process which has to be done by hand. At this point, let us make a distinction between the internal identification, which is the computer's name for a person, and his external identification, which is the way the anthropologist recognizes him. In the method proposed here these names need not be the same and, as we shall see, we do not need to know (or even want to know) the internal "name" of an individual.

The effect of separating the internal and the external names is that these two representations of the data become much more independent of each other. We have, of course, taken on the additional task of programing the computer to make the translation from external names to internal names. This is not too difficult when taken as a separate problem. If we assume for the moment that this translation can be accomplished, what characteristics would we like the representation of the data to have?

The ideal for an external representation is that it should be as easy as possible to get the data into the required format. Another consideration is that it should be as easy as possible for the anthropologist to specify the people or problem in which he is interested to his program. In general the external representation of the data should be convenient for the people on the outside. By the same token the internal representation should be convenient for the computer and the programer. What does this entail? There are three general considerations: space, run time, and programing ease. At the moment, in most computer systems, either a problem will fit in the existing memory or it does not run. The effect of this has been that, if the program and data did fit, there was no reason to try to economize further, and if they did not, their space requirements had to be reduced at all costs. With the advent of multiprograming and better auxiliary storage devices, this situation is changing, and in the future the efficiency with which storage is used will not be such a dichotomous variable. It will, however, remain an important one. The time it takes the computer to accomplish a specific task can be markedly reduced if the data the program needs are readily available to it without having to search for them. This usually costs space, and so these two goals are often in opposition to each other. The concept of programing ease is harder to specify, but some questions are much easier to answer with the data in one format rather than another. An example from anthropology illustrating the effect of format is the fact that it is easier to find the identity of Ego's father's father in a patrilateral society than in a matrilateral one because of the way the data would be organized.

The unique feature of kinship data is the large number of cross-references which make it up. Thus for every Ego we must know father, mother, siblings, wives or husbands, and children. It is clear that if we list for every Ego all his, or her, children and all his, or her, siblings there will be a great deal of redundancy in the data. In the solution to this problem given below, a certain amount of programing ease and computer time is sacrificed in order to avoid using space in the computer to hold this redundant information.

Since one person will have more immediate relatives than another, we would like to be able to vary the amount of space allocated to each person rather than making every record big enough to hold the largest possible record. We can do this, however, only if we are prepared to rearrange this allocation of the computer's memory when additional data or corrections become available. Because of the difficulty of collecting data in the field, a computer system for handling such data must be able to update and correct such data easily in order to get the most out of it as possible.

A third consideration to be borne in mind when thinking about a computer system for kinship data is the fact that the data are not collected primarily for their own sake but in order to help the anthropologist to understand other phenomena observed in the culture. For this reason it is important to leave open the possibility of including other variables in the data. What these variables will be and how they should enter into an analysis of the data must be determined by the anthropologist.

The general scheme that I suggest is to generate a record for each person referenced in the data. This will tell where to find the record corresponding to each of this person's immediate relatives. Thus the record of any Ego will tell where to find his father's record, which in turn will tell where to find his (Ego's father's) father's record, etc. In this manner it is possible to move from a person's record to that of any of his relatives and each person in the chain provides the link (or pointer) to the next person in the chain. Now, it is apparent that as far as the computer program is concerned, a person is his record, and the internal name of a person is the location in memory of his record. For all the internal workings of the computer this is all that is ever needed to identify a person. When the time comes to communicate with the outside world, however, the computer will need to know the outside name as well as the internal one. For this reason the outside name needs to be incorporated into each record. Since the amount of room in memory taken by the preceding records will determine where in memory a person's record is (and so what the internal name of a person will be), the program that loads the data will have to keep track of where each person's record goes and see to it that all references to him are to this location. Although this would be a ghastly chore to do by hand, it is quite straightforward for the computer, and indeed it is a problem that computer science solved early in its career. To the computer expert this is the problem of relocating a program and its data in such a way that all the program's references to itself and to the data remain correct.

Before going into the details of the specific method proposed here, there are several loose ends which must be cleaned up. One of these is how to reference Ego's siblings without introducing an inordinate amount of redundancy, and how to handle the problem of multiple husbands and wives. The solution to the sibling problem is to have each sibling in a family point to (i.e., reference) the next, say, in order of age just to be specific. Thus the oldest would point to the next oldest and so forth down to the youngest, who would point to the oldest, so that no matter where the circle was entered all siblings could be found by continuing far enough. In this system a parent will point to his oldest child by a marriage and all his children of that marriage can be found from that one. The solution of the multiple marriage problem is to list all of Ego's spouses (and the eldest child of each marriage) as part of Ego's record. Since the number of spouses varies, this solution entails including in each record a number that indicates how long the record is (or equivalently how many wives Ego had).

Both these solutions are arbitrary to some extent, and for some purposes other solutions might well be more appropriate. For example, Ego does not need to list his wife (or wives) if he lists the eldest child of each marriage. In this system Ego's wife would be his child's mother. This would require the creation of dummy children for childless couples and considerable programing effort to find such relationships as first-wife's second husband.

Another problem is that some data will, of necessity, be missing, and something must be inserted for the phrase "father unknown." The solution turns out to be surprisingly easy. A completely zero record is created at location zero, and whenever data are missing a zero pointer is inserted. Any program that gets referenced to zero will stay there because all of "zero's" pointers point to itself. Hence, "zero's" father's mother's husband is still "zero." The implication of this is that a program does not need to check at each step of a search to see if that step led to an existing relative, but can wait until the end. If it was not successful in finding an existing relative it will have found "zero."

Throughout the following discussion I shall assume that everybody has been given a unique number as an external name. This is not so much because the computer could not handle alphabetic names as because the effort to get the computer to distinguish between two people with the same name did not seem worth the programing effort.

I will now describe the system in detail by going through an example step by step. In order to distinguish between internal and external I shall use Roman numerals for external names and Arabic numerals to refer to machine locations and internal names.

Table 1 shows the raw data in anthropological notation. When optical readers become perfected, it will be possible to give data to the computer in such a format. Table 2 shows what the data look like on the data cards. There is one card per person giving Ego's name, sex, father, mother, next youngest sibling, first spouse, their oldest child, second spouse and the oldest child of that marriage, etc. All references are to a person's outside name, and any corrections or updating need involve only

Table 1.   Raw Data.

```
                I      II
                Δ  =  O
                   |
           ┌───────────┐
   O  =  Δ  =  O        Δ
   III   IV   V        VI
```

Table 2.   Data Cards.

Ego	Sex	Fa	Mo	Sib	Sp1	Ch1	Sp2	Ch2
I	+	0	0	0	II	V	0	0
II	−	0	0	0	I	V	0	0
III	−	0	0	0	IV	0	0	0
IV	+	0	0	0	III	0	V	0
V	−	I	II	VI	IV	0	0	0
VI	+	I	II	V	0	0	0	0

Table 3.   List Format.

	a.	*b*	*c*	*d*	
l1	Sex	Ego	Fa	Mo	
l2	*n*	Sib	Sp1	Ch1	
l3	—	—	Sp2	Ch2	} as needed
ln	.	.	.	.	

one or two cards. To record a new marriage, the wife's name must be put on the husband's card and the husband's name on the wife's. To record a new child, his card must be added to the deck. His sibling will be the oldest child in the family, and the card of his next oldest sibling must be changed so that the name of the new child is entered as that child's sibling. A first child must be entered on his father's card and also on the mother's card. It would be possible to avoid this duplication except for the problem that often one or the other parent is not known. As shown in Table 2, people who are not known are entered as zero.

In phase one, these data cards will be loaded into an array in memory called the population list, and in phase two external names will be changed to internal names. The arrangement of an individual record in memory is shown in Table 3. This format was used on the Burroughs B5500 at Stanford. This computer has a 48-bit word size, so that each computer word could hold a small number and three pointers. Thus four pieces of information can be stored in each computer word. The amount of information which can be stored in a word will vary with the computer. The difficulty of getting at part of a word also varies from one programing language to another. It is possible to get around this by putting only one piece of information in each computer word, but this will require more words of memory for a given amount of data. For the rest of this discussion I will assume the format shown in Table 3.

Sex is indicated by the sign of the first word of the record. Ego, father, and mother are put into positions b, c, and d, respectively. The second word holds the number of wives, n, the next youngest sibling, the first wife (or husband), and the eldest child of that marriage. If Ego did not have more than one spouse, that is all of the record; if there were more spouses, more words will be added to the record as needed. The shortest record will be two words long, while there is no fixed limit to the longest.

Table 4 shows the population list as it looks at the end of phase one. The computer generates this list, one card at a time. As it reads each card, it loads the data from that card into the next available storage locations. The first card's record goes into locations 2 and 3 because locations 0 and 1 are reserved for "Mr. Zero," whose only positive information is that he (or she) had only one spouse. The phase one program counts the number of spouses on each data card and thus figures out the number of

Table 4. Pass One.

Loc	a	b	c	d
0	+	0	0	0
1	1	0	0	0
2	+	I	0	0
3	1	0	II	V
4	−	II	0	0
5	1	0	I	V
6	−	III	0	0
7	J	0	IV	0
8	+	IV	0	0
9	2	0	III	0
10	0	0	V	0
11	−	V	I	II
12	1	VI	IV	0
13	+	VI	I	II
14	1	V	0	0

spouses for itself. While it is loading the data cards in phase one, the program is also building the dictionary, which is shown in Table 5. The dictionary is simply a list, the ith entry of which is the location of the record (i.e., internal name) of the person whose external name is "i." To be a little more specific about how this is done, the load program has a pointer that is the location of the next vacant position on the population list. When the next card is read, the value of this pointer is stored in location "Ego" of the dictionary and the record on that card is then added to the data list, starting with the location indicated by the pointer. The pointer is then advanced to the next empty location and the process is repeated with the next data card.

Table 6 shows the population list after the end of phase two. All the names have been changed from external names to internal names except that of Ego, the name in position b of the first word of each record. This translation can be done quickly and easily by using the dictionary. To find the internal name corresponding to

5. Dictionary.

Ext	I	II	III	IV	V	VI
Int	2	4	6	8	11	13

Table 6. Pass Two.

Loc	a	b	c	d
0	+	0	0	0
1	1	0	0	0
2	+	I	0	0
3	1	0	4	11
4	—	II	0	0
5	1	0	2	11
6	—	III	0	0
7	1	0	8	0
8	+	IV	0	0
9	2	0	6	0
10	0	0	11	0
11	—	V	2	4
12	1	13	8	0
13	+	VI	2	4
14	1	11	0	0

person *ZZZ*, we just look at the *ZZZ*th entry in the dictionary and there is his internal name. To find the external name corresponding to an internal name *XXX* we look at the *b* part of the *XXX*th word on the population list.

The flexibility of this system is illustrated by the fact that, if the first person in the data set should marry again, the internal names of everyone else would be increased by one. Only the cards of him and his new wife would have to be changed by a person using the program, and the loader program would do the rest automatically. Another feature is that the system is not dependent upon the order of the data cards, although this will affect the internal name assignments.

The data used to illustrate the system do not include any nongenealogical information. There is no problem in modifying the system to include such information, since one simply allocates a position in the data card format for this material and also a place for it in the internal format. The last word of the internal representation could, for example, contain blood type, age, and socioeconomic status at puberty. The rest of his record would remain the same.

2. Function of the Computer

In this part I discuss the functions a computer could perform for anthropologists interested in studying kinship data. For the moment I ignore the question of cost and paint a picture, to some perhaps a nightmare, of what might be done. After exploring the possible gains I will discuss the cost briefly. Even so, it is difficult to define precisely what one means by possible. It would be possible, for example, to study the migrations of nomadic tribes using the techniques of aerial surveillance developed by the military; however, it does not seem to be a likely project. The things I will consider as possible will be things for which present technology can provide the tools and for which an interested group of graduate students could provide the programing talent.

Any computer system will need programs that check the data for inconsistencies and holes. For example, it should check that all the siblings that point to each other do indeed have the same parents, or that all males are listed as husbands of their wives. Every checking procedure that can be relegated to the computer both increases the confidence in the further analysis of the data and decreases the time required to get the data into the computer (since less time is needed for hand checking).

One of the more valuable aspects of having a computer system is that, if data can be sent from the field and put into the computer, they can be checked and the information necessary to correct them collected while the investigator is still in the field. This idea could, in some cases, be extended so that the research done in the second part of a field trip took advantage of analyses done on data collected during the first phase. The programing for such a project would be done in advance, and the data collection would be planned so that a minimum of hand coding would be required before the data were punched onto cards or put on other input media. The amount of time the anthropologist in the field will have to wait for the results of these analyses will depend on the speed of communication and the time required to punch the cards. The computer time will be negligible.

With the advent of timesharing, it will be possible for an anthropologist in, say, the American Southwest, to have a teletype in a "not too distant" town which would put him in direct communication with the computer. How much value such a facility would add to the time spent in the field would have to be determined by each field worker for himself.

Some examples of programs that could be written to answer specific questions of kinship data follow.

The first question that comes to mind is, given two persons in the population, how are they related. This question has been investigated to some extent by Coult and Randolph (1965). It was in the process of developing such a program that the program described in the first section was written. One problem in writing this sort of program is in defining what one wishes to consider legal links. Is Ego's wife's brother's wife to be considered a relative? When the data are from a highly interrelated population, the user may be swamped with types of relationships which do not interest him.

Another program, or series of programs, would exhibit the data in various formats. One would specify a person and have all his descendants through the male line, or through the female line, exhibited. A variant of this program might display all of Ego's ancestors in a suitable format. Such displays could be either on a line printer or, what would be more useful to the anthropologist, they could be on a television screen. Systems where the user can sit at a remote station, interrogate his data and have the answers displayed on a scope within seconds are currently under development. They will be very appealing if they can be made practical.

Another example of a possible program is one that would list, or perhaps just count, the number of pairs of people who stand in a specified relationship to each other. Thus one might ask how many people could have married a specific relative, as well as how many people did.

The possibility of including other variables with the kinship data was mentioned in connection with the data organization. If this is done, programs could be written which would answer a variety of questions relating these variables to the kinship structure. A simple example is that if date of birth were recorded one could inquire whether the difference between a husband's age and his wife's differed for different types of marriages. Another question is whether cousins tend to marry younger than other types of marriage partners.

At this point it is clear that, with sufficient ingenuity, a program can be written to answer any well-formulated question, and most of these questions could be answered without a computer. One would like to know (1) if the computer provides an easier method of obtaining these answers and (2) are there questions which only a computer can answer. The answer to the first question is that to find the answer for one set of data by writing a computer program is probably harder, but if the program can be used on subsequent sets of data the overall effort may be much less.

I now turn to the second question. One of the things only a computer can provide is the power to answer the same questions as current methods of analysis for larger and larger bodies of data. As departments of anthropology send teams of researchers to the same locality year after year, the sheer mass of data collected will require computer methods for analysis. A second advantage, which has already been referred to, is fast turnaround time. Once a program to answer a specific question has been developed, it is then possible to apply that program to other bodies of data very quickly.

These considerations are not particularly compelling, however, and I believe that if the computer is to earn its salt in anthropology it will be because there are deeper and more complicated analyses to be done. Only if these can be formulated into computer programs will the computer have really been utilized. I feel that it is a fundamental mistake to think of the computer as a way of extending "classical" methods. The computer should also be viewed as an instrument that encourages its user to develop new methods. If this is to happen in anthropology, it is clear that anthropologists will have to write these programs. Only a person who sees both the capabilities of the computer and the needs of anthropology will be able to utilize the one to help the other. Such people can come only from anthropology. Indeed, the principal cost of any effort to use the computer in anthropology will be that the programing talent has to come from graduate students in anthropology. This cost will manifest itself in such forms as giving foreign language credit for learning a programing language. Anthropology will take to the computer most successfully at universities that have departments of computer science. These departments provide students with access to a variety of programing languages and computer techniques as well as people who can advise them. It is at these places that new techniques such as the use of optical scanners and visual displays will first become available, and the people ready to utilize these developments will get the most immediate benefit from them.

The computer was originally conceived of as a calculating engine, and many people in the computing field have been slow to appreciate its potential for handling other than numerical types of information. As the behavioral sciences evolve increasingly more interesting and significant applications, this bias towards calculation will decrease. As this happens, the behavioral scientist can expect the professional computer expert to contribute more to the solution of his problem. It is also likely that some of the peculiarities of his problems will receive increasing consideration in the design of computer systems. Thus, as people from anthropology learn more about computers, they will increase the interest of computer people in their problems.

References

Coult, Allan D., and R. R. Randolph
1965 "Computer Methods for Analyzing Genealogical Space," *American Anthropologist* 67: 21–29.

Gilbert, J. P., and E. A. Hammel
1966 "Computer Simulation and the Analysis of Problems in Kinship and Social Structure," *American Anthropologist* 68: 171.

Hymes, D., ed.
1965 *The Use of Computers in Anthropology* (The Hague: Mouton and Company).

CLASSICAL METHODS

3

Introduction

Chapple's paper summarizes over 25 years of research on the measurement of interaction and points in the direction of a general mathematical theory of interaction. The basic notions of the theory are impressively simple. The two fundamental primitive notions are those of an action and an inaction, or silence. The primary postulate is that "each individual . . . has a fundamental rhythm . . . within which the ratio [of time spent in action to time spent in inaction] tends to approach a constant."

The full theory attempts to account for, among other things, the accommodation of the periods and action/silence ratios of two interacting individuals with different fundamental periods (tempos, rhythms) and/or different basal action-to-silence ratios. This entails empirical derivation of measures of dominance, persistence, interaction latency, and so on.

Although the mathematical model is not yet fully formulated, Chapple expresses the firm conviction that the appropriate approach is the deterministic one of classical physics rather than a stochastic one. The mathematical relationships involved in the basic model (the initial state equations) appear to be certainly nonlinear and most likely of considerable complexity. Chapple suggests the necessary mathematics is not yet available but might be furnished by a general theory of relaxation oscillators.

Chapple envisages extending the basic two-person interactional model to encompass cultural constraints on interaction by the introduction of n-person interactional situations. At this point, cultural factors would be treated mathematically by probabilistic handling of the entry and exit of the various potential actors via initiation and termination probabilities.

A full understanding of the paper may require some reading of Chapple's experimental work, which is fully referenced in the text and bibliography.

Since the late 1930s, the author and his associates have been concerned with developing the theory of interaction, as more and more situations, both human and animal, have been investigated through interaction measurement. This work is increasingly coming to be supplemented by other researchers, and the rapid growth in

The contributors to the development of interaction measurement over almost 30 years are too many to be listed, since often they made an important but unwitting contribution merely by asking what significance, if any, a particular pattern of reaction to stress might have, thus forcing us to try to find out. The logic in this paper has been remarkably benefited by the critical comments of Martha Field Chapple, who, in addition, in her own right has been a major contributor to more rigorous experimental methods, and by Richard Sheldon, who has patiently gone over its several versions to see if its potential mathematical implications are clearly stated and who revised the Introduction.

Opportunity to carry on some of the work reflected here and , in particular, to develop more comprehensive and efficient methods of data collecting and data analysis was aided by support through NSF grant G22691 and NIMH grant MH–06245.

Toward a Mathematical Model of Interaction:
Some Preliminary Considerations

8

ELIOT D. CHAPPLE

biology of studies of free-ranging animals has played an important role in increasing our understanding of the phenomena with which we have to deal.

It seems to be necessary to refer to the subject, for the present time at least, as interaction measurement, since the term "interaction" has, in the last 30 years, taken on a wide variety of meanings. Studies of interaction have come to be regarded as coterminous with small group theory, which was explicitly not my intention when I defined the term operationally in my early work (Chapple 1940; Chapple and Coon 1942). Interaction was, of course, used occasionally in the sociological literature long before then, but merely as a synonym for interpersonal relations or associations and, sometimes, for communication.

Our research has been based on the assumption that the methods of the exact sciences may prove equally powerful if applied to the study of human behavior. Until this approach is thoroughly tested in the "behavioral sciences" and found wanting, one cannot, other than philosophically, argue convincingly that the science of human interaction is *ipso facto* essentially different from the older sciences. If one is to apply the methods of these sciences to behavior, two things are necessary. First, one must renounce a global view of behavior or society and instead attempt to isolate a relatively small number of variables that can be systematized to deal with relatively limited aspects of behavior. This approach, which has been called by Lindsay and Margenau (1957) the method of elementary abstraction, is universal throughout the exact sciences. Second, one must seek variables that can be defined operationally and can be measured in equally spaced (interchangeable) units along some dimension, so that a full set of the tools of mathematical analysis can be applied to them; another way of saying this is that the operations of measurement used must yield units that are isomorphic with arithmetic. Otherwise we are limited to ordering inequalities, with coincident reduction in mathematical versatility. In our research, the variables used are the physical activity (actions), or lack of it (inactions), of individuals interacting with one another, and the measurement is that of the duration in time of these actions and inactions (silences).

When individuals, human or animal, interact, they characteristically alternate their actions and inactions. Thus when two people are talking together, one talks while the other listens and vice versa, although there are also interruptions when both talk at the same time and there are periods when both are silent. In a first approximation, it is the pattern of these actions and silences—their length, sequences, and the way they fit together—with which interaction measurement is concerned. However not all interaction is verbal. Nodding the head and other similar gestures are familiar examples of nonverbal actions that carry more or less definite meaning, and there are other actions (for example, those that we group under the heading "restlessness") that are clearly connected with the interactional situation. Furthermore, there is strong evidence that the rate or degree of an individual's activity is determined in good part by physical and chemical processes within the body—in, for example, the autonomic nervous system—and if, for some reason, activity in the form of speech is inhibited, it will appear in some other form of bodily movement. Such movements are thus "meaningful" and should be taken into account, particularly because there are significant cultural, social, and individual differences in the degree to which speech is "permitted" in various situations while the other person is talking. If one expects to make comparisons cross-culturally and cross-species, as well as between individuals within any single group, total activity is the only measurement that will yield high reliability. For all these reasons, plus the requirement that the variables under study be defined operationally, the measurement of actions cannot be restricted simply to the measurement of speech durations.

In interaction measurement, the beginnings and endings of actions are operationally defined by observation of the contractions and relaxations of muscle systems (in the human, primarily those of the face and head, often associated with sound, which is ordinarily coincident with visible movements of the mouth). In other words, the visible (or aural) beginning of a contraction of a muscular system, identified for the strain or species as a pattern of action (or response) used in associations with others, is the cue for the observer to start his measurement; relaxation of the muscle system to a state of completion or a shift to another system (particularly in animals) marks the end of the measurement. The measurements are made by an observer, who has a set of keys connected electrically to a recording device running at a constant speed. One key is assigned to each of the subjects under observation. When a subject begins an action, the observer presses the appropriate key and holds it down until the action ends. Hence, the start of the action (or inaction) is coincident with the starting of the clock: when the behavioral ending is detected, the clock, so to speak, is stopped, though beginning again with the next state. Thus a recording is made of the durations and sequences of all the actions and intervals of inaction (silence in the conversational sense) and the overlap, when both are acting or are inactive, of the individuals under observation.

The notion of restricting oneself rigorously only to the measurement of time intervals of interaction in order to understand the phenomena of human relationships strikes many persons as almost absurd or far too abstract and limited in what one can learn. How can the rich fabric of language and the almost infinite nuances which the rapidly developing "ethnography of communication" (Hymes 1964) is identifying in each and every context of situation between people be so arbitrarily ruled out of consideration? Though a book by the author (Chapple 1970) describes in detail the biological evidence that supports the tenability of this point of view, it may be worth commenting briefly on the problem so that the implications of what follows thereafter, directed towards the construction of a mathematical model, will seem less abstract.

The test of a scientific procedure is not whether it is reasonable from *a priori* considerations, but whether it works. Does it enable one to discover uniformities in the data under study such that meaningful predictions can be made and subjected to experimental test? We have found that the measurement of the time intervals of actions and interactions besieges the investigator with a multiplicity of such uniformities. By a simple change in terminology, one can call many of these uniformities measurements of personality. They can be subjected to tests as predictors of future behavior in the same way that personality appraisals based upon the content of communications can. Because of the precise nature of our measurements, we have found it possible to make quite precise predictions of how people will interact in ongoing situations. This method has the great virtue of applying the same measurements to the individual and the interpersonal situation in which he interacts. Since the latter is what every method hopes to be able to predict, it is extremely useful not to have to change criteria and techniques of describing behavior.

Under these circumstances, the question about the significance of content in interactional analysis is this: Would the addition of some way of measuring content, if such could be found, to the measurement of interaction, enable us to improve predictions to a degree that would justify undertaking the extraordinarily difficult and time-consuming task of interpreting content? (In assessing the difficulty of this task we have to recognize that not only do symbols shift their meanings between cultures and subcultures and change these meanings as time goes by, but we have to face the fact that in the last analysis the meaning is intensely individual and idiosyncratic.) We cannot, of course, give a precise answer to this question at the present time. But we can say that, at least in many cases, the content appears to be subordinate to or produced by the interactional situation.

This is particularly true when we are dealing with content that has emotional connotations. Two questions are here involved. First, it can be shown that highly significant changes in interactional behavior take place in conjunction with interpersonal stress, and these constitute the temperamental (or transference) reactions that are decisive and measurable indicators of emotional states (Chapple et al. 1954). Second, a very large number of observations of behavior changes are correlated with changes in autonomic nervous system activity, the system that controls and activates the organs with which even the layman is aware "emotion" is associated. The secretion of adrenalin and noradrenalin, of acetylcholine and ACTH, affect the heart rate, blood pressure, the gastrointestinal tract, respiration, the superficial vessels of the skin, even the hair, and above all the whole skeletal muscular system. Major changes in interactional behavior, in mood, and in all the associated phenomena of emotion result. Injection of a particular chemical transmitter like adrenalin produces important behavioral changes whether or not a precise "emotion" occurs, which can be identified intuitively (Gellhorn and Loofbourrow 1963). Actually the interplay of adrenalin, or acetylcholine, or ACTH are involved in subjective notions of "emotional" states. The interrelations of interaction and the autonomic nervous system can at least be sketched with some certainty and, for those interested in these relationships, a book by the author (Chapple 1970) treats the problem in more detail than is possible in this paper. In other words, it can be demonstrated that the affective aspects of interaction are measurable in terms of the changes in interaction patterns which the operation of the autonomic nervous system brings about, and, in this view, the meaning of content is dependent upon the interactional and autonomic states.

The Nature of the Model

In order to formulate a mathematical model of human interaction, I have tried to make explicit the fundamental uniformities that have been discovered over many years of investigation and state them as working hypotheses. Much of the research has required the isolation and definition of the constituent variables so that they can be measured with precision. The hypotheses as to their interrelationships cannot yet be given in equation form, but enough data exist to suggest how this formulation might be approached.

Three sets of equations appear to be necessary: (1) a deterministic set that describes the initial equilibrium state of the individual—his "basic nature"—and represents the boundary conditions for treating him as a system.[1] In this sense, experimental variation of the boundary conditions requires selecting different individuals, with different values of their parameters, for investigation. (2) A deterministic set which must include the initial equilibrium state equations (1) but where additional parameters describe the ways in which a given individual with his particular parametric characteristics will adjust to different kinds of interactional situations over a defined period of time—in a first approximation, over a 24-hour period. We are here concerned with the cumulative changes in interaction potential, which can be thought of as changes in the net positions of the variables constituting the equilibrium system state such that increases or decreases in the thresholds and magnitudes of reaction of the separate variables are building up.[2] (3) A probabilistic set in which the state equations (2) of a given individual—and those others with whom he interacts in any organizational system—provide parameters whose magnitudes, durations, and frequencies are a function of the probabilities that interaction may or may not take place with any given other. These probabilities result from constraints imposed by three cultural categories or dimensions,[3] i.e., spatial location, sequenced activity flow (work flow is one type of such ordering of actions), and communicative patterning.

[1] Though it may be unnecessary to say so for the general reader, it should be emphasized, for those who tend to think of equilibrium as a "static" state, that we are only concerned in biological (and interactional) processes with *dynamic* equilibrium in which the balancing relationships are between *rates*. Further, the properties of the equilibrium manifested occur in what is defined as a steady-state system, i.e., a state in which the system parameters change slowly over time, e.g., in the maturation process of the organism.

[2] Although the mathematical problems are complex, these equations might well be stated as "functionals" (Volterra 1930), which are used in physics to solve what are called problems of "hereditary mechanics," An example would be those studies of the effects of torsion on a wire, where the cessation of the twisting force is not followed by a return by the wire to its initial state since elastic fatigue and hysteresis have induced a change in state that is not reversible and must be taken into account in predictive formulations.

[3] The definition of these cultural categories or dimensions and their relation to interaction is treated at length in Chapple (1970).

The Basic Interaction Rhythm

Only a slight familiarity with the measurements of an individual's alternations of action and inaction is needed to suggest the *possible* existence of a regularity in the durations of each, masked by what the other(s) is doing. It was for this reason that a major part of our early work was devoted to developing standardized methods of interacting within an interviewing context (Chapple 1949, 1952) so that high reliability (replication) would be obtained if the individual were reinterviewed by the same or another interviewer who followed the programed procedure carefully (Matarazzo *et al.* 1959).

It turned out to be necessary to follow a rigorous, nondirective content pattern. In addition, one could not allow the interviewer to vary his behavior unsystematically. The duration of each response or interval of nonresponse is, therefore, quantitatively programed and controlled by a signal system visible only to the interviewer. At the beginning, and for at least 15 minutes, the interviewer does not interrupt, verbally or nonverbally, waits a fraction of a second (0.5 sec) to be sure the subject has stopped before responding and limits his response to 5 seconds. After the initial period of adaptation, varying for different individuals, the variation in durations decreases markedly in "normal" individuals and the values of actions and inactions approach what can be regarded as "basal" levels. Though the purpose of the interview is to conduct a series of experiments, using the interviewer as the independent "variable," these data on the basal state (in remarkable contrast to that manifested by schizophrenics, Chapple *et al.* 1960) suggest the existence of a stable rhythm both of the durations and the tempo at which each action begins.[4]

One cannot be certain about the degree of stability of this rhythm since one cannot conjure away the influence of the other person entirely. The only alternative would be to persuade an individual to talk to himself in isolation. Unsystematic observations of persons asked to carry on a monologue, or of those under drugs or having organic brain damage, suggest that the durations of actions and inactions are indeed highly regular (Jaffe *et al.* 1964). Some of our early attempts to make such studies indicated, however, that accurate experiments can only be conducted in a soundproof room without visual cues, i.e., the observer must be behind one-way glass. Any cues, whether visual or auditory, appear to entrain a change in the values of the "interaction" sequence, whose effects will last for varying intervals of time depending on the person and his state.

---

[4] It should be emphasized that not all persons achieve a "basal" level by the end of 15 minutes (this is particularly true for many types of psychiatric patients). Those familiar with this standardized interview from the literature will realize that not all potential experimental patterns are included in what follows. Since this is not intended as a discussion of interview design, suffice it to say here that there are criteria for determining the probabilities that the 15-minute period has elicited what can be called a basal period—with minimal variability of the component variables—or whether a longer interval of time or repeated interviews may be necessary. In preparation is a paper discussing such designs but, as of this moment, it is sufficient to say that for practical purposes—given a limited period of time available (slightly over an hour), the standardized interview of the literature has been very effective both in terms of reliability and validity.

Though one could wish for more experimental evidence (there are, however, sound physiological grounds giving additional support), we can state as a working hypothesis that these alternations of actions and inactions are essentially periodic and, in a state of isolation, their durations repeat themselves with minimal variation. Since present methods of observation exclude the measurement of intensity of action— because of the operational difficulty of continuously measuring amplitude both of sound (which varies as a function of phonemic position) and nonverbal action and because high predictive accuracy has been obtained without these measures— the waveform of the periodic function would approximate that of a square wave.[5] Behaviorally (and operationally), the alternation of tension and relaxation which characterizes the interaction rhythm, as well as of many noninteractional rhythms, suggests that a better fit will be obtained by describing the process as that of relaxation oscillations, analogous to those so intensively studied by biologists as circadian rhythms (Aschoff 1960; Pittendrigh 1960). Since the tension phase is the one dependent on chemical energy, the shifts in durations of actions and inactions and in the period of the oscillations can be related to physiological and biochemical factors set in motion by the process of interaction.

Although the model of the interaction pattern as a relaxation oscillator best fits the assumptions suggested by the data, the mathematical complications make analysis too difficult in a first approximation because of the nonlinear fluctuations introduced by other persons. Therefore, if we let A symbolize an action and S a silence or inaction, we may state our working hypothesis as follows: each individual i has a fundamental rhythm with a period T (i.e., with a frequency $1/T$) within which the ratio A/S tends to approach a constant, K_i $(A + S = T)$. For the purposes of this paper, since the term "frequency" is used in statistical studies to refer to F, the distribution of the variate, we shall use the term "tempo" for $1/T$.

Interrelations of the Basic Rhythms in Two-Person Interaction

Let us assume that two persons come to an interactional situation *de novo* (with no previous happenings to disturb their basic rhythms). Each will have his own tempo and A/S ratio whose constituent durations of action and inaction are limited in length by the value of $1/T$. Since our hypothesis, as an induction from experience, is that their alternating patterns are reciprocal, i.e., that in a rough approximation one acts while the other is inactive, a preliminary phase shift takes place to set this alternation in motion.

Except in rare cases, when perfect synchronization takes place because $K_i = 1/K_j$ and $1/T_i = 1/T_j$, which we will refer to as *complementarity*, they will be unsynchronized,

---

[5] Treatment of the measurements as a square wave is based upon this operational simplification since presently we are not able *reliably* to measure the amplitude or intensity. Studies of circadian rhythms suggest, however, that amplitude is a function of duration (Aschoff 1960) and some experiments recently begun indicate that to increase durations to the individual's maximum, much greater physical motion—e.g., walking, gestures, raising the voice—are necessary, whereas reduction in durations requires a marked inhibition of intensity of movement.

either with both individuals acting at the same time or both being simultaneously inactive. When only two individuals are involved, we shall, for convenience, refer to the unsynchronized portions of their interaction as either *double actions* or *double inactions* or, to use a less accurate (even for the human) but more euphonious term, *double silences*. For two individuals, i and j, at any one moment of observations, there are only four possible states:

1. i acting/j not acting   (i acting alone $= i_0$).
2. j acting/i not acting   (j acting alone $= j_0$).
3. i acting/j acting   (double action).
4. i not acting/j not acting   (double silence).

When double actions or double silences occur, identifying the state does not, of course, tell who is responsible. Hence, we identify the preceding state from which it was a transition; this tells us whether i or j was acting alone and was either interrupted or not responded to. To determine the outcome, we must wait for the next transition state, when one or the other is acting alone. As we shall see, we characterize the ending of the double action or double silence, respectively, as having been brought about by one or the other dominating, i.e., continuing to act or initiating, i.e., starting to act after both are silent. Whenever state 1 alternates with state 2 and no instances of states 3 or 4 are observed, complete synchronization exists, and the A/S and $1/T$ for one is described as the *complement* of the other.

Although one might find two persons whose rhythms are so unyielding that they make no attempt to adapt to the other, ordinarily at least one, and usually both individuals, will begin to shift his values to approach complementarity.[6] Each individual differs in the degree to which he can shift (and how long he can maintain it), some people being much more capable of variation (flexibility) than others. In addition, they will vary in the relative degree of variability between tempo and the action-inaction ratio, with the latter usually having the greatest potential for change since one can, after all, be relatively silent or relatively talkative at the same tempo.

From data obtained in standardized interviews, one can make the hypothesis that each person has upper and lower limits to the durations exhibited in his actions and inactions and, of course, his tempos. If the frequency with which he begins to act (his tempo), does in fact have such a limit, then the A/S ratio can only be approximately constant in the intermediate tempo range. Once maximum or minimum tempo limits are reached, either the action or inaction duration is reduced to a minimum, and the A/S ratio must become asymptotic.

Although we have not had the resources to carry out an extensive computational

[6] If both were absolutely fixed, unvarying, and noncomplementary, which is unlikely even for extreme psychotics, then once the phase relationship has been adjusted so that the two alternating series are maximally interpolated, we can easily compute the durations and frequencies of the double actions and double silences, given the values of A/S and $1/T$ for the two individuals.

program, the data suggest that an individual's values shift (when interacting and "hunting," in the cybernetics sense, for synchronization within his limits) to values that are definitely related functionally to his "basal" values. In other words, each person can be considered to have a spectrum or, more properly at this stage, a multi-modal set of tempos, actions, and inactions which may be internally related as multiples (or harmonics) of the basal values. This would be in accord with our hypothesis that we are dealing, in interaction data, with periodic functions.

In examining the measurements of the alternating durations of actions and inactions, one finds from time to time a "run" of intervals in which the quantitative values are highly regular. However, most commonly, the values occur irregularly. It is tempting to consider that the phenomena are entirely stochastic, or primarily so, and that the waveform is random or obscured by random components. The temptation comes from the relative ease with which stochastic methods can be applied to data of this sort (Altmann 1965; Jaffe et al. 1964). Yet observation of interactional situations in a wide variety of settings and analysis of the data obtained under controlled situations strongly support the intuitive feeling that the interplay of two (or more) interaction rhythms is lawful and capable of deterministic formulation. There are uniformities in what happens to A/S and $1/T$ when perfect synchronization (complementarity) is not attained and the variables through which these take place can be precisely defined and measured. However, they cannot yet be derived from fundamental laws or principles since functional expression of their mutual dependence is still beyond our present mathematical capacities.

In introducing the discussion of these specifically "interactional" variables, i.e., those characterized by the occurrence of a double action or a double silence as one of the constituent sequential transition states, it is important to emphasize that the quantitative value measured for any one person is in part a product of the other. Thus if i interrupts j, the length of time i persists in his interruption, and the resulting duration, is a consequence not only of his persistence but of the other person's. Obviously, if j gives up after a few seconds and stops acting, enabling i to dominate, then we are unable to state how long i might have persisted before stopping. Consequently, the measurement of this evidence of his persistence against competition is a *joint* product of both persons and is thus not predictive of how long he might have persisted—only of how long he does, given measured amounts of persistence on the part of the other person. Only by observing i with others or by experimentally determining, in a programmed interview, how long he continues double-acting when the interviewer varies his durations of persistence systematically, are we able to make definitive statements.

Similarly, if a double silence occurs when both persons are inactive, the length of the latency or pause before one or the other responds is equally jointly determined, since one cannot tell how long a period of time would have elapsed before i would take the initiative, if j has already beaten him to it. The implications of these dependencies will be clearer when we describe the individual variables which can be isolated in both types of situations.

We shall begin by discussing the variables that can be defined when double actions (interruptions, if this word is not assumed to involve intent) occur which we shall classify as the dominance variables. As is evident from the last two paragraphs, the elements in a double action consist of the *latency of onset* before the interruption begins, how long it lasts, its *persistence*, and who outacted the other and so obtained an instance of *dominance*. In the double-silence situation, comprising the initiative variables, we measure the *latency of response*, or interval of time before one or the other takes the *initiative* by beginning to act, and the *duration of the initiative* once it is under way; these will be discussed immediately after the dominance variables.

The Dominance Variables

Latency of Onset of Double Action Before an interruption (double action) occurs, ordinarily some time has elapsed during which, the person to be interrupted has been talking alone. (Very rarely, both persons will begin to act simultaneously after both have been inactive.) The duration of this latency of onset of the interruption is the first of the dominance variables that can be isolated. The data suggest that the point in the duration of the individual acting alone, i.e., where this occurs, has differential effects on the course of the action. If we assume that, for individual i, the duration of the action required by his fundamental rhythm is sufficiently long so that an ending to this action can be attributed to the double action, then one can make several hypotheses about the impact of an interruption of a fixed duration. If it occurs at the beginning of an action, after a few seconds for example, i is more liable to stop acting (and to be dominated) than if considerable time has elapsed. By contrast, if j's interruption takes place in what would be the middle of the action duration, as determined from the A/S and $1/T$ variables, then not only does the interruption not cause j to win by dominating i—at this point in the action, only a much longer interruption would have this effect—but it appears to lengthen i's action, almost as if through resonance. However, if j's interruption occurs towards the end of i's action, it acts as an effective cutoff such that i ends somewhat before he "normally" would, i.e., as determined from his basal rate. Repetition of such cutoffs progressively damps the length of i's actions and begins to shift the tempo and the A/S ratio, separately or together.

The fact that i is dominated not only marks the end of his action, whatever the requirements of his basic rhythm happen to be, it also is the beginning of his inaction and affords the opportunity for j to act in his turn without having to persist any longer. Thus being dominated shifts the *phase* of i's rhythm and, in turn, makes possible j's establishment of his rhythm, assuming he encounters no competition in return. On the other hand, if the interruption occurs in the middle of i's action and j is overridden, then j's A/S ratio remains fractional, even though he may be acting at the same tempo as he would if he had won. It is interesting to note that equivalent findings have been described for circadian rhythms in the effects of light signals in shifting the phase of the rhythm, depending on where they occur in the activity-rest cycle (Bruce 1960).

Persistence in Interruptions Once an interruption begins, the length of time both continue is called their *persistence*. Individuals vary considerably in their capacity to sustain this persistence in the face of competition; some people are unable to continue an interruption for very long, though this may differ in whether they were the interrupter or the interrupted. As indicated in discussing latency of onset, the persistence duration will vary depending on where the interruption occurs. Given a similar location in the action duration, however, these individual differences show up.

Persistence is, of course, the variable through which dominance over the other person is achieved. Thus the frequency with which one person is able to dominate depends on the persistence level of his competition (and where, in the other's actions, he interrupts). If the people with whom he associates have little capacity to persist, he can achieve a relatively high degree of dominance, even though, with other groups, there might be very few individuals with such low persistence levels.

One cannot, of course, determine the capacity of an individual i to persist from those cases in which the other individual j gives up and is dominated, since we do not know how long i would have continued. Accordingly, in order to estimate the degree to which i can persist, we have to select only those cases in which j continued and dominated i, expressing these durations as a function of the position of the interruption in j's actions. However, the durations of i's persistence intervals when he wins are associated with stabilizing or reestablishing his fundamental rhythms through dominance, and are relevant in determining the particular people with whom he prefers to interact.

When i is acting and j interrupts and loses, the duration of j's action and his persistence involve the same action. If i's action continues and j again interrupts and loses, j's A/S and tempo continue to be equivalent to his *persistence* and *latency of onset*. Under these conditions, it is possible that the tempo and A/S modalities previously operating may shift to new levels in the face of i's continuing action, but at present we simply do not have enough data to support such a hypothesis.

The Dominance Rate The end result of every double-action situation is that one person dominates by continuing to act and the other is dominated and stops acting (except for the rare cases when both stop acting simultaneously). If i is interrupted by j and dominates, and so continues his action, there is no shift in phase for i, but j has lost his turn in the alternating sequence of phase shifts which constitute the interaction pattern; i.e., where i acts, j is inactive, and when i stops acting, j begins to act with varying degrees of synchronization. On the other hand, if i is dominated by j, the alternation does occur, altered in its complementary character by the lack of synchronization resulting from the interruption. The outcome of the interruption, therefore, no matter which person is responsible for the double action, is quite different in its effects on the alternating rhythm of "give and take."

In addition, the person responsible for the interruption must also be taken into account. If i's tempo triggers off the onset of an action during a period when j is already acting, a loss by i due to the location of the interruption in j's action, and/or his inability to persist sufficiently long to dominate, reduces the duration of his action (coterminous with his persistence). Either his A/S ratio will then shift (if his inactions remain constant) and his tempo increase or, if he characteristically tries to maintain a constant ratio, his silences will become much shorter and his tempo will speed up even more. Alternatively, he will appreciably increase his silences in length if his tempo is to remain constant. When j interrupts and wins, similar changes will be set in motion, but their impact on i's A/S and $1/T$ will be less marked except where they occur early in the course of i's action.

Maintenance Duration When dominance occurs (i.e., when the other person stops acting), the winner of the double action continues, by definition. How long he continues is not merely a function of his natural action pattern; the fact of winning, of dominating, alters the duration of action thereafter, in ways which are idiosyncratic for individuals. Some stop sooner than their basal rate would indicate, as if the effort of dominating reduces their capacity to continue acting. Others, of course, increase their durations. Dominance, in other words, serves to shift their action duration level to a higher range. Where the other person recycles his tempo and again interrupts, the repetition of the attempt, coming in the middle of an established action is easier to overcome as pointed out in the discussion of the cycling factor.

The Dominance Hypothesis

A fundamental hypothesis in interaction theory is that each individual tries to maintain a constant balance between the number of times he dominates and the number he loses. Clearly, this cannot be achieved by any i in interacting with a particular j, since the latter may be highly persistent and dominant: rather it is assumed that, over a limited period of time, probably the 24 hours of the circadian rhythm, the pluses and minuses balance themselves out and a net position is achieved, characteristic of that person. Compensatory shifts, therefore, take place during the day as any i moves from one j to another, seeking to reestablish a balance if disturbed, to make up for a cumulative deficit which, it must be emphasized, occurs jointly in dominance *and* in the manifestation of the fundamental A/S and $1/T$ rhythms. Short-term deficits, even within a single contact, are stressful for the individual and are followed by measurable changes in the basic interaction rhythms: longer-term deficits (i.e., for much longer than 24-hour periods) may force shifts in the initial state equations of the individual.

Since we are still concerned with describing the dominance variables, our present concern is not these state equations, but rather the hypothesis of a dominance rate. From the foregoing, it should be evident that the effects of dominating or being dominated depend on the outcome with regard to the pattern of alternation and the shifts produced in the A/S and tempo rhythms and, from the point of view of any i or *j*, whether he was impelled to interrupt or had to confront, and persist against, the interruption of another.

In early work, we combined total dominances for *i* with the total number of instances which he lost, usually expressed as a ratio or percentage, but this clearly was inadequate. We now separate the wins and losses for all double actions in which *i* was the interrupter and, as a separate figure, those in which *j* interrupted *i*. Highly significant differences are found between the two types of combinations, particularly under the standardized conditions of the experimental interview, so that it seems evident that this kind of separation is necessary in any general formulation. We shall thus assume that there is a significant difference between the dominance variables in those instances when *i* is acting, and *j* interrupts and loses, and the opposite situation where *j* is acting, and *i* interrupts and loses. Differential rates need also to be obtained by comparing the instances in which each interrupter wins and the alternation sequence is approximately maintained. In both types of situations, one can then determine the nature of the interdependence of these variations in rates with the A/S and $1/T$ variables of the basic rhythms of the individuals concerned.

A few words should be said here about the use of fixed ratios or percentages as opposed to the determination of rates. Within any contact of individual *i* with another individual *j* or with all the $(j_1, \ldots, j_n)$ he encounters during the day or in any specified period, the number of trials (double actions) and their distribution over time is of first importance. Hence, if someone wins 90% of his encounters but only has nine during the whole period, this is hardly comparable to the individual who, for whatever reason, has a thousand. More important, the sequential ordering of wins or losses has to be taken into account, since being dominated repeatedly in a long contact with one *j* has demonstrably different effects on *i*'s basic interaction rates than if the wins and losses are more evenly distributed. In addition, repetitive domination, as can be demonstrated experimentally, may only be "tolerated" within characteristically specific limits by different people; thereafter, a major shift in A/S ratio and tempo and in the dominance and initiative variables may take place. Therefore, percentages or ratios must be taken with a considerable amount of salt. Under controlled conditions, they have some utility, but even there one needs to inspect the actual sequence carefully to determine idiosyncratic differences.

Last, it should be pointed out that in any interactional contact, either person may be able to inhibit the occurrence of interruptions by him, and do so, in which case the dominance variables for which he is responsible reduce to zero. This does not necessarily mean that he synchronizes perfectly, since to achieve this kind of adjustment, he may repeatedly show latency of response. How he reacts to the other person's interruptions may, of course, alter this capacity to synchronize by shifting his A/S and tempo to levels where such synchronization is no longer possible; but, for varying lengths of time, depending on his capacity to shift his fundamental rhythms, he may be able to eliminate his double actions as a significant set of variables.

The Initiative Variables

Latency of Response When a double silence (inaction) occurs, that is to say, when one person ends his action and the other does not respond immediately, we can begin to measure its duration. Empirically (and in the case of psychiatry, clinically), we are much more liable to notice the occurrence of latency of response, which we may also refer to as pauses, hesitancies, etc., than interruptions. How long this pause or latency lasts is determined by the onset or initiation of a new action by one of the individuals interacting; the various possibilities have formal similarities to the double-action situation.

If i ends his action and j fails to respond, either i or j can initiate the action that brings the latency to an end. If j, after a shorter or longer interval of time, begins to act, the alternating sequence of interaction is maintained. Some semblance of complementarity may thus be preserved, modified by the length of the latencies where true synchronization did not occur. Let us say that j's silence or inaction began when i started his action and the *hesitancy*—as this condition is referred to by us—may well be an expression of the expected duration of the S variable for j under these conditions and the tempo at which he acts. On the other hand, it is well known that such hesitancies are associated with various psychiatric conditions and may be consistent in their duration even with variations in the length of i's actions.

In other words, one could regard the latency, if it showed evidence of shifting to synchronize more closely with i's durations, as a cybernetic phenomenon in which synchronization took place through a hunting process, particularly with individuals whose tempos and A/S ratios are far from complementary. In these cases, we would expect to see a reduction in latencies if i's action durations and tempo are relatively constant. (To make the point, we have to assume that i is not going through a similar adjustment process.) If the latencies do not show this adaptive feature, or even have an inverse relationship to i's actions, various types of "psychiatric" possibilities are indicated.

Where j's hesitancies are of appreciable length, j's tempo is much slower than i's, and this may produce, as in many types of nondirective interviewing—psychoanalytic or otherwise—an increase in the length of i's actions and consequently a shift in his A/S ratio, bringing the tempos more into line. This is, of course, a common technique to get people to talk for longer intervals, but unfortunately is not blindly applicable to every kind of personality.

In contrast to this alternation between i and j, characterized by hesitancy before responding by one or both individuals, i having stopped and finding that j is not responding may wait no longer and initiate another action himself. In this event, more obviously than in the double-action analogue, j has lost his turn and the alternation between i and j has been broken. This type of latency, where i takes the initiative without waiting for j, we refer to as *quickness*. Our measures of the duration of the latency which i can allow before his A/S and tempo set him in motion again (in contrast to those of hesitancy) demonstrate that there are highly significant differences between individuals in these two aspects of what might be thought a single variable.

People vary remarkably in the length of time they can tolerate not getting a response; for some, it is a matter of a few seconds; more commonly much longer intervals can occur before the pressures build up to initiate. If i finally takes the initiative while j is not responding, we can assume that the double silence preceding the initiative is an accurate measure of i's limit of bearable nonresponse or quickness. In the hesitancy situation, where j finally does respond, the duration of the latency only tells us that i's limits are longer than that number of seconds; it does, however, give us an accurate measure of j's hesitancy at that particular point in the interaction.

If i's quickness is quite short, or alternatively j's hesitancy quite long, so that i's range causes him to initiate within its limits, then the repetition of an action by i lengthens j's silence interval by the length of i's action (assuming no double action) and slows down his tempo. Repeated failure by j to respond, resulting in a repetition of i's taking the initiative, can bring about changes in the A/S ratio and tempo of i. These ordinarily take the form, differing for individuals, of marked acceleration or deceleration of tempo with coincident shifts in the intervals of silence as well as in the durations of the actions initiated which together make up the A/S relationship.

Initiative Durations Once the initiative has been taken by one or the other person, its duration is not necessarily determined by the A/S and $1/T$ variables. Where hesitancy characterizes the latency of response, it is uncertain whether the durations of the initiative differ significantly from those to be expected if closer synchronization occurred. There is evidence to suggest that long hesitancies are associated with decreasing durations of action, but these take place in psychiatric conditions. It is probable that where the latencies are a function of the cybernetic hunting process, or of a slow tempo characteristic of the individual, one would find that the initiatives (operationally so defined) are not different in duration from those to be expected from the A/S and tempo variables.

On the other hand, when the latency lasts long enough for i—the person whose action was not responded to—to take the initiative, the durations of such initiatives can be widely different. Some people become shorter and shorter in their initiative durations, but vary between those who manifest shorter and shorter intervals of silence (and hence a speeded up tempo) or become increasingly silent; others may talk for longer and longer intervals as if the lack of response was a signal for substantial increase over basal levels. There is also a common pattern of reaction where i's repeatedly taking the initiative will set j in motion with a long interval of reaction whose magnitude is far greater than previously manifested. This only occurs after he fails to respond and i takes the initiative away from him, so to speak. The particular pattern manifested by the individual is idiosyncratic for him and represents his reaction to the very specific stress which nonresponse sets up for every individual. Its relevance for consideration among the factors going into a mathematical model, apart from initiative duration and quickness, lies in the observation that the changes in durations taking place in repetition show characteristics of exponential and other nonlinear functions which shift the basic periodic functions in determinable ways.

The Initiative Rate As in the case of dominance, the rate at which initiative is taken by any given individual is regarded, by hypothesis, as a balance, over a 24-hour period—between the number of times he initiates and the number of times he is initiated to. Such a discrimination has for many years been applied to new events, but it also has to include the initiatives taking place within the on-going interaction of the event itself. In order to achieve this balance, therefore, any individual i will increase his initiatives to others if his relationship with a particular person j has reduced his net position. Throughout the day, compensatory activity by i occurs in taking the initiative, avoiding situations where he will be initiated to or, when he is ahead on balance, being willing to respond, though on other occasions, with the same person, he might not.

So, too, the interplay of initiative durations, latencies, and his basal rhythms affect the initiative rate. Very brief contacts, even though someone else initiates to him, have different functional significance than a sustained initiative duration. In determining the initiative balance, one has to distinguish between hesitancy and quickness situations. One might argue that an action by j after an interval of hesitancy following the ending of i's action does not constitute "initiative" at all, because the pattern of alternation of phases by each remains unbroken, though not accurately synchronized. On the other hand, if we are forced into the position of asking how much time has to elapse before one could regard such an action as initiative, we will lose the cumulative effect of being able to take the initiative after long latencies (instead of encountering repeated initiatives by the other person), the importance of which has been proven in many psychotherapeutic situations. Provided the two situations are kept separate and, if desired, labeled "initiative$_h$" and "initiative$_q$," with their mutual relationships being dependent on further analysis, we can avoid confusion.

In addition, in a first approximation to analysis, it may be useful to separate out those initiatives of new events in which neither person was previously in interaction from those in which the initiative to a third person is an immediate consequence of the interaction of two others, one of whom is the initiator for that event. This is analogous to the reciprocal initiative just discussed, except that j initiates to j_1 instead of back to i; its frequency of occurrence and differential importance is recognizably dissimilar to those initiations of new events by one person, without prior interaction for an appreciable period.

A few words should also be said about the significance of initiative (of whatever sort) in making possible the triggering off of the periodic function which the interaction rhythms represent. Since a fundamental hypothesis of interaction theory is that each individual requires a constant amount (implicit, of course, in the idea of a periodic function) of interaction with a sufficient degree of complementarity, and hence manifestation of his basic rhythms, inability to initiate significantly reduces the possibilities of achieving such needed outlets. People whose initiative rate is very low may be able to maneuver themselves into spatial proximity with those who will initiate to them and, in so doing, provide the complement for those with high initiative rates. But they are dependent either on proximity or an established relationship with an initiator; if either of these conditions vanishes, with no substitute, a sharp diminution in manifestation of interaction is a consequence.

It is important to emphasize, however, that the patterns of initiation, differentiated by the quickness and hesitancy variables, apply to the initiation of new events. Thus, it is expected in all societies that reciprocal initiation is an essential element in a relationship, analogous to the interval of time elapsing before j responds to i. Further repetition of initiative with varying frequencies and at various intervals characterizes the relationships of individuals where the initiator is trying to establish interaction, continuing until he gets a response, or alternatively, where the repetition of initiations without allowing time for reciprocal initiations is a source of disturbance.

Terminations of Interaction

Although the process of interaction, for the individual, may appear almost continuous, nevertheless it is clear that each person has varying degrees of capacity to terminate the interaction (Chapple 1940). Such terminations are necessary, either because the adjustment in the interaction is disturbing in one or another of the described ways or because the sheer fact of acting longer than the base rhythm permits, or at values of the spectrum which are hard to maintain (even if maladjustment is not evident in the dominance and initiative variables), forces a break and a need to bring the interaction to an end.

The latency found in ongoing interaction brings the interaction to an end, either by the initiative of the same person when his quickness limit is reached, or by the other person in a delayed reaction to the expected alternating pattern. Yet the same discriminations also occur in the initiation by i or j of a "new" event, i.e., where there has been a definite break in the interaction. Operationally, it is not easy to set up completely unambiguous criteria for defining a new event. Empirically, we feel sure that a "certain" length of time has to elapse, but how much?

We can begin with the distinction that events on successive days (or at longer intervals) are new: in general, we would also hold that if i interacts with person j_2 after interacting with j_1, this would constitute a new event. If i and j_1 have been in interaction and j_2 is in the same room—within interactional distance spatially, but not interacting—we would be entitled to use the same criterion. Even where set events take place, alternating with pair events when more than two people are present (a "set" event is defined as that case where i initiates to $(j_1, \ldots, j_n)$ and they respond simultaneously) the occurrence of a set event followed by a pair event between i and j would operationally constitute a new event. In the same way if i initiates to j_1 who in turn initiates to j_2 with no significant break in the interaction, each of these would be regarded as new.

The most difficult decision comes when two persons are spatially contiguous, e.g., sitting in chairs in the same room, both reading, and have not been interacting for that "certain" length of time. Assuming it is important to make this distinction when one looks up from his book and speaks to the other, an approximate method is to determine whether the interval of noninteraction exceeds some multiple of their separate tempos; this criterion is less clearly definable, however.

The problem of defining the criteria for the new event is necessarily bound up with the question of terminating one. Clearly, by beginning to interact with a person j_2, the interaction with j_1 has been ended, even if only temporarily. If i does not respond to j_1's last action, then i has terminated the interaction and, as Kendon (1965) and others have pointed out, this is related to the postural positions adopted by i and, in particular, by the direction of the gaze. Thus if i looks away from j_1 (if he physically moves away, the problem is simple), at the same time not responding, it is liable to represent the termination of the action, since it appears from such studies as have been conducted that *looking toward* is the signal for the other person to act next and also, as Kendon points out, a signal that the person acting (speaking) either is trying to elicit a response (in order to dominate) or is bringing his action to an end.

We have by no means obtained sufficient evidence to determine unambiguous criteria for all situations to be able to say that termination has occurred, although in most cases the decision is simple. In some instances, the individual who acts last has in fact terminated the interaction, but he does this only by combining such an ending with a shift in gaze and posture, e.g., by beginning to look at papers on his desk, turning back to his work and the like. Hence both actions and inactions can be terminations.

Notes on the Initial State Equations

The purpose of defining a set of initial equilibrium state equations for the individual is to be able to estimate the values of the several variables under basal conditions and the degree to which known amounts of synchronization or the various types of asynchronization alter the individual's basal values. We are not concerned, in this section, with the effects of cumulative changes in these variables over a 24-hour or longer period, but only with what we can properly regard as the boundary conditions that have to be taken into account in setting up the "hereditary" equations for long periods of time.

For our present purposes, we shall assume: (1) that all others with whom an individual interacts during a day (or longer) may be regarded as a single person, j; and (2) that the differences in the parameters of the state equations of each of such persons can be regarded as the analogue of a series of experiments in which we program interaction of varying quantitative properties for him to encounter. These same assumptions can be carried over into the next set of equations, but at that point we must take into account the cumulative effects of interaction, whereas here we are conducting (by assumption) each experiment at the point when the individual is in his basal situation.[7]

If the interaction patterns of the two individuals are regarded as relaxation oscillators, and hence periodic functions, the curve for i would be the sine wave expression of a square wave while the curve for j would be the sine curve, displaced to be 180° out of phase. Under such conditions, then, perfect complementarity would take place and, in our simplifying assumptions, given $A/S_i = K_i$ and so on, $K_i = 1/K_j$ and $1/T_i = 1/T_j$.

Inasmuch as perfect complementarity (or even a close approximation thereto), sustained for a long period of interaction is rare, the equilibrium states that characterize an individual involve only partial complementarities. For example, the tempos may be equal, but the A/S ratios are not reciprocals of one another. In addition, *both* the initiative and dominance rates have their complementarities, marked by correlative changes in the underlying double-action and double-silence variables, so that one may often find, for example, persisting pairs of individuals with conjoint complementarities in which one person is high in dominance, the other extremely low, or one who takes the initiative and the other who waits passively for the partner to initiate.

It is also possible for partial complementarities to occur at specific modal points in the A/S and tempo values, but not at others. For example, an individual i may be able to interact with high synchrony with another person j as long as his A/S ratio equaled 2.0 and the tempo is on the order of 10 seconds. If the A/S ratio shifts to very high values and the tempo becomes much slower, i.e., when individual j is talking in long bursts and is silent very briefly, adjustment might become quite asynchronous for i because he is unable to adjust at the other modality. Since we believe that each person has a basal or fundamental rhythm, the capacity to adjust or not to do so may occur at the *fundamental* or in one of the modalities whose proportionate contribution and significance is far less. This is why one can find people able to interact with high complementarity in certain cultural activities, e.g., games or sports, yet who find it difficult to spend an evening together.

The equations that delineate the model must, therefore, be able to manage the mutual relations of the several groups of variables—the basal rhythm and its modalities, and the dominance and initiative variables. This does *not* mean that a given initiative rate must *ipso facto* be accompanied by a given dominance rate. What it does mean is that changes in one variable may produce changes in others, but not necessarily linearly and still less as a positive relationship. For example, if every time

---

[7] The title of this section, as well as the title of the paper, means exactly what it says; we are by no means far enough along to formulate these equations in any organized system. However, I shall attempt to indicate, in words, something of the nature of the relationships of the several interactional variables already described and this may suggest to the mathematically sophisticated reader how these equations could tentatively be written.

an individual starts to speak he is interrupted and dominated, and if, as a result, his action durations become shorter and shorter, not only may his silences become longer but his hesitancies may increase significantly in length and his initiative rate shift (one way or the other) in consequence. One could then say that the shift in hesitancy values is a function of the increase in silence coincident with the increase in the speed with which the other person starts to interrupt and the length of the conjoint persistences.

As various discussions of the effects of administering the standard experimental interview have demonstrated (Chapple 1953), characteristic patterns of asynchrony repeated for a given number of times, e.g., interrupting, not responding (with varying time parameters), have the effect of disturbing the system in predictable ways, both by shifting the A/S ratios and tempo and the initiative and dominance variables. When the disturbance is removed and the other person (interviewer in these experiments) returns to a pattern of synchrony (and complementarity for him), compensatory changes in these variables, often involving major shifts outside the basal values, take place—the degree and direction (and the particular variables affected) being idiosyncratic for the individual. Only after these values work themselves out, in what are called transients since they represent the intermediate states before the return to equilibrium, does the individual return to his basal conditions.

In general, the transients for each variable appear to be nonlinear, usually exponential in form, and are often parametrically described by a major shift in the origin (e.g., the position on the ordinate) as well as by the positive or negative slope. In this formulation, durations are plotted on the ordinate and the absolute sequence on the abscissa. These major shifts (by comparison to the basal levels) give us an empirical description of the severity of the reaction (emotionally and behaviorally) and have been described in general terms elsewhere (Chapple *et al.* 1954; Chapple and Sayles 1961). They provide us with precise measures of the degree of stress imposed on the system, which is also measured directly during the intervals when it is being applied. However, it is an induction from many such observations that the extent of the shift in the component variables during the stress period is by no means sufficient to predict the parameters of the compensatory changes once the stress is removed.

It may be worth commenting here for those interested in the analysis of the frequency distributions of interaction measurements that, in an early paper (Chapple 1940), having indicated that the frequency distributions of durations of actions and silences could be best fitted by a negative exponential (J-shaped curve), $F = ae^{-bt} + ce^{-dt}$, I discovered that the slopes of the frequency distributions for long and short actions and silences were functionally related and, no matter with whom the individual was interacting, the resulting slope of the function was invariant for him. This statistical (and functional) finding would support the present point of view that there is a mutual dependence between A/S equaling K and the constant value of $1/T$. More important, if we are here dealing with square waves, the frequency distribution, of course, given a regular periodic function, would be Gaussian. The exponential character of the frequency distributions of A, S, and K in free interaction could then be regarded as the result of the influences of the initiative and dominance variables, which are exponential. Their contributions from a statistical point of view, in biasing the normal curve, could be expressed as a function of the degree of synchronization.

To return to sketching the elements to be taken into account in formulating the initial state equations, in a first approximation we can regard the A/S rhythm and tempo for individual i as the dependent variable in the equations with the independent variables including the initiative and dominance variables, and some coupling quantities derived from the A/S rhythms of the two individuals. Stated in other words, the A/S rhythm (including $1/T$, of course) for i is the output-controlled variable and the input signal variable is j's A/S and $1/T$. To this must be added the double-action and double-silence variables, which represent disturbances or, in control theory terms, the error signals. The various, probably nonlinear, processes by which the system tries to adjust to complete complementarity would require some type of time-dependent operators with the steady state or state of equilibrium being represented by the equation for complementarity.

The only way in which one can determine the characteristics of the system is to carry out a series of experiments, of the type we have been undertaking in designing our programmed interviews, in which constant-input-variable states at selected fixed values of the disturbance (double-action double-silence) variables are introduced. Since nonlinear formulations of the type envisaged, even if within the framework of a generalized relaxation oscillator model, are highly abstruse (and beyond our mathematical competence), I can only suggest that we might begin with a set of equations— to define the equilibrium state—in which each of these input variables is separated out and tested systematically for its effects on the output-dependent variables. We would, therefore, have an equation for latency of response in which j finally took the initiative, another for that case when the latency continued so long that i took the initiative, and we would need to differentiate each by the length of the initiative duration. And similarly, for interruptions. In addition, we would be required to vary the basic rhythms of j at least as some regular multiple of the values exhibited.

Though this type of approach may appear to be a very large order, particularly because it assumes that a useful mathematical framework for highly nonlinear relaxation oscillators will become available, a great deal can be done by carrying out the experiments on a systematic basis. In addition, one can take courage from the fact that this kind of formulation appears to be necessary for biological systems generally, and much mathematical effort is being put into work designed to break the nonlinear bottleneck. Furthermore, the biological systems involving respiration, body temperature, the heartbeat and the skeletal muscles as well as endocrine function also appear to be controlled by relaxation oscillators and seem to provide the components of the basic rhythms of the interaction pattern.

The Individual as a System in Equilibrium

If we can develop initial state equations for the individual which describe the processes by which he adapts to the interaction patterns of others, we shall then have to introduce parameters into these equations which describe the cumulative changes in the initial state variables over time. To do so may be relatively simple once the state equations themselves are worked out, but I suspect that this is not so. It is better to separate the two processes, since the values obtained through measuring the individual's interaction with others, even for a single day, will clearly manifest compensatory changes. The parameters derived will, in part, depend on the character of the adjustment and the "net positions" of the variables at the particular time of the day that a new event begins. Deviations occurring in these parameters, therefore, set limits on the interaction requirements for further interaction of given degrees of complementarity or its obverse.

We are assuming that the initial state equations can be obtained by methods presently being employed in the experimental interview (Chapple 1953) with the obvious qualification that, for scientific purposes at least, several interviews with different quantitative programs would be necessary. For these "hereditary" equations (Volterra 1930), though we can still regard individual i as interacting with only one individual j whose range of behaviors is comparable to those already established in the initial state equations, we now have to deal with the fact that, in everyday life, interaction does not take place in programmed quantitative doses. On the contrary, interaction with any single person will fluctuate, almost from moment to moment, from one set of double-action double-silence variables to another, with varying degrees of duration in each, so that regular repetitions of any single set are the exception rather than the rule. In consequence, the quantities, which we have suggested may be functionals, take their values from the sequential range of each of the variables in the initial state equations and will require operators by which their mutual relationships over time are interrelated. In other words, the cumulative effects of intermittent alternations of i's dominating j, sometimes in the middle of an action, on occasion at the beginning, interspersed with intervals in which he does not respond to j, but takes the initiative and also manages brief intervals of synchronization, will require ways of bridging these mutual effects.

In addition, as these parameters are cumulatively time dependent, the individual will be continually involved in compensatory processes. These will either maintain or restore his equilibrium state and, if possible, increase the level of complementarity or, where "optimum" adjustment has been attained, try to continue this state and the event which produces it. Hence, if a particular relationship has a high degree of complementarity (the term here refers to a high level of approximation of this state, not necessarily to complete achievement), he will try to prolong the state as long as possible. As a consequence, he is reducing negative values of the parameters of the relevant variables and approaching a stable manifestation of his basal rhythms. This does not mean, of course, that the other person with whom he is interacting is necessarily also approaching *his* basal rhythms; he may be operating at a pattern of synchronization peripheral to his basal requirements, as does the psychotherapist or any of the other persons whose role requires them to manage, to some degree at least, a pattern of minimal synchronization.

Where complementarity is low, and where the nature of the lack of synchronization is to disturb the initial state equations so that transient reactions of varying degrees of magnitude occur and prolong themselves [what we have elsewhere called "temperamental reactions" (Chapple *et al.* 1954; Chapple and Sayles 1961)], then the individual will endeavour, if he can, to bring the interaction to an end. Actually, to state it in these terms is insufficiently precise since, in most cases, the changes in his interaction variables, resulting from the occurrence of stress, may in turn result in stress for the other person. As synchronization decreases, and A/S and $1/T$ variables get more and more out of phase and complementarity, the occurrence of a long silence with no one taking the initiative, or the appearance of a third person, enabling one or the other to seek compensatory adjustment, will be sufficient to end the event. Such ending of events can be observed even where the two individuals do not move spatially from where they may be sitting, for example, with a double silence becoming prolonged after sequential shifts in the several values of the variables relevant to their interactional lack of adjustment.

In a first approximation to a formulation of these "hereditary" equations, we have postulated that the parameters describe the cumulative changes over a 24-hour period. This is based upon the importance to the organism of the circadian rhythm and to the fact that sleep appears to act, among other things, as a means through which the equilibrium is restored. Since the evidence from the many studies of circadian rhythms indicates that the major physiological functions, including endocrine activity, follow a daily cycle, with overactivity as an interdependent component, it seems reasonable to assume that, in most steady-state systems where major disturbances are not evidenced in the values assumed by the parameters, one can hypothesize a kind of reestablishment of equilibrium on a daily basis. In addition, evidence from circadian studies indicated that the total amount of activity per cycle is a constant (though this too can be shifted experimentally). By hypothesis, therefore, we can assume that the amount and quantitative properties of the individual's system equations for the day approach a constant. Empirical observations have long suggested that if individuals have "too much" interaction, they endeavor to reduce it as the day wears on; if too little, they try to make up in the evening for what they have missed during the day. Such unsystematic evidence is, of course, not sufficient to demonstrate the tenability of the hypothesis, yet it enables one to test its utility by continuous observation of an individual over 24 hours on a repeated basis.[8] Probably no one reaches the end of his day with his interactional accounts neatly balanced; yet if one remembers that we can properly regard the individual variables as approaching limits, then we can assume that, within such limits, equilibrium can be maintained.

It should be realized that I am not ignoring the occurrence of substantial overdrafts, or the reverse, in many individuals' interactional course. Varying types of cultural situations may require abnormal amounts of interaction, or they may be facilitated by the use of drugs like caffein or amphetamine, by alcohol, and even by sustained degrees of high complementarity. In contrast, all sorts of restrictions on interaction are imposed, from solitary confinement on. In general, compensatory changes may take place when these conditions are prolonged; the fact that they may be managed within limits without always entailing major shifts in the equilibrium state argues for the importance of the circadian alternation of waking and being asleep. This explains why attempts to shift the personality, e.g., brainwashing and other types of sensory deprivation, are grounded on the interruption of the wake-sleep cycle (Sargant 1964).

Apart from these more obvious types of interference with the complete adequacy of the 24-hour-parameter formulation, there is little doubt but that long-term cumulative changes do occur, and that these require the introduction of other parameters of heredity. The working hypotheses of the etiology of psychiatric disorder, when these are not so strictly stated as to exclude the possible influences of interpersonal relations, assume that substantial and continuing maladjustment results in a fundamental disturbance of the state of equilibrium such that a new state, with quite different parametric values, comes into being. Although one can criticize the rigor of the evidence adduced by various investigators like Bowlby (1962), Spitz (1945), etc., experimental work by Harlow (1962), Jensen et al. (1964) on monkeys and many studies of similar situations in laboratory animals below the primate order support the hypothesis that these changes take place during the maturation of the neonate. In addition, a wealth of clinical material can be interpreted to support the hypothesis that particular types of personality (where they can be interactionally defined) are more vulnerable to stress than others and suggest that rigorous methods of interaction measurement might be used to prove the point. This is not to say that physiological,

[8] Twenty-four hour observations of individuals or groups have very rarely been carried out, even by nonquantitative procedures. Roberts (1965) in Zuni studies on three different small kin groups, dictated a continuous account of what each individual was doing and recorded the exact clock time, roughly every minute, from the time that the first individual got up in the morning until the last one went to bed. Barker and Wright (1951) did a similar study of a seven-year-old boy but included a good deal of interpretation of the "meanings" of events to the boy.

We ourselves have been able to measure the activity, location and postural position, and interaction (but contact duration, not interaction as here described) for one schizophrenic patient over the entire 24 hour period, a patient whose intervals of sleeping were short.

biochemical, and genetic factors are not involved, but there seems little reason to question the evidence that interaction is the overt manifestation of the reactions of a total endocrine and biochemical system.

We can, therefore, contemplate in the long run the necessity of introducing into our system equations for the individual, parameters which will describe these changes over months and years. For the present, the 24-hour formulation is difficult enough, but once it is managed and the equations provide a satisfactory fit of the data, long-range parameters should not be hard to add.

Cultural Categories as
Probabilistic Constraints of Interactional Systems

Up to this point in the discussion, we have been concerned only with the considerations that appear relevant in describing the interactional properties—and the equations to describe them—for the single individual. By necessity, this requires us to consider the other person—and this means all other persons—so that we are now prepared to consider the situation in which varying numbers of individuals interact. These may be simple or complex and, for our purposes, we shall refer to them as organizations or institutions (Chapple 1940; Chapple and Coon 1942). In contrast to the foregoing, the formulation of equations which will adequately describe what takes place in organizations requires the introduction of probabilistic factors derived from the culture of the particular group under study.

When we observe the interactional events for given individuals over the day, it is immediately evident that they differ remarkably in length and, of course, in the number of people with whom each individual interacts, either in pair events or in group situations. Thus if we return to the equations which we hopefully believe can be established for each person with whom we are concerned, we realize that their contribution in terms of complementarity or lack of adjustment, even of the number of variables entering into the equations from our measurements, is highly variable. A greeting, or a word and gesture and an answering response, between two people makes little parametric contribution to the system equations; a large number of events, in fact, the largest number, are very short, since various studies, beginning with Molina's classical analysis of the length of telephone conversations (1927), have shown that they are distributed in a negative exponential (a die-away curve) $F = ae^{-bt}$.

As a consequence, although we established our equations for individual i on the basis of all other persons $j_1, \ldots, j_n$ as representing a single j, we now have to separate them out in their sequential place in a network of relations making up i's daily round. At each point established by a new event, i.e., with a person different from the one with whom he was interacting, we have to estimate the cumulative position of his parameters and the resources which the cultural dimensions of his organizational situation provide for further interaction.

In so doing, though the constituent interactions that make up the individual's equilibrium state equations over the circadian period occur as events, the components of which are deterministic, their occurrence at a particular time are to a considerable extent affected by considerations of probability. No matter how an individual's net position may cry out for interaction with friend or family member to compensate for the events in which he has been repeatedly dominated, his organizational situation sets constraints on who is available and when he will be free to seek relief in another organization system. In other words, freedom to initiate or be initiated to, or for interaction to optimum length, is by no means available to the individual, since cultural constraints control, to a considerable extent, the "who does what, with whom, when, where and for how long," which is the substance of organizational (or social) observation (Chapple 1953).

I have elsewhere (Chapple *et al.* 1954) used the analogy, for culture, of the ways chemical processes are controlled. It may be helpful to quote it to make clear the part these cultural categories play in interaction.

They provide a set of contraints on the interaction patterns that comprise the organizational structure, just as the test tubes and complicated glass linkages of the chemistry laboratory control the rates at which chemical processes can occur. To perform a different experiment using the same compounds, the chemist changes his arrangement of tubes and beakers and piping; so, to follow the analogy, without changing the personalities, any change in the cultural elements that results in altering the flow of contacts, changes the organizational relationships of the individuals who make it up. As in the chemical analogy, the personality constituents of the organizational system in turn bring about modifications in its structure, even where the cultural constraints remain fixed, for each individual's interactional needs differ if he is to achieve a state of equilibrium in his relations with others.

For the purposes of analysis of their specific effects on interaction, three categories can be said to subsume cultural phenomena. If we are not being too precise in the mathematical sense, these categories may be regarded as dimensions since they order interactions within probabilistic limits. They are (1) *relative spatial location*; (2) *sequenced activity flow* (work flow in technology); and (3) *communicative patterning*. If we take up each in turn, their mode of operation can be described in the following way.

Spatial Distance The effects of space on interaction are so obvious that little systematic attention has been paid to the many ways in which cultures use the relative spatial location of individuals in three dimensions to inhibit or foster interaction, or even to emphasize the use of particular patterns as opposed to others. Hall (1959, 1966) has done much to make explicit its importance by bringing together work from animal and human studies, but he is more concerned with the communicative aspects than with their operational character.

Clearly, physical separation prevents interaction. In many societies, there is little or no way for interaction to take place, though relatively short distances may be bridged very inadequately by some kind of signal system. Even the telephone is more limited than the Bell System would have us think; not only is the interaction restricted to the verbal, but there are practical limits for most people in terms of the time when calls can be made, their frequency, and how long they may last. Whatever the organization—business, government, even the family—the fact that an individual with whom it is necessary to interact is in a distant community, or even in a different building, drastically reduces the possibilities of interacting with him.

The natural environment and its influences at particular stages of culture as well as the differentiation of space through architectural means (taken broadly to include the modification of the landscape) separate individuals and may effectively prevent their interaction, often for long periods of time. Even within a building, these constraints operate significantly. The probabilities of interacting with someone are far higher if he is in the same office or an adjacent one than if he is on a different floor. Moreover, the degree of specialization of rooms for various purposes, say within a house, can set up areas like a bedroom, which may exclude all others or at least certain others, so that free access to interaction with all the individuals in a system can take place only in common meeting areas. There is no particular reason to labor the point, and in any case the implications are discussed in more detail by Chapple (1968).

Alternatively, the enforcement of proximity by the amount of available space increases the probabilities of interaction. The members of a family living in a one-room house can achieve privacy (and separation from interaction) only by leaving it. People working together whose proximity is fixed by geographical propinquity, at adjacent desks in an office or a schoolroom, at the same workbench or in the same bed, cannot get away from each other, and interaction is difficult to avoid. Further, the scope of available interaction, though obviously also mediated by the technology, is strongly influenced. Man and wife in the same bed can add tactile interaction as well as speech and gesture; how close the desks are together or positions at a work-bench can alter the probabilities of interaction and, in turn, the noise level in the room may play an important part.

Not only can horizontal space act as a constraint, but vertical differentiation does likewise and, in addition, can facilitate interaction of a particular sort, e.g., the speaker on a platform, the king on his throne. When this is supplemented by related horizontal space—the long path to the chancel in a cathedral—spatial differentiation can make the carrying out of particular patterns of interaction for specified periods easier and, in particular, controlling (or at least making more probable) the likelihood that individuals in certain locations can initiate while others respond.

Occupation of space by a given individual over time establishes his association with it and the patterns of interaction used by him toward others and others toward him. Extensive studies of animals and humans have brought into focus the importance of territoriality, using this term in its general sense, both for individuals and for groups. Encroachment on this territory by someone taking the initiative creates conflict and struggles for dominance; the winner, moving toward *his* space, which might be temporarily occupied by another, forces the other to respond immediately to his initiative by moving elsewhere. Interesting studies have been carried out on the lower animals, showing that the capacity to be dominant varies as a function of the distance from the individual's territory. Clearly its significance depends on the interactional context, e.g., the incursion of a toddler or of an adult male, but within these limits, for many groups, distance for both animal and human takes on dimensional implications.

In the two books referred to, Hall sketched out a scale of distance ranges based on the limitations imposed by the human sensory apparatus on perceptual discrimination. If we restrict ourselves to sight and hearing, with touch only possible at zero distance, his idea that patterns of interaction differ depending on how far people are apart can be used to set up a probabilistic scale for experimental testing. He points out that at about 25 feet and more, facial detail is hard to see; between 12 and 25 feet the voice level must be raised and more expressive gestures used. On the other hand, interactional intensity is likely to be much greater when people touch each other or when they are not more than 2 or 3 feet apart. Whether the ranges he uses or any modifications thereof provide a better fit of the data, it is quite clear that the intervals are logarithmic and that, expressed as a function of interactional intensity, the probabilistic expression would turn out to be hyperbolic.

As it turns out (Chapple, 1970), not only are the visual and auditory receptors (and, of course, the tactile) capable of being categorized along a distance scale, but there is now very substantial evidence neurologically and physiologically with regard to the biological processes which cause animals to maintain spatial distance. Berlyne (1965) has reviewed the evidence on curiosity or exploratory behavior and discussed the ways in which the reticular formation of the brain and the limbic area increase the state of arousal and elicit spontaneous activity. The process, broadly called orientation, is concerned with the focusing of attention after a change in stimulus and is demonstrated by changes in the animal's direction (a) by body movement and (b) by actual movement toward the stimulus. Although the significance of the orientation process cannot be discussed further here, the evidence makes quite clear that the dimension of spatial distance is based on biological properties and that the intervals on a distance scale, developed for a species, can be assigned very accurate probabilistic values as to the likelihood of particular patterns of interaction taking place.

Cultural Sequencing Although we are accustomed to think of work flow as a special characteristic of industrial organizations, where, as in the assembly line, the division of labor requires individuals to perform their special activities in an ordered sequence, all cultural forms, where the division of labor (or, better, the differentiation of actions) has developed, evidence these orders. Thus a ritual or ceremony in a religious institution is ordinarily performed by two or more people; sometimes, of course, it requires the presence of many, and even such simple tasks as preparing family meals or washing the dishes usually involve a division of labor, formal or informal.

Wherever such sequenced activity flows occur, the order of initiation of actions is defined with relatively high probabilities, altered, of course, by spatial factors, since proximity increases the probabilities, and by the communicative patterning, as we shall see. These chains of actions, performed in sequence, again present the semblances of a dimension and are, in fact, the organizing factor on which the structure of both simple and complex institutions is based. Each step in the chain requires a time duration for the activity (or interaction itself) to be accomplished, and each step is dependent upon the completion of the prior step by the antecedent individual.

In the case of cultural sequencing, the dimensional form is made up of an ordered array of individuals with the dimensional distance between two people depending on the number of relational steps between them. In addition, all the persons contained within the array are mutually dependent on one another and are separate from all others at the sequence's beginning and ending steps. Although, by definition, these sequences require a division of labor, they are necessarily built up on the fixed action sequences available to the organism. The sequences necessarily take a temporal form for, as Marler and Hamilton (1966) point out, if different acts could occur in random order, the skeletal-muscular system would be in a state of chaos. Further, the temporal behavior sequences are the repertoire through which the basic biological rhythms—of activity and interaction—are expressed. Since they are temporally determined and controlled, synchronization of actions and interactions making them up is a necessary consequence. They are the basis on which organizational complexity is developed.

Cultural sequences, therefore, define the probabilities that specific individuals either will or will not interact with one another; depending on the technological development or the nature of the flow, this probability may be as high as 1.0—in the cases of ritual—dropping to much lower levels in industrial settings where conveyors or other systems are in operation. Even here, however, though direct initiative may not be possible between individuals performing adjacent steps, interferences in the flow can set in motion interactional changes within a group of workers at a particular step; and sequenced initiatives (flowing both ways) do occur between supervisors and other specialized personnel like inspectors and engineers (Chapple and Sayles, 1961).

Since these flows include interaction events, the nature of the communicative transaction, e.g., in selling women's hosiery versus living room furniture, sets up quite different tempos and A/S ratios as well as initiative and dominance variables. So, too, a manufacturing operation specializing in the production of single units requires much more extensive interaction of particular types, while in ceremonies the content of the interaction is usually highly standardized.

Communicative Patterning Although, from recent literature, one might come to the conclusion that communication, in its broadest "ethnographic" sense (Hymes *et al.* 1964), is the primary determinant of interaction, it, too, establishes only probabilities within which interaction may or may not occur and, more important, specific patterns of interaction. As indicated briefly in the Introduction, there is no necessary reason to believe that the individual's equilibrium state equations will not override the content structure. As an example, the direct question, asked after a series of long actions by individual i, as mentioned earlier, can either be answered by a very short action, thereby shifting both A/S and $1/T$ radically, or it can be answered with individual i continuing his basal rhythm at the previous values. The test is, did or did not a change in interaction take place?

The communication-patterning dimension can be broken down into two categories of subdimensions, the first subdivision deriving from the biological properties of communication, both verbal and nonverbal. These consist of (a) fluctuations in amplitude or intensity of sound or movement; (b) changes in intonation or pitch; (c) variations in timbre or tonal quality; and (d) changes in quickness of movement or articulation rates, i.e., not the separation of action durations by inaction intervals. Although the properties of these four subdimensions vary, and are difficult to measure accurately with our present technology on a continuous basis, paricularly their nonverbal manifestations, they can all be treated dimensionally by the same analytical procedure, either within any given sequence of interaction or in comparing one person with another.

The means for so doing lie in the fact that, within limits, each individual adapts to the presenting values and their fluctuations in the other person. *Only* if there is an excursion outside these limits to which one quickly becomes "tuned" do the probabilities of altering the interaction rhythm change. In other words, amplitude becomes significant if there is a change from the normal range to very loud or soft speech. Similarly a shift in pitch operates the same way, although particular patterns,—for example, the pitch-contour of interrogation—have a higher probability of changing the interaction pattern than that of running up and down the scale. Modulations of timbre, from a wider spectrum frequency to a narrow one, and for that matter intonation rate, also vary within limits. Therefore, to construct a dimensional scale for each, one has to utilize the techniques of statistical process control, that is, to measure or estimate the average level and its expected limits of variation (the mean and the standard deviations) and to develop an interval scale for deviations outside the band widths for *each* individual. The dimensional values are therefore positive or negative steps away from the limits.

Of course, the mean value (and the limits) for some individuals often differ considerably from others. People who appear always to shout or gesture widely offer a vivid contrast from those with limited pitch-contours as again contrasted to those who shift "automatically"; and those with "rich" voices where the timbre is a complex set of frequency vibrations in contrast to flat monotonal speakers have idiosyncratic influences on the other person, often sufficient to alter the interactional pattern because the presenting deviations of the normal range make adjustment difficult.

The second category of subdimensions involves the evocative properties of the symbols used. Though they occur within interaction durations and their communicative (response-eliciting) capacity is modified by the subdimensions just described, they can, of course, affect the probabilities on their own. One obvious type is denotative. By word or gesture, one person can designate one or more others as the addressees from whom a response is expected. It does not follow that this response will happen automatically, but the probabilities are high in many situations that others present will not reply when it is unintended by the sender. Further, the symbols may indicate, through cultural conditioning again, the pattern of interaction to be manifested, e.g., an employment interview, a selling transaction, entering the confessional.

A discussion of the process through which symbols take on meaning cannot be included in this paper. However, it is obvious and well demonstrated in work both with animals and humans (Chapple, 1970) that this takes place through a process of accretion where repetition in a series of contexts of situation results in the symbol standing for some uniformity of occurrence which characterizes the events making up these contexts. In effect, learning or conditioning (whatever term is preferred) results in a series of abstractions from the contexts of living, and these abstractions are graded by degree of inclusiveness into what are called levels of abstractions.

Each level actually represents a category with the greatest specificity of reference to the individual event. If we were to assume arbitrarily that we were beginning in any cultural situation *de novo*, then the word "father" might be used to refer to a person who has just behaved toward one in a particular way. As life, and interaction, goes on, the word takes on a highly complicated set of meanings built up out of the emotional-interactional contexts in which the two persons have taken part. Alternatively, the term may be used for broader and broader degrees of inclusiveness for many individuals in a relationship to some one person—the priest as Father, the ruler as Father of his Country, and so on. Without needing to labor the point, one can see how symbols can be ranged on a scale either vertically (hierarchically) or longitudinally by the levels of abstraction which they represent; in fact, the dimensional character of symbols is denoted by the practice of referring to abstractions (and defining them) as first-order, second-order, and as many higher orders as one can identify. For scaling purposes, then, one can hypothecate that the evocative properties of symbols is a function of the level of abstraction which they represent—the higher the level, the greater the impact.

Granted that such a scale presents semantic difficulties since often only examination of the total context (and other contexts) will tell one, particularly in the longitudinal case, whether saying the word "Father" is simply denotative and indicates that one would like to interact (this constituting the content of the initiation of action), or whether it is at a higher level, usually indicated by shifts in amplitude, pitch and timbre: "Oh Father, Dear Father, Come Home with Me Now." Thus, symbols vary in their evocative capacity, in the degree to which they are selected as those which are liable to have the most "meaning" emotionally for the other person, with shifts in voice and gesture accompanying their use and their juxtaposition in the communicative sequence. How evocative is then determined by success in producing a response and the extent of its quantitative properties, including the rhythms of responding by which the repetition of such symbols structures the interaction patterns of the responders. Thus the symbolic elements set up constraints on the tempos of the individuals interacting and can build toward synchrony or asynchronous adjustment. Moreover, the train of association of symbols in a communicative sequence provides a framework within which idiosyncratically required durations of actions (and inactions) can occur, although beginnings and endings can be obliterated or emphasized in terms of the linguistic content of speech. Again, these are probabilistic elements, since the actual pattern of interaction which is observed and measured may override the grammatical and semantic constraints of the communication process. Nevertheless, the language of any people evidences the remarkable elaboration of its rhythmic substrates, for the emotional impact of the symbol or symbols can structure responses to the beat required by the speaker. Conversely, where there is increasing lack of synchronization, the symbols lose their effects and the speaker his audience.

Moreover, particular cultural situations themselves may increase the probabilities to a relatively high degree. These include rituals, ceremonies, and theatrical performances, where words, and often gestures and bodily movements, are prescribed and followed to the letter. Yet the rhythm, and often the relative distribution of action and silence, as well as the initiative and dominance variables, are capable of wide variation, not only as a consequence of the idiosyncratic characteristics of an individual personality, but as a means of varying the "meaning." Occasionally, one may have the opportunity to see (or arrange) a play in which the actors deliberately change their interaction patterns, using the same words, and play it first as a comedy, and then as a tragedy. Slowness of pace or long latencies immediately shift the viewer's expectations to the tragic; very fast pace and frequent interruptions are obvious elements in the pattern of humor.

The Elaboration of Roles from the Cultural Categories Although not directly relevant to the mathematical formulation, it is worth pointing out that interrelations between elements of these categories combine to make up distinguishable patterns of interactions commonly referred to by the term "role." Actually, one should more properly refer to subroles or a spectrum of roles, rather than assume that the usual role label, whether it be applied to being a mother, a salesman, a doctor, or whatever, has specific quantitative definition. More properly, in a stricter definition they can be referred to as interaction forms (Chapple 1970) analogous to musical forms, since they represent a sequential arrangement of elements. These interaction forms vary quantitatively as a function of the situation that elicits them. For any given individual, they are further varied by the limits of his interactional properties. Thus there is not one interaction form for being a salesman; there are clearly defined differences depending on the type of selling being done, whether it be insurance, selling consumer goods to a dealer, or working as a salesman in a department store. Here we have validated seven quite different patterns, depending on the pace, the sequencing and the spatial relations, e.g., selling women's hosiery at a counter, men's clothing from racks, or moving around the floor of the furniture department selling a living room "suite" (Chapple 1957).

Further, even a relatively unambiguous "role" like that of selling has other quite interactionally distinct interaction forms which make it up: a salesman may supervise, transmit inquiries to other areas, negotiate (when the customer wants to return a purchase), etc. In more complex roles like that of mother or doctor, the interaction patterns are highly varied, for mothers (or doctors) interview, supervise, sell, and perform a variety of interaction forms, however well or badly, in their relationship to children or patients.

The significance of these interaction forms lies in the fact that particular combinations of variables, quantitatively varied, are selected out (and can be learned to a considerable extent) by the interplay of the individuals involved in the relationship; effective performance can be shown to be related to the degree to which the individual is able to behave in a particular quantitative pattern, and not another. From the point of view of this paper, the importance of "roles" lies in the fact that they represent an intersection of the three cultural categories described above such that probabilities can be much more highly specified for particular patterns of interaction than for others. Again, idiosyncratic factors play an important part. Many individuals are unable to perform the interaction form called for by the situation simply because the parameters of their basic state equations cannot be fitted within its constraints. "Role disharmony," then, within any cultural situation, increases the probability of disturbance, if not for both members of the relationship, certainly for one of those taking part.

The Probabilistic Equations

The assumption that both the initial state equations for each individual, as well as the system equations representing the cumulative effects of changes in his state parameters over time, are deterministic is, in my opinion, a most useful way of looking at the phenomena. In effect, we are saying that whatever the event in which the individual interacts, the nature of his reactions to that event are functionally determined by the equations describing the properties of his equilibrium state. On the other hand, it is equally true that the occurrence of just that particular event with that particular person at given stages in each of their equilibrium states is probabilistic, since cultural constraints act to interfere with what might otherwise be an entirely closed system.

Thus when we turn to consider the interrelations of a group of individuals, whose individual reactions we can formulate deterministically, our organization model would regard each event as carrying with it a set of parameters derived from the system equations of the two individuals with specific degrees of complementarity or maladjustment. The impact of these parameters would, in addition, be a function of the event's duration and the interval of time during which one or the other was not in interaction thereafter.

Since interaction is a transitive process (which is why we can treat all the persons with whom individual i interacts as representing a single j in his equilibrium state equations), compensatory interactions depend on the probabilities that given individuals are available, or for that matter not available, due to the operation of the cultural constraints. Durations, frequencies, and opportunities to initiate are thus in large part probabilistic. Choice of one person in contrast to another with expected contributions to equilibrium or disequilibrium is dependent both on actual availability within a spatial location and a contiguous position in the sequenced activity flow; it also involves encountering a communicative pattern as part of an interaction form that may or may not be interactionally satisfactory.

By analogy with the nuclear model, the organizational system of relationships of however many individuals may be regarded as consisting of interactional packets of varying amounts of adjustment (and thus of emotional impact), occurring with varying frequencies and durations, partly controlled by the interactional requirements imposed by each person's equilibrium state equations and partly by the probabilities which the cultural categories interpose. Thus the organizational equilibrium equations that ultimately should be formulated will have quite different properties than those for the individual; in fact, for many persons, equilibrium of the system means disequilibrium for them, with compensatory interaction only to be managed through membership in other organizations to which some other part of the 24-hour period can be devoted.

Actually, the absolute number of persons available for interaction, even without the differentiation introduced by cultural categories, requires us to be concerned with probability *if* we are to attempt to describe the relational system of any given number of individuals. The mere appearance within interactional range of a third person is sufficient to complicate the formulation, since one is no longer able to regard all the interaction of any person i as limited to pair (dyadic) interaction with each particular j. Instances occur in which the action of one person (commonly his initiation of an action) is followed by actions of the other two more or less simultaneously, and these conjoint synchronizations have to be taken into account. I have called such occurrences, "set (or group) events" (Chapple 1940), and continuous observation of the interaction of groups of people indicates that they are interspersed with the more characteristic, and longer lasting, pair events. In rituals and ceremonies, in public meetings and, above all, in military activities, these set events may follow a rhythm in their own right, with alternation of action and inaction, precisely as with pairs, except that one member of the relationship is multiple (and, of course, there are also situations where more than one person may be initiating synchronously to the group or alternating interactionally with them).

The important thing about these set events is that they organize individuals in groups vis-à-vis one another and habituate them to respond sequentially. In fact, they are the basis for the structuring or organization of relationships, since they polarize individuals in common positions in the interactional sequence. Although there has been much use in the literature of such phrases as "power structures," "dominance hierarchies," and the like, assumed to be based on the dominance of i over j, which then entitles him to initiate at a later date to j, the fact is that *no* hierarchy can be based on pair events, since there is no ordering of individuals into a common position with regard to one another—only a percentage difference in the number of times that one or the other takes the initiative.

When these set events take place with any frequency, the interplay of the cultural categories tends to differentiate the ordering of the individuals so that they fall into classes holding the same position in the interaction sequence. There then develops an ordered sequence of such classes or groups which I have called "sets" (though, since we are now concerned with mathematical models, they should more properly be called "interactional sets") (Chapple 1940). The definition of an interactional set is that it consists of an aggregate of interactional relations of such a nature that every individual in the set is a member of one of three primary classes or relationships:

1. A class of individuals who only initiate.
2. An intermediate class, which may have many subclasses, $2a$, $2b$, ..., $2n$, who respond to members of Class 1 when they initiate and who, in turn, initiate to members of Class 3.
3. A terminal class of individuals who only respond, and never initiate, in set events to members of Classes 1 and 2. At some time, every initiator takes part in a set event with two or more individuals in the responding class, thereby making evident in overt action his relative position.

This does not mean that individuals in the lower classes in the interactional set do not initiate to those above them; they may do so in pair events, and there are extensive cultural patterns by which relative position and appropriate directional interaction in set events are maintained.

It is easy to recognize that these interactional sets provide the operational definition of hierarchies. In simple cultures, only Class 1 and Class 3 may be present; in more complicated organizations such as large corporations or governments or in the army, Class 2 is differentiated into a number of subclasses. Interactional sets are not, however, only hierarchical in the traditional sense. The constraints of sequenced activity flow as well as the other correlative cultural categories produce other interactional sets that structure the relations of the individuals and produce *other* directional polarities, so that a Class 1 individual in one set may be in Class 3 in another, e.g., the president of a company having to respond with the other members of his management to the union. These interactional sets, differentiated by the cultural dimensions, form the basis of complex organizational systems. They are by no means static and fixed; they fluctuate as a function of the cultural situations and the equilibrium states of the constituent individuals.

In this paper, we cannot be concerned with the problem of the model of the complex organization since its successful formulation, even the preliminary description of its properties, depends on adequate definition of the state equations of the individual. Nevertheless, it is worth emphasizing the unique importance of synchronous response patterns in set events for individuals, since this common simultaneity has very direct stabilizing effects on the individual's interaction rhythms. How it does this is still not clear, yet there is no question that both animals and humans (treated as separate, purely linguistically) have highly developed patterns of group response. Among the mammals at least, this is enforced by dominance on the part of the members of the higher class in the set. Individuals and groups try to shift their relative positions by various means, from nonresponse to open conflict. In other publications (Chapple 1940; Chapple and Coon 1942; Chapple 1962), some of the basic properties of complex organizations as systems have been described and, in a future publication, I hope to be able to bring these together in a useful form. For our purposes here, the set events must be regarded as predominantly occurring within the framework of the cultural constraints (and for the lower animals, the interdependence of environment and patterns of adaptation thereto and to one another) whose influence cannot be disregarded in a final formulation of the mathematical models that combine individuals and groups into one common framework.

References

Altmann, Stuart A.
1965 "Primates: Communication and Social Interactions," *Science* 149:886–887.
Aschoff, Jurgen
1960 "Exogenous and Endogenous Components in Circadian Rhythms," in *Cold Spring Harbor Symposia on Quantitative Biology*, Vol. 25 (New York: Long Island Biological Association), pp. 11–28.
Barker, R. G., and H. F. Wright
1951 *One Boy's Day: A Specimen Record of Behavior* (New York: Harper and Brothers).
Bowlby, J., *et al.*
1962 "Childhood Bereavement and Psychiatric Illness," in *Aspects of Psychiatric Research*, D. Richter, ed. (London: Oxford University Press), pp. 262–293.
Bruce, V. G.
1960 "Environmental Entrainment of Circadian Rhythms," *Cold Spring Harbor Symposia on Quantitative Biology*, Vol. 25 (New York: Long Island Biological Association), pp. 29–48.
Chapple, E. D.
1940 "Personality Differences as Described by Invariant Properties of Individuals in Interaction," *Proceedings of the National Academy of Sciences* 26:10–16.
1949 "The Interaction Chronograph: Its Evolution and Present Application," *Personnel* 25:295–307.
1952 "The Training of the Professional Anthropologist: Social Anthropology and Applied Anthropology," *American Anthropologist* 54:340–342.

1953 "The Standard Experimental (Stress) Interview as Used in Interaction Chronograph Investigations," *Human Organization* 12:23–32.
1957 "Report on the Selection and Placement of Sales People with the Interaction Chronograph for the Associated Merchandise Corporation," N.Y. Unpublished monograph.
1962 "Quantitative Analysis of Complex Organizational Systems," *Human Organization* 21, No. 2, pp. 67–80.
1970 *Culture and Biological Man* (New York: Holt, Rinehart & Winston).

Chapple, E. D., and C. S. Coon
1942 *Principles of Anthropology* (New York: Henry Holt & Company).

Chapple, E. D., and L. R. Sayles
1961 *The Measure of Management* (New York: Macmillan).

Chapple, E. D., *et al.*
1954 "Behavioral Definitions of Personality and Temperament Characteristics," *Human Organization* 13:34–39.
1960 "Interaction Chronograph Method for Analysis of Differences between Schizophrenics and Controls," *A.M.A. Archives of General Psychiatry* 3:160–167.

Gellhorn, E. and G. N. Loofbourrow
1963 *Emotions and Emotional Disorders* (New York: Hoeber).

Hall, Edward T.
1959 *The Silent Language* (New York: Doubleday and Company).
1966 *The Hidden Dimension* (New York: Doubleday and Company).

Harlow, H. F., and Harlow, M. K.
1962 "Social Deprivation in Monkeys," *Scientific American* 207, No. 5:136.

Hymes, Dell, *et al.*
1964 "Toward Ethnographies of Communication," *American Anthropologist*, John J. Gumperz and Dell Hymes eds., 66, No. 6, pt. 2, pp. 1–34.

Jaffe, Joseph, *et. al.*
1963 *Proceedings of the 1963 Rochester Conference on Data Acquisition and Processing in Biology and Medicine*, K. Enslein, ed. (New York: Pergamon).
1964 "Markovian Model of Time Patterns of Speech," *Science* 144:884–886.

Jensen, Gordon D., *et al.*
1964 "Effects of the Early Environment on Interaction Development," in *Advances in Child Development*, N. Wagner, ed. (New York: Random House).

Kendon, Adam
1965 "Some Functions of Gaze Direction in Social Interaction," Institute of Experimental Psychology, Oxford University (unpublished).

Lindsay, R. B., and H. Margenau
1957 *Foundations of Physics* (New York: Dover Publications).

Matarazzo, J. D., *et al.*
1959 "A Technique for Studying Changes in Interview Behavior," in *Research in Psychotherapy* (Washington, D.C.: American Psychological Association).

Molina, Edward C.
1927 "Application of the Theory of Probability to Telephone Trunking Problems,"
Bell System Technical Journal 6:461–494.

Pittendrigh, C. S.
1960 "Circadian Rhythms and the Circadian Organization of Living Systems,"
Cold Spring Harbor Symposia on Quantitative Biology, Vol. 25 (New York: Long Island
Biological Association), pp. 159–184.

Roberts, J. M.
1965 *Zuni Daily Life* (New York: Taplinger).

Sargant, W.
1964 *Battle for the Mind* (Baltimore: Penguin Books).

Sommer, R.
1959 "Studies in Personal Space," *Sociometry* 22: 247–260.

Spitz, R. A.
1945: "Hospitalism: An Inquiry into the Genesis of Psychiatric Conditions in
Early Childhood," in *The Psychoanalytic Study of the Child* (New York: International
Universities Press), p. 53.

Volterra, V.
1930 *Theory of Functionals and of Integral and Integro-Differential Equations* (New York:
Dover Publications).

4

PROBABILISTIC METHODS

Introduction

Hoffmann applies the theory of finite Markov chains to the age-grade system of the Galla tribes of Ethiopia. According to the ethnographer, each man enters the age-grade system at the moment his father leaves it—regardless of his own age—and remains in the system exactly forty years. Hoffmann is concerned with specifying the nature of the social and demographic conditions under which such a system can remain stable, if any, and under what conditions it may be expected to change in a given direction.

Hoffmann takes as his criterion of stability that there not be a long-run increase in the proportion of older men in the younger age-grades. (There are five age-grades, each of eight years' duration, in the system.) He models the system as a three-state finite Markov chain where the states are essentially *youth*, *adult*, and *senior citizen* and the transition probabilities express the likelihood that the son of a man who entered the lowest age-grade as, say, a youth, will himself enter the system as a youth, adult, or senior citizen. Hoffmann selects arbitrary but reasonable transition probabilities, which do not reflect any apparent bias toward stability. Since all the transition probabilities are positive, the chain is regular and Hoffmann applies the fundamental theorem of regular Markov chains to derive the limiting probability vector. For the transition probabilities selected, this comes out to be **26% *youths*, 45% *adults*, and 28% *senior citizens*, a not unreasonable result.**

Hoffmann argues that this type of approach can have the advantages of (*a*) revealing types of social ideology which require highly special demographic conditions to remain stable and (*b*) pointing out particular types of empirical observations that should be made to get a deeper understanding of stability and change in social systems.

What is a stable culture? Is a tribe likely to persist as described in an ethnography at one point in time or must it inevitably evolve into a different configuration? Is it possible to develop a model that would permit anthropologists to predict the future of a tribe?

Such models break into several types. Some are decision procedures that differentiate complementary cultural processes inherent in observed data. Others abstract ongoing cultural phenomena by including time among their variables. Binford's "'Red Ocher' Caches from the Michigan Area: A Possible Case of Cultural Drift" (1963) is an example of the first type. Binford's model analyzes the changes in shape of cache blades from different sites over time. It determines whether these changes arise from the establishment of daughter communities or from the random variation to be expected among independent villages. This paper is an example of the second type. It abstracts certain features of Ethiopian age grades and predicts their future course.

Models can transform a culture into some point of the future in two ways.

Markov Chains in Ethiopia **9**
HANS HOFFMANN

Deterministic models specify exactly which of several alternative configurations will follow any given configuration as the culture moves through time. *Stochastic* models specify the probabilities governing the transitions from state to state. The precision of deterministic models makes them obviously desirable, but they often do not survive for long in the raw and complex world of reality. When a deterministic model is developed in anthropology, it often has a severely restricted scope. Stochastic (or probabilistic) models circumvent this limitation. However, they merely specify the relative probabilities of the various configurations that could follow any given configuration. This type of prediction is less precise than that provided by deterministic models. However, since stochastic models can more readily encompass the world as it is, their contribution to anthropological theory is likely to be greater. This paper develops a stochastic model of cultural evolution.

Cultural stability and cultural evolution are two aspects of the same phenomenon. Hence a model of cultural stability may, if sufficiently general, also serve as a model of cultural evolution. That is, an analysis of the conditions necessary for cultural stability can often illuminate why (and perhaps even how) a tribe may change. From a logical point of view it would seem that knowledge of cultural stability is a prerequisite for the understanding of cultural evolution. From a practical point of view it appears that conditions necessary for stability are more accessible to analysis than are general statements about culture change. One is tempted to recall a parallel case in mathematics where a refractory subject—elliptic integrals—yielded its secrets once the inverse problem—elliptic functions—was attacked by Abel. The stochastic model developed in this paper reflects the reciprocal nature of cultural stability and culture change.

This paper will be developed in terms of ethnographic data from Ethiopia. Among the Shoa Galla government operates through a system of age grades of the Gada, or cycling, type. Murdock (1959: 326) describes their structure as follows:

One basic system prevails throughout both the pastoral and sedentary Galla tribes. This consists of five grades, typically named the Daballe, Folle, Kondala, Luba, and Yuba grades. Age sets, in which membership endures for life, spend eight years successively in each grade, with a spectacular ceremony marking each transition. When there are five, a son belongs to a set bearing the same name as his father's, and is initiated into the first grade when his father retires from the fifth, i.e. exactly forty years later.

It is evident that the stability of Galla communities is threatened by the arbitrary interval of 40 years that is interposed between the generations. Since this interval is often greater than the actual chronological difference between generations, the ages of some of the people in the grades may become progressively greater. This can result in humiliation and incongruity. An old man, entering the first grade, would be required to abstain from sexual activity and to wander around with its youthful members begging food from the married women. Further, if he should die before attaining the higher grades, important administrative, judicial, and priestly offices may go unfilled.

Is it possible to predict under what conditions this state of affairs will not arise? That is, is it possible to deduce from the formal structure of the Shoa Galla age grades necessary conditions that will ensure cultural stability? If this were the case, it would be possible to look for these conditions during field work and to predict whether this institution would remain stable or not.

A Deterministic Model of the Gada System

This question gave rise to the following deterministic model of the evolution of the Gada system, which transforms a small segment of Galla culture n generations into the future (Hoffmann 1965):

$$A_{n+1} = A_1 + nk - \sum_{i=1}^{n} P_i,$$

where A represents the age of a person when joining the first grade and P his age as he becomes a father. Subscripts denote generations and k the number of years any person remains in all of the various age grades. The model specifies exactly the age at which a distant offspring will enter the first grade, given the age at which his ancestor n generations before entered them.

From this model the stability of a particular Gada system can be deduced as follows. It was postulated that a realistic (i.e., stable) relationship between age and role behavior can be maintained if, between any arbitrary number of generations, the ages at which an ancestor and his distant offspring entered the first grade are equal. It is easy to deduce from the model that this criterion will be met if the *average* age of parenthood from Ego to the father of his distant offspring were equal to the number of years one spent in the grades; i.e., if

$$1/n \sum_{i=1}^{n} P_i = k,$$

then the postulated condition $A_{n+1} = A_1$ is met. This criterion is intuitively evident when considering adjacent generations. It is less obvious, however, that severe oscillations in ages of parenthood can also result in a stable culture. This surmise requires a mathematical demonstration.

Deterministic models have many uses in science. They abstract the intrinsic structure of empirical data such as the Gada system. This permits one to classify such data according to criteria of structural identity. Further, the abstractness of such models facilitates their application in unsuspected empirical contexts. For example, a century ago Maxwell predicted the existence of radio waves from his model of electromagnetic phenomena. These were duly found by Hertz in 1888. Today Maxwell's model has wide application in such recent developments as the electron microscope. In anthropology, the model of the Gada system was used by the writer merely to deduce a criterion for the stability of age grade systems. Another anthropologist, immersed in totally different problems, may deduce from it empirical consequences of even wider and more exciting significance.

On the other hand, this model of the Gada system has severe limitations. It deals only with one-dimensional father-son links and ignores the branching of descent lines representing siblings. Nor does it consider a tribe as a social entity consisting of a bundle of different descent lines. In other words, the model abstracts only a narrow slice of the Gada system rather than its entirety. This particular defect could be surmounted without leaving the realm of deterministic models. Mathematically a clutch of siblings is equivalent to a set of father-son links. Each of these can then be evaluated separately by the model. From such computations one can make an informal (and perhaps a formal) estimate of the degree of stability of Galla culture.

This solution is treacherous. While the revised model abstracts a more extensive portion of the Gada system it obscures a second liability of the original model, namely that it abstracts features of the tribe that may have no existence. Further, such unjustified exuberance will characterize any similar deterministic model of ongoing social systems. The model transforms any given family into some point of the future where it may no longer exist. This occurs because the model contains no restrictions on the length of the father-son chain that it abstracts. The subscript n, denoting number of generations, is not confined within some boundaries. Empirically this would mean that any father-son chain will continue indefinitely, that male heirs will always be produced in any given family. Obviously this is absurd. The most diligent of Galla progenitors will at times be the frustrated father of all-female offspring.

Why then was the original model published at all? It remains a valid and useful device for deducing a criterion for the stability of Galla culture. It is not, however, sufficiently general to describe Galla culture as an ongoing social phenomenon. The model permits one to say: "The Gada system will work if, for any given chain of father-son links that is observed to be n generations long,

$$1/n \sum_{i=1}^{n} P_i = k."$$

It does not, however, permit one to say that any given chain of father-son links *will* endure for n generations. We cannot predict *exactly* how long any chain will be because no one can (as yet) control the sex of his offspring. Further, random fluctuations in the physical environment such as floods or epidemics may carry off males before they can participate in the Gada system. We can predict only the most probable lengths of such chains; i.e., after much statistical evaluation of much census data we can predict *approximately* how long any chain is likely to endure. In other words, a deterministic model, which would predict this information exactly, cannot realistically be proposed. Instead we must be content with the more oblique probabilistic information generated by stochastic models.

Anthropological theory is not unique in having this intrinsic limitation. Feynman (1963: 2–6), commenting on the nature of quantum mechanics, notes that

... it is not possible to predict *exactly* what will happen in any circumstance. For example, it is possible to arrange an atom which is ready to emit light, and we can measure when it has emitted light by picking up a photon particle.... We cannot, however, predict *when* it is going to emit light or, with several atoms, *which one* is going to. You may say that this is because there are some internal "wheels" which we have not looked at closely enough. No, there *are* no internal wheels; nature, as we understand it today, behaves in such a way that it is *fundamentally impossible* to make a precise prediction of *exactly what will happen* in a given experiment.

A Stochastic Model of the Gada System

Formal criteria for the stability of a cultural system are an abstraction of various empirical conditions. These must be aired and agreed upon before there is much point in describing them mathematically. We noted earlier that the stability of Galla culture is threatened by a disparity between chronological age and cultural role; for example, an old man entering the first grade would have to abstain from sexual activity and wander around begging food from married women. Hence it is desirable that the first grade should consist largely of adolescents. At this point we postulate that the absolute number of age grade members is less crucial than the relative number. If most of the candidates for initiation are adolescents, the culture remains tranquil. If most of them are older men, there will be much psychological distress and much pressure to ignore or change the Gada system. We suggest that this will occur whether "most of the candidates" refers to 10 or to 100 of them. This is not to say that 10 misfits will generate as much pressure as 100 of them. It does say that *even* 10 misfits will threaten the Gada system if these happen to comprise three-quarters of that age grade.

The Gada system consists of five patrilineages moving through time. They are staggered eight years apart, i.e., a newly formed age set from one of these lineages is initiated into the system every eight years. Thus any one lineage contributes an age set to the system once every 40 years. The model will abstract each patrilineage separately.

Every 40 years a patrilineage injects a new set into the Gada system. This set may enhance or disturb the stability of the system during its tenure in the five grades. However, since there are five such patrilineages, the imbalance created by one may be absorbed by the others. This more general problem will be set aside for the moment. Instead we will investigate the effect on cultural stability of any one of the patrilineages.

Any age set has many numerical properties, such as the number of its members, or the distribution of their ages. Such properties may be called vectors because they describe the set at a point in time. The history of age sets (or of a patrilineage) can be described by the changing values of the components of this vector. This model predicts these changes as the patrilineage moves through time.

At this point an expansion of terminology becomes necessary. A vector describing an age set may consist of a single component (number of people in that set). More commonly it contains several different components: number of people in their teens, number of people in their twenties, number of people age 30 or older. In the literature of Markov processes (the mathematical structure underlying this model) these components are customarily called "states." The boundaries of states are arbitrarily defined, according to the problem at hand. Here we partition any vector into three states as follows: s_1 = ages 13–19, s_2 = ages 20–29, s_3 = ages 30 or older. Vectors are recorded as n-tuples of numbers. If there are 100 males in an age set of a patrilineage at a point in time distributed among the states as follows: 25 in s_1, 55 in s_2, 20 in s_3, then the vector is written (25, 55, 20). This model is more concerned with the proportion rather than the absolute number of people in each state. Such information can also be written in vector notation: (0.25, 0.55, 0.20). By definition, the n components of such a vector add up to one. Because of this property it is called a probability vector. Further, since it describes the states at the beginning of an arbitrary time sequence, it is called an initial probability vector.

We noted earlier that an age set about to enter the grades must consist largely of adolescents if the Gada system is to survive. That is, s_1 should encompass a substantial proportion of age set members, while s_3 should include only a small proportion of people. Further, there should not be much drift in population from s_1 to s_3 as new age sets are formed, although a drift in the reverse direction is desirable. The model discussed in this paper predicts the direction and intensity of such drifts.

Consider two contiguous age sets (i.e., that are 40 years apart) on the eve of their respective initiations into the Gada system. Males in the earlier set will produce sons at various times, all of whom enter the Gada system at the same time but at different ages. That is, a father may contribute sons to a variety of states in the later set. This raises the question of where the sons came from, i.e., how may sons in s_1 were born of s_1 fathers, of s_2 fathers, of s_3 fathers? Assume that these figures are 10, 55, and 5. This relationship between the two age sets can be recorded as follows:

$$
\begin{array}{c}
\text{sons} \\
\begin{array}{ccc} s_1 & s_2 & s_3 \end{array} \\
\text{fathers } \begin{array}{c} s_1 \\ s_2 \\ s_3 \end{array} \left(\begin{array}{ccc} 10 & & \\ 55 & & \\ 5 & & \end{array} \right).
\end{array}
$$

To complete this hypothetical example, assume that 100 s_2 sons have the following origin: 25 from s_1 fathers, 60 from s_2 fathers, and 15 from s_3 fathers. Comparable figures for s_3 sons may be 30, 35, and 5. These data can be entered in the array

$$
\begin{array}{c}
\begin{array}{ccc} s_1 & s_2 & s_3 \end{array} \\
\begin{array}{c} s_1 \\ s_2 \\ s_3 \end{array} \left(\begin{array}{ccc} 10 & 25 & 30 \\ 55 & 60 & 35 \\ 5 & 15 & 5 \end{array} \right).
\end{array}
$$

At this point the entries in the array are converted to fractions such that each row adds up to one:

$$\begin{pmatrix} 10/65 & 25/65 & 30/65 \\ 55/150 & 60/150 & 35/150 \\ 5/25 & 15/25 & 5/25 \end{pmatrix}.$$

This transformed array may be read: "10/65 of the sons of s_1 fathers entered the Gada system in s_1, 25/65 of the sons of s_1 fathers entered the Gada system in s_2, and so on." We need not assume as in the previous model that each father had only one son, or that each male in the earlier set contributed at least one offspring to the second set. A final step of data processing converts the fractions of the array into decimals, which results in a modest saving of space and an increase in clarity:

$$\begin{pmatrix} 0.154 & 0.384 & 0.462 \\ 0.367 & 0.400 & 0.233 \\ 0.200 & 0.600 & 0.200 \end{pmatrix}.$$

Thus far the array (or matrix) has been treated as a passive information storage device. The model will now endow it with a more active and autonomous existence. First of all, an entry in the matrix states that 0.154 of the sons of s_1 fathers entered the Gada system in s_1. This is a statement of frequency that may be rephrased in the language of probability theory: "There is a probability of 0.154 that the son of an s_1 father will enter the Gada system in s_1." Mathematically these statements are equivalent. The matrix specifies the relative probabilities of each of the nine possible transitions from the state of a father to that of his son. Hence it is called a matrix of transition probabilities. This matrix is the stochastic model that transforms the Gada system from one point in time into the future.

The reciprocal nature of culture change and cultural stability is reflected in this model. We shall first use it to describe a part of Galla culture (namely a single patrilineage) as an ongoing social phenomenon. Specifically the model predicts the proportion of people found in the various states of an age set 40 years in the future. Further, if the transition probabilities remain relatively constant, the model will project the patrilineage into a sequence of points 40 n years into the future (where n is any whole integer from one on). This is accomplished as follows. A probability vector and a matrix of transition probabilities can be multiplied together. Their product is another probability vector which predicts the distribution of people among the states of an age set one "generation," i.e., 40 years away. This multiplication is defined by

$$(a, b)\begin{pmatrix} c & d \\ e & f \end{pmatrix} = (ac + be, ad + bf).$$

Using the data from the preceding example, we have

$$(0.25, 0.55, 0.20)\begin{pmatrix} 0.154 & 0.384 & 0.462 \\ 0.367 & 0.400 & 0.233 \\ 0.200 & 0.600 & 0.200 \end{pmatrix} = (0.28, 0.44, 0.28).$$

Thus the model predicts that there will be a slightly higher proportion of sons in s_3 than there were fathers a generation ago, and that this extra population has drifted into s_3 from s_2. The history of this patrilineage is becoming somewhat ominous.

It must be pointed out that this prediction could have been seen directly from the data used to calculate the matrix. However, the prediction for 80, 120, ... years in the future could not have been determined by inspection. These predictions are carried out by raising the matrix to higher powers, according to the following rule:

$$\begin{pmatrix} a & b \\ c & d \end{pmatrix}\begin{pmatrix} e & f \\ g & h \end{pmatrix} = \begin{pmatrix} ae + bg & af + bh \\ ce + dg & cf + dh \end{pmatrix}.$$

Hence we have

$$\begin{pmatrix} 0.154 & 0.384 & 0.462 \\ 0.367 & 0.400 & 0.233 \\ 0.200 & 0.600 & 0.200 \end{pmatrix}^2 = \begin{pmatrix} 0.260 & 0.490 & 0.250 \\ 0.270 & 0.451 & 0.279 \\ 0.291 & 0.437 & 0.272 \end{pmatrix}.$$

To predict the proportion of people in the various states two generations (80 years) in the future, we multiply the initial vector (generation zero) by the second power of the transition matrix:

$$(0.25\ 0.55.\ 0.20)\begin{pmatrix} 0.260 & 0.490 & 0.250 \\ 0.270 & 0.451 & 0.279 \\ 0.291 & 0.437 & 0.272 \end{pmatrix} = (0.27.\ 0.46.\ 0.27).$$

If the transition probabilities have remained about the same, the vector

$(0.27, 0.46, 0.27)$

constitutes this prediction. Earlier fears about the stability of this patrilineage seem less justified from a perspective of 80 years.

The utility of this model for describing Galla culture as an ongoing social phenomenon clearly hinges on whether the transition probabilities remain stationary or not. The inverse problem of cultural stability, however, can be discussed in any event. If they do remain stationary, the Gada system would be described as Markovian in nature. (A process defined in terms of a finite number of possible states is termed Markovian only if the probability of passing from one particular state to another is defined and is independent of prior states of the process.) Many genetic processes, chemical reaction kinetics, the spatial distribution of galaxies, and other phenomenon can be assumed to be Markovian (Bharucha-Reid 1960). On the other hand, this issue has received less attention in the behavioral sciences. Intergenerational occupational mobility as analyzed by Prais (1955: 56–66) appears to be Markovian, whereas attitude or behavior change through time does not (Coleman 1964). It is essential for our understanding of behavioral science data that it be screened for various intrinsic mathematical properties such as this one. A number of statistical aids that facilitate this project exist (Anderson and Goodman 1963: 241–262.)

Thus far the model abstracts the Gada system as an ongoing social phenomenon but can only project it into a future of successive 40-year intervals. It is possible to strengthen it so that its time perspective will encompass an unlimited number of such intervals at a glance. This brings the ultimate fate of any patrilineage within the Gada system into view. The mathematical machinery that constitutes the model is called a Markov chain. At this point a further assumption must be added, namely that some power of the transition matrix has no zero entries. This condition seems to pose few problems in the present context. We are now dealing with a regular (as opposed to an absorbing) Markov chain. The matrix of transition probabilities of a regular Markov chain has a remarkable property. As it is raised to higher and higher powers, it approaches a new matrix whose rows are identical. We represent one of these row vectors by (a_1, a_2, a_3). This vector is called the limiting vector for that Markov chain because it will not change when multiplied by the matrix of transition probabilities. Thus it represents the equilibrium proportions for that particular chain. When the age set members are distributed among the states in the proportions (a_1, a_2, a_3) the patrilineage has attained stability and will continue to duplicate this age set indefinitely (or until the matrix itself changes).

Regular Markov chains have another property of considerable interest. The limiting vector is independent of the initial probability vector. The early history of a patrilineage is not relevant to its future; only the matrix of transition probabilities determines what this future will be.

The isolation of the limiting vector proceeds as follows. First of all, the theorem under discussion guarantees the existence of a unique limiting vector associated with any regular Markov chain. Further, the theorem states that the limiting vector remains invariant when multiplied by the transition matrix. Hence the following matrix equation will hold:

$$(a_1, a_2, a_3) \begin{pmatrix} 0.154 & 0.384 & 0.462 \\ 0.367 & 0.400 & 0.233 \\ 0.200 & 0.600 & 0.200 \end{pmatrix} = (a_1, a_2, a_3),$$

which results in the three equations

$$0.154a_1 + 0.367a_2 + 0.200a_3 = a_1,$$
$$0.384a_1 + 0.400a_2 + 0.600a_3 = a_2,$$
$$0.462a_1 + 0.233a_2 + 0.200a_3 = a_3,$$

from which the limiting vector $(0.26, 0.45, 0.28)$ is readily computed.

The ultimate fate of this patrilineage is described by this limiting vector. If the data are Markovian, then the proportion of people in the three states will eventually become $s_1 = 0.26$, $s_2 = 0.45$, $s_3 = 0.28$. These values are not radically different from the initial vector $(0.25, 0.55, 0.20)$. Thus this patrilineage may be considered stable.

Conclusions

Following Braithwaite (1953) we will distinguish between a calculus and a model. A calculus is an abstract mathematical structure, a model its interpretation within an empirical context. Markov chains are the calculus here, transitions between age grades their interpretation. It remains a perennial question in science whether a particular interpretation of a calculus is valid or not. If the transition matrices are constant in Galla culture, then the interpretation is valid. At the present state of anthropological knowledge this is clearly a matter of conjecture rather than of fact. What then is the value of this discourse?

We have shown that the crucial data for evaluating the stability of Galla culture consist of the transition probabilities between age grades rather than of the number of people at one point in time. The initial vector is largely irrelevant; it is the transition matrix that determines the future of a patrilineage.

If we are unwilling to postulate the invariance of the transition matrix, it is still possible to use the model as a decision procedure. The limiting vector of an observed transition matrix is readily calculated. Then one can state: "This pattern of transitions is/is not compatible with the stability of the Gada system."

If, on the other hand, we are willing to postulate the invariance of the transition matrix, then the model abstracts the history of that patrilineage as an ongoing social phenomenon as its oscillations approach the limiting vector. It is a model of cultural evolution that enables an anthropologist to predict the future of the tribe.

References

Anderson, T. W., and Leo A. Goodman
1963 "Statistical Inference about Markov Chains," in *Readings in Mathematical Psychology*, R. Duncan Luce, Robert R. Bush, and Eugene Galanter, eds., Vol. I (New York: John Wiley & Sons).

Bharucha-Reid, A. T.
1960 *Elements of the Theory of Markov Processes and their Applications* (New York: McGraw-Hill Book Company).

Binford, Lewis R.
1963 "'Red Ocher' Caches from the Michigan Area: A Possible Case of Cultural Drift," *Southwestern Journal of Anthropology* 19: 89–108.

Braithwaite, R. B.
1953 *Scientific Explanation* (New York: Cambridge University Press).

Coleman, James S.
1964 *Introduction to Mathematical Sociology* (New York: Free Press).

Feynman, Richard P., Robert B. Leighton, and Matthew Sands
1963 *The Feynman Lectures on Physics* (Reading, Mass.: Addison-Wesley Publishing Company).

Hoffmann, Hans
1965 "Formal Versus Informal Estimates of Cultural Stability," *American Anthropologist* 67: 110–115.

Murdock, George Peter
1959 *Africa* (New York: McGraw-Hill Book Company).

Prais, S. J.
1955 "Measuring Social Mobility," *Journal of the Royal Statistical Society* 118: 56–66.

Introduction

Romney attacks the problem of assessing the degree of subgroup endogamy in an endogamous overall population composed of a finite number of subgroups, not necessarily of the same size.

In the special case of subgroups of equal size an appealing measure is apparent. Suppose there are k subgroups. Then there are k types of endogamous marriage and $\binom{k}{2} - k$ types of nonendogamous (exogamous) marriage. If we let $\bar{d}$ stand for the mean number of marriages in the k endogamous types and $\bar{o}$ for the mean number in the nonendogamous type, then overall subgroup endogamy is given by

$$\varepsilon = \frac{\bar{d} - \bar{o}}{\bar{d} + \bar{o}},$$

where ε is the proportion of those individuals who would be expected to marry exogamously under random mating who, in fact, have married endogamously.

However, the trick is to make a sensible calculation where the subgroups are unequal in size and/or contain unequal numbers of men and women. The general problem is to deal with a data matrix of the following form, where the entry a_{ij} is the number of recorded marriages between a male of subgroup i and a female of subgroup j.

Males	Females			
	Subgroup 1	$\cdots$	Subgroup k	
Subgroup 1	a_{11}	$\cdots$	a_1k	$a_1.$
.	.	$\cdots$	.	.
.	.	$\cdots$	.	.
.	.	$\cdots$	.	.
Subgroup k	a_{k1}	$\cdots$	a_{kk}	$a_k.$
	$a._1$	$\cdots$	$a._k$	N

No special constraints are allowed on the row and column totals. The logic of the problem here resides in the fact that we do not wish our measure to be affected by the number of groups or their relative sizes or sex ratios. Otherwise put, we imagine a two-stage process: in stage one couples meet on a random basis. The probability of meeting of any given couple-type (say male of group i and female of group j) is, of course, dependent on the proportions of the total population comprised by males of group i and females of group j. At stage two, our couple marries, or fails to marry, with a probability independent of the probability of their having met. Only the stage two probability represents a cultural predilection for endogamy

Measuring Endogamy **10**
A. KIMBALL ROMNEY

(exogamy) independent of the size and sex composition of actual groups. No existing measure of endogamy (e.g., Nicholl's index, cited by Ayoub, M. R., 1959, "Parallel Cousin Marriage and Endogamy: a Study in Sociometry," *Southwestern Journal of Anthropology* 15: 266–275) corresponds to pure marriage choice probabilities, independent of "meeting probabilities"; more precisely, none is independent of disparities in row and column totals. The problem thus stated is of some generality and not necessarily restricted to the endogamy/exogamy interpretation.

Romney's approach is to normalize the matrix to one in which all row and column sums are equal by use of a successive approximations (iterative) procedure. This involves alternate multiplications by two $k \times k$ diagonal matrices, whose entries in the diagonal cell a_{ii} are each the desired row (column) total divided by the row (column) total resulting from the previous multiplication. In practice all the desired row and column totals are taken as 100. An Appendix contains an algorithm for the iteration procedure furnished by William H. Geoghegan. The procedure is fully explained and exemplified in the text.

The result of the iteration procedure is a transformed data matrix whose row and column sums are all approximately 100. Then ε and functionally related measures are calculated on the transformed matrix.

Romney has not shown analytically that the iterative transformation of the data matrix preserves the desired properties. However, two independent computer simulations of some hypothetical data by Michael Burton and Roy G. D'Andrade, which are based directly on the two-stage marriage probability model, give results very close to Romney's procedure.

There are further indications that the iterative procedure does in fact produce the desired results. Thus ε and derivative measures may be calculated, not only overall, but for each pair of subgroups. On this basis, various hypotheses may be formed to account for the full marriage distribution. These hypotheses are expressed in what Romney calls a ratio table, which is a $k \times k$ hypothetical data matrix. This matrix is iterated back to the original marginals by the same procedure. The resulting cell frequencies are then compared to the original data, a close fit indicating that the theory embodied in the ratio table in fact accounts for the data.

Romney applies the full procedure to three sets of real data. In each case he succeeds in constructing a ratio table which, when iterated back to the original marginals, produces an excellent fit to the original data.

This paper suggests a procedure for the description and analysis of the patterns of marriage among a set of intermarrying groups. In addition, it provides some quantitative measures to express the strength of endogamy or exogamy among these groups.

The present procedures are limited to situations in which there is some endogamous population that is subdivided into a set of intermarrying groups. The procedures are not usually applicable in other situations.

Analysis begins with empirical data arranged in the form of a double polytomy represented in the accompanying table. Classification A divides the population into

Males	Females				
	A_1	A_2	$\cdots$	A_k	Total
A_1	a_{11}	a_{12}	$\cdots$	a_{1k}	$a_1.$
A_2	a_{21}	a_{22}	$\cdots$	a_{2k}	$a_2.$
$\vdots$	$\vdots$	$\vdots$	$\vdots$	$\vdots$	$\vdots$
A_k	a_{k1}	a_{k2}	$\cdots$	a_{kk}	$a_k.$
Total	$a._1$	$a._2$	$\cdots$	$a._k$	N

k groups $A_1, A_2, \ldots, A_k$. The groups may be lineages, sibs, religions, social classes, barrios, or whatever.

N represents the total number of married couples included in the study.

$a_1., a_2., \ldots, a_k.$ represent the number of males in each of the respective groups while $a._1, a._2, \ldots, a._k$ represent the number of females in each group.

a_{11}, a_{12}, etc., represent the number of married couples for each cell. For example, a_{12} represents the number of couples where the males are from group A_1 and the females are from group A_2.

The procedures described in this paper require complete data in the form just given.

In the model to be presented, the marriage process is conceptualized in two stages. In the first stage, male-female pairs "meet." In the second stage, those who "meet" either marry or do not marry. The probability of a male in a given group meeting a female in a given group is determined by the relative sizes of the different groups. The notion of "meeting" divides the population distribution into categories; e.g., a simple categorical distinction might be males meeting females of the same group versus males meeting females of a different group. The second stage posits differential preferences or probabilities of marriage in the different categories, e.g., the odds are 4 to 1 in favor of marrying a person of the same group versus marrying a person of a different group (regardless of how likely such a "meeting" may be). The indices that we propose are estimates of the strength of preferences in the second stage. The basic question that we are asking is to what extent one category of marriage partners is preferred over another.

The proposed measures are most easily understood in the case where there are equal numbers of individuals in each group and where there are equal numbers of males and females in each group. This situation focuses upon stage two since the probability

Table 1. Hypothetical Case of Two Intermarrying Groups of Equal Size.

Males	Females		
A_1	A_1	A_2	Total
A_1	70	30	100
A_2	30	70	100
Total	100	100	200

of meeting someone in any group, one's own or another, is the same. Table 1 illustrates such a situation, with just two groups, where we have hypothesized 100 males and 100 females in each of two groups. The proposed measure of endogamy is ε, and the formula is as follows:

$$\varepsilon = \frac{\bar{d} - \bar{o}}{\bar{d} + \bar{o}},$$

where $\bar{d}$ is the mean size of the diagonal cells and $\bar{o}$ is the mean size of the off-diagonal cells.

The computation for Table 1 is

$$\varepsilon = \frac{70 - 30}{70 + 30} = 0.4.$$

ε takes all values from -1 (complete exogamy) to $+1$ (complete endogamy). It also has the property of being zero when there is no tendency toward either endogamy or exogamy. In larger tables it may be computed between specified groups as well as for the overall table. It may also be computed for special patterns, e.g., marriage in a circle. It is independent of N and of the number of intermarrying groups. The ε of 0.4 calculated for Table 1 may be interpreted as indicating that 40% of those individuals who would have married outside their own group under conditions of random assortment actually married inside their own group. Two additional expressions of marriage preference derived from ε are useful. The proportion of people marrying within their own group is 0.7. We represent this by p. In terms of odds, it is $2\frac{1}{3}$ to 1 in favor of marrying within a person's own group. We represent this as R for the ratio of the proportion marrying in a person's own group.

ε, p, and R are related by the following formulas:

$$\varepsilon = 2p - 1, \qquad p = \frac{\varepsilon + 1}{2}, \qquad R = \frac{\varepsilon + 1}{1 - \varepsilon},$$

$$\varepsilon = \frac{2R}{1 + R} - 1, \qquad p = \frac{R}{1 + R}, \qquad R = \frac{p}{1 - p}.$$

Table 2. Hypothetical Case of Two Intermarrying Groups of Unequal Size.

Males	Females A_1	A_2	Total
A_1	126	24	150
A_2	24	26	50
Total	150	50	200

These indices are not applicable to tables where the marginals are unequal. When the marginals are unequal, then the probabilities of "meeting" people in a person's own category change. Since the indices above are meant to represent the preference of individuals at stage two, they should not be affected by unequal marginals. The way unequal marginals are handled is discussed with reference to Table 2.

Table 2 presents some hypothetical data in which the intermarrying groups are unequal in size. The problem is how to normalize a table such as Table 2 in order to compare marriage preferences between this situation and that in Table 1. Another way to express this is to ask how many marriages of each kind would have been expected to occur (holding marriage preferences constant) if there were equal numbers of people in each group (and equal numbers of males and females in each group).

Given a table with unequal marginals such as Table 2, we desire to normalize to a situation in which there are exactly 100 men and 100 women in each group (see the Appendix). This is done by an iterative process in which all rows are adjusted to 100. Columns are then adjusted, rows readjusted, etc., until both rows and columns are approximately correct. This procedure provides a good approximation. Exact solutions are difficult and beyond the scope of this paper.

In the above example, we begin by dividing 150 into 100 (equals 0.6667) and multiplying through the first row. Then divide 50 into 100 (equals 2.0) and multiply by the second row. The whole solution appears below.

Begin with   Gives:

126	24	150	first row times 0.6667	84	16	100
25	26	50	second row times 2.0	48	52	100
150	50	200		132	68	200

The columns are now corrected by multiplying through by appropriate corrective factors (0.7576 for the first column and 1.4706 for the second column) to get new row total

63.6364	23.5294	87.1658 × 1.4724
36.3636	76.4706	112.8342 × 0.8863
100	100	200

73.0062	26.9938	100
32.2275	67.7725	100
105.2337	94.7663	200
×0.9503	×1.0552	

69.3753	28.4846	97.8599 × 1.0219
30.6247	71.5154	102.1401 × 0.9790
100	100	200

70.8925	29.1075	100
29.9830	70.0170	100
100.8755	99.1245	200
×0.9913	×1.0088	

70.2772	29.3646	99.6418 × 1.0036
29.7228	70.6354	100.3582 × 0.9964
100	100	200

70.5298	29.4702	100
29.6167	70.3833	100
100.1465	99.8535	200
×0.9985	×1.0015	

This process yields the approximate solution (rounded and interpolated):

70.46	29.54	100
29.54	70.46	100
100	100	200

We call this process normalization by iteration. It enables us to reduce tables of any size to a standardized form in which each group has exactly 100 males and 100 females. The indices ε, p, and R are always computed from normalized tables. The three values for Table 2 are $\varepsilon = 0.4092$, $p = 0.7046$, and $R = 2.385$. We can thus state that Table 1 and Table 2 exhibit very similar degrees of intensity of endogamy.

The iteration procedure may also be used to provide expected frequencies for tables with unequal marginals, given a particular degree of endogamy. For example, we might like to know the exact expected number of marriages in which the ε value corresponds to Table 1 and the marginals correspond to Table 2. Here we begin with a normalized table (Table 1) and we desire to produce the expected frequencies where group A_1 has 150 males and 150 females and where A_2 has 50 males and 50 females.

In the preceding example we begin by dividing 100 into 150 (equals 1.5) and multiplying through the first row. Then divide 100 into 50 (equals 0.5) and multiply the second row. The example is worked through now.

Begin with				Gives:		
70	30	100	first row times 1.5	105	45	150
30	70	100	second row times 0.5	15	35	50
100	100	200		120	80	200

The columns are now corrected by multiplying through appropriate corrective factors (1.25 for the first column and 0.625 for the second column) and the process continued from columns to rows, rows to columns, etc.

131.25	28.125	159.375×0.9412
18.75	21.875	40.625×1.2308
150	50	200

123.5294	26.4706	150
23.0769	26.9231	50
146.6063	53.3937	200
$\times 1.0231$	$\times 0.9364$	

126.3889	24.7881	151.1770×0.9922
23.6111	25.2119	48.8230×1.0241
150	50	200

125.4049	24.5951	150
24.1803	25.8197	50
149.5852	50.4148	200
×1.0028	×0.9918	

125.7526	24.3927	150.1453 × 0.9990
24.2474	25.6073	49.8547 × 1.0029
150	50	200

125.6309	24.3691	150
24.3181	25.6819	50
149.9490	50.0510	200
×1.0003	×0.9990	

The approximate solution (rounded and interpolated) is

125.67	24.33	150
24.33	25.67	50
150	50	200

In this example we began the iteration with normalized frequencies. The same answer would have been obtained had we used $p = 0.7$ in the diagonal cells and $1 - p = 0.3$ in the off-diagonal cells. Similarly, the R could be used with $R = 2\frac{1}{3}$ in the diagonal cells and 1 in the off-diagonal cells. We have found the R measure generally most convenient as will become clear.

The expected numbers obtained by iteration represent the outcome predicted by the model of the two-stage marriage process. The unequal size of groups affected the probability of "meeting" and the ε provided an estimate (in this case, arbitrary) of preference for one's own group. In order to check the model and to clarify its operation, we designed a computer simulation of the process. A description of this simulation will help in understanding the model.

Suppose that we have two urns. Urn 1 contains 150 black marbles and 50 white marbles. Urn 1 represents the males in Table 2. Urn 2 contains 150 black marbles and 50 white marbles. Urn 2 represents the females in Table 2. We thus have a table with the following marginals:

Males Urn 1	Females Urn 2		
	A_1 black	A_2 white	
A_1 black	a	b	150
A_2 white	c	d	50
	150	50	200

The procedure for the computer simulation was as follows:

1. Draw a marble from Urn 1 at random (this corresponds to drawing a male from the village at random).

2. Draw a marble from Urn 2 at random (this corresponds to drawing a female from the village at random).

3. Compare the colors of the marbles (this is equivalent to determining whether or not they are from the same group). The probability that they are from the same group can be thought of as the probability of meeting someone from one's own group. Similarly, the probability of their being different colors represents the probability of people from different groups meeting. This completes stage one of the model.

4. If the marbles are of the same color (group), assign them a probability of marrying of 0.7 and use a random draw to determine whether or not they do marry. If they are different colors, assign them a probability of marrying of 0.3 and use a random draw to see whether or not they do marry. If marriage takes place in either circumstance, enter the marriage in the table and do not replace the marbles in the urns. If marriage does not take place, return the marbles to their respective urns and rerandomize each urn. This corresponds to stage two of the model.

5. Continue this process until both urns are empty.

Two independent computer simulations of the foregoing process were carried out. Roy D'Andrade wrote one program and ran 51 simulations. Michael Burton independently wrote a program and carried out 39 simulations. Since there is only one degree of freedom in a 2×2 table, we present data for the d cell only (endogamous marriages between A_2 males and A_2 females). The results for $p = 0.7$ and $1 - p = 0.3$ are as follows (results of the iteration are included for comparison):

D'Andrade simulation ($n = 51$)   25.00,

Burton simulation ($n = 39$)   25.90,

Romney iteration   25.67.

These figures for the simulation represent means of all trials.

Table 3. Data from Aguacatenango.

Males	Females A_1	A_2	A_3	
A_1	46	6	1	53
A_2	8	24	5	37
A_3	2	13	8	23
	56	43	14	113

It is important to note that the proposed indices of endogamy are completely independent of the number of males and females in each group. They represent the tendency to marry someone from one's own group irrespective of the probability of meeting someone in one's own group.

The utility of the indices may be illustrated in the analysis of some empirical data. The village of Aguacatenango in Chiapas, Mexico, was completely censused in 1964 by the author and Sara Nerlove. The village consists of two main barrios and a series of small outlying settlements adjacent to Barrio 2. We were able to obtain complete data on origins of 113 current marriages. These data are shown in Table 3. A_1 is Barrio 1, A_2 is Barrio 2, and A_3 is the series of outlying settlements. The first step in the analysis is to normalize the data by iteration. The normalized data for Aguacatenango are shown in Table 4.

The various indices are as follows:

$\varepsilon(1,2)$	$=0.65$	$p(1,2)$	$=0.83$	$R(1,2)$	$=4.79$
$\varepsilon(1,3)$	$=0.87$	$p(1,3)$	$=0.93$	$R(1,3)$	$=14.30$
$\varepsilon(2,3)$	$=0.27$	$p(2,3)$	$=0.64$	$R(2,3)$	$=1.74$
Overall $\varepsilon=0.58$		Overall $p=0.79$		Overall $R=$	3.77

Table 4. Normalized Aguacatenango Data (rounded to nearest whole number).

Males	Females A_1	A_2	A_3	
A_1	81	13	6	100
A_2	15	53	32	100
A_3	4	34	62	100
	100	100	100	300

The three ε figures with subscripts indicate the degree of endogamy among groups taken two at a time. The greatest degree of endogamy is found between groups 1 and 3 with an ε of 0.87. The R score equals 14.3. This may be interpreted as indicating that the odds (or preferences) are 14.3 to 1 in favor of marrying in a person's own group as between groups 1 and 3. An examination of Table 4 shows that the different indices form an ordered set with group 1 intermarrying most with group 2 and least with group 3, while group 2 intermarries most with group 3 and least with group 1. This corresponds to the geographic setting of the three groups, since Barrio 2 lies between Barrio 1 and the outlying settlements adjacent to Barrio 2.

It is possible to see whether or not the overall ε is sufficient to account for the observed pattern. The overall ε tells us the mean amount of endogamy on the assumption that all groups are intermarrying equally. In order to make this calculation, we form a table from overall R and iterate back to the original marginals. The appropriate ratio table is as follows:

3.77	1	1
1	3.77	1
1	1	3.77

The 3.77 may be interpreted to indicate that, in the village as a whole, the odds are 3.77 to 1 that an individual will marry into his own group, other things being equal, i.e., that the groups were of the same size. When the ratio table is iterated back to the original marginals, we obtain the following:

40.4	9.3	3.3	53
8.0	26.7	2.3	37
7.6	7.0	8.4	23
56	43	14	113

The cell frequencies here represent the theoretical expectation on the assumption that all groups are intermarrying equally among each other, where the odds are 3.77 to 1 that marriage is within own group, other things being equal. The calculated χ^2 with these frequencies as the theoretical expected and the frequencies in Table 3 as the observed is 12.5 (corrected for continuity). This size χ^2 with 4 degrees of freedom lies between the 0.02 and the 0.01 level of significance. We thus conclude that there is a real difference in the amount of intermarriage among different groups.

We can construct a ratio table utilizing all three ratios as follows:

$$R(1,2) = 4.79, \qquad R(1,3) = 14.3, \qquad R(2,3) = 1.74.$$

First, place largest ratio on diagonal and a 1 in the appropriate cells; thus,

	A_1	A_2	A_3
A_1	14.3		1
A_2		14.3	
A_3	1		14.3

where 14.3 is the largest ratio and the 1 is placed in cells 1,3 and 3,1. Next divide the other ratios into the largest and enter in appropriate cells, e.g., 4.79 goes into 14.3 about 3 times (2.99) so 3 is entered in cells 1,2 and 2,1. Similarly, as ratio (2,3), which is 1.74, goes into 14.3 about 8.2 (8.22) times, 8.2 is entered in cells 2,3 and 3,2. The completed table appears as follows:

Ratio Table for Aguacatenango

	A_1	A_2	A_3	
A_1	14.3	3	1	18.3
A_2	3	14.3	8.2	25.5
A_3	1	8.2	14.3	23.5
	18.3	25.5	23.5	67.3

The ratio table iterated back to original marginals (rounded to nearest whole numbers) gives

Men   Women

	A_1	A_2	A_3	
A_1	46	6	1	53
A_2	8	24	5	37
A_3	2	13	8	23
	56	43	14	113

Note that this corresponds to the original data and therefore verifies that the three indices are sufficient to account for the pattern of observed endogamy.

We can summarize to this point by suggesting a general informal algorithm for the analysis of a given set of data. The steps involved are as follows: (1) Arrange the observed data in the form shown on the first page of the article. (2) Obtain a normalized table by iteration where each group consists of 100 males and 100 females. (3) Compute the indices for the overall table and for each pair of intermarrying groups according to the formulas given above. (4) Examine the indices and form hypotheses about the pattern that seems most appropriate to the data. From these hypotheses some recomputation of summary indices may be necessary. On the basis of the hypotheses, form a table of ratios. (5) Iterate the table of ratios back to the original marginals. (6) Test the correspondence between the expected frequencies obtained in step 5 and the original data. The expected frequencies obtained in step 5 may be used as the theoretical frequencies in a χ^2 test with appropriate attention to small numbers. If the correspondence is close, the analysis is complete. If the obtained χ^2 is too large, go back to step 4 and form a new set of hypotheses.

We will illustrate the application of the algorithm on data published by Ayoub on a Druz Arab society (Ayoub 1959). Table 5 shows her original data. Ayoub does not distinguish males and females. Each marriage is seen as a mutual choice and appears twice. There is also marriage outside the village. Thus the data do not correspond to the assumption inherent in the model. For these reasons, the following exercise is to be taken as illustrating the method and not as a definitive substantive finding. Unfortunately, anthropological literature is almost devoid of data in the form needed for the computation of the suggested indices.

Step 2 involves normalizing the original data by the iterative procedures. Table 6 presents the data in normalized form. Step 3 involves the computation of the indices. Since there is very little marriage between the M family and the N family, we compute only those indices that refer to the subgroups within each of these larger groupings.

Table 5. Observed Frequency Distribution of Marriages by Lineage and Origin of Spouse (Ayoub 1959: 270).

Lineage	Origin of Spouse								
	MA	MB	MC	MD	NA	NB	NC	ND	R
MA	42	10	4	13					69
MB	10	22	3	6	1	1			43
MC	4	3	14	4					25
MD	13	6	4	60					83
NA		1			18	0	2	4	25
NB		1			0	18	6	6	31
NC					2	6	14	0	22
ND					4	6	0	18	28
C	69	43	25	83	25	31	22	28	324

Table 6. Ayoub's Data in Normalized Form.

	MA	MB	MC	MD	NA	NB	NC	ND	
MA	55.6	17.8	10.3	15.6	0	0	0	0	100
MB	18.6	55.0	10.8	10.1	2.6	2.2	0	0	100
MC	10.2	10.3	69.4	9.3	0	0	0	0	100
MD	15.5	9.6	9.2	64.9	0	0	0	0	100
NA	0	3.9	0	0	72.8	0	8.7	15.1	100
NB	0	3.4	0	0	0	54.5	22.9	19.8	100
NC	0	0	0	0	9.0	23.2	68.3	0	100
ND	0	0	0	0	15.5	19.9	0	65.1	100
	100	100	100	100	100	100	100	100	800

These indices are as follows:

Family M indices

ε_{AB} = 0.50	p_{AB} = 0.75	R_{AB} = 3.0
ε_{AC} = 0.72	p_{AC} = 0.86	R_{AC} = 6.1
ε_{AD} = 0.59	p_{AD} = 0.79	R_{AD} = 3.9
ε_{BC} = 0.71	p_{BC} = 0.85	R_{BC} = 5.9
ε_{BD} = 0.72	p_{BD} = 0.86	R_{BD} = 6.1
ε_{CD} = 0.76	p_{CD} = 0.88	R_{CD} = 7.3
Overall ε = 0.666	Overall p = 0.833	Overall R = 4.99

Family N indices

ε_{AB} = 1	p_{AB} = 1	R_{AB} =
ε_{AC} = 0.78	p_{AC} = 0.89	R_{AC} = 8.0
ε_{AD} = 0.64	p_{AD} = 0.82	R_{AD} = 4.5
ε_{BC} = 0.47	p_{BC} = 0.73	R_{BC} = 2.8
ε_{BD} = 0.50	p_{BD} = 0.75	R_{BD} = 3.0
ε_{CD} = 1	p_{CD} = 1	R_{CD} =
Overall ε = 0.707	Overall p = 0.854	Overall R = 5.83
Adjacent ε = 0.595	Adjacent p = 0.798	Adjacent R = 3.94
0.5975	0.7975	3.95

For family M the simplest hypothesis is that the odds are about 5 to 1 in favor of marriage with own group and otherwise random among lineages. This assumes that the overall indices would adequately describe marriage among the lineages within the M family. In order to test this hypothesis, we form a ratio table as follows (rounding the ratio to 5):

5	1	1	1
1	5	1	1
1	1	5	1
1	1	1	5

By iterating this table back to the original marginals, we obtain the following theoretically expected frequencies

	MA	MB	MC	MD	
MA	47.05	6.68	4.72	10.55	69
MB	6.68	23.47	3.35	7.50	41
MC	4.72	3.35	11.71	5.22	25
MD	10.55	7.50	5.22	59.73	83
	69	41	25	83	218

Using these figures as the theoretical frequencies, we perform a test using the original data and come out with a χ^2 equal to 4.66 (corrected for continuity). For nine degrees of freedom, this lies between the 0.9 and 0.8 level of significance. We conclude that for family M a single index figure is sufficient. An adequate description is that the odds are approximately 5 to 1 that a person will marry within his own lineage and otherwise at random.

An examination of the indices for family N suggests a slightly more complex description. Since there is no intermarriage between C and D nor between A and B, let us assume that marriage is preferred with a person's own group, with odds about 4 to 1, or with adjacent group, where adjacency is defined as the arrows in the accompanying diagram:

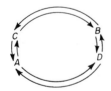

By reordering the groups, we obtain the following table of ratios for family N:

Ratio Table for Family N

	C	B	D	A
C	3.94	1	0	1
B	1	3.94	1	0
D	0	1	3.94	1
A	1	0	1	3.94

Iterating these figures back to the original marginals, we obtain

	C	B	D	A	
C	14	4	0	4	22
B	4	21	5	0	30
D	0	5	19	4	28
A	4	0	4	16	24
	22	30	28	24	104

These figures show a very close correspondence to the original data and verify the description.

We may summarize Ayoub's data as follows: family N has a slight edge over family M in overall endogamy among its lineages. This difference is probably not significant. There is no internal pattern among the lineages of family M. There is an internal pattern among the lineages of family N as described earlier.

Let us compare this interpretation to that given by Ayoub. She borrows Nicholl's index for homogamous choice. "This index will be denoted h_{ij} and may be written:

$$h_{ij} = (O_{ij} - E_{ij})/R_i - E_{ij}, \text{ when } O_{ij} > E_{ij}$$
$$h_{ij} = (O_{ij} - E_{ij})/E_{ij}, \text{ when } O_{ij} < E_{ij}$$

The range of the index is from -1 to 1, and it is calculated for every cell in the table" (Ayoub 1959:272).

Table 7 gives Nicholl's index for the data.

Table 7. Index of Preference[a] of Lineage i for Marriage with Lineage j (Ayoub 1959: 273).

Lineage Origin of Spouse								
	MA	MB	MC	MD	NA	NB	NC	ND
MA	0.52	−0.27	−0.57	0.03	−1.00	−1.00	−1.00	−1.00
MB	0.06	0.39	−0.48	−0.13	−1.00	−0.56	−1.00	−1.00
MC	−0.12	−0.40	0.49	−0.01	−1.00	−1.00	−1.00	−1.00
MD	−0.14	−0.64	−0.64	0.67	−1.00	−1.00	−1.00	−1.00
NA	−1.00	−0.80	−1.00	−1.00	0.70	−1.00	0.03	0.07
NB	−1.00	−0.84	−1.00	−1.00	−1.00	0.53	0.15	0.11
NC	−1.00	−1.00	−1.00	−1.00	0.02	0.19	0.62	−1.00
ND	−1.00	−1.00	−1.00	−1.00	0.08	0.12	−1.00	0.60

[a] $O_{ij} - E_{ij}/R_i - E_{ij}$, when $O_{ij} > E_{ij}$. $O_{ij} - E_{ij}/E_{ij}$, when $O_{ij} < E_{ij}$.

Ayoub then comments on this table as follows:

We may now note that Lineage *MD*, with an index of 0.67, is evidently the most endogamous of the lineages of Family *M*, that Lineage *MA* is the next most endogamous, with a 0.52, that Lineage *MC* follows, and that Lineage *MB*, though above 0, seems to be relatively indifferent to marrying into itself. Considering Family *N* in Table 5 we learn that an even stronger proclivity for lineage endogamy is apparent. The indices of marriage preferences between lineages in both families are regularly negative, or very low, which is not surprising inasmuch as each lineage has so over-selected itself that it commonly has no more choices left to bestow on others. There does not seem to be any clear pattern of secondary preference of any one lineage for another, nor of indirect exchange in a ring among several. (Ayoub 1959:272)

Note that the rank order of the groups is different between the present procedure and Ayoub's use of Nicholl's index. The reason for this discrepancy is that Nicholl's index is affected by relative size of groups (it is also affected by the size of the matrix). The use of the algorithm and model suggested in this paper gives a more precise and explicit picture of endogamy patterns in Druz Arab society than previous measures such as Nicholl's index.

Up to this point, all of the examples have displayed data that are symmetrical, or nearly so, about the diagonal. One special property of symmetrical matrices, not true of asymmetrical ones, is that each index obtained from the complete matrix is the same as that obtained by taking any two groups and doing the calculation separately. Thus, normalizing each 2×2 table by itself gives the same index as when the whole table is normalized. This is true in general for any size symmetrical table. One can take any subset of groups in general and get the same indices as when the whole set is normalized.

For example, take 2×2's for Aguacatenango and do the normalization by iteration, as follows:

Original data

	A_1	A_2			A_1	A_3			A_2	A_3	
A_1	46	6	52	A_1	46	1	47	A_2	24	5	29
A_2	8	24	32	A_3	2	8	10	A_3	13	8	21
	54	30	84		48	9	57		37	13	50

Normalized

	A_1	A_2			A_1	A_3			A_2	A_3	
A_1	82.4	17.6	100	A_1	93.5	6.5	100	A_2	64.1	35.9	100
A_2	17.6	82.4	100	A_3	6.5	93.5	100	A_3	35.9	64.1	100
	100	100	200		100	100	200		100	100	200

$$\varepsilon = 0.65 \qquad \varepsilon = 0.87 \qquad \varepsilon = 0.27$$
$$p = 0.83 \qquad p = 0.93 \qquad p = 0.64$$
$$R = 4.79 \qquad R = 14.30 \qquad R = 1.74$$

These correspond to the indices obtained when all three groups were considered together earlier in the paper.

Asymmetrical tables involve some additions to the model. We can illustrate these additions on a hypothetical case. Consider the 3×3 matrix of a magic square and assume it represents a complex pattern of marriage among three groups. The magic square is

Magic Square

A_1	A_2	A_3	
4	9	2	15
3	5	7	15
8	1	6	15
15	15	15	45

The indices are as follows:

$(1,2) = -0.14$	$p(1,2) = 0.43$	$R(1,2) = 0.75$
$(1,3) = 0$	$p(1,3) = 0.5$	$R(1,3) = 1$
$(2,3) = 0.15$	$p(2,3) = 0.58$	$R(2,3) = 1.375$
$(c) = 0.6$	$p(c) = 0.8$	$R(c) = 4$

where c represents special marriage rule of marrying in a "circle" as follows:

A_1 men marry A_2 women,
A_2 men marry A_3 women,
A_3 men marry A_1 women.

The preceding indices are computed directly from the table because it is normalized to equal marginals. The procedure for obtaining the original table from the indices is as follows: (1) construct a ratio table ignoring the marriage in a circle rule. This comes from the values of R according to procedures described earlier. The table comes out as follows:

	A_1	A_2	A_3
A_1	1.375	1.833	1
A_2	1.833	1.375	1.375
A_3	1	1.375	1.375

This table is normalized to the original marginals to obtain the following figures (rounded to whole digits):

5	6	4
6	4	5
4	5	6

All off-diagonal cells are summed and divided by $R + 1$, where R is the ratio of the rule of marriage in a circle. Thus

$$\frac{\sum \text{off-diagonal cells}}{R + 1} = \frac{30}{5} = 6.$$

To obtain the final result, shift half of the result around the matrix according to the rule, e.g., take 3 from cell (3,1) and add it to cell (1,3), etc. This gives the original table of the magic square.

An empirical example of marriage in a circle is the Purum data as reported by White (White 1963). These data also illustrate the importance of examining the constraints imposed by unequal marginals. We will discuss the last problem first.

Take the marginal data for three intermarrying sets of sibs—Thao (T), Marrim and Kheyang (M-K), and Parpa and Makan (P-M). The data are (White 1963)

Males	Females			
	T	M-K	P-M	
T				26
M-K				50
P-M				52
	19	63	46	128

The rules may be stated as follows:
1. T males must marry P-M females,
M-K males must marry T females,
P-M males must marry M-K females.
2. Follow rule one insofar as possible and then marry to constraints of marginals.

The number of "perfect" marriages according to rule 1 is limited by smallest marginal relevant to the cell. Thus we get

	T	M-K	P-M	
T	0	0	26	26
M-K	19			50
P-M	0	52	0	52
	19	63	46	128

which shows the maximum possible "correct" (by rule 1) marriages given the marginals. Only two cells remain unconstrained by the marginals, and they allow only one possible distribution of cases as follows:

	T	M-K	P-M	
T	0	0	26	26
M-K	19	11	20	50
P-M	0	52	0	52
	19	63	46	128

This table shows the best fit to the two marriage rules. Compare it to the observed data

	T	M-K	P-M	
T	0	0	26	26
M-K	19	13	18	50
P-M	0	50	2	52
	19	63	46	128

Note that normalization by iteration on the observed data gives the following:

Normalized

	T	M-K	P-M	
T	0	0	100	100
M-K	100	0	0	100
P-M	0	100	0	100
	100	100	100	300

Thus the iteration procedure leads directly to rule 1 of marriage in a circle. There is a deviation of only two marriages out of 128 from rule 1, given the constraints imposed by the marginal frequencies. Of course, once the marginal restraints are noticed, the iteration is superfluous in this case.

Discussion

An algorithm has been presented that facilitates the analysis of the patterns of inter-marriage among the subgroups in a population. Indices are suggested which measure degree of preference independent of the number of intermarrying groups and of the relative size of the groups. The model assumes that the universe is an endogamous population and examines the patterns of intermarriage among the subgroups. No assumption is made about the nature of the subgroups. They may be clans, lineages, social status groups, religious groups, etc.

The model is not applicable where substantial numbers of the intermarrying population are not included in the universe. It is important to realize that when census data are available, for example, from only one subgroup, it is meaningless to make statements about the degree to which that single subgroup is exogamous or endogamous. This is so since there is no estimate of the total population of which the subgroup is a part. Consider, for example, the case of Aguacatenango (see earlier). We might say that in Barrio 1 (A_1), approximately 87% of the males marry women of their own group, while in the outlying barrios (A_3), 35% of the males marry women of their own group. If one investigator had only data on Barrio 1 and another investigator had data only on the outlying barrios, they would come to different conclusions about endogamy. Yet both are parts of the same system.

In talking about Pul Eliya, Leach says, "thus, while it is certain that the intensity of endogamy within the total community has at all times been high, it is probable that the remembered genealogies tend to exaggerate this endogamy" (Leach 1961 : 168). This statement leads one to believe that the proportion of marriages where both spouses were from Pul Eliya would be high. The actual reported percentage, as calculated from data on page 83, is 20%. In order to know whether 20% represents a tendency toward endogamy or exogamy, it is necessary to provide some reasonable model that enables one to calculate expected frequencies for comparison with observed frequencies. The present model may be too limited to handle situations such as Pul Eliya. Some additional factors would be needed to be taken into account. The factor of distance seems to be a likely candidate in cases similar to that of Pul Eliya. The major point is that whatever models we use to describe endogamy and marriage patterns, we must provide for a comparison of the actual distribution of the data with some explicit and well-rationalized hypothetical distribution.

The indices suggested for the model described in this paper measure the strength of endogamy as revealed by actual marriages as enumerated in census materials. These observed patterns may be compared to ideal patterns elicited in interviews conducted to determine the extent to which the ideal patterns are practiced.

It should be noted that the iterative procedure gives an approximate solution. The approximation seems reasonably close and can be used with reasonably sized samples. Formal proofs and exact methods will be published elsewhere.

It is hoped that the present effort will add to the precision of measuring endogamy in one special situation and that it will help to stimulate the development of models for more complicated circumstances.

* Several people have contributed important ideas and help in crucial stages of the development of the ideas in this paper. I want particularly to thank Roy D'Andrade for doing the original computer simulation for getting expected frequencies. Michael Burton wrote an independent simulation program and was also responsible for writing a program for obtaining normalized tables through iteration. The original suggestion that iteration might provide an approximation to the sampling problem was provided by William Geoghegan, who also wrote the matrix notation for the iteration. Sara Nerlove did a major share of the data collection in Aguacatenango. Frederick Mosteller is working on exact solutions that will result in technical publications elsewhere. I have also benefited from talking with Paul Kay.

Appendix

The following matrix notation for the iterative procedure was provided by William Geoghegan.

Suppose that we have an $m \times n$ matrix $M^{(1)}$ and wish to adjust its column and row sums to a set of specified values. The following iterative procedure is satisfactory for this purpose.

Let

$$M^{(1)} = \begin{pmatrix} a_{11} & a_{12} & \cdots & a_{1n} \\ a_{21} & a_{22} & \cdots & a_{2n} \\ \vdots & \vdots & & \\ a_{m1} & a_{m2} & \cdots & a_{mn} \end{pmatrix}.$$

Let the column vector

$$R = \begin{pmatrix} r_1 \\ r_2 \\ r_3 \\ \vdots \\ r_m \end{pmatrix}$$

represent the row sums that we wish to achieve, and let the row vector

$$C = (c_1, c_2, c_3, \ldots, c_n)$$

represent the column sums we want.

For the iterative procedure, let $M^{(i)}$ be the ith estimation matrix ($M^{(1)}$, our starting matrix, is also the first estimation matrix). The process involves constructing a series of these $M^{(i)}$, each successive one of which more closely approximates the desired vectors R and C in its row and column totals, respectively.

For any $M^{(i)}$ let

$$R^{(i)} = \begin{pmatrix} r_1^{(i)} \\ r_2^{(i)} \\ \vdots \\ r_m^{(i)} \end{pmatrix}$$

represent its row sums and

$$C^{(i)} = (c_1^{(i)}, c_2^{(i)}, \ldots, c_n^{(i)})$$

represent its column totals. We now construct two diagonal matrices $T^{(i)}$ and $Q^{(i)}$ as follows. Let $T^{(i)}$ be an $m \times m$ diagonal matrix with entries $t_{jj}^{(i)} = r_j / r_j^{(i)}$ (major diagonal entries) and $t_{jk}^{(i)} = 0$ for $j \neq k$. That is,

$$t_{jk}^{(i)} = \begin{cases} \dfrac{r_j}{r_j^{(i)}} & \text{for } j = k \\ 0 & \text{for } j \neq k \end{cases} \quad (1 \leq j, k \leq m).$$

Similarly, let $Q^{(i)}$ be an $n \times n$ diagonal matrix with entries $q_{jj}^{(i)} = c_j / c_j^{(i)}$ and all others equal to zero. That is,

$$q_{jk}^{(i)} = \begin{cases} \dfrac{c_j}{c_j^{(i)}} & \text{for } j = k \\ 0 & \text{for } j \neq k \end{cases} \qquad (1 \leq j, k \leq n).$$

We also require two error vectors, E_r and E_c, which represent the degree of approximation we want to achieve.

$$E_r = \begin{pmatrix} e_1 \\ e_2 \\ \vdots \\ e_m \end{pmatrix}, \quad \text{where } e_i = e_j \text{ for all } 1 \leq i, j \leq m.$$

For example, E_r might be

$$\begin{pmatrix} 0.01 \\ 0.01 \\ 0.01 \end{pmatrix},$$

$E_c = (e_1, e_2, \ldots, e_n)$, where $e_i = e_j$ for all $1 \leq i, j \leq n$. For example, E_c might be $(0.01, 0.01, 0.01)$.

Finally, let M^1 be an $m \times n$ matrix (one of the estimation matrices) which gives a reasonable approximation to the desired row and column sums. It is the estimation matrix we wish to obtain from $M^{(1)}$.

The iteration proceeds as follows:

1. Begin with estimation matrix $M^{(1)}$.
2. If $|R_i - R_i^{(1)}| \leq E_{r_i}$ and $|c_j - c_j^{(1)}| \leq E_{c_j}$, then take $M^{(1)} = M^1$, and stop.[1]
3. If not, then $M^{(2)} = T^{(1)} \times M^{(1)}$.
4. If $|R_i - R_i^{(2)}| \leq E_{r_j}$ and $|c_j - c_j^{(2)}| \leq E_{c_j}$ for all i, j then $M^{(2)} = M^1$, and stop.
5. If not, then $M^{(3)} = M^{(2)} \times Q^{(2)}$
6. Repeat the test (see 2 and 4). If it passes, then $M^{(3)} = M^1$.
7. If it fails, then $M^{(4)} = T^{(3)} \times M^{(3)}$; and so on, alternating the use of $T^{(i)}$ and $Q^{(i+1)}$ until the test succeeds. For any stage i of the process,

$$M^{(i)} = T^{(i-1)} \times M^{(i-1)} \text{ if } i \text{ is even}$$

and

$$M^{(i)} = M^{(i-1)} \times Q^{(i-1)} \text{ if } i \text{ is odd}.$$

References

Ayoub, Millicent R.
1959 "Parallel Cousin Marriage and Endogamy: a Study in Sociometry," *Southwestern Journal of Anthropology* 15: 266–275.

Leach, E. R.
1961 *Pul Eliya—A Village in Ceylon* (Cambridge, England: Cambridge University Press).

White, Harrison C.
1963 *An Anatomy of Kinship* (Englewood Cliffs, N.J.: Prentice-Hall).

[1] For vectors $A = (a_1, \ldots, a_k)$ and $B = (b_1, \ldots, b_k)$, we say $A \leq B$ just if $a^i \leq b_i$ for all a_i in A and b_i in B.

Introduction

Kozelka and Roberts attack the following problem: Two sets of m informants are drawn from two presumably distinct populations. Each informant is assigned the task of ranking (with respect to a given criterion) some number of objects, not necessarily the same number for both sets of informants. The degree of concordance (consensus) in each set of informants is given by Kendall's coefficient of concordance W. Do the populations represented by the two sets of informants differ significantly in the degree of concordance (agreement) on the ranking task? Put another way, are the W statistics sufficiently close for the two sets (now samples) of informants so as to admit the conclusion that the population analogues of the W statistics (or some other measure) are, for anthropological purposes, identical?

After an examination of the literature on this problem, the authors conclude that the various approaches to date are of two types: (1) those that sacrifice naturalness of measurement to tractability of the mathematical model, and (2) those that make the converse sacrifice.

They then advocate the use of Tukey's "jackknife." For each set of m informants, calculate m nearly independent measures of W by omitting one informant from the calculation of each estimate. Then set confidence limits on the population parameter to which W presumably corresponds by using Student's t statistic with $m - 1$ degrees of freedom.

One is now equipped to handle certain clear cases in a reasonable fashion. An example of such a clear case is presented. American and Japanese informants were set the task of ranking social distance between themselves and the occupants of statuses marked by kin terms. The 20% confidence levels on the coefficients of concordance in the two samples were identical for one version of the ranking task and showed considerable overlap in another version. This suggests that American and Japanese speakers

* This investigation was supported primarily by Public Health Service Grant MH 04161-03, National Institute of Mental Health, and secondarily by Public Health Service Grant MH 08161-02, National Institute of Mental Health. The authors are grateful to Robert J. Smith for his permission to publish materials here which will also be published in a forthcoming monograph by John M. Roberts, Robert J. Smith, and Robert M. Kozelka. We have profited from discussions with Frederick Mosteller, John W. Tukey, John Gilbert, and others attending the conference on statistics and anthropology held in Santa Fe, New Mexico, in 1965, where an earlier version of this paper was presented.

Within the context of this symposium a word should be said about the present collaboration of a statistician and an anthropologist. In a number of published research reports and in a number of forthcoming papers, the statistician provided important, but essentially auxiliary, support to an anthropological inquiry. In the present instance the anthropologist, who makes no claims to statistical competence, provided auxiliary support in terms of providing data, an interest in the problem of concordance expressed in terms of providing research support for a substantial period of time, and the like. It is an instance of a well-established working relationship which has endured for more than a decade and which has resulted in mutual profit.

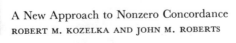

A New Approach to Nonzero Concordance

ROBERT M. KOZELKA AND JOHN M. ROBERTS

generally do not differ substantially in the tendency to agree among themselves on such rankings.

The authors conclude with a discussion of the importance of the concept of consensus, or sharing of culture, in anthropological theory. It is hard to resist agreement with the position that anthropologists, who are theoretically interested in problems of consensus and sharedness of culture, might profit from awareness of statistical methods dealing with concordance.

The paper also represents a recent institutional innovation, collaboration of an anthropologist and a mathematician. More such collaboration must surely benefit anthropology and may also raise some problems of interest to mathematicians.

When a sample of m informants each rank n objects, the problem of measuring agreement among the informants has been solved. Measures proposed by Friedman (1937:675–701), by Kendall (1962), by Kruskal and Wallis (1952:583–621) and by Mosteller and Tukey (1954) are functionally related. Since much of the work on this problem has been done in England and follows Kendall's notation, this paper will use his "coefficient of concordance," defined as

$$W = \frac{12}{n^3 - n} \sum_{k=1}^{n} \left(\sum_{i=1}^{m} \frac{r_{ik}}{m} - \frac{n+1}{2} \right)^2,$$

where r_{ik} is the rank of the kth object by the ith informant.[1] This is related to, e.g., Friedman's measure χ^2_{Fr} by the formula $\chi^2_{\text{Fr}} = m(n-1)W$. A complete discussion of the rationale behind these measures may be found in the works in which they are defined.

The problem of measuring similar agreement in a population, however, is not so unanimously determined. In the case of zero population concordance, which may be thought of either in terms of independence between all members in the population of judges or in terms of random rankings, it is well agreed that the case is essentially that of random permutations of the integers $1-n$. Such considerations form the basis of the discussion by Friedman and of a somewhat more general paper by Pitman (1938:322–385); these authors look at the problem as one of analysis of variance. Tests for nonzero concordance thus become tests for nonrandom ranking and reduce to the familiar χ^2 variable.

If the sample value W is shown to be significantly different from zero by a test of the form described, one is led to conclude that the informants in the sample have some degree of agreement, and it is a natural extension of the sample to try to measure such nonzero agreement in the population. Such a population measure is *not* generally

---

[1] An effort has been made to keep the notation consistent throughout the paper; hence some notations have been changed from their original or the common format.

agreed upon, and several attempts at a suitable formulation have been made. Daniels (1950: 171–181) considered two natural extensions: (1) a finite population of N objects ranked according to each of m different qualities, from which a sample of size n is drawn, and (2) a finite population of M members, each of which is an n-tuple of the natural numbers 1 to n in some order; a sample of size m is drawn from this population. Following the second of these ideas, Stuart (1951: 33–42) determined the first four moments of the quantity $\sum k_1^2$ under the assumption of identical means of all population rankings and then took the limit for large M. [The quantity k_1^2 represents the square of the difference between any of the n variates and $(n+1)/2$.] Stuart, and Linhart (1960: 476–480) following him, essentially define population concordance in terms of cumulants corresponding to the various k statistics. [For a complete discussion of cumulants and related k statistics, see Tukey (1956: 37–54).] Since Stuart's results depend on the assumption of equal mean ranks in the population, they are not applicable to the kind of problem we choose to discuss, nor, indeed, to ranking problems not related to analysis of variance.

Linhart, carrying Stuart's method in a slightly different direction, defines nonzero population concordance the same way and then uses the difference of Stuart's statistics for the two populations to test for equality of population concordances. (This is directly the problem with which we are concerned.) One sets $d = \sum (k_1^2 - h_1^2)$, where k_1 and h_1 are the first k statistics (measured from the mean) for the first and second groups, respectively. Linhart finds $E(d)$ and $\mathrm{var}(d)$ in terms of cumulants, approximates the necessary values by substituting back the corresponding k statistics, and tests equality by assuming a normal distribution for the variable d. Apparently he is not any happier with the last assumption than is the reader, for he quotes Kendall (1950) on the outstanding problem of ranking theory being that of specifying a population with a tractable number of parameters, and then he remarks, "As long as that problem has not been solved, one has to be satisfied with crude methods, similar to those suggested here." He finishes the paper by applying his result to sets of data similar to those that gave rise to the present paper. Unfortunately his data are not given in a form suitable to the purposes of this paper (the original rankings are condensed into a cumulative form), and the data as given seem to present a prima facie case of different nonzero population concordances.

One of the first systematic attempts to reduce the number of parameters in ranking problems to a manageable size was made by Ehrenberg (1952: 82–97), who sets π_{ab} equal to the proportion of judges in a population who ranked objects u_a and u_b as $u_a \prec u_b$ ($\prec$ means "is ranked with a smaller number than") and defined the population concordance by the coefficient

$$\gamma = \binom{m}{2}^{-1} \sum_{a<b} (2\pi_{ab} - 1)^2.$$

He notes that one need only consider $\pi_{ab} \geq \frac{1}{2}$ and that

$\gamma = 0$ if and only if $\pi_{ab} = \frac{1}{2}$ for all pairs$\Big\}$ yields $\Big\{$minimum$\Big\}$ concordance.
$\gamma = 1$ if and only if $\pi_{ab} = 1$ for all pairs$\Big\}$ yields $\Big\{$maximum$\Big\}$ concordance.

Then intermediate values of γ arise from one of the following:

1. $\pi_{ab} = \pi$, $\frac{1}{2} < \pi < 1$, for all pairs (a, b). Then,

$$\gamma = \binom{m}{2}^{-1} \sum_{a<b} (2\pi - 1)^2 = (2\pi - 1)^2.$$

Hence, if $\pi = \frac{3}{4}$ for all pairs, we have $\gamma = \frac{1}{4}$; however, a coefficient of concordance $\gamma = \frac{1}{2}$ corresponds to a common π value of 0.85.

2. $\pi_{ab} = 1$ for a fraction π of the $\binom{m}{2}$ pairs and $\pi_{ab} = \frac{1}{2}$ otherwise. Then

$$\gamma = \binom{m}{2}^{-1} \sum_{a<b} (2\pi_{ab} - 1)^2 = \pi,$$

which is intuitively appealing.

3. π_{ab} takes on values other than $\frac{1}{2}$ or 1 for some pairs. Note that as in case 1, even though π is constant, the *same* informants may not agree on all pairs, only the *same proportion* of informants. This seems intuitively unappealing.

This approach to population concordance is also studied by Babington Smith (1950), who assumes the π_{ab} are independent; by Bradley and Terry (1952), who assume π_{ab} may be written as $\pi_a/(\pi_a + \pi_b)$; and inferentially by other writers who approach the problem via paired comparison methods. An excellent summary of these approaches as attempts to measure agreement in general qualitative data may be found in the articles by Goodman and Kruskal (1954: 732–764; 1959: 123–163).

In a variant of the preceding, Mallows (1957: 114–130), having postulated a known *a priori* ranking, defines a generalized matching coefficient

$$A(n) = \sum_{j=1}^{n} \alpha_{jk_j},$$

where k_j is the rank by one informant of an object ranked j by another informant. He then shows that various choices for the measure α_{jh} yield well-known coefficients; i.e., $\alpha_{jh} = (j - h)^2$ yields Spearman's rank correlation coefficient. Although most of the work is concerned with agreement only between *pairs* under various restrictions, he uses the fact that the average of m Spearman coefficients equals $(mW - 1)/(m - 1)$ to get an estimate of

$$\phi = \sqrt{\frac{\pi}{1 - \pi}},$$

where π is as above and is constant for all pairs. Then for any ranking $u^{(j)} = u_1 \prec u_2 \prec u_3 \prec \cdots \prec u_n$, he sets $s_j = \binom{n}{2}\tau_j$, where τ_j is Kendall's tau coefficient of correlation between $u^{(j)}$ and the *a priori* "correct" ranking. Then under the null hypothesis

$\pi = \frac{1}{2}$, or for "small" deviations from it, he finds $\bar{s} = \sum s_j/m$ is distributed approximately

$$N\left(E = V_0 \log \sqrt{\frac{\pi}{1-\pi}}, \quad \left[V_0 - \frac{27E^2}{25n}\right]\frac{1}{m}\right),$$

where

$$V_0 = n(n-1)\,(2n+5)/18.$$

While this may be satisfactory from a theoretical point of view, given his assumptions, it does not solve the problem in the case of large deviations from the null hypothesis, which is the situation faced in the kind of problem here studied.

A completely different approach, one in terms of cumulative distribution functions, is attempted by Sathe (1962), who postulates the *cdf* of a random variable z_{ik} to be

$$F(z_{ik}) = F(z + \varepsilon + \zeta_i + \eta_k).$$

As usual in such models, he assumes that the z_{ik}'s are independent and $\sum \varepsilon = \sum \eta_k = 0$ but

$$\zeta_i = \theta_i/\sqrt{m}.$$

Then the quantity $\bar{\theta} = \sum \theta_i/n$ serves as a measure of agreement to test $H_0 : \theta_i = \theta_i'$ for all i, i'. He shows that as m becomes large the *pdf* of χ^2_{Fr} tends to be noncentral χ^2 (central if H_0 holds) with noncentrality parameter proportional to $\sum(\theta_i - \bar{\theta})^2$. One may, then, although Sathe does not do so, choose the noncentrality parameter as the measure of concordance, with the sample estimate presumably given by the value of the usual estimator of such a parameter. Tables of the noncentral χ^2 are now quite generally available, but the problem of testing equality of two noncentrality parameters is still, to our knowledge, unsolved. Some question remains, however, about the assumption of independence of the z_{ik}'s. Viewed as a model related to analysis of variance it may be reasonable, but as a model for sets of ranks running from 1 to n it seems untenable.

All in all, one may view the problem of nonzero concordance rather like that of utility some years ago. Someone has commented that economists knew the properties of utility but were not able to measure it, while psychologists could measure it but did not know how it behaved. The natural extensions, to a population, of the sample concordance coefficient by Pitman and Stuart led to intractable mathematics. On the other hand, formulations by Mallows and others which admit a usable limiting distribution led to a measure of population concordance which was either unnaturally restricted or peculiar when compared with the well agreed upon sample coefficient. Goodman and Kruskal, who make a convincing case for defining any measure of agreement in terms of probabilities of preferences, handle only the case $m = 2$. Indeed it may be that S. N. Roy was correct when he told one of the present authors (per-

Table 1. Basic Parameter Values for Concordances (Roberts, Smith, and Kozelka, n.d.).

	Long Form	Short Form
English	$m = 6$ informants	$m = 26$ informants
	$n = 77$ kin terms	$n = 15$ kin terms
	$W = 0.829$	$W = 0.815$
Japanese	$m = 6$ informants	$m = 26$ informants
	$n = 64$ kin terms	$n = 16$ kin terms
	$W = 0.868$	$W = 0.780$

sonal communication) that he felt it was impossible to measure concordance by a one-dimensional quantity. Unfortunately, the conversation was never pursued, but the impression left was that he favored something like an appropriately chosen hyperplane or envelope. Such formulations are well beyond the scope of this paper.

The instance of nonzero concordance that gave rise to the present considerations appears in a paper by Roberts, Smith, and Kozelka (n.d.). Two sets of informants, one of American English background and one of Japanese background, ranked kin terms by a constant-sum ratio scale method. This led, for some but not all of the informants, to a patterned response that was measurable but not comparable between informants. In an effort to include all of the data, as well as to make comparisons within and between groups, the ranks of the kin terms made up the concordance matrices. Two data forms were used. Table 1 shows the results. All of the sample concordance coefficients are significantly different from zero. Since both kinships systems are of the same (Eskimo) type but differ rather markedly in the individual terms that appear, and since a heuristic argument can be made for a difference between cultures concerning kin cohesiveness, the problem of testing difference of nonzero concordance is pertinent.

Following a suggestion by F. Mosteller, a technique developed by Tukey (1958:617) and others was used. This technique, called a "jackknife" to indicate a tool that is ordinarily used not for delicate work but which is adaptable to a variety of approximate results, is sufficiently uncommon so that a brief description is warranted. If a single statistic D is computed from m data points, the problem is to obtain sufficient independent measurements of D to produce useful confidence limits on the corresponding population parameter Δ. Let D_i be the same statistic as D but computed on all data points except the ith, and write

$$D_i^* = mD - (m - 1)D_i \qquad (i = 1, 2, \ldots, m).$$

Then the values D_i^* constitute m nearly independent observations, as may be seen by using the sample mean statistic $\bar{x}$, whence each

$$\bar{x}_i^* = m\bar{x} - (m-1)\bar{x}_i = m(\sum x/m) - (m-1)[(m-1)[\{(\sum x) - x_i\}/(m-1)]$$

is just the ith observation x_i. Then one obtains confidence limits for Δ from the D_i^* by using Student's t statistic computed on $m-1$ degrees of freedom in the usual fashion. (An extensive example of the jackknife may be found in Mosteller and Wallace 1964.)

Lacking a direct test for the difference (or ratio) of two significantly nonzero concordance values, a possible procedure is to examine pairs of confidence intervals for nonvoid intersection. While such a procedure may fail to give satisfactory results in the most general situation (suppose that 90% intervals overlap but 80% intervals do not—what significance should be claimed?), it may be informative in extreme cases. If two short intervals corresponding to a small degree of confidence overlap, one feels confident (!) that a case for equality of parameters may be made; conversely, if two long intervals corresponding to a high degree of confidence are disjoint, distinct values of the parameters seem ensured. The former case applies in the present situation; the data are shown in Table 2.

The original data were in the long forms, but in an effort to reduce the computation involved and get reasonable sample sizes, a short form was chosen which admitted hand computations. The items in the short form were *not* chosen at random from the long form but were selected consciously to provide a broad coverage of major terms. (Hence the discrepancy between concordance values for the two forms within a culture is not germane at the moment—if the forms are used for further investigation, some other selection of items may be used.) Since one may wonder whether the jackknife assumption of a t distribution for the resulting adjusted statistics is legitimate for nonnormal data with samples as small as 6, the emphasis will be on the short-form data. Although originally the larger samples were desired for another purpose, one must admit that if the jackknife has any claim to validity at all that samples of sizes 21 and 26 should be sufficient.

Table 2. Approximate Confidence Intervals by the "Jackknife" Technique.[a]

Long Form English	Japanese	Confidence Coeff.	Short Form English	Japanese
(0.72, 0.98)	(0.75, 095)	98%	(0.72, 0.90)	(0.64, 0.92)
(0.78, 0.92)	(0.75, 0.95)	90%	(0.74, 0.88)	(0.68, 0.88)
(0.80, 0.91)	(0.81, 0.89)	80%	(0.75, 0.87)	(0.70, 0.87)
(0.82, 0.89)	(0.82, 0.88)	60%	(0.77, 0.85)	(0.72, 0.85)
(0.83, 0.87)	(0.83, 0.87)	40%	(0.77, 0.85)	(0.73, 0.83)
(0.84, 0.86)	(0.84, 0.86)	20%	(0.78, 0.84)	(0.74, 0.82)

[a] Since the intervals are computed from the adjusted statistics, they do not center on the sample W's of Table 1.

The fact that the 20% confidence intervals overlap appreciably does not, of course, allow us to conclude that the population concordances are identical, or to make a probability judgment about such a conclusion. The results are such, however, that if one had to proceed on the basis of a decision of identity or nonidentity of concordance, or at least on the basis of highly similar population concordances, a loss function that dictated the decision of nonsimilarity from these data would be decidedly skew. The results may be sufficiently indicative, say, to point the direction and emphasis of further field research dependent on concordance (see the following), even though an appropriate statistical coefficient is lacking.

One further check on the jackknife, of a negative sort, might proceed as follows (this goes beyond the original recommendation): since the adjusted statistics are assumed approximately t-distributed in the means, some sort of near-normality must be present in the values themselves. If this is the case, one should be able to use the common tests for equality of variances and means. Such tests may not strengthen but at least they should not deny the conclusions based on the confidence intervals. Computations in the short-term case yield an F value for variances of 1.69 compared with a 5% value (20, 25 d.f.) of 1.99, and a t value for means of approximately 0.5 on 45 d.f. Both of these results are in accord with the interval computations.

Conclusion

The problem of nonzero population concordance may be thought of as a variation of the Heisenberg uncertainty principle: if we define it properly, we cannot measure it in a natural fashion, whereas if we measure it naturally we have considerable doubt about what we are measuring. The jackknife technique of approximate confidence intervals from approximately independent observations attacks the problem in the latter formulation. By taking a well agreed upon sample quantity we get approximate confidence limits on whatever the appropriate population analogue may be. Although the results may not be supremely satisfying from the theoretical point of view, at least for the data studied the results tend to confirm observation and allow any practical decisions concerning further anthropological work based on the concordance concept. The mathematics based on natural extensions of sample concordance is unwieldy, and no probabilistic formulation of nonzero population concordance admits the natural sample quantity. Hence we find ourselves rather at the point of the student who, when asked if he knew any theological implications of Heisenberg's uncertainty principle, replied, "If I can determine God's position, I may then never hope to measure His velocity."

Anthropological Comment

This is a statistical paper, but since it is a contribution to the symposium on mathematical anthropology, it is appropriate to discuss, at least briefly, its relevance to anthropological concerns. An interest in concordance is pertinent to the larger anthropological problem of the degree to which cultural features (whether traits, patterns, attitudes, values, or whatever) must, can, or should be shared by the members of a culture. To be sure, the relevant literature cannot be reviewed here, but it is possible to consider at least briefly the importance of the concept of "shared" in contemporary anthropological thought.

The publication *Culture: A Critical Review of Concepts and Definitions* (Kroeber and Kluckhohn 1952) attests to the salience of this concept in the older literature. This is plain, for example, in the definition cited from Linton's *The Study of Man*:

The culture of any society consists of the sum total of the ideas, conditioned emotional responses, and patterns of habitual behavior which the members of that society have acquired through instruction or imitation and which they share to a greater or less degree. (Linton 1936:288)

Again, the following excerpt from a paper by Murdock is illuminating:

Habits of the cultural order are not only inculcated and thus transmitted over time; they are also social, that is, shared by human beings living in organized aggregates or societies and kept relatively uniform by social pressure. They are, in short, group habits. The habits which the members of a social group share with one another constitute the culture of that group. This assumption is accepted by most anthropologists, but not by all. Lowie, for example, insists that "a culture is invariably an artificial unit segregated for purposes of expediency.... There is only one natural unit for the ethnologist—the culture of all humanity at all periods and in all places...." The author finds it quite impossible to accept this statement. To him the collective or shared habits of a social group—no matter, whether it be a family, a village, a class, or a tribe—constitute, not an "artificial unit" but a natural unit—a culture or subculture. (Murdock 1940:365)

Numerous other citations could be made from Kroeber and Kluckhohn and from other sources as well. It is enough to say here that anthropologists have long manifested both explicit and implicit interest in the sharing of culture.

In addition to the theoretical literature dealing with the subject, many ethnographic sources pay attention to the typical or modal situation, to consensus, to ranges of variation in individual and group behaviors, to agreement on themes, values, value orientations, and so on. In the main, though, it would appear that the ethnographic literature follows the general line of the theorists with little deviation and with a minimal amount of empirical examination.

More recently Wallace has supplied a new view on the subject in his book, *Culture and Personality* (Wallace 1961), where he gives serious consideration to the problem of sharing. The following quotation does not serve to present his full argument, but it indicates the degree to which he differs from some of the earlier writers:

Indeed, we now suggest that human societies may characteristically *require* the non-sharing of certain cognitive maps among participants in a variety of institutional arrangements. Many a social subsystem will not "work" if all participants share common knowledge of the system. It would seem therefore that cognitive *non*-uniformity may be a functional desideratum of society (although by the criteria we have used above, it is certainly not a formal prerequisite any more than is uniformity). For cognitive non-uniformity sub-serves two important functions: (1) it permits a more complex system to arise than most, or any, of its participants can comprehend;

(2) it liberates the participants in a system from the heavy burden of knowing each other's motivations. (Wallace 1961: 39–40)

Very importantly, Wallace concludes that a "sharing of motives is not necessary to a sharing of institutions" (Wallace 1961: 30). Rather than contradicting the earlier writers it would appear that Wallace makes a case for the most careful consideration of this problem in both theoretical and descriptive terms. It is worth noting that quite independently a compatible, but different exploration of the subject was made by Roberts (1964), who suggests a similar conclusion. Clearly the problem is not a superficial one.

The line of inquiry leading to the present study began with the position stated by Murdock in the cited quotation. Stimulated by Murdock's thinking, Roberts studied the three Ramah Navaho households which had been selected by the expert judge, Kluckhohn, as being the three most similar households in the Ramah Navaho community for differences and for similarities (Roberts 1951). This was followed by a study, as yet unpublished, which attempted to measure and compare the cultural control of individuals. There was a further consideration of the problem in a series of studies (which will not be cited here) dealing with a Zuni multiple-role small-group net. One of these studies involved the comparison of the American English and Zuni color terminologies (Lenneberg and Roberts 1956), and this study led to an interest in the high-concordance code (cf. Roberts 1965; Roberts, Smith, and Kozelka n.d.).

The problems of studying sharing at the ethnographic level are great, but the same problems can be studied with some neatness and precision in the field of the high-concordance code, the linguistic code on which there is agreement on the meanings of the elements in the code and on the relationships among them (cf. Roberts 1965: 38). Many questions can be asked: Can the amount of agreement be stated quantitatively? Is it possible to compare degrees of concordance and on this basis make inferences about the state of cultural integration, the rapidity of cultural change, the amount of diffusion, and the like? What levels of concordance must be maintained if there is to be both efficient communication and storage? Many other questions can be asked, but as yet few answers have been provided by our research. It is to be hoped that this line of inquiry can be broadened and extended in the future.

References

Arveson, J. N.
1969 "Jackknifing U-Statistics," *Annals of Mathematical Statistics* 40: 2076–2100. In this article Arveson proves J. W. Tukey's conjecture on the *t*-distribution.
Babington Smith, B.
1950 "Discussion on Symposium on Ranking Methods," *Journal of the Royal Statistical Society*, Ser. B, 12: 182–191.
Bradley, R. A., and M. E. Terry
1952 "The Rank Analysis of Incomplete Block Designs," *Biometrika* 39: 324–345.

Daniels, H. E.
1950 "Rank Correlation and Population Models," *Journal of the Royal Statistical Society*, Ser. B, 12:171–181.

Ehrenberg, A. S. C.
1952 "On Sampling from a Population of Rankers," *Biometrika* 39:82–87.

Friedman, M.
1937 "The Use of Ranks to Avoid the Assumption of Normality Implicit in the Analysis of Variance," *Journal of the American Statistical Association* 32:675–701.

Goodman, L. A., and W. H. Kruskal
1954 "Measures of Association for Cross Classification I," *Journal of the American Statistical Association* 49:732–764.
1959 "Measures of Association for Cross Classifications II," *Journal of the American Statistical Association* 54:123–163.

Kendall, M. G.
1950 "Discussion on Symposium on Ranking Methods," *Journal of the Royal Statistical Society*, Ser. B, 12:182–191.
1962 *Rank Correlation Methods*, 3rd ed. (New York: Hafner Publishing Company).

Kroeber, A. L., and C. Kluckhohn
1952 *Culture: A Critical Review of Concepts and Definitions*, Papers of the Peabody Museum of American Archaeology and Ethnology, Vol. XLVII, No. 1 (Cambridge, Mass.: Harvard University), p. 223.

Kruskal, W. H., and W. A. Wallis
1952 "Use of Ranks in One-Criterion Variance-Analysis," *Journal of the American Statistical Association* 47:583–621.

Lenneberg, E. H., and J. M. Roberts
1956 *The Language of Experience: a Study in Methodology*, Memoir 13 of the International Journal of American Linguistics, Indiana University Publications in Anthropology and Linguistics (Bloomington, Ind.: Indiana University).

Linhart, H.
1960 "Approximate Tests for *m* Rankings," *Biometrika* 47:476–480.

Linton, R.
1936 *The Study of Man* (New York: D. Appleton-Century Company).

Mallows, C. L.
1957 "Non-Null Ranking Models I," *Biometrika* 44:114–130.

Mosteller, F., and J. W. Tukey
1954 "Data Analysis, Including Statistics," in *Handbook of Social Psychology*, G. Lindzey, ed. (Reading, Mass.: Addison-Wesley Publishing Company).

Mosteller, F., and D. L. Wallace
1964 *Inference and Disputed Authorship: The Federalist Papers* (Reading, Mass.: Addison-Wesley Publishing Company).

Murdock, G. P.
1940 "The Cross-Cultural Survey," *American Sociological Review* 5, No. 3:361–370.

Pitman, E. J. G.
1938 "Significance Tests Which May Be Applied to Samples from Any Populations. III The Analysis of Variance Test," *Biometrika* 29:322–385.

Roberts, J. M.
1951 *Three Navaho Households: A Comparative Study in Small Group Culture*, Papers of the Peabody Museum of American Archaeology and Ethnology, Vol. XL, No. 3 (Cambridge, Mass.: Harvard University).
1964 "The Self-Management of Cultures," in *Explorations in Cultural Anthropology*, Ward H. Goodenough, ed. (New York: McGraw-Hill Book Company), pp. 435–454.
1965 "Kinsmen and Friends in Zuni Culture: A Terminological Note," *El Palacio* 72/2:38–43.

Roberts, J. M., R. J. Smith, and R. M. Kozelka
n.d. "Value and Codability," (manuscript).

Sathe, Y. S.
1962 "Studies of Some Problems in Nonparametric Inference," University of North Carolina Institute of Statistics Mimeo Series 325. Chapel Hill.

Stuart, A.
1951 "An Application of the Distribution of the Ranking Concordance Coefficient," *Biometrika* 38:33–42.

Tukey, J. W.
1956 "Keeping Moment-Like Computations Simple," *Annals of Mathematical Statistics* 27:37–54.
1958 "Bias and Confidence in Not-Quite-Large Samples" (abstract), *Annals of Mathematical Statistics* 29:614.

Wallace, A. F.
1961 *Culture and Personality* (New York: Random House).

Introduction

Majone and Sanday consider the problem of attaching distance, or equivalently similarity, measures to discrete characteristics distributed over a sample of data points. The locus used as an example is the set of 21 binominal variables distributed over the sample of societies treated in the Driver and Sanday paper in this volume. The mathematical problem is, however, independent of this particular locus and is, as the authors state, a rather general question in the field of numerical taxonomy.

The authors argue for the use of metrics in the strict sense as similarity/proximity measures. In particular they argue against the use of the Pearson r for nominal data.

Sanday and Majone are concerned with distance/similarity between characteristics. They define the carrier or truth set of a characteristic as the subset of sample points each of which has that characteristic. Various metrics of distance (dissimilarity) between pairs of characteristics are then defined as positive functions of the number of sample points in the symmetric difference (exclusive disjunct) of the carriers of the two characteristics. The distance metric that is exemplified with the Driver and Sanday data may be expressed as the ratio between (1) the number of sample points in the symmetric difference of their truth sets to (2) the number of sample points in the union of their truth sets. Majone and Sanday, in fact, express their metrics in more general terms, for reasons suggested in the following.

Several well-known similarity measures are derived in a novel way and their mutual relations are made clearer.

The general formulation is in terms of probability distributions over the carriers. This approach allows a more general class of metrics to be defined than are treated in detail in the paper. In particular, Majone and Sanday suggest that for some purposes nonuniform probability measures might be assigned to the set of data points. That procedure would produce distance metrics that could not be expressed simply in terms of the number of data points in various truth sets. Such metrics might, however, be especially useful in cases of logical inclusion of characteristics and generally in cases of highly uneven distributions of characteristic frequencies.

* This paper is the product of the collaboration between a mathematical statistician (Majone) and an anthropologist (Sanday). Sanday raised the problem and related the general procedure to numerical taxonomy in anthropology; Majone supplied the mathematical basis of the procedure. The paper is, of course, the joint responsibility of both authors. We wish to personally thank Harold E. Driver for his encouragement in the writing of this paper and for putting at our disposal funds for the reanalysis of the data contained in Driver and Sanday (1970). The work of G. Majone was supported in part by a grant under Contract NONR 760(24) N R 047-048 with the U.S. Office of Naval Research.

12

On the Numerical Classification of Nominal Data
GIANDOMENICO MAJONE AND PEGGY SANDAY

The discussion in this paper falls in the general area of numerical taxonomy, a field of growing importance in all the life sciences. The methodological questions treated here are, we believe, of common interest to all taxonomists, regardless of their specific fields of specialization. The data that are used, however, come from cultural anthropology. The class of data to which the discussion refers is of the nominal dichotomous type, a class fairly common to anthropological research.

Attempts to use quantitative methods for the classification or clustering of subject or ethnic units are old in anthropology.[1] In general, the steps followed in numerical classification are as follows:

1. Determination of units to be classified.[2]
2. Selection of a suitable sample. (If the sample is to be drawn from a population of ethnic units, attention must be given to the problem of historical factors.)[3]
3. The comparison of each unit with every other to determine the degrees of similarity. Similarity is usually measured by some coefficient of association and the results displayed in a matrix of similarities.[4]
4. The application of an appropriate numerical technique to the matrix of similarities for the derivation of groups or clusters of units.[5]

Once the problems inherent in steps 1 and 2 have been satisfactorily dealt with, of prime importance is the choice of the measure of similarity. Many of the problems incurred in the numerical classification of nominal data can be traced to the use of the correlation coefficient. For example, both the problems of the negative interdependency of the variables discussed by Driver and Sanday (1970) and, the problem of the unequal frequency of occurrence in the sample of the units to be classified (discussed in the following) are magnified by the choice of a correlation coefficient as the measure of similarity.

Whatever method is used to cluster the units under analysis (see step 4), the results depend on the type of coefficient used, as remarked by Guilford (1952:32) in connection with the use of factor analysis. All classifications of complex phenomena should employ some index of distance between the units being grouped (Driver 1965:30). Taxonomic distance has been measured in a variety of ways. Sokal and Sneath (1963) list 16 different coefficients of similarity. Much is known about their respective properties and usefulness, but, to the best of our knowledge, no systematic study of their metric character seems to have been undertaken. The desirability of

[1] For an extensive survey of the use of numerical classification in all fields of anthropology see Driver (1965). For a critical analysis of the history and methods of numerical classification in the field of ethnology in particular see Driver (in press).
[2] For a discussion on the determination of units see Driver (1965).
[3] For the problems of sampling consult Chaney and Driver (n.d.); Naroll and D'Andrade (1963); and Naroll (1961).
[4] For an example of step 3 see the matrix of ϕ coefficients for 21 variables in Driver and Sanday (Chapter 14, Table 1, p. 270).
[5] Two such techniques are the cluster and the factor analysis model utilized by Driver and Sanday (1970). For an example of how these steps are followed in biological taxonomy see Bailey (1967:133–153).

using a metric distance in classification stems from the fact that a metric distance satisfies the property of transitivity (to be defined). The importance of this property is recognized by Driver (in press) when he observes that "if the concept of correlation or association is to have a useful meaning in comparative ethnology, two variables which correlate or associate perfectly and positively with a third must correlate or associate perfectly and positively with each other."

This paper will explore the metric properties of a class of similarity measures suitable for analyses which have as a goal the clustering of nominal dichotomous characteristics. There is no loss of generality in restricting attention to dichotomous characteristics, since any nominal characteristic assuming, say, m values can always be expressed in terms of m dichotomous mutually exclusive categories. Since the clustering was applied to characteristics and not to individuals (or societies), we will usually employ this term in the text. But it should be understood that our discussion applies to any type of taxonomic units or variables. The data reported by Driver and Sanday (1970) will be analyzed using a metric distance derived as a particular case of the general class. The clusters derived from the matrix of similarities will then be compared with the clusters derived by the same authors.

The Metric Properties of Measures of Proximity

In this and the following section we will introduce the mathematical axioms that formalize our intuitive notions of distance. This will allow us to give a precise meaning to the class of similarity measures commonly used in clustering problems.

A *distance function* or *metric* over a set S is a real-valued function defined for all pairs (x, y) of points of S and satisfying the following properties:

D_1 $d(x, y) \geq 0$; $d(x, y) = 0$ if and only if $x = y$;

D_2 $d(x, y) = d(y, x)$;

D_3 $d(x, z) \leq d(x, y) + d(y, z)$, for all points x, y, and z in S.

D_3 is the familiar triangle inequality, expressing the transitivity of the proximity relation. Thus if x is close to y and y is close to z, then x will be close to z. (The importance of the transitivity relation for comparative ethnology is expressed by Driver in the statement quoted earlier.) A set S with a distance function d is called a *metric space*.[6]

Notice that if d is any metric and M a positive real number, we can always define a new metric d' by setting

$$d'(x, y) = \frac{M \cdot d(x, y)}{1 + d(x, y)}.$$

The new metric is bounded above by M. To prove the triangle inequality for d',

---

[6] It is to be noted that here d is being used as a generic term denoting any function meeting the requirements of the definition of a distance function.

one uses the fact that if r, s, t are real numbers such that $r + s \geq t \geq 0$, then

$$\frac{r}{1+r} + \frac{s}{1+s} \geq \frac{t}{1+t}.$$

We shall give an application of the d' metric below.

Some familiar examples of metric spaces are

a. The real line, where the distance $d(x, y)$ is the absolute difference $|x - y|$.

b. Two, three, or n-dimensional Euclidean space, whose distance is given by

$$d(x, y) = \sqrt{\sum_{i=1}^{n} (x_i - y_i)^2}.$$

c. n-dimensional vector space with the non-Euclidean distance

$$d(x, y) = \frac{1}{n} \sum_{i=1}^{n} |x_i - y_i|.$$

The latter metric is known to taxonomists as the mean character difference (see Sokal and Sneath 1963 : 146), and has been used in anthropology at least as early as 1932 (e.g., Czekanowski 1932).

Closely related to these metric notions is a measure of proximity in terms of angular distance. Angular distance is defined through the inner product and characterizes Euclidean space. The coefficient of correlation (often used as a measure of similarity) between vectors x and y is defined by the expression

$$r(x, y) = \frac{\sum_{i=1}^{n} (x_i - \bar{x})(y_i - \bar{y})}{\sqrt{\sum_{i=1}^{n} (x_i - \bar{x})^2 \sum_{i=1}^{n} (y_i - \bar{y})^2}}.$$

It is known from linear algebra (Hadley 1961) that in an n-dimensional vector space this expression is simply the cosine of the angle between vectors $x - \bar{x}$ and $y - \bar{y}$. Thus this coefficient (and its derivatives such as the ϕ coefficient) measures proximity in terms of angular distance; in the corresponding Euclidean metric, distances are measured in units of standard deviation.

There is a literally endless variety of possible metrics on a given set. Choice of the appropriate metric must depend on the nature of the problem and the type of available data. In this respect there is no one privileged distance, in spite of the fact that some taxonomists seem to think that Euclidean distance is the only "true" distance (Sokal and Sneath 1963 : 146).

Some Problems in the Use of the Correlation Coefficient in Cluster Analysis

The concepts introduced in the preceding section can be used to clarify some important methodological points. In the presence of a variety of ways of measuring distance, the researcher should obviously choose the method that fits the data and the problem rather than follow blindly established practice. This particularly applies to the uncritical use of correlation coefficients or related techniques. The popularity of such statistical indices seems to outdistance by far their usefulness, in spite of warnings by competent statisticians. Thus Tukey (1954:721) asks: "Does anyone know when the correlation coefficient is useful, as opposed to when it is used? If so, why not tell us? What substitutes are better for which purposes?" Gradually, however, difficulties in the use of correlation techniques are being brought to the attention of anthropologists. Two important difficulties stemming from the nature of the data will be discussed in the following.

The correlation coefficient as a similarity measure is unsuitable for the grouping of a set of units consisting of n subsets each containing m mutually exclusive units (as is the case with the set of 21 sociological variables discussed by Driver and Sanday). As these authors point out, the units contained in each subset will be negatively correlated, with the result that the classification device (in this case factor analysis) may extract artifactual taxa reflecting nothing more than the negative interdependence of the units within a subset.

The correlation coefficient is even more unsuitable when the frequency of occurrence in the sample of the units to be clustered is greatly unequal; for example, when a number of units are present in almost all the sample members and others present in very few of the sample members. This can be readily seen in the 2×2 table by checking to see if $a + b$ differs greatly from $a + c$. The difficulty stems from the fact that the greater the difference in frequency of occurrence between two variables (units) in a sample, the smaller will be the maximum correlation between them. The formula for the maximum correlation between two variables of unequal frequency is given in Ferguson (1941:324).[7]

Geometrically, it is not hard to see why correlation methods may be unsuitable as clustering devices, particularly in the case of unequal frequencies. As observed in the preceding section, the correlation coefficient measures proximity in terms of angular distance. Suppose we have to decide whether to cluster z with x or with y, as in Figure 1, where the units are represented as vectors in a suitable coordinate system.

If we are using maximum correlation the decision will depend on a comparison of the cosines of the two angles θ_1 and θ_2. In the situation depicted in Figure 1, for example, z would be clustered with y (since $\cos \theta_2 > \cos \theta_1$), even though z would be considered closer to x in terms of Euclidean and other distances. The dotted line through the origin is the boundary between the region where a unit is clustered with x and the region where it is clustered with y.

Clustering by correlation can be appropriate when all the vectors have the same length (norm), which is the case of equal frequencies, in a suitable coordinate system. In such a case the terminal points of the vectors will lie on the surface of an n-dimen-

---

[7] For a discussion of how this problem, when it occurs among a number of variables to be factor analyzed, affects the factor analysis results see Sanday (1967).

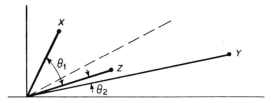

Figure 1. Clustering by maximum correlation.

sional hypersphere so that they can differ only in the direction and magnitude of their angular distances (see Figure 2).

This is the geometric significance of a procedure often recommended when using correlation techniques, namely the normalization of the data by subtracting the mean and dividing by the standard deviation. The points will then be distributed on the surface of the n-dimensional sphere of radius one, when distances are measured in units of standard deviation. However, this procedure becomes practically meaningless when applied to nominal data.

A Class of Metrics Suitable for Nominal Dichotomous Data

In the preceding section we have pointed to problems in the use of the correlation coefficient. Because of these difficulties, we suggest that another type of measure, one that is based only on a counting operation and satisfies the properties of a distance function, be employed.[8] In this section we introduce formally a class of such measures. We then show that two of the oldest and simplest coefficients of similarity known to anthropologists, Kroeber's[9] W and T (or S_1 and S_2, as these coefficients are called by Bailey 1967; or S_{SM} and S_J, as they are called by Sokal and Sneath 1963), can be derived as important special applications of our procedure. Also, the coefficient of Rogers and Tanimoto (Sokal and Sneath 1963) can be simply related to the basic metric.

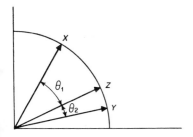

Figure 2. Clustering by maximum correlation in the case of equal frequencies.

[8] Driver (1939: 297–306) shows with actual data that correlation coefficients and coefficients related to the measures to be discussed give similar results where variables occur with equal frequency. This is to be expected in the light of our discussion on the correlation coefficient (see Figure 2).
[9] See Driver (in press) for the history of the use of these methods.

Consider the set S of all the elements of the sample under consideration. An element of S often will be referred to as a "point." Given two subsets A and B we define the following set-theoretic operations and relations (for more details see Kemeny, Snell, and Thompson 1957):

1. $A \cup B$ (union): all points of S which belong to A or to B or to both sets.
2. $A \cap B$ (intersection): all points which belong both to A and to B. For convenience we will often write AB instead of $A \cap B$.
3. $\tilde{A}$ (complementation): all points of S which do not belong to A.
4. $A \subset B$ (inclusion): all points of A which also belong to B; $A = B$ means $A \subset B$ and $B \subset A$.
5. $A \triangle B = (\tilde{A} \cap B) \cup (A \cap \tilde{B}) = \tilde{A}B \cup A\tilde{B}$ (symmetric difference); see Figure 3.
6. 0 (the empty or null set): the subset of S which contains no points.

Let $K_1, K_2, \ldots, K_m$ be m characteristics (units). To each K_i we associate a set $S_{K_i} \subset S$, which will be called the *carrier* or *truth set* of property K_i. S_{K_i} is the set of all elements of the sample which have property K_i. Equivalently, if the characteristics are coded in binary form (0 or 1), S_{K_i} is the set of points where $K_i = 1$. Logical relations among the characteristics entail set-theoretic relations among the corresponding truth sets. Thus, if K_i logically implies K_j, in the sense that K_j is present whenever K_i is, we have in the given example $S_{K_i} \subset S_{K_j}$ (see Figure 4). We proceed now to introduce a metric in the space of characteristics.

A probability P on (the subsets of) S can be thought of as a distribution of weights (masses) on the points of S such that the sum of the weights of all the points is equal to unity. The probability of a subset A is the sum of the weights attached to its points. In particular, if all points in S are given the same weight (the uniform probability measure) then $P(A) = N(A)/N(S)$, where $N(A)$ is the number of points in A, and $N(S) = n$ is the total number of elements in the sample. The collection $\mathscr{A}$ of all subsets of S will now be made into a metric space by defining the distance between any two sets A and B in $\mathscr{A}$ as follows:

$$d(A, B) = P(A \triangle B) = P(A\tilde{B}) + P(\tilde{A}B).$$

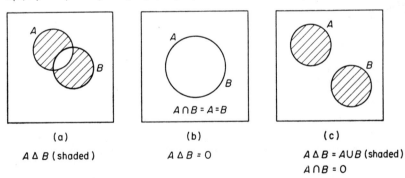

(a)	(b)	(c)
$A \triangle B$ (shaded)	$A \triangle B = 0$	$A \triangle B = A \cup B$ (shaded)
		$A \cap B = 0$

Figure 3. Symmetric difference.

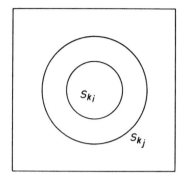

Figure 4. Logical implications: $S_{K_i} \triangle S_{K_j} = \tilde{S}_{K_i} S_{K_j}$.

We now show that this expression does indeed define a metric. It is clear that $d(A, B) = d(B, A)$, and that $d(A, B) = 0$ if and only if $A = B$ (since all our sets are finite, a set of zero probability is in fact empty; in the case of infinite sets we would have to introduce classes of equivalent sets). To verify the triangle inequality, consider a third set C in $\mathscr{A}$. Since

$$A\tilde{B} = A\tilde{B}C \cup A\tilde{B}\tilde{C},$$

we have

$$A\tilde{B} \subset \tilde{B}C \cup A\tilde{C},$$

so that

$$P(A\tilde{B}) \le P(\tilde{B}C) + P(A\tilde{C}).$$

Similarly,

$$P(\tilde{A}B) \le P(\tilde{A}C) + P(B\tilde{C}).$$

Combining the two inequalities we have

$$P(A\tilde{B}) + P(\tilde{A}B) \le P(A\tilde{C}) + P(\tilde{A}C) + P(B\tilde{C}) + P(\tilde{B}C);$$

i.e.,

$$d(A, B) \le d(A, C) + d(C, B),$$

which is the desired property.

The distance between characteristics will now be defined in terms of distances between their carriers by setting, for any two characteristics K_i and K_j,

$$d(K_i, K_j) = d(S_{K_i}, S_{K_j}) = P(S_{K_i} \triangle S_{K_j}).$$

Because of the triangle inequality, we always have

$$d(K_i, K_l) \leq d(K_i, K_j) + d(K_j, K_l),$$

so that if K_i is close to K_j, and K_j to K_l, then also K_i is close to K_l.

The following facts, which are obvious from the definition of the distance, are worthy of notice.

a. If $d(K_i, K_j) = 0$, then the two characteristics have the same carriers.

b. If one of the two terms, $P(S_{K_i} \tilde{S}_{K_j})$ or $P(\tilde{S}_{K_i} S_{K_j})$, but not both, is zero, then one of the carriers is contained in the other. This means that one of the characteristics logically implies the other, a fact which may be of special interest to the researcher (see the following).

c. Finally, if

$$d(K_i, K_j) = P(S_{K_i}) + P(S_{K_j}),$$

then K_i and K_j are mutually exclusive since their carriers are disjoint (cf. Figure 3c).

The definition of distance introduced above gives a whole class of metrics. Particular distances correspond to particular choices of a probability measure. For instance, choice of the uniform probability on S gives the metric d_1:

$$d_1(K_i, K_j) = \frac{N(S_{K_i} \tilde{S}_{K_j}) + N(\tilde{S}_{K_i} S_{K_j})}{N(S)}.$$

In the familiar notation of the 2×2 table we have

<table>
<tr><td></td><td></td><td colspan="3" align="center">K_j</td></tr>
<tr><td></td><td></td><td>1</td><td>0</td><td>Totals</td></tr>
<tr><td rowspan="2">K_i</td><td>1</td><td>$N(S_{K_i} S_{K_j}) = a$</td><td>$N(S_{K_i} \tilde{S}_{K_j}) = b$</td><td>$a + b$</td></tr>
<tr><td>0</td><td>$N(\tilde{S}_{K_i} S_{K_j}) = c$</td><td>$N(\tilde{S}_{K_i} \tilde{S}_{K_j}) =$
$N(S) - a - b - c = d$</td><td>$c + d$</td></tr>
<tr><td></td><td>Totals</td><td>$a + c$</td><td>$b + d$</td><td>n</td></tr>
</table>

Thus

$$d_1(K_i, K_j) = \frac{b + c}{n},$$

and

$$1 - d_1(K_i, K_j) = \frac{a + d}{n}.$$

This is Kroeber's W, so that $1 - W$ is an actual metric distance in the space of characteristics.

The inclusion of mutual absences, as in W, usually results in an artificial increase in similarity (Driver in press). To obtain a measure of taxonomic distance which does not present this disadvantage, consider

$$d_2(K_i, K_j) = \frac{P(S_{K_i} \triangle S_{K_j})}{P(S_{K_i} \cup S_{K_j})},$$

which corresponds to the choice of the conditional probability $P(S_{K_i} \triangle S_{K_j} \mid S_{K_i} \cup S_{K_j})$. Using again the uniform probability on S we have

$$d_2(K_i, K_j) = \frac{N(S_{K_i} \tilde{S}_{K_j}) + N(\tilde{S}_{K_i} S_{K_j})}{N(S_{K_i}) + N(S_{K_j}) - N(S_{K_i} S_{K_j})} = \frac{b + c}{a + b + c}.$$

Kroeber's T can now be obtained from d_2 since

$$1 - d_2(K_i, K_j) = 1 - \frac{b + c}{a + b + c} = \frac{a}{a + b + c}.$$

Notice that both metrics vary between 0 and 1. The upper bound 1 is actually achieved by d_2 in the case of characteristics with disjoint carriers.

A coefficient, recently proposed by Rogers and Tanimoto (Sokal and Sneath 1963), is defined by

$$S_{RT} = \frac{m}{n + u},$$

where $m = a + d$ and $u = b + c$; unmatched pairs carry twice as much weight as matched ones in the denominator. This coefficient (called S_3 by Bailey 1967), too, can be simply related to our general metric. It will be recalled that if d is any metric, and M any positive constant, a new metric d' can be obtained from d by taking

$$d'(x, y) = \frac{M \cdot d(x, y)}{1 + d(x, y)}.$$

In this expression take $M = 2$ and $d = d_1$. Then

$$d_1'(K_i, K_j) = 2 \frac{(b + c)/n}{1 + (b + c)/n} = \frac{2u}{n + u}$$

so that

$$1 - d'(K_i, K_j) = 1 - \frac{2u}{n + u} = \frac{n - u}{n + u} = \frac{m}{n + u},$$

which is precisely S_{RT}.

An Example

In this section we present a reanalysis of the 21 sociological variables reported in Driver and Sanday, using d_2 as the distance measure. For the matrix of similarities see Table 1. (Note that in this matrix 1 corresponds to maximum and 0 to minimum distance.)

Once a suitable metric has been introduced in the space of characteristics, there is a variety of techniques currently used to form clusters. All such techniques have advantages and disadvantages, and there does not seem to exist at present any compelling reason to prefer one clustering method over all others. More research is needed to develop techniques of cluster analysis with optimal properties. Naturally, the optimality of a technique depends on the intended applications. For instance, we may form clusters in order to select variables for discriminatory analysis (assignment of units to two or more existing classes). In this case, it would seem reasonable to say that a clustering technique is optimal if it minimizes the distances within clusters relative to between-cluster distances. The discovery of the appropriate algorithm would probably require the solution of difficult problems of combinatorial analysis and integer programing. For other purposes, however, different notions of optimality may be more appropriate.

Table 1. Matrix of Similarities
(1 corresponds to maximum and 0 to minimum distance).

	1	2	3	4	5	6	7	8	9
1. Iroquoian cousin terms	0.000								
2. Bifurcate collateral avuncular terms	0.718	0.000							
3. Eskimo cousin terms	0.989	0.887	0.000						
4. Bilocal or neolocal residence	0.965	0.781	0.836	0.000					
5. Patrilocal residence	0.728	0.631	0.911	1.000	0.000				
6. Bilateral descent	0.840	0.579	0.855	0.718	0.543	0.000			
7. Hawaiian cousin terms	0.984	0.717	0.967	0.795	0.628	0.394	0.000		
8. Lineal avuncular terms	0.976	0.984	0.884	0.840	0.720	0.657	0.601	0.000	
9. M-S avoidance	0.831	0.731	0.960	0.861	0.796	0.770	0.858	0.956	0.000
10. F-D avoidance	0.918	0.796	0.971	0.900	0.859	0.859	0.895	0.981	0.427
11. Generation avuncular terms	0.986	0.993	0.973	1.000	0.980	0.984	0.969	0.987	1.000
12. Matrilocal residence	0.900	0.871	0.959	1.000	1.000	0.879	0.877	0.964	0.816
13. Bifurcate merging avuncular terms	0.825	0.901	0.936	0.915	0.824	0.856	0.893	0.993	0.708
14. Avunculocal residence	0.938	0.992	1.000	1.000	1.000	1.000	1.000	1.000	0.961
15. Matrilineal descent	0.862	0.921	0.952	0.978	0.971	1.000	0.975	0.970	0.856
16. Crow cousin terms	1.000	0.943	1.000	0.959	0.988	0.979	1.000	1.000	0.857
17. M-D avoidance	0.959	0.924	1.000	0.939	0.960	0.927	0.939	0.975	0.813
18. F-S avoidance	0.940	0.915	1.000	0.935	0.930	0.908	0.937	0.978	0.688
19. Patrilineal descent	0.791	0.818	1.000	0.968	0.740	1.000	0.963	0.981	0.863
20. Omaha cousin terms	0.988	0.929	1.000	0.917	0.900	0.974	1.000	1.000	0.802
21. Descriptive cousin terms	1.000	0.984	1.000	0.982	0.993	0.994	1.000	1.000	0.987

In the present study we have obtained our clusters by the use of elementary linkage analysis, a technique presented in McQuitty (1957). Its advantage lies mainly in the speed with which results can be obtained. (The 21-variable matrix was analyzed into objectively determined types in less than a half-hour, all operations with only pencil and paper.) Elementary linkage analysis is a technique for deriving clusters from a matrix of similarities such that every variable in a particular cluster is closer to at least one other variable in that cluster than it is to any variable not in the cluster. The disadvantage of the method is that variable x can be assigned to only one cluster. Thus, if there are variables in other clusters which variable x is close to, this relationship is lost.

The results of applying this technique to Table 1 are shown in Figure 5. Each cluster is formed by a reciprocal pair. A pair of variables i and j are reciprocal if i is closer to j than it is to any other variable and j is closer to i than to any other variable. Cluster I is formed by the closest two variables, Cluster II by the next closest, and so on. Once the reciprocal pairs have been found, each member of the pair is investigated for those variables closer to that member than to any other variable. These variables are then investigated for those closest to them, and so on, until all variables have been included in a cluster. The descriptive cousin term variable is left out of the analysis because it occurs in only 2 of the 260 societies of

10	11	12	13	14	15	16	17	18	19	20	21
0.000											
1.000	0.000										
0.875	0.880	0.000									
0.825	0.961	0.731	0.000								
0.979	1.000	1.000	0.944	0.000							
0.947	0.902	0.617	0.695	0.861	0.000						
0.897	0.889	0.717	0.789	0.960	0.575	0.000					
0.674	1.000	0.930	0.963	1.000	1.000	0.971	0.000				
0.673	1.000	0.894	0.885	0.967	0.912	0.854	0.621	0.000			
0.833	0.958	1.000	0.845	1.000	1.000	1.000	0.981	0.969	0.000		
0.774	0.967	0.985	0.838	1.000	1.000	1.000	0.941	0.909	0.630	0.000	
1.000	1.000	1.000	1.000	1.000	1.000	1.000	1.000	1.000	0.976	1.000	00.00

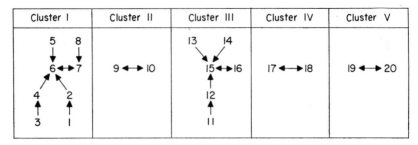

Cluster I	Cluster II	Cluster III	Cluster IV	Cluster V
5 8 ↓ ↓ 6◄►7 ↗↖ 4 2 ↑ ↑ 3 1	9 ◄► 10	13 14 ↘ ↙ 15◄►16 ↑ 12 ↑ 11	17 ◄► 18	19 ◄► 20

Figure 5. Clustering by elementary linkage analysis (numbers correspond to variables named in Table 1).

the sample and its closest index of association is 0.976. (For a more complete illustration of the procedure see McQuitty 1957.)

There are four major clusters that in general conform to the clusters isolated by Driver and Sanday. Cluster I is clearly a bicentered cluster; Cluster II an avoidance cluster; Cluster III a matricentered cluster; Cluster IV an avoidance cluster; and Cluster V a patricentered cluster. Clusters II and IV illustrate Driver's (1966:141) point that same-sex avoidances correlate higher with each other than with cross-sex combinations. The interesting feature of these clusters, not shown in the Driver and Sanday clusters, is the illustration of how the terminological variables associate with the descent and residence variables. Some of these associations, however, show up in the factor analysis results reported by these authors. Factor analysis is not a satisfactory technique to use for this type of data because factors are extracted which are artifacts reflecting the negative interdependency of the variables (see Driver and Sanday 1970) and the unequal frequency of occurrence of some of the variables. (For a discussion of how unequal frequency of occurrence can result in artifactual factors see Sanday 1967.)

It is suggested that analyses having as a goal clustering or classification should utilize more information than that provided by the matrix of similarities. Some relationships that may be of potential significance for the task of clustering may be lost if only the distances are used. In particular, the relationship of inclusion (see Figure 4) may escape the analyst unless he independently analyzes the frequency cells of all the 2 × 2 tables.

Ordinarily the relationship of inclusion will yield a low distance measure between the respective variables. However, in the case of two variables that differ widely in their frequency of occurrence, this may not be the case. A case in point is the relationship between patrilineal descent and patrilocal residence. Patrilineal descent may be said to imply patrilocal residence in the sense that when the former occurs the latter also occurs (see Figure 6 for a diagram of this relationship). This is not a complete example of inclusion since there are three cases when patrilineal descent occurs without

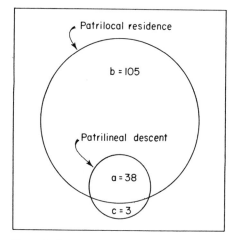

Figure 6. Occurrence of patrilineal descent with patrilocal residence.

patrilocal residence. However, it must be kept in mind that these three cases may be due to data errors or to the lag phenomenon discussed by Driver and Schuessler (1967:343) for patrilineal descent. These data offer other examples of the relationship of inclusion. Some of the variables exhibiting this relationship are, however, close in distance and are therefore indicated in the clusters. Those cases of inclusion for which this is not true are

1. M-D avoidance (one exception) ⊂ Bilateral descent
2. M-D avoidance   ⊂   M-S avoidance
3. M-D avoidance   ⊂   F-D avoidance
4. M-S avoidance (two exceptions) ⊂ F-S avoidance

The exact meaning to be attached to logical implication in comparative ethnology studies needs to be clearly specified. The discussions of Driver (1966) and Jorgenson (1966) on historical versus psychofunctional factors are suggestive for the under-standing of the meaning of this type of relationship when it occurs between subject units. A clustering technique that takes into consideration the relationship of inclusion remains to be devised.

Conclusions

Coefficients already well known to taxonomists have been obtained here by a formally different method and no new measure of similarity or distance has been explicitly introduced. We have indicated why the metric properties of any proposed coefficient of similarity should be clearly stated and fully exploited. There seems to be no reason to treat coefficients of similarity and measures of taxonomic distance as distinct concepts.

In conclusion, some remarks on the possible applications of the method introduced here are in order. First, in our definition of distance probability measures other than the uniform distribution used above can be chosen. This would correspond to assigning unequal weights to the taxonomic units. Although unequal weighting is usually criticized in numerical taxonomy, one can imagine situations in which this procedure would have advantages similar, for instance, to those of feature weighting techniques in pattern recognition. For example, with respect to the type of data analyzed here one might want to assign proportionally greater weight to characteristics that are seen to have special importance but which are carried by only a few elements of the sample.

Finally, the terminology of set theory and the associated visualization by means of Venn diagrams can be of great help in numerical taxonomy. The systematic representation of logical statements about the sample in terms of sets permits the utilization of the powerful formalism of Boolean algebra in the discovery of complicated relationships among the units. The value of these logicomathematical procedures has already been proven in such nonquantitative fields as medical diagnosis (cf. Ledley and Lusted 1962). There is no reason why they should not prove equally useful to the anthropologist and the numerical taxonomist.

References

Bailey, Norman T. J.
1967 *The Mathematical Approach to Biology and Medicine* (New York: John Wiley and Sons).

Chaney, Richard P., and Harold E. Driver
(in press) "Cross-Cultural Sampling and the Tylor-Galton Problem," in *A Handbook of Method in Cultural Anthropology*, R. Naroll and R. Cohen, eds. (New York: Natural History Press).

Czekanowski, J.
1932 "Coefficient of Racial Likeness und Durchschnittliche Differenz," *Anthropologische Anzeige* 9:227–249.

Driver, Harold E.
1939 "Culture Element Distributions: X, Northwest California," *University of California Anthropological Records* 1:297–433.
1965 "Survey of Numerical Classification in Anthropology," in *The Use of Computers in Anthropology*, D. Hymes, ed. (The Hague, Mouton and Company), pp. 301–344.
1966 "Geographical-Historical versus Psycho-Functional Explanations of Kin Avoidances," *Current Anthropology* 7:131–160.
(in press) "Statistical Studies of Continuous Geographical Distributions," in *A Handbook of Method in Cultural Anthropology*, R. Naroll and R. Cohen, eds. (New York: Natural History Press).

Driver, Harold E., and Peggy R. Sanday
1966 and 1970 "Factors and Clusters of Kin Avoidances and Related Variables," *Current Anthropology* 7:169–176, and chapter 14 in this volume.

Driver, Harold E., and Karl F. Schuessler
1967 "Correlation Analysis of Murdock's 1957 Ethnographic Sample," *American Anthropologist* 69: 332–352.

Ferguson, George A.
1941 "The Factorial Interpretation of Test Difficulty," *Psychometrika* 6: 323–329.

Guilford, J. P.
1952 "When Not to Factor Analyze," *Psychological Bulletin* 49: 26–37.

Hadley, G.
1961 *Linear Algebra* (Reading, Mass.: Addison-Wesley Publishing Company).

Jorgensen, Joseph G.
1966 "Geographical Clusterings and Functional Explanations of In-Law Avoidances: an Analysis of Comparative Method," *Current Anthropology* 7: 161–169.

Kemeny, John G., J. Laurie Snell, and Gerald L. Thompson
1957 *Introduction to Finite Mathematics* (Englewood Cliffs, N. J.: Prentice-Hall).

Ledley, R. S., and L. E. Lusted
1962 "Medical Diagnosis and Modern Decision Making," in *Mathematical Problems in the Biological Sciences, Proceedings of Symposia in Applied Mathematics*, Vol. XIV (Providence, Rhode Island: American Mathematical Society).

McQuitty, Louis L.
1957 "Elementary Linkage Analysis for Isolating Orthogonal and Oblique Types and Typal Relevancies," *Educational and Psychological Measurement* 17: 207–229.

Naroll, Raoul
1961 "Two Solutions to Galton's Problem," *Philosophy of Science* 28: 15–39.

Naroll, Raoul, and Roy G. D'Andrade
1963 "Two Further Solutions to Galton's Problem," *American Anthropologist* 65: 1053–1067.

Sanday, Peggy R.
1967 "Some Problems in the Use of Factor Analysis for the Classification of Naturally Occurring Categories in Cross-Cultural Data," paper presented at the 66th Annual Meeting of the American Anthropological Association, Washington, D.C.

Sokal, Robert R., and Peter H. A. Sneath
1963 *Principles of Numerical Taxonomy* (San Francisco: W. H. Freeman and Company).

Tukey, Y. W.
1954 "Unsolved Problems of Experimental Statistics," *Journal of the American Statistical Association* 49: 706–731.

Introduction

Roberts, Strand, and Burmeister apply scaling and preference-mapping methods to the formerly qualitative concept "systemic culture pattern."

Chief among their several results are first that individual patterns of preference for items of clothing can be quantitatively mapped in a way that is both objective and intuitively satisfying, second that the maps show systematic distinctions between respondents who are bearers of distinct cultures, and third that intercultural differences in systemic pattern are in the directions predicted by culture historians.

Subjects are requested to respond to each of pair of items such as (two pairs of shoes and three shirts versus one pair of shoes and four shirts), where the stimuli are the 1,176 members of the Cartesian product of the sets $\{x$ shirts $|x = 0, 1, \ldots, 6\}$ and $\{y$ pairs of shoes$|y = 0, 1, \ldots, 6\}$. Responses take the form of preferences expressed as one of the ratios 1/9, 2/8, 3/7, $\ldots$, 9/1.

From these data average preferences for each of the 49 item-pairs (e.g., two pairs of shoes and three shirts) are calculated; similarly average contrasts against all other items are obtained. The preference and contrast scores are then charted on a seven by seven array, and isobars are drawn showing regions of similar preference or contrast. These operations are performed on both individual and aggregate data.

A glance at the figures shows that this procedure leads to interesting and readily interpretable results. For example, Figures 1, 2, and 3 each show clear preference configurations, and each is quite distinct from the others.

The authors also discuss in some detail the interpretation of the preference versus the contrast scores. The approach has also been successfully applied to preferences in family composition first in this paper in a preliminary way and much later in Puerto Rico (G. C. Myers and J. M. Roberts, 1968, "A Technique for Measuring Preferential Family Size and Composition," *Eugenics Quarterly*).

Cultural patterns have long been a salient and explicit interest in general anthropology (see the works of Kroeber, Kluckhohn, Benedict, and others), but this may no longer be the case. A cursory examination of recent textbooks and general books in anthropology suggests that, while anthropologists continue to study the phenomena often treated in the older literature under the rubric of "pattern," they no longer use the rubric. Thus, while Kroeber published a chapter on "patterns" almost as a matter of course in the revised edition of his well-known work on general anthropology

This investigation was supported primarily by Public Health Service Grant MH 04161-03, National Institute of Mental Health, and secondarily by Public Health Service Grant MH 08161-03, National Institute of Mental Health. The authors are grateful to Robert M. Kozelka for helpful suggestions and to the Cornell Computing Center for donation of time.

13

Preferential Pattern Analysis
JOHN M. ROBERTS, RICHARD F. STRAND, AND EDWIN BURMEISTER

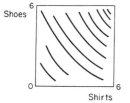 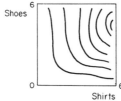 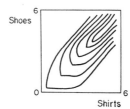

Figure 1. American male.　Figure 2. Indian male.　Figure 3. Chilean female.

(Kroeber 1948:311–343), no comparable treatment appears in the most recent textbooks. Moreover, the elaborate pattern terminology and classification, such as that published by Kluckhohn (Kluckhohn 1941:109–130) seems to have disappeared from view.

Nevertheless, the rubric of patterns may still be pertinent to contemporary interests. The present paper, for example, revives an interest in pattern analysis at a descriptive level and lays the groundwork for future research that may yield interesting generalizations.

The Systemic Pattern Broadly speaking, this study deals with "systemic patterns," a class of pattern which has been defined by Kroeber in the following way:

A second kind of pattern consists of a system or complex of cultural material that has proved its utility as a system and therefore tends to cohere and persist as a unit; it is modifiable superficially, but modifiable only with difficulty as to its underlying plan. Any one such systemic pattern is limited primarily to one aspect of culture, such as subsistence, religion, or economics; but it is not limited areally, or to one particular culture; it can be diffused cross-culturally, from one people to another. Examples are plow agriculture, monotheism, the alphabet, and, on a smaller scale, the *kula* ring of economic exchange among the Massim Melanesians. What distinguishes these systemic patterns of culture—or well-patterned systems, as they might also be called—is a specific interrelation of their component parts, a nexus that holds them together strongly, and tends to preserve the basic plan. This is in distinction to the great "loose" mass of material in every culture that is not bound together by any strong tie but adheres and again dissociates relatively freely. As a result of the persistence of these systemic patterns, their significance becomes most evident on a historical view. (Kroeber 1948:312–313)

More specifically this investigation is concerned with the major systemic pattern of "tailored garments." The two following quotations provide enough background on this pattern for present purposes. Chapple and Coon state:

Tailored Garments. Life in the boreal forest and the tundra requires something better, something that will keep a person warm and still not hamper his movements. The answer to this is tailored clothing, including shirts or coats, trousers, boots or shoes, and gloves or mittens. The people who are most perfectly adapted to a climate of extreme cold from the standpoint of clothing, are the Eskimo. They are so good at tailoring warm, lightweight outdoor clothing, that arctic explorers prefer Eskimo costumes to anything that they can bring from home. Throughout the boreal forests of Europe, Asia, and North America, tailored clothing made of furs and skins are worn by everyone. In the grasslands and temperate forests of the Old World, these garments are also used in modified form. The Chinese costume is tailored, and so is that used by the Central Asiatic nomads, the Mongols and Turks. Trousers are better on horseback than breech-clouts, and the Scythians, notable equestrians of antiquity, probably introduced them to Europe. Our male costume is derived, through medieval proto-types, from this same Asiatic source. (Chapple and Coon 1942: 119–120)

The same authors state:

The ideal desert footgear is the sandal, worn in the Sahara, the Arabian desert, and the deserts of India, as well as in those of the New World. It also penetrated, in antiquity, the Mediterranean area. The northern type of footgear, developed as part of the tailored clothing complex, is the complete foot covering of leather, which takes the form of the moccasin in North America, and of the boot in Asia. From this Asiatic footcovering come our modern Occidental boot and shoe. (Chapple and Coon 1942: 120)

Kroeber also says:

For instance, Occidental civilization, Ancient Mediterranean, and East Asiatic are each characterized by a distinctive, long-term basic pattern of clothing. In comparison with our fitted clothing, Greek and Roman clothing was draped on the body. While this statement is not wholly exact, it is true comparatively. Sleeves were little developed, trousers lacking, the waist of clothing was not fitted in to follow the body, the general effect accentuated the fall of drapery and the flowing line. The Roman toga was a wrap-around blanket. One did not slip into it like a coat, one adjusted it to hang in proper folds.

After prevailing for many centuries, this basic pattern of dress began to crumble and become transformed toward the end of the Roman Empire, when the old Hellenic-Latin religion had yielded to Christianity and the total Mediterranean civilization was disintegrating and at the point of gradually being replaced by the beginnings of our Occidental one. Trousers, in spite of protests and counter legislation, were adopted from the barbarians. Sleeves came into general use. During the Dark Ages, the transition was gradually accomplished. The fitted clothes might be pretty well concealed under a long coat or cloak, as in the sixth-century mosaics of the Eastern Emperor Justinian and the Empress Theodora; but they were there. By the Middle Ages, they were in the open; and their pattern is still the fundamental pattern of our own clothing. The characteristic of this, in contrast with ancient clothing, is that it is cut and tailored, fitted to the figure. (Kroeber 1948: 332)

These quotations attest to the fact that the European clothing complex is a systemic pattern; that it is a northern adaptation contrasting with the nudity pattern of the rain forests and the breechclout and robe pattern of the Mediterranean world and elsewhere; and that, in general, its geographical distribution is increasing rather than diminishing.

Internal Systemic Pattern Analysis Thus far the discussion of "tailored garments" has the ring of "culture history," and indeed most studies of systemic patterns have been culture historical in intent. The present inquiry, however, seeks to go beyond this traditional purpose. More specifically, it is concerned with a form of comparative preferential pattern analysis which provides information both on the internal structure of the systemic pattern and on other anthropological topics.[1]

This inquiry uses operations with the pattern nomenclatures in making inferences about the internal structure of the systemic pattern. All such patterns, of course, are coded linguistically in the languages of their host cultures so that they, and their component elements, can be easily discussed. Commonly most nomenclatures contain loan words derived from the language of the culture originating the pattern. Often, of course, the host culture receiving the pattern provides its own terminology; but even here the new nomenclature is usually the equivalent of the old in that the same elements in the pattern are named. In the case of high-concordance patterns, i.e., those patterns known by the vast majority of adults in a culture, the linguistic codes for the patterns are well designed for general communication since they have been forged in the fires of millions of discussions of the pattern. Indeed, these pattern nomenclatures are themselves high-concordance codes.[2] This linguistic integration of the pattern into the language of the host culture is most important. The study described herein is built on the assumption that operations with terms for pattern elements, e.g., shirts and shoes, can support inferences about the pattern itself, e.g., tailored clothing, the people who share in it, and the host cultures that accommodate it.

Preference and Contrast The foregoing discussion of the systemic pattern has served to define the setting in which the two psychocultural variables of preference and contrast will be considered. Indeed, these variables rather than clothing constitute our primary concern. The two variables, however, are not easily defined. "Preference" is treated here as being equivalent to "subjective utility" or "The utility or satisfaction an article gives to an individual based upon his personal judgment and desires rather than upon market judgment" (Webster 1963:2276). "Contrast," on the other hand, is used in an ordinary sense, "to exhibit especially antithetically the differences and relative worth of" (Webster 1963:496). Both terms will be defined operationally later in the paper.

We offer the following hypotheses pertaining to preference and contrast:

1. Operations with combinations of element terms drawn from a systemic pattern nomenclature permit inferences about the systemic pattern as a whole on the basis of determined preference and contrast values.

2. The greater the preferences for elements in the pattern the greater the integration of the systemic pattern into the host culture.

[1] This concern with the systemic pattern and its internal structure emerged in large part from a collateral line of research devoted to the study of games and related phenomena (Roberts, Arth, and Bush 1959; Roberts and Sutton-Smith 1962; Sutton-Smith, Roberts, and Kozelka 1963; Roberts, Sutton-Smith, and Kendon 1963; Sutton-Smith and Roberts 1964; Roberts 1965b; Roberts, Hoffmann, and Sutton-Smith 1965; Roberts, Thompson, and Sutton-Smith 1966; and Sutton-Smith and Roberts 1967).
[2] As a matter of fact this study is a continuation of an interest in the high concordance code (cf., Lenneberg and Roberts 1956; Schneider and Roberts 1956; Roberts 1965a; Kozelka and Roberts, n.d.; and Roberts, Smith, and Kozelka, n.d.).

3. The greater the contrasts values, the greater the integration of the systemic pattern into the host culture.

4. Preferences and contrasts can be mapped, and the resulting pattern projections are useful in pattern analysis.

Various subsidiary hypotheses can be derived from the above statements, but it is not necessary to list them here.

Research Design

There are advantages to using the tailored clothing complex as the systemic pattern for study. This pattern has had a very long culture history, and it is readily identifiable wherever it occurs. This complex is dominant and high in concordance over a vast geographical area, and there is a larger area where it is a familiar alternate form. Some unsystematic sampling has indicated that the principal elements of the pattern are coded linguistically in various host cultures in much the same way, and that the "fit" between the linguistic code dealing with the pattern and the pattern itself is particularly good. Moreover, it can be assumed that all persons who share in the tailored clothing complex value the possession of some clothing as against none and various combinations of articles of clothing as against other articles even in a situation where those articles do not represent transferable property.

Within the tailored clothing complex the elements of the shirt and the shoe were selected for special consideration. They are elements in the core complex which do not have close associative meanings such as those found in such common expressions as "hat and coat" or "shirt and trousers." Still, these two elements constituted a sufficiently important subset of the set of elements making up the complex to permit inferences about the pattern as a whole. In this study, then, the English words "shirts" and "shoes" were used with the stipulation that the word "shoes" pertains to pairs of shoes rather than to single shoes. Furthermore, subjects were asked to consider the word "shirts" as referring to men's white shirts and the word "shoes" as referring to pairs of men's black leather oxfords.

Seven married couples participated in the original test. The subjects ranged in age from 19 to 31 years. In all cases the husbands were students at Cornell University, and the wives had completed at least a secondary school education. Four of the couples were native Americans; the three remaining couples were from France, Turkey, and Chile. Later, three additional male students from India, Cameroun, and Egypt were added as subjects.

The eight American and the two French informants constituted a northern group where high concordance and high integration could be expected in the host cultures. The other subjects constituted a miscellaneous southern group representing host cultures where the tailored clothing complex and collateral ideas about property have not always been dominant, although in each instance the men habitually wore shirts and shoes and everyone in the group was entirely familiar with the complex.

The prediction was made that the members of the northern group would display higher preference and contrast values than the members of the southern group.

The 17 subjects dealt with two sets: Shirts = {0 shirts, 1 shirt, 2 shirts, 3 shirts, 4 shirts, 5 shirts, and 6 shirts} and Shoes = {0 pr. shoes, 1 pr. shoes, 2 pr. shoes, 3 pr. shoes, 4 pr. shoes, 5 pr. shoes, and 6 pr. shoes}. In the study, subjects were asked to deal with the 49 elements in the Cartesian product of the two sets: Shirts × Shoes = {(0 shirts, 0 pr. shoes), (0 shirts, 1 pr. shoes), (0 shirts, 2 pr. shoes), . . . , (6 shirts, 6 pr. shoes)}. Each element in the Cartesian product will hereafter be termed a "shirt-shoe combination." Each subject expressed his preference for one of a pair of shirt-shoe combinations. Since all possible pairs were used each subject judged between 1,176 pairs of shirt-shoe combinations.

In expressing preferences, the men were asked to make their choices in terms of their own prospective use of the combinations, but the women were asked to act as though they were choosing to satisfy their family's needs. In order to remove monetary considerations, the subjects were instructed to imagine themselves in a situation in which they had no shirts or shoes, but in which they could obtain their choices in each situation without having to pay for them. They were further instructed to imagine that once they had obtained a quantity of shirts and shoes, they could not sell or give away the clothing. The clothing was strictly for personal use (in the case of the men) or for the husband's use (in the case of the women).

Use was made of a constant-sum ratio scale[3] in this inquiry, but from the subject's viewpoint, he had only to express his choice of one of two shirt-shoe combinations in terms of one of the following ratios: 1 : 9, 2 : 8, 3 : 7, 4 : 6, 5 : 5, 6 : 4, 7 : 3, 8 : 2, and 9 : 1. The shirt-shoe combination pairs were presented orally in random order. As each pair was given to the subject, he marked the ratio expressing his preference for one shirt-shoe combination as against the other on a specially prepared IBM card with an electrographic pencil. The two shirt-shoe combinations were also printed on the card. Thus, a typical card might read "5 shirts 4 shoes . . . 6 shirts 0 shoes." Each subject completed 1,176 cards.

This set of judgments permitted the mapping of both the preferences and the contrasts. The two variables, then, were functions of the same judgments. Fundamentally, preferences involved a choice for one combination as against another. Thus, all subjects, regardless of cultural background or sex, preferred the combination "(6 shirts, 6 pr. shoes)" as against the combination "(0 shirts, 0 pr. shoes)." The contrast variable, on the other hand, fundamentally represented the clearness of the choice. Here, a subject's judgment between any two points is a measure of the degree to which he differentiates the points. A judgment of 9 to 1 between points a and b indicates a strong subjective contrast between a and b, while a judgment of 5 to 5

[3] Torgerson (1958:105) reports that the constant-sum method was advocated over two decades ago by Metfessel (1947:229–235) and Comrey (1950:317–325). For a recent application of the method, see Roberts (1965a) and Kozelka and Roberts (n.d.).

between a and b indicates no subjective contrast between the two points. An informant could display greater contrast in rejecting the combination "(0 shirts, 0 pr. shoes)" as against some other combination than in selecting the combination "(6 shirts, 6 pr. shoes)" as against some other combination. The preference maps, then, show an increasing preference for the higher shirt-shoe combinations, whereas the contrast maps show high contrast in rejecting the lower valued or deficit shirt-shoe combinations and high contrast in preferring the higher-valued shirt-shoe combinations. The lower contrasts occur with shirt-shoe combinations of intermediate value.

Statistical Procedures The foregoing explanation does not do justice to the statistical procedures used. These are now explained in some detail.

Preference The preference for each combination of shirts and shoes is computed by the constant-sum method for determining ratio-scale values, and the procedure followed is that described by Torgerson (Torgerson 1958:108–112). Perhaps it should be stated here that economists are primarily interested in measures of preference (utility) in order to predict behavior under uncertainty, and the works of Von Neumann and Morgenstern (1947), Savage (1954), and many other recent authors are concerned with obtaining a cardinal measure of utility which is unique up to a linear transformation (an interval scale). Our approach to the measurement of preferences may be termed "classical" in that it in no way involves decisions under uncertainty; rather subjects are asked to judge their preferences between riskless options. Stevens (1959) offers an argument in support of this approach.

In using the constant-sum method each combination of shirts and shoes is compared with every other combination; thus, for n combinations of shirts and shoes there are $n(n-1)/2$ paired comparisons. In making a comparison, the subject is asked to divide 10 "votes" between the two combinations in the proportion that indicates the ratio of his preference of one combination against the other; thus, a division of nine votes for combination a and one vote for combination b indicates a 9 to 1 preference for a over b. We implicitly assume that subjects can do better than estimate equal intervals; a subject must be able to judge the *ratio* of his preference for a over b, e.g., $9:1$, $7:3$, or $4:6$. The ratio judgments are entered as elements of an $n \times n$ matrix $\mathbf{R}$; the element on the ith row and the jth column is therefore the ratio for the comparison of combination i to combination j. The principal diagonal of the matrix will contain only ones, indicating the ratio of the comparison of a combination with itself. One-half of the matrix is now filled in; the remaining elements are entered as the reciprocals of their corresponding elements in the other half of the matrix; that is, the element in the jth row and the ith column is the reciprocal of the element in the ith row and the jth column.

The jth column of this matrix contains n elements, each element being the comparison-ratio of combination j with each of the n combinations (including itself). The *preference* of combination j is defined as the geometric mean of the elements in column j (Torgerson 1958:110). All n preference values fall on a ratio scale. Thus letting P_j

denote the preference value of combination j, $j = 1, \ldots, n$, we have uniquely determined any ratio of the form P_j/P_i. Multiplying all values P_j by a positive scalar will leave the latter ratios unchanged, which is precisely the definition of a ratio scale: preference values are determined uniquely up to a multiplicative constant. Following Torgerson, the *unit* of the scale is defined as the geometric mean of the n preference values (i.e., the geometric mean of the n preference values equals one). Since the point (0 shirts, 0 shoes) was included among the paired comparisons, the above procedure implies that the preference value of the (0, 0) point will be positive, a result that may not be intuitively appealing. However, a discussion of this and related difficulties with the procedure used is beyond the scope of our present study, although we agree that they are important in principle and must be faced before our results can be interpreted with complete rigor.

Note also that the unit of the preference scale is not invariant across subjects. The problem of interpersonal comparisons is one which plagues all psychophysical measurement, and we simply must ignore it if we are to attempt any research of the type presented here. Nevertheless, it is important to realize that what may be an insurmountable *theoretical* question may also be *empirically* unimportant. For a discussion of this viewpoint, cf. Stevens (1966: 540):

How should we regard these individual differences in range, or in exponent? Admittedly it would be something of a miracle if everybody's judgments followed exactly the same function for delinquency, loudness, or anything else. Perhaps the variations in how people use numbers and how they regard ratios are no more than the inevitable noise that characterizes these complex processes. The fact that two of the lines in Fig. 13 have different slopes may mean that the two observers in question have different mechanisms at work in their auditory systems, but it may also mean that the two observers happen merely to differ about what they consider an apparent ratio. Further experiments may decide the point. In the meantime, there is growing evidence that the differences in the observed exponents, for a reasonable sample of observers, have one of the very important properties of noise—namely, the capacity to be averaged out. Note, for example, in Fig. 12 how nearly the average estimations by the police officers agree with the average estimations by university students. It is the stability of the function from group to group that makes the result useful.

The computation of preference is facilitated by the use of logarithms. The elements in matrix **R** are replaced by their logarithms, forming matrix **L**; the logarithms in column j are added and divided by n and the result is the logarithm of the preference of combination j. This procedure is summarized in the formula

$$\log P_j = \frac{1}{n} \sum_{i=1}^{n} \log r_{ij},$$

where P_j is the preference of combination j, n is the total number of combinations, and r_{ij} is the ratio judgment of combination i compared to combination j.

Contrast The ratio judgment between any two combinations is an indication of the subject's contrast in his choice. A ratio judgment of 9 to 1 between combinations a

and b indicates a high contrast in regard to both the choice of a and the nonchoice of b. Conversely, a judgment of 5 to 5 between a and b indicates no contrast whatsoever. In comparing any two combinations i and j, a measure of the contrast associated with j with respect to i may be obtained from the ratio judgment between the two combinations; if the judgment is r_{ij}, the contrast measure is r_{ij} or $1/r_{ij}$, whichever is the greater; we will denote by c_{ij} the concept "the greater of r_{ij} and $1/r_{ij}$." Thus c_{ij} is always greater than one. For example, if i versus j has a judgment of 6 to 4, the contrast of j with respect to i is $6/4 = 1.5$, indicating a slight contrast between i and j. We may now define the *contrast* of combination j with respect to the total pattern as being the geometric mean of c_{ij} for all values of i.

Computation of contrast is again simplified by the use of logarithms. In matrix **L** the element of the ith row and the jth column is identical to the element in the jth row and the ith column except for sign; if r_{ij} is less than one, the sign of the logarithm will be negative. As already stated, c_{ij} is defined as the greater of r_{ij} and $1/r_{ij}$; since $\log r_{ij} = -\log(1/r_{ij})$ and c_{ij} is greater than one, $\log c_{ij} = |\log r_{ij}|$. The formula for the contrast of combination j is

$$\log C_j = \frac{1}{n} \sum_{i=1}^{n} |\log r_{ij}|,$$

where C_j is the contrast associated with combination j, n is the total number of combinations, and $|\log r_{ij}|$ is the absolute value of the logarithm of the ratio judgment of combination i compared to combination j.

Total Pattern It is advantageous to have statistics that will give a representation of the characteristics of the entire pattern. We admit, however, that this task is ambitious and one requiring further theoretical justification, but we can let our results speak for themselves. As a summary statistic to represent contrast, we shall choose the geometric mean of all contrast values C_j. Thus

$$\log C_M = \frac{1}{n} \sum_{j=1}^{n} \log C_j,$$

where C_M is the *mean contrast* over the entire pattern.

A convenient statistic to represent the total preference pattern is the arithmetic mean of all preference values. Thus

$$P_M = \frac{1}{n} \sum_{j=1}^{n} P_j,$$

where P_M is the *average preference* over the entire pattern.

Results

The results obtained through the use of the scaling technique are presented in Tables 1 and 2. It should be noted in the case of the preference values that each member of the northern group of respondents (American and French) displays a higher average preference value than any member of the southern group (Fisher test $p = 0.00005$). Again, the members of the northern group have both lower and higher values for specific combinations in the list than any member of the southern group. The members of the northern group also have higher mean contrast values (cf. Table 2) than the members of the southern group (Fisher test $p = 0.00005$).

The American respondents can be viewed as a distinctive group because they can be distinguished from all others in having higher average preference values (Fisher test $p = 0.0009$) and higher mean contrast values (Fisher test $p = 0.0009$). This simply means that the relationships noted for the groups hold even if the two French respondents are treated as deviant cases.

The data presented in Tables 1 and 2 may be used in constructing maps of the preferential patterns of the individual respondents in order to facilitate the task of cultural interpretation and evaluation. These maps portray the square pattern field of 49 data points and give the values of each shirt-shoe combination in the field at each data point. The "contour lines" of each map are provided by plotting the indifference curves (the lines connecting points of either equal preference value or equal contrast value depending upon the map) in the pattern field. These maps constitute a "projection" of the preferential pattern and they permit a visual assessment of the pattern which could not be made by examining Tables 1 and 2.

Fortunately, the preferential pattern maps can be made by a computer, and this procedure was followed in the course of the present study. The computer maps, however, are too detailed for presentation here. Instead, illustrative examples are given in the figures which follow, and in these figures only a few of the relevant indifference curves are plotted.

Figure 1 presents the preference map for the American man displaying the highest mean contrast and the highest preference variance (U.S. 7M, Tables 2 and 1). This map shows a strong preference for the larger combinations of shirts and shoes and the bias in favor of shirts. Figure 2 presents the preference map of the American male who displayed the lowest preference variance and mean contrast values in the American group. Figure 2 contrasts with Figure 1 in showing less of a bias in favor of shirts and a relatively higher preference for some of the lower combinations of shirts and shoes. The other six Americans had preference maps lying between these two extremes.

It will be recalled that the Indian male provided preference variance and mean contrast values which were very close to those of the lowest American. His preference map is given in Figure 3. It can immediately be seen that the preference pattern for the Indian is quite different from either of the Americans shown in Figures 1 and 2. His maximum preference value, for example, is 7.25, and it occurs at the six shirts and three pairs of shoes data point, whereas in both cases the American maximum is 8.61, occurring at the six shirts and six shoes data point. Figure 3 also shows a slight

TABLE 1 -- PREFERENCE VALUES

SHIRTS	SHOES	U.S. 7M	U.S. 7F	U.S. 3M	FR 2F	U.S. 3F	U.S. 6M	U.S. 6F	U.S. 4F
0	0	.12	.12	.12	.12	.12	.12	.12	.12
0	1	.13	.15	.15	.13	.15	.15	.14	.14
0	2	.14	.16	.23	.16	.18	.17	.17	.19
0	3	.15	.15	.34	.18	.22	.18	.19	.24
0	4	.18	.17	.46	.23	.34	.21	.22	.33
0	5	.21	.19	.80	.30	.33	.24	.25	.35
0	6	.21	.22	.91	.33	.37	.24	.28	.48
1	0	.20	.18	.13	.14	.13	.15	.14	.15
1	1	.30	.32	.23	.29	.27	.37	.37	.24
1	2	.31	.37	.34	.35	.37	.41	.43	.37
1	3	.38	.39	.64	.45	.56	.47	.47	.37
1	4	.41	.44	.93	.60	.68	.56	.54	.51
1	5	.43	.52	1.50	.73	1.09	.60	.73	.66
1	6	.59	.56	2.26	.79	1.19	.65	.85	.78
2	0	.24	.23	.15	.19	.15	.20	.18	.21
2	1	.55	.56	.30	.44	.33	.59	.55	.38
2	2	.62	.69	.52	.69	.61	.76	.73	.58
2	3	.71	.73	.73	.79	.91	.78	.77	.72
2	4	.77	.77	1.35	1.05	1.29	.91	.92	.98
2	5	.90	.91	2.68	1.18	1.88	1.08	1.31	1.08
2	6	1.01	.98	3.99	1.42	2.57	1.09	1.61	1.33
3	0	.28	.31	.17	.22	.19	.22	.21	.22
3	1	1.01	1.06	.33	.62	.51	.88	.76	.61
3	2	1.12	1.09	.82	1.13	.79	1.13	.98	1.03
3	3	1.35	1.34	1.30	1.50	1.48	1.51	1.41	1.49
3	4	1.46	1.47	2.31	1.71	2.41	1.55	1.55	1.72
3	5	1.66	1.46	3.60	2.04	3.07	1.86	2.40	1.92
3	6	2.05	1.74	5.30	2.38	3.61	2.10	2.61	2.10
4	0	.39	.38	.22	.26	.25	.23	.23	.34
4	1	1.58	1.76	.46	1.00	.64	1.36	1.22	.91
4	2	1.76	2.02	.96	1.59	1.20	2.16	1.92	1.43
4	3	2.28	2.30	1.59	2.68	1.84	2.42	1.81	2.22
4	4	2.78	2.66	3.10	3.21	3.16	2.81	2.62	2.98
4	5	3.12	2.98	4.40	3.32	5.11	3.21	3.41	3.23
4	6	3.63	3.16	5.70	4.05	6.01	3.35	3.52	4.06
5	0	.62	.39	.24	.30	.33	.28	.27	.42
5	1	2.26	2.67	.61	1.31	.87	1.81	1.58	1.38
5	2	3.51	3.38	1.28	2.33	1.58	3.44	3.23	2.66
5	3	4.02	4.13	2.11	4.39	2.93	4.27	3.80	3.78
5	4	4.47	4.34	3.87	4.86	4.59	4.57	4.67	4.59
5	5	5.25	5.12	5.70	5.91	6.58	4.94	5.50	4.94
5	6	6.01	4.71	6.93	6.13	7.87	5.91	5.65	6.01
6	0	.58	.49	.31	.41	.43	.31	.32	.47
6	1	3.13	4.32	.64	1.81	1.04	2.00	1.91	1.64
6	2	5.25	5.41	1.33	4.25	2.07	4.50	3.83	3.89
6	3	6.58	6.58	2.63	6.11	3.40	6.58	5.86	6.15
6	4	7.19	6.76	5.68	6.58	5.32	7.19	6.96	7.19
6	5	7.87	7.87	7.31	7.87	7.19	7.87	7.87	7.74
6	6	8.61	8.37	8.61	8.61	8.61	8.61	8.61	8.61
AVERAGE PREFERENCE		2.01	1.98	1.96	1.98	1.98	1.98	1.95	1.92

TABLE 1 -- PREFERENCE VALUES

		SUBJECT							U.S. Average
FR	U.S.	IND	CAM	EGY	TURK	CHILE	CHILE	TURK	
2M	4M	8M	9M	1M	5F	2F	1M	5M	AV
.12	.12	.15	.15	.23	.26	.35	.14	.24	.12
.15	.16	.21	.22	.28	.43	.49	.27	.35	.15
.19	.22	.22	.25	.29	.45	.52	.32	.42	.18
.23	.34	.22	.27	.28	.52	.60	.43	.47	.22
.28	.45	.22	.36	.29	.66	.49	.54	.54	.29
.36	.66	.23	.43	.33	.74	.56	.65	.56	.36
.38	1.05	.22	.58	.31	.87	.51	.72	.61	.42
.14	.13	.20	.20	.24	.30	.47	.27	.34	.15
.27	.21	.43	.29	.38	.41	4.15	.46	.53	.27
.33	.31	.59	.34	.42	.52	1.16	.50	.49	.36
.44	.42	.47	.45	.44	.60	.78	.59	.60	.45
.57	.62	.59	.48	.44	.80	.58	.70	.68	.57
.84	1.02	.50	.67	.45	.85	.56	.87	.72	.77
.99	1.89	.51	.84	.53	1.29	.58	1.02	.98	.99
.16	.17	.21	.29	.28	.32	.53	.36	.44	.19
.41	.28	.75	.40	.64	.46	1.55	.51	.49	.41
.65	.49	.94	.55	.65	.65	5.44	.90	.87	.61
.70	.74	1.03	.70	.73	.81	1.77	.90	.94	.76
.96	1.15	.88	.97	.67	1.07	.88	1.11	.96	1.01
1.44	1.58	.88	1.21	.62	1.26	.65	1.23	.95	1.35
1.84	2.41	.75	1.48	.78	2.15	.50	1.51	1.23	1.70
.23	.23	.23	.41	.29	.38	.54	.45	.51	.23
.70	.43	1.07	.60	.91	.57	.70	.55	.67	.63
.89	.60	1.56	.63	1.18	.71	1.48	.98	.86	.90
1.34	1.20	1.64	1.05	1.01	.98	6.58	1.51	1.82	1.35
1.71	1.70	1.78	1.54	1.11	1.32	1.71	1.37	1.24	1.73
2.51	2.68	1.39	1.60	1.16	1.92	.74	1.81	1.33	2.26
2.62	3.30	1.17	2.14	1.17	2.58	.58	2.05	1.61	2.72
.30	.29	.23	.54	.41	.49	.52	.57	.58	.29
1.02	.67	1.78	1.11	1.35	.86	.65	.80	.94	.94
1.75	1.02	2.88	1.35	1.95	.95	.82	1.11	1.20	1.44
2.09	1.59	3.01	1.63	2.10	1.46	1.85	1.52	1.39	1.92
2.45	2.85	2.40	2.41	1.82	1.51	7.19	2.69	2.83	2.82
2.89	3.72	2.27	3.51	1.78	2.42	2.30	2.22	2.09	3.58
4.11	5.23	2.11	3.75	2.05	3.57	.81	2.52	2.07	4.26
.32	.51	.27	.79	.57	.48	.53	.71	.70	.39
1.42	.83	2.66	1.28	2.75	.75	.60	.94	.97	1.30
2.37	1.62	4.32	2.05	3.91	1.20	.59	1.22	1.27	2.26
3.02	2.34	4.77	2.93	3.86	1.59	.93	1.76	1.72	3.16
4.05	4.00	4.01	3.54	4.26	1.95	1.90	2.50	2.43	4.25
4.64	5.52	4.02	4.62	4.23	3.81	7.87	3.05	4.43	5.37
5.81	6.89	3.10	5.20	3.65	4.82	1.98	3.19	2.51	6.18
.34	.68	.24	.89	.59	.69	.50	.82	.79	.46
2.04	1.21	2.24	1.42	4.36	1.02	.60	1.10	1.07	1.67
4.41	2.06	6.90	2.05	5.46	1.43	.57	1.50	1.36	3.05
5.18	2.99	7.25	3.55	5.96	2.12	.72	2.13	1.97	4.51
6.13	5.10	5.75	5.35	5.43	2.66	.77	2.58	2.51	6.14
7.74	7.52	5.44	5.17	4.98	2.94	2.38	3.57	2.70	7.57
8.46	8.61	4.06	5.96	5.32	3.81	8.00	5.28	6.80	8.56
1.88	1.83	1.81	1.60	1.69	1.31	1.58	1.32	1.30	1.86

TABLE 2 -- CONTRAST VALUES

SHIRTS	SHOES	U.S. 7M	U.S. 7F	U.S. 3M	FR 2F	U.S. 3F	U.S. 6M	U.S. 6F	U.S. 4F
0	0	8.61	8.61	8.61	8.61	8.61	8.61	8.61	8.61
0	1	8.61	7.79	8.09	8.19	8.01	7.40	7.74	7.65
0	2	8.61	7.72	7.97	8.10	8.07	7.23	7.32	6.49
0	3	8.61	7.79	7.41	7.87	7.84	7.34	7.66	6.19
0	4	8.00	7.92	6.97	7.46	7.08	7.13	7.79	5.19
0	5	8.23	8.37	6.06	7.43	6.51	7.02	7.71	5.27
0	6	8.33	7.92	7.03	7.08	6.04	7.11	7.62	5.07
1	0	7.87	7.17	8.61	8.33	8.46	7.19	7.67	7.42
1	1	7.52	7.66	7.53	7.34	6.63	8.46	8.46	6.55
1	2	7.25	7.26	7.96	7.27	7.06	8.46	8.10	6.47
1	3	7.65	7.72	8.14	7.68	7.53	8.19	8.19	6.45
1	4	8.14	7.37	8.19	7.58	7.68	7.92	7.71	6.28
1	5	7.18	6.70	7.53	7.39	6.60	7.43	6.90	5.47
1	6	7.31	5.96	7.30	7.06	6.89	7.06	6.44	5.26
2	0	7.59	7.92	8.23	7.71	8.46	7.05	8.01	6.37
2	1	7.94	7.79	7.53	7.11	7.04	7.68	7.72	5.86
2	2	7.65	7.22	7.67	7.92	7.19	7.62	7.32	6.25
2	3	7.65	8.23	7.28	7.33	7.21	6.89	7.31	5.60
2	4	8.07	7.96	7.42	7.97	7.47	7.42	7.55	6.38
2	5	7.85	8.03	8.61	7.75	8.10	7.71	7.07	6.73
2	6	7.38	8.46	7.57	7.40	7.79	7.66	6.54	5.97
3	0	7.31	7.14	8.09	6.85	7.58	7.23	7.62	6.27
3	1	7.94	8.33	7.68	7.37	7.75	7.31	7.35	5.54
3	2	7.92	7.87	7.02	7.64	7.20	7.19	7.25	6.18
3	3	8.37	7.89	7.31	7.96	7.15	7.42	7.60	6.85
3	4	7.06	8.10	8.10	7.79	7.74	7.71	7.68	6.29
3	5	8.33	8.00	7.55	7.89	7.97	7.39	7.29	6.85
3	6	8.61	8.01	7.72	7.83	8.37	7.43	7.58	7.03
4	0	7.07	7.07	7.68	6.97	6.94	6.92	7.07	4.70
4	1	7.92	8.37	7.89	7.31	7.46	6.86	6.88	6.26
4	2	7.80	8.46	7.47	7.49	7.39	7.58	7.37	5.84
4	3	8.00	8.37	7.32	8.05	8.46	7.97	7.46	6.88
4	4	8.14	7.93	8.33	8.61	8.46	7.68	7.97	7.43
4	5	8.37	7.74	8.23	8.33	8.46	8.33	7.58	7.49
4	6	8.14	8.46	8.30	8.16	8.61	8.23	7.58	7.36
5	0	6.10	6.79	7.43	6.99	6.67	7.51	7.46	4.22
5	1	7.12	7.58	7.25	6.17	6.95	6.37	6.06	5.17
5	2	8.61	8.30	7.26	7.41	7.50	7.71	7.92	6.32
5	3	8.23	8.46	8.09	8.23	8.61	8.46	7.54	7.74
5	4	8.37	8.33	7.93	8.33	8.61	8.10	8.46	8.33
5	5	8.23	8.01	8.30	8.46	8.61	8.01	8.33	7.87
5	6	8.61	8.07	8.30	8.16	8.61	8.46	8.37	8.05
6	0	5.62	6.69	7.25	6.39	6.08	7.26	8.05	3.99
6	1	7.37	7.40	7.45	7.03	7.10	5.94	5.60	4.07
6	2	8.23	8.01	6.96	7.04	7.03	7.29	6.71	6.10
6	3	8.61	8.61	7.75	8.46	7.62	8.61	7.66	8.05
6	4	8.61	8.09	7.32	8.61	8.33	8.61	8.33	8.61
6	5	8.61	8.61	8.00	8.61	8.61	8.61	8.61	8.45
6	6	8.61	8.37	8.61	8.61	8.61	8.61	8.61	8.61
AVERAGE CONTRAST		7.89	7.83	7.70	7.68	7.61	7.59	7.55	6.38

TABLE 2 -- CONTRAST VALUES

		SUBJECT							U.S. Average
FR	U.S.	IND	CAM	EGY	TURK	CHILE	CHILE	TURK	Average
2M	4M	8M	9M	1M	5F	2F	1M	5M	Av
8.61	8.61	6.68	6.87	4.57	4.90	2.84	6.94	4.25	8.61
7.19	7.62	5.21	4.59	3.96	3.18	2.18	3.96	3.04	7.53
6.76	6.78	5.25	4.46	3.62	2.92	2.11	3.44	2.62	6.68
6.16	5.36	5.41	4.13	3.74	2.66	1.99	2.75	2.59	5.84
5.99	5.05	5.12	4.23	3.54	2.59	2.09	2.72	2.27	5.23
6.19	4.36	5.27	4.20	3.39	2.51	2.14	2.34	2.30	4.76
5.95	3.88	5.11	3.29	3.33	2.40	2.08	2.43	2.35	4.31
8.03	8.23	5.48	5.16	4.25	3.50	2.32	3.88	3.13	7.15
6.26	6.94	5.67	4.12	3.44	2.73	7.97	2.87	2.63	6.27
6.70	5.73	5.31	4.11	3.62	2.67	3.51	2.50	2.61	6.19
5.87	5.47	5.95	3.62	2.97	2.73	2.14	2.58	2.41	5.92
5.84	4.61	5.73	3.49	2.81	2.58	1.85	2.28	2.22	5.47
5.07	4.28	5.65	3.18	3.28	2.80	2.10	2.21	2.35	4.71
4.39	4.83	5.92	3.17	3.19	2.60	1.96	2.22	2.46	4.24
7.32	7.18	5.11	4.17	4.07	3.61	2.08	3.07	2.70	6.45
6.08	6.41	5.54	3.30	3.54	3.15	3.63	2.75	2.68	5.83
6.48	5.71	5.24	3.26	3.59	2.35	8.23	2.66	2.41	5.97
6.46	4.89	5.07	3.50	3.36	2.48	3.94	2.32	2.33	5.57
5.81	5.55	5.94	3.54	2.92	2.58	2.38	2.22	2.42	5.50
5.43	4.78	5.29	3.85	3.13	2.43	1.97	2.12	2.24	5.18
5.99	4.80	6.14	3.86	3.23	3.19	2.20	2.21	2.10	4.66
6.22	6.09	5.26	3.56	4.05	3.07	1.91	2.80	2.41	6.12
6.01	5.74	5.57	3.52	3.27	2.55	2.37	2.61	2.22	5.15
5.99	5.06	5.91	2.96	3.51	2.38	3.18	2.52	2.17	5.59
6.64	5.85	6.02	3.28	3.45	2.61	8.61	2.97	2.76	5.93
6.13	5.70	5.62	3.62	3.35	2.57	3.55	2.58	2.61	5.62
6.31	5.80	4.98	3.39	3.19	2.69	2.41	2.68	2.49	5.45
6.03	5.52	5.00	3.79	3.33	3.14	2.23	2.61	2.48	5.40
5.44	5.01	4.87	3.16	3.61	2.69	2.12	2.45	2.45	5.51
5.30	4.90	5.65	3.43	4.25	2.52	2.05	2.16	2.17	4.73
6.16	5.35	5.76	3.48	3.79	2.83	2.09	2.44	2.60	5.19
6.28	5.59	5.78	4.46	3.99	2.49	4.36	2.42	2.42	5.47
6.35	6.49	5.03	4.21	3.23	2.97	8.61	3.51	3.71	6.14
6.63	6.85	4.78	4.93	3.79	3.21	3.81	2.86	2.77	6.50
6.61	6.95	5.25	5.00	3.40	3.84	2.37	2.79	2.86	6.27
5.40	4.07	5.14	3.22	3.17	2.96	2.29	2.31	2.12	4.74
4.47	4.73	5.11	3.33	4.64	2.57	1.89	2.21	2.42	4.20
6.03	4.80	6.78	4.08	5.56	2.11	2.09	2.27	2.33	5.06
6.34	5.51	6.50	4.44	4.78	2.41	2.23	2.37	2.54	6.03
7.17	6.63	5.78	4.61	4.80	2.46	3.45	2.93	2.80	6.84
7.29	7.22	6.07	5.23	4.87	4.31	8.61	3.39	4.58	7.41
7.88	7.53	5.69	5.69	4.03	5.07	3.58	3.30	2.83	7.39
5.21	3.51	4.87	3.04	3.03	2.45	2.23	2.36	2.06	4.63
5.03	4.38	4.47	3.65	5.28	2.58	1.83	2.22	2.11	3.86
6.69	4.97	7.38	3.66	6.07	2.85	1.96	2.46	2.38	4.68
7.02	5.82	7.25	4.81	5.96	3.04	2.32	2.53	2.48	5.91
7.33	6.54	6.19	5.75	5.52	3.49	2.09	3.02	2.88	7.34
8.46	8.23	6.06	5.65	5.44	3.93	3.94	3.63	3.01	8.28
8.46	8.61	4.86	5.96	5.41	4.47	8.46	5.28	6.80	8.56
6.29	5.68	5.55	4.00	3.84	2.89	2.83	2.73	2.61	5.74

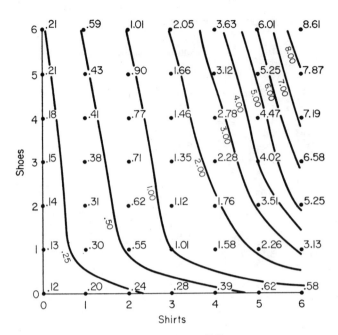

Figure 1. Preference map—United States 7M.

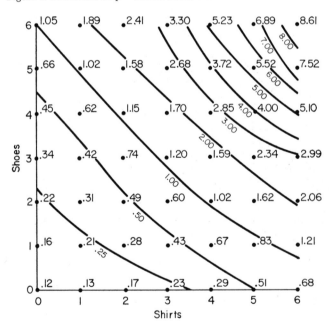

Figure 2. Preference map—United States 9M.

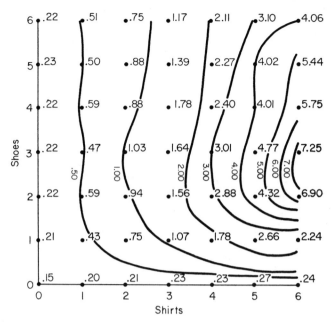

Figure 3. Preference map—India 8M.

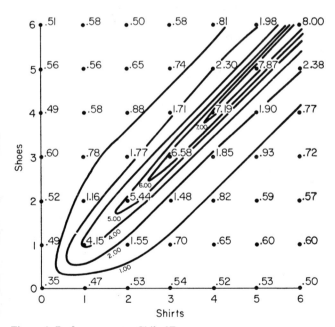

Figure 4. Preference map—Chile 1F.

"ensemble" effect in that there appears to be a value attached to the right proportion of shirts to shoes.[4]

The "ensemble" effect, however, is portrayed in extreme form in the preference map of the Chilean female (Figure 4). Plainly, in this preference map the combinations of one shirt and one pair of shoes, two shirts and two pairs of shoes, three shirts and three pairs of shoes, four shirts and four pairs of shoes, five shirts and five pairs of shoes, and six shirts and six pairs of shoes are preferred greatly to nearby combinations. The proportion of shirts to shoes is important to this particular respondent.

In general the preference maps have similar conformations, although the differences and similarities among informants can be readily seen in the course of only a cursory inspection. The contrast maps are equally easily read, but their contours are very different because of the fact that combinations for which there are both low and high preferences display high contrast. Again, the similarities and differences among respondents can be readily seen.

Figure 5 shows the contrast map of the Indian male whose preference map was given in Figure 3. A comparison of Figures 3 and 5 reveals the differences in the two forms

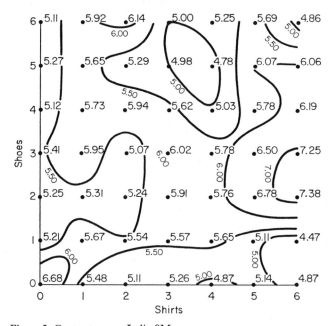

Figure 5. Contrast map—India 8M.

[4] A pure "ensemble" effect exists when shirts and shoes are *always* wanted in the same proportion, say two shirts to one pair of shoes. In this case we would theoretically expect that the indifference contours would all be L-shaped with every corner lying along a line through the origin with slope two.

of maps. For the contrast map the areas of low contrast should be noted in relationship to the areas of high contrast. In all probability, as the discussion will indicate, the
contrast map is a more informative document in cases of low mean contrast than for
cases of high mean contrast, since in the latter instance the contrast maps can almost
be inferred from the preference maps. We would expect, of course, that subjects who do
not have well-formed preferences ("are undecided") will exhibit large numbers of
5 : 5, 4 : 6, and 6 : 4 votes, which, in turn, will be reflected by low mean contrast.

Thus far it has been demonstrated that the preference and contrast values can be
determined for each of the 49 shirt-shoe combinations and that these values can be
mapped. Attention has been called to the summary statistics of preference variance
and mean contrast. Since further consideration of the results will involve some interpretation, this treatment will appear in the discussion section that follows. Before
turning to this discussion, it would be well to deal briefly with two additional descriptive problems: (1) the degree to which a summary or composite statement of
pattern can be made and (2) the degree to which this approach can be extended to
other patterns.

Composite Maps The eight American respondents appear to share in the same
general cultural pattern as far as shirts and shoes are concerned, although admittedly
the female respondents do not wear men's shirts and shoes. Figure 6 shows the composite preference map of all respondents obtained by averaging their original

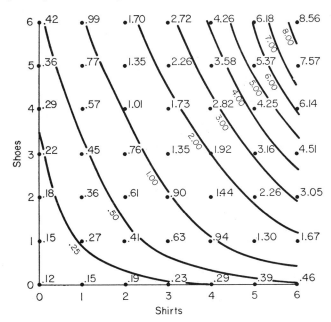

Figure 6. U.S. average preference map.

judgments and then processing these judgments as if they had been produced by a single respondent. The procedure used for averaging judgments is given by Torgerson (1958: 105–106): the arithmetic mean of the votes for each combination is computed, and the ratio judgment between any two combinations is taken to be the ratio of the average number of votes assigned to each combination. Figure 7 presents the accompanying composite contrast map. Later in the discussion section it will be argued that such a composite map does constitute an appropriate projection of the general cultural pattern even though individual patterns of judgment may not be precisely comparable.

A word can be said about concordance. Kendall's W, a measure of concordance, was computed for both preference and contrast for two groups, the eight Americans and the two respondents from France constituting one group and the remaining respondents constituting the second group. Kendall's W for the first group for preference was 0.95, and for the second group it was 0.84. It was predicted in advance that the predominantly American group would have a higher concordance than the other. Still, there is a great deal of agreement among the members of each group.

The situation is different with contrast. Here the predominantly American group had a Kendall's W of 0.60 and the composite group of remaining respondents had a Kendall's W of 0.45. Again, as predicted, the predominantly American group had a higher concordance.

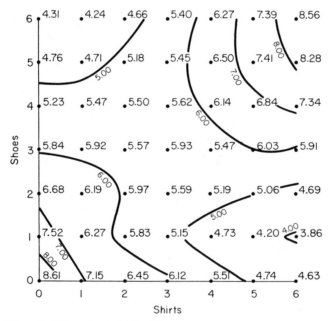

Figure 7. U.S. mean contrast map.

It is difficult to do anything with these statistics in anything other than an ordinal way. Still, it can be asserted that there is greater agreement among the members of the predominantly American group than among the members of the composite group for both preference and contrast. Again, there is greater agreement for the members of both groups in the area of preference than there is in the area of contrast. Perhaps it can be asserted that the higher the concordance for any variable, the greater the integration of the pattern into the culture. Here the northwest European pattern is clearly more highly integrated than that of the composite, quasi-Mediterranean pattern.

Another Preferential Pattern The methods of description illustrated thus far need not be restricted to certain systemic patterns. They can be used in any instance

Table 3. A Woman's Family Pattern.

Boys	Girls	Preference	Contrast	Boys	Girls	Preference	Contrast
0	0	0.48	2.41	3	4	0.85	4.59
0	1	1.85	3.45	3	5	0.45	4.60
0	2	3.68	5.25	3	6	0.29	4.49
0	3	2.71	4.10	4	0	1.67	4.20
0	4	1.62	3.81	4	1	1.97	4.34
0	5	1.04	3.50	4	2	1.59	4.86
0	6	0.52	3.72	4	3	0.89	4.33
1	0	1.91	3.57	4	4	0.60˙	3.74
1	1	7.16	7.40	4	5	0.33	4.91
1	2	7.59	7.59	4	6	0.24	4.95
1	3	4.51	6.14	5	0	0.85	3.83
1	4	2.11	4.80	5	1	0.94	4.15
1	5	0.88	3.96	5	2	0.72	4.61
1	6	0.46	4.08	5	3	0.48	4.10
2	0	2.86	4.39	5	4	0.39	4.53
2	1	7.20	7.20	5	5	0.26	5.02
2	2	6.02	6.93	5	6	0.17	5.95
2	3	2.95	4.96	6	0	0.50	4.11
2	4	1.47	4.96	6	1	0.55	4.41
2	5	0.77	4.42	6	2	0.41	4.17
2	6	0.39	4.42	6	3	0.32	4.56
3	0	2.31	3.80	6	4	0.24	5.29
3	1	5.00	6.56	6	5	0.19	5.42
3	2	3.02	5.36	6	6	0.15	6.50
3	3	1.83	5.27				

Average Preference 1.74; Mean Contrast 4.66

where the Cartesian product of two pattern elements is interesting. Thus, over the world there is a good deal of interest in the number of children in the ideal family. Figure 8 shows the preference pattern of one female American respondent for boys and girls, and Figure 9 gives the accompanying contrast map. Note that in this instance the field was large enough to provide for the phenomenon of closed indifference curves. Note, too, that some combinations of boys and girls had lower preference values than no children at all.

Perhaps the same closed curves would have appeared if it had been possible to have had many more combinations of shirts and shoes judged. We expect that indifference curves will be closed contours when a maximum preference value is attained for a particular combination; the latter combination is then a saturation point, and, if the saturation point is unique, all other points (combinations) have lower preference values.

It might be noted that several years after the completion of the above maps, the same technique was used in mapping the preferential family size and composition of 18 Puerto Rican women. Indeed, the same cards and programs developed for the shirt and shoe study were used. The results of this investigation have already been published (Myers and Roberts 1968) and further extensions of this mapping technique are being made now.

Discussion

The more interesting results of this inquiry are essentially descriptive and methodological. The most salient finding, of course, was the differentiation of the northern group from the southern group on the basis of preferential pattern or, to be even more specific, the differentiation of the American group of respondents from all others. This finding requires discussion.

High preference values are the result of strong preferences for some combinations and strong rejection of others. Individuals displaying these values seem to know exactly where they stand; they must share in a pattern which is well integrated at both the individual and cultural levels. Again, high mean contrast is the result of making sharp discriminations in judging combinations of elements as against other combinations. Here again, the pattern is likely to be well integrated. If, in addition to these overall measures, however, the indifference curves have the same shapes and the same patterns with all informants, the pattern must be well integrated at the individual and cultural levels. Figures 6 and 7, then, illustrate a pattern which is well integrated —at least this is our hypothesis.

It is argued, but not proven here, that evidences of integration (including concordance statistics) which hold for combinations of two such elements as shirts and shoes are enough to support the statement that the pattern as a whole, e.g., tailored clothing, is well integrated. We do not have data on tailored clothing as a whole, but arguments can be advanced to support the statement that the total pattern is well integrated as far as the northern group is concerned.

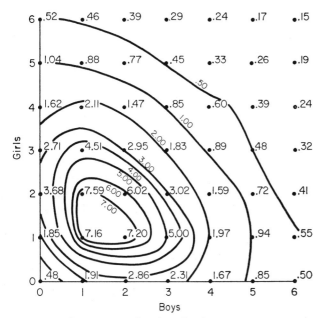

Figure 8. Preference map—American female.

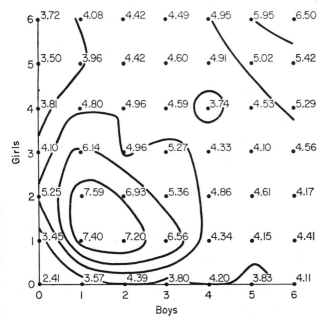

Figure 9. Contrast map—American female.

Shirts and shoes represent an adaptation to a northern environment; even to this day the same environment provides negative sanctions against intrusive patterns. Every summer one can see intrusive "robes and sandals" on northern college campuses in the form of actual sandals and loose sport shirts—the academic procession, of course, is known for its sleeved robes, although the solemn marchers never wear sandals. In areas devoted to sunbathing, it is even possible to see the tropical breech-clout (e.g., the bikini), but these intrusive patterns vanish with the snows of winter. The dominant pattern remains that of shirts and shoes, or, more largely, tailored clothing.

Shirts and shoes are also property and the accumulation of property is generally accepted as one form of achievement. Perhaps the northern cultures are more achieving and people from these cultures might well prefer more property than less without too much reference to the particular kind of property. If, however, the members of the northern group have stronger preferences for property, this value only contributes to the integration of the tailored clothing pattern in the general culture.

There are undoubtedly many other factors as well. Shirts and shoes have had a longer and more enduring culture history in the northern regions than they have had in the southern. If factors of tradition and sentiment are important, they may be less strong in the south, where alternate patterns of clothing have existed before and where they may well exist again.

It would be possible to expand on the point that tailored clothing is well integrated into the cultures of the United States and France, but it is likely that any reader will accept this statement on the basis of his own experience. Would he, for example, accept the notion that the pattern is less well integrated in the cultures of the southern informants?

Certainly the informants from Egypt, India, and Cameroun had exposure to alternate patterns of clothing. Indeed, the Cameroun respondent had worn robes. It is certainly possible to say that tailored clothing is not as well integrated in these cultures as in those of the United States and France on the basis of simple inspection. With the Turks and Chilians no direct statements can be made, although it would be interesting to learn the degree to which they, as individuals, were familiar with clothing variants and to determine their attitudes toward property.

It can still be argued, then, that tailored clothing is more integrated in the cultures of the northern group than it is for the cultures of the southern group. Furthermore, attitudes toward shirts and shoes may be representative of attitudes toward other elements in the clothing complex. Finally, the shirts and shoes preferences and contrasts presented here may be acceptable indices of the differences in integration of the total pattern in the cultures of the two groups.

When this study was initiated, the mapping of preferences was the principal concern, but as the study progressed the mapping of contrast values gained in interest. Contrast is a dimension of preference which merits further research in its own right.

Unfortunately, it was impossible to study the same subjects again, for they, with one exception, were no longer available when all of the data had been analyzed. The single exception was the Indian respondent (Indian 8M, Tables 1 and 2) whose preference and contrast maps appear in Figures 5 and 7. He provided additional information of some significance.

A list was made of those preference values appearing in Table 1 for the Indian respondent which were either the same or within 0.02 of each other in value. In three cases with high-valued combinations it was necessary to list values that varied by 0.03, 0.04, and 0.04 respectively. This last adjustment was necessary in order to provide some examples from the upper end of the distribution as compared with the numerous examples from the lower end. It was then assumed that these values were equivalent or almost so. In all except two instances, however, the contrast values for the pairs of data points differed. In 54 instances, then, the preference values were essentially the same and the contrast values were different, thus making it possible to study contrast with preference held constant.

Other work in the fields of codes and models and with kin terms has suggested that the lower the contrast, the greater the curiosity about the item or combination. Thus, it was argued that the Indian respondent would be more interested in stories about combinations with low contrast than in stories about combinations of shirts and shoes with high contrast. The question was put to him in the case of each of the elements in the pairs of shirt-shoe combinations. Here, where preference values were held constant, it was predicted that he would favor hearing a story about the combination in each pair which had the lowest contrast. In 35 (65%) of the 54 trials the choice favored the hypothesis (exact binomial test $p = 0.02$).

The distribution, however, of the contrast values suggested that if contrasts were very close in value, they ought to be treated as being roughly equivalent, and in such cases no prediction could be made since there was too little difference to permit discrimination. In other words, if the two contrast values differed only by 0.01, it was not likely that one could expect the predicted response on the part of the informant more frequently than one could expect by chance. When the 33 cases in which the contrast differs by 0.200 or more are considered, we find that in 26 of the 33 (79%) choices, the combination selected favored the hypothesis (exact binomial test, $p = 0.00066$). Perhaps, then, the hypothesis should read: if preference values are equivalent for different data points and if the contrast values for the same data points differ by 0.20 or more, those data points having the lower contrast values will also be those in which the subject has the greatest curiosity or potential model involvement. It is worth noting, incidentally, that there is no obvious relationship between these curiosity preferences and direct judgments of shirt-shoe combinations.

Clearly more should be done with contrast. Perhaps high contrast and high preference make for stability of a cultural pattern, one which would be stable even in the presence of new and relevant information. If, however, new information is continually entering the system and if from time to time this information has a bearing on the choice of combinations, then cultural change affected by new information is most likely to occur in and around the data points for which there is low contrast; for it is precisely in these areas that the respondents are most likely to entertain new ideas. Thus, the combination having the lowest contrast value for the Indian is the combination of 6 shirts and 1 pair of shoes with a contrast value of 4.47. If he were told that the people whom he most admired always owned shirts in the ratio of six shirts to one pair of shoes, this new information might well affect his preference value for this combination of 2.24. On the other hand, if he had already had high contrast values for this combination, he might not be too interested in new information affecting this choice. Thus, in situations of equilibrium or low change, low contrast is relatively meaningless. In a shifting system, however, low contrast values may well point toward pattern areas that are vulnerable to future cultural change.

At the very least, the operations with preference and contrast suggest that subjective utility is a multidir sional affair and that no point is truly the same in value as another point if it does not have the same value on all dimensions. No attempt was made to effect such a transformation, but it is not improbable that the dimensions discussed are similar to those figuring in the semantic differential research of Osgood and others.

There is no harm in ending with a final speculation. Perhaps the closed indifference curves mentioned briefly in this paper represent a phenomenon that should be considered in the anthropological analysis of systems of property destruction and free distribution (e.g., the potlatch) which have occurred in numerous primitive societies in response to acculturation.

In conclusion, a descriptive technique of preferential pattern analysis has been described, a technique which may have its ethnographic uses particularly in the field of systemic patterns. More specifically, the American pattern was described and contrasted with the responses of individuals from a number of countries. Here the northern group of respondents was clearly different from the southern group. In addition, the differences between preference and contrast were considered and there was some speculation about the implications of this research for the understanding of cultural dynamics. Finally, as is always the case, the present study has laid a foundation for future research and indeed continuation of this line of inquiry in the field of family preference (Myers and Roberts 1968) has already been completed.

References

Chapple, E. D., and C. S. Coon
1942 *Principles of Anthropology* (New York: Henry Holt & Company).
Comrey, A. L.
1950 "A Proposed Method for Absolute Ratio Scaling," *Psychometrika* 15:317–325.

Kluckhohn, C.
1941 "Patterning as Exemplified in Navaho Culture," in *Language, Culture, and Personality*, Essays in memory of Edward Sapir, Leslie Spier, A. Irving Hallowell, and Stanley S. Newman, eds. (Menasha, Wisc.: George Banta Company, Inc.).

Kozelka, R. M., and J. M. Roberts,
n.d. "A New Approach to Non-Zero Concordance" (manuscript).

Kroeber, A. L.
1948 *Anthropology* (New York: Harcourt, Brace and Company).

Lenneberg, E. H., and J. M. Roberts
1956 *The Language of Experience: a Study in Methodology*, Memoir 13 of the International Journal of American Linguistics, Indiana University Publications in Anthropology and Linguistics (Bloomington, Indiana: Indiana University).

Metfessel, M.
1947 "A Proposal for Quantitative Reporting of Comparative Judgments," *Journal of Psychology* 24:229–235.

Myers, G. C., and J. M. Roberts
1968 "A Technique for Measuring Preferential Family Size and Composition," *Eugenics Quarterly*, 15:164–172.

Roberts, J. M.
1965a "Kinsmen and Friends in Zuni Culture: a Terminological Note," *El Palacio* 72/2:38–43.
1965b "Oaths, Autonomic Ordeals, and Power," in "The Ethnography of Law," Laura Nader, ed. *American Anthropologist* 67, No. 6, pt. 2:186–212.

Roberts, J. M., M. J. Arth, and R. R. Bush
1959 "Games in Culture," *American Anthropologist* 61:597–605.

Roberts, John M., and Michael L. Forman
n.d. "Riddles: Expressive Models of Interrogation," in *Directions in Sociolinguistics: Ethnography of Communication*, John Gumphz and Dell H. Hymes, eds. (New York: Holt, Rinehart, and Winston), in press.

Roberts, J. M., H. Hoffmann, and B. Sutton-Smith
1965 "Pattern and Competence: a Consideration of Tick Tack Toe," *El Palacio* 72/3:17–30.

Roberts, J. M., and F. Keonig
1968 "Focused and Distributed Status Affinity," *Sociological Quarterly*, 9:150–157.

Roberts, J. M., R. J. Smith, and R. M. Kozelka
n.d. "Value and Codability" (manuscript).

Roberts, J. M., and B. Sutton-Smith
1962 "Child Training and Game Involvement," *Ethnology* 1:166–185.
1966 "Cross-Cultural Correlates of Games of Chance," *Behavior Science Notes* 1:131–144.

Roberts, J. M., B. Sutton-Smith, and A. Kendon
1963 "Strategy in Games and Folk Tales," *Journal of Social Psychology* 61:185–199.

Roberts, J. M., W. E. Thompson, and B. Sutton-Smith
1966 "Expressive Self-Testing in Driving," *Human Organization* 25:54–63.

Savage, L. J.
1954 *The Foundations of Statistics* (New York: John Wiley & Sons).

Schneider, D. M., and J. M. Roberts
1956 "Zuni Kin Terms," Note Book No. 3, Monograph 1, Laboratory of Anthropology, The University of Nebraska. Reprinted by Human Relations Area Files Press in 1965 in *Behavior Science Reprints*.

Stevens, S. S.
1959 "Measurement, Psychophysics, and Utility," in *Measurement: Definitions and Theories*, C. W. Churchman and P. Ratoosh, eds. (New York: John Wiley & Sons).
1966 "A Metric for the Social Consensus," *Science* 151:530–541.

Sutton-Smith, B., and J. M. Roberts
1964 "Rubrics of Competitive Behavior," *Journal of Genetic Psychology* 105:13–37.
1967 "Studies of an Elementary Game of Strategy," *Genetic Psychology Monograph* 75:3–42.

Sutton-Smith, B., J. M. Roberts, and R. M. Korelka
1963 "Game Involvement in Adults." *Journal of Social Psychology* 60:15–30.

Torgerson, W. S.
1958 *Theory and Methods of Scaling* (New York: John Wiley & Sons).

Von Neumann, J., and O. Morgenstern
1947 *Theory of Games and Economic Behavior*, 3rd ed. (Princeton, New Jersey: Princeton University Press).

Webster
1963 *Webster's Third New International Dictionary of the English Language* (Springfield, Mass.: G. & C. Merriam Company).

Introduction

Driver and Sanday study the intercorrelations among 50 ethnological variables on 277 ethnic units in North America. The variables deal with various aspects of kinship terminology, descent, residence, avoidance patterns, language family, and culture area.

A cluster analysis of the intercorrelations among a subset of 21 sociological variables is done. The authors then compare the results with the results of a factor analysis they perform on the same intercorrelation matrix. The authors point out that one of the major distinctions between any cluster analysis and any factor analysis method is that the former assigns a given variable *in toto* to one (or more) clusters while the latter assigns parts (of the variance) of the variable to various factors. They suggest that by applying both sorts of analyses to the same data and comparing the results, certain new insights may be gained.

A factor analysis of the full set of 50 variables is then performed and the ethnological implications of the various analyses and their comparisons are discussed.

The authors also discuss the problem of interpreting the results of a factor analysis performed on variables not all of which are logically independent.

This article is a sequel to a much longer paper in *Current Anthropology* by Driver (1966). It includes tabulated and documented data on 277 ethnic units in North America. This paper is almost identical to that published in *Current Anthropology* by Driver and Sanday (1966) but it does not repeat the large 50 × 50 matrix. Before writing the first paper on avoidances, Driver computed ϕ coefficients for all the interrelations among 50 North American variables of culture area, language family, residence, descent, kin terms, and avoidances (Driver and Sanday 1966: Table 3). Because the matrix was far from simple, he decided not to present it all at once, but to select small groups of correlations and present them when and where they had direct bearing on some aspect of the problem. After the first paper was finished, he returned to a consideration of the 50-variable matrix with a view to carrying out a factor analysis of the data.

Driver first made several trials at sorting the 21 social variables by inspection. On the fourth trial, after a few hours of recopying and cutting and pasting, he came up with the arrangement shown in Table 1. Positive ϕ's of 0.20 or higher, significant at less than 0.001, are shown in boldface. Clusters are further made obtrusive by enclosing them in boxes.

There are four major clusters in Table 1. At the upper left is a bicentered cluster, in the middle a matricentered cluster, immediately to the right and below an avoidance cluster, and at the extreme lower right a patricentered cluster. The bicentered cluster has mostly negative correlations with all the other clusters, a few of them quite

Table 1. φ Coefficients for 21 variables.

	No.	1	2	3	4	5	6	7	8	9	10	11	12	13	14	15	16	17	18	19	20	21
Descriptive cousin terms	1	.20[a]	-.05	-.04	-.08	.06	-.03	.08	-.05	-.02	-.01	-.04	-.04	-.03	-.06	.04	.04	-.03	-.02	-.03	.08	-.01
Lineal avuncular terms	2	-.05	.78[a]	.32	.41	.03	.05	-.58	-.28	-.07	-.10	-.18	-.20	-.19	-.37	-.30	-.24	-.16	-.08	-.20	-.23	.16
Bilateral descent	3	-.04	.32	1.00[a]	.49	.24	.15	.01	-.20	-.15	-.24	-.62	-.17	-.35	-.39	-.14	-.11	-.01	.09	-.34	-.66	.01
Hawaiian cousin terms	4	-.08	.41	.49	.90[a]	.07	-.25	-.10	-.49	-.02	-.16	-.31	-.08	-.30	-.31	-.21	-.11	-.09	.02	-.33	-.31	.06
Bilocal or neolocal residence	5	.06	.03	.24	.07	.96[a]	.15	.10	-.21	-.10	-.09	-.17	-.25	-.07	-.12	-.05	-.03	-.01	.03	.03	-.14	-.61
Eskimo cousin terms	6	-.03	.05	.15	-.25	.15	.72[a]	.04	-.18	.00	-.06	-.02	-.08	-.07	-.07	-.14	-.11	-.13	-.09	-.13	-.17	-.05
Bifurcate collateral avunc. terms	7	.08	-.58	.01	-.10	.10	.04	.76[a]	-.17	-.15	-.07	-.12	-.08	-.05	-.31	.09	.16	.04	.11	-.02	.09	.00
Iroquoian cousin terms	8	-.05	-.28	-.20	-.49	-.21	-.18	-.17	.86[a]	-.06	.19	.08	-.02	-.17	.06	.05	-.07	.01	-.02	-.16	.18	.14
Generation avuncular terms	9	-.02	-.07	-.15	-.02	-.10	.00	-.15	-.06	.25[a]	-.03	.16	.24	.16	.02	-.12	-.09	-.06	-.05	.01	.03	-.09
Avunculocal residence	10	-.01	-.10	-.24	-.16	-.09	-.06	-.07	.19	-.03	.68[a]	.40	-.08	.12	.21	.14	.05	.09	.06	-.05	-.07	-.19
Matrilineal descent	11	-.04	-.18	-.62	-.31	-.17	-.02	-.12	.08	.16	.40	1.00[a]	.45	.60	.39	.14	-.02	.10	-.05	-.14	-.18	-.34
Matrilocal residence	12	-.04	-.20	-.17	-.08	-.25	-.08	-.08	-.02	.24	-.08	.45	.95[a]	.38	.25	.15	.05	.08	.05	-.12	-.21	-.55
Crow cousin terms	13	-.03	-.19	-.35	-.30	-.07	-.07	-.05	-.17	.16	.12	.60	.38	.76[a]	.31	.19	.12	.21	.04	-.10	-.14	-.28
Bifurcate merging avunc. terms	14	-.06	-.37	-.39	-.31	-.12	-.07	-.31	.06	.02	.21	.39	.25	.31	.63[a]	.25	.12	.12	-.01	.23	.12	-.16
M-S avoidance	15	.04	-.30	-.14	-.21	-.05	-.14	.09	.05	-.12	.14	.14	.15	.19	.25	.60[a]	.68	.52	.36	.29	.04	-.13
F-D avoidance	16	.04	-.24	-.11	-.11	-.03	-.11	.16	-.07	-.09	.05	-.02	.05	.12	.12	.68	.60[a]	.50	.53	.31	.15	-.03
F-S avoidance	17	-.03	-.16	-.01	-.09	-.01	-.13	.04	.01	-.06	.09	.10	.08	.21	.12	.52	.50	.56[a]	.65	.06	.06	-.08
M-D avoidance	18	-.02	-.08	.09	.02	.03	-.09	.11	-.02	-.05	.06	-.05	.05	.04	-.01	.36	.53	.65	.54[a]	.04	-.06	-.08
Omaha cousin terms	19	-.03	-.20	-.34	-.33	.03	-.13	-.02	-.16	.01	-.05	-.14	-.12	-.10	.23	.29	.31	.06	.04	.79[a]	.55	.09
Patrilineal descent	20	.08	-.23	-.66	-.31	-.14	-.17	.09	.18	.03	-.07	-.18	-.21	-.14	.12	.04	.15	.06	-.06	.55	1.00[a]	.31
Patrilocal residence	21	-.01	.16	.01	.06	-.61	-.05	.00	.14	-.09	-.19	-.34	-.55	-.28	-.16	-.13	-.03	-.08	-.08	.09	.31	.97[a]

[a] SMC values.

high. The correlations between the matricentered and patricentered clusters are all negative, with one high value. Avoidances have mostly low positive relationships with the matricentered cluster, and both low positive and negative correlations (the positive being slightly more numerous) with the patricentered cluster; the relation of avoidances to the bicentered cluster is mostly low negative.

The contrast between internal and external relationships is greatest with the avoidance cluster, where internal relationships are much higher. For the other three clusters, the positive internal relationships of each are of about the same magnitude as the negative external relationships with the other two. The avoidance cluster, therefore, is the most independent of the four. The four avoidances have closer relations to each other than to any of the other variables in the matrix.

Although we do not claim that any novel ideas arose in our minds from viewing these clusters in a single matrix, the technique nevertheless provides a useful summary of the behavior of all 21 variables with respect to each other. Such a summary does not obscure the individual correlations, which may be read and appraised one at a time. If negative as well as positive correlations are considered in the clustering, as is the case in Table 1, it is possible to anticipate in part the contrasts that will appear in the factors.

Given a large matrix of intercorrelations, where there is some notion based either on theory or previous work, that the variables form natural groups, the statistical techniques of cluster analysis and/or multiple-factor analysis can be utilized to demonstrate the presence of such groups. The clusters of Table 1 demonstrate that the data are not chaotic, that there are groupings. The application of factor analysis to these data is now advisable, for while in cluster analysis each variable is usually placed in a cluster as a unit, in factor analysis different portions of the variance may be assigned to different factors (Fruchter 1954).

In any factor matrix, every variable will usually have a loading of some magnitude on every factor. In the simplest cases to interpret, a variable will have a high loading on only one factor and a very low loading on the others. In some cases, such as the factor matrix reported below, a variable may have a high loading on more than one factor. In such cases it is to be remembered that each factor is composed of a constellation of variables, and it is this constellation which is to be interpreted as measuring a common dimension. For example, in Table 2, matrilineal descent appears with a high loading on two factors—one which includes avunculocal residence, and one which includes matrilocal residence. This fact is not surprising since both kinds of residence are functionally related to matrilineal descent.

Factor Analysis of the 21 Sociological Variables
The Dependence of the Variables A look at the 21 sociological variables demonstrates that there are five classes of variables: (1) four avoidance variables; (2) six cousin-term variables; (3) four avuncular-term variables; (4) three descent variables; and (5) four residence variables. The four avoidance variables are not dependent in

Table 2.   Varimax Factor Loadings for 21 variables.

		I	II	III	IV	V	VI	VII	Com.
Descriptive cousin terms	1	.036	−.032	−.053	.016	.057	−.092	−.004	.017
Lineal avuncular terms	2	.264	−.225	.230	.113	−.034	**.704**	.051	.685
Bilateral descent	3	**.446**	.058	**.691**	**.409**	.131	.107	−.054	.877
Hawaiian cousin terms	4	.197	−.076	**.396**	**.424**	.083	.362	**.532**	.802
Bilocal or neolocal residence	5	.247	−.021	.020	.050	**.916**	−.045	−.109	.917
Eskimo cousin terms	6	.041	−.136	.130	.108	.082	.004	**−.763**	.637
Bifurcate collateral avunc. terms	7	.135	.119	.071	.127	.044	**−.778**	−.030	.662
Iroquoian cousin terms	8	.145	−.085	.027	**−.572**	−.292	**−.508**	.111	.712
Generation avuncular terms	9	−.302	−.132	−.052	.076	−.036	.042	.030	.121
Avunculocal residence	10	−.034	.109	.029	**−.676**	.074	.092	.043	.487
Matrilineal descent	11	**−.731**	.007	.024	**−.559**	.008	.086	−.077	.860
Matrilocal residence	12	**−.850**	.072	.176	.148	.009	−.127	.152	.820
Crow cousin terms	13	**−.659**	.183	.002	−.163	.038	.066	−.151	.522
Bifurcate merging avunc. terms	14	**−.409**	.157	−.317	−.303	.010	.108	−.065	.404
M-S avoidance	15	−.118	**.722**	−.157	−.107	.018	−.089	.007	.578
F-D avoidance	16	−.006	**.764**	−.194	.051	−.006	−.076	.020	.630
F-S avoidance	17	−.047	**.742**	.059	−.095	−.012	.005	.026	.566
M-D avoidance	18	.066	**.692**	.101	.009	.018	−.022	.068	.498
Omaha cousin terms	19	.060	.226	**−.766**	.142	.072	.023	−.041	.668
Patrilineal descent	20	.141	−.080	**−.882**	.011	−.173	−.210	.151	.901
Patrilocal residence	21	**.464**	−.078	−.174	.104	**−.809**	.096	−.047	.928
Proportion of total variance		.197	.180	.175	.127	.125	.122	.074	

the manner that the other variables are, since a society may have more than one avoidance variable. However, no society may be scored for more than one variable from the remaining four classes (except for a few cases involving kinship terminology). Thus, when the correlation between, for example, bilateral descent and patrilocal residence is computed, the absence cells include all the other variables in the descent or residence classes. Therefore, there are a number of negatively interdependent variables in each class. This violates the requirement of the factor analytic model that the variables must be linearly independent. Because of their interdependence, the variables in each class will be negatively correlated, and the worst one can expect from the factor analysis is that variables from the same class will appear on a factor with high negative and high positive loadings (reflecting the negative interdependence). As will be seen, this is the case for several of the factors.

It is doubtful whether the interdependence of the variables in a class would influence the manner in which a factor cuts across classes. Therefore, if it were discovered that variables from different classes associate in some meaningful way on a factor, factor analysis could be used as a probing device in spite of the interdependence of the variables.

Table 2 demonstrates mixed results. Factors I, II, III, IV, and VI are consistent with what an anthropologist would expect; they cut across classes, but they also reflect high negative correlations within the same class. Factors V and VII are artifactual factors in that they reflect only negative correlations between the variables of single classes. Because the negative interdependence of the variables within classes probably has little influence on the way the factors cut across classes, there is some justification for using factors I, II, III, IV, and VI in interpretation. However, because of the violation of the factor-analytic model, we cannot claim to have proved that they are real factors.

Estimating Communalities The number of factors in the common factor space is determined in part by the values placed on the diagonal of self-correlations in the matrix. If these values are unity (1.00), the number of common factors will equal the number of variables (Harman 1960b: 69). Since the problem here is to reduce the correlation matrix to a small number of common factors, the diagonal should contain an estimate of communalities. The communality of a variable is the proportion of the total variance in common with the other variables in the analysis. The problem of estimating these communalities, as the self-relationships are called, is a problem of extreme importance in the multiple factor approach. Since there is no *a priori* knowledge of the values of the communalities, some method of approximation must be used.

Many solutions to this problem have been proposed (see Harman 1960b : 69–96). One of the better solutions for approximating communalities is the squared multiple correlation (SMC) of each variable with the remaining $n - 1$ variables (Harman 1960b:89). The SMC's have been called the "observed communalities" since they measure the predictable common variance among the observed correlations. An important property of the SMC is that it provides a lower bound for the communality.

The method used to obtain the SMC's for each of the 21 variables was one suggested by Harman (1960b: 89). This is to calculate the inverse R^{-1} of the correlation matrix R (with unities on the diagonal). The SMC for variable z_i is given by

$$\text{SMC}_i = 1 - 1/r^{ii},$$

where r^{ii} is the diagonal element of R^{-1} corresponding to variable z_i. The resultant values were placed on the diagonal of the correlation matrix (Table 1) and inputed to the biomedical computer program (Dixon 1964) which was selected and run by Sanday. It computes a principal component solution and performs an orthogonal rotation to the Varimax criterion. The algorithms used by this program are reported in detail in Harman (1960a) for the principal components solution and in Kaiser (1959) for the Varimax rotation.

In order to determine the number of factors to be rotated, the output of this program was inspected for the trace of the latent roots (eigenvalues). After the first seven factors the latent roots are small and diminish very slowly close to zero. The decision was made to rotate seven factors. The rotated factor matrix is reported in Table 2. The loadings at 0.400 or higher are shown in boldface. The order of the factors from left to right is that of the proportion of total communality given at the bottom. The order of variables is that of Table 1. When factor loadings are arranged in this manner, the relation of clusters to factors is transparent.

Factor I opposes three matricentered variables and bifurcate merging to bilateral descent and patrilocal residence. The latter two variables show one high negative correlation each (Table 1) with one of the matricentered traits. Factor II gives high positive loadings on the four avoidances but no negative contrast higher than that for lineal avuncular terms, -0.225. Avoidances, therefore, constitute the most independent factor as well as the most independent cluster. Factor III opposes two patricentered variables to two bicentered variables, one of which has a high negative correlation with patrilineal descent. Factor IV groups matrilineal descent, avunculocal residence, and Iroquoian kin terms together and opposes them to two bicentered variables. The inclusion of Iroquoian kin terms in the first half of the contrast was unanticipated from the clustering. Factor V opposes bilocal or neolocal residence to patrilocal residence, reflecting their artifactually high negative correlation. Factor VI contrasts bifurcate collateral and Iroquoian kin terms with lineal terms and, at a lower level, Hawaiian terms. The positive relation of the first two values was not anticipated from the ϕ of 0.17 in the clustering, but a high and medium ϕ for the two contrasting relationships are to be expected. Factor VII opposes Eskimo to Hawaiian kin terms, an artifactual relationship hardly anticipated from a negative ϕ of -0.25.

Turning to the individual variables in Table 2, bilateral descent and Hawaiian kin terms are the most ubiquitous, with heavy to medium loadings on three or four factors. Iroquoian terms, matrilineal descent, and patrilocal residence each show high or medium loadings on two factors. Descriptive cousin terms exhibit almost zero loadings throughout, which matches its almost zero correlations with all other variables (Table 1). Generation avuncular terms fare little better. The other 14 variables are loaded on only a single factor at the medium to high level.

On the whole, the factors of Table 2 match the clusters of Table 1 more closely than anticipated, due in part to the negative interdependence of pairs of variables within each of the four topical classes of the data: residence, descent, avuncular terms, and cousin terms. In light of the proportion of total communality of the factors (Table 1, bottom), the most novel idea produced by the factors is probably the splitting of the matricentered cluster into two factors, one with matrilocal residence and the other with avunculocal.

Analysis of all 50 Variables

The Dependence of the Variables Each of the two additional classes of variables, culture areas and language families, has many negative interdependencies within it (Driver and Sanday 1966: Table 3). However, each class consists of so many mutually exclusive categories (16 culture areas, 13 language families) that the negative correlations are quite low and have little effect on the factors. There is not a single instance in Table 3 of the present paper in which two culture areas or two language families are heavily loaded with opposite signs on the same factor, as was the case with the 21 variables, where two factors were artifactually produced by oppositions within a single class of variables. On the other hand, in Table 3 a new kind of factor appears in which there are only two medium or high loadings, one on a culture area and the other on a language family: factors IX, X, XI, XIII, and XIV. Other factors cut across several classes of variables: e.g., factor II, six classes; and factors I and V, five classes.

Estimating Communalities The SMC's for the 50 variables could not be computed due to the impossibility of getting an accurate inversion of the correlation matrix. This was probably due to the deviant relationships of culture areas and language families; e.g., the Yukon Subarctic and Mackenzie Subarctic correlate 0.45 and 0.54, respectively, with Athapaskan language family, but −0.03 with each other. Another approximation to communality had to be used; in this case the highest correlation of each row was placed in the diagonal. This method is called by Harman (1960:56) an "arbitrary approximation to communality," as opposed to a "complete approximation to communality" such as the squared multiple correlation coefficient used earlier. The same computer program was used for the factor analysis. Since the latent roots diminish very slowly close to zero after the first 15 factors, only 15 factors were rotated. The results are reported in Table 3. (Contrasting type faces have the same limits as in Table 2.)

The factors of Table 3 show a number of differences from those of Table 2. Factor I,

Table 3. Varimax Factor Loadings for 50 Variables.

		I	II	III	IV	V	VI
Descriptive cousin terms	1	.008	.030	.024	.121	.029	—.008
Lineal avuncular terms	2	.240	.256	—.186	**—.545**	—.028	—.150
Bilateral descent	3	**.466**	**.509**	.168	—.238	—.217·	—.155
Salish language family	4	.108	.089	—.129	—.234	—.063	.113
Plateau culture area	5	.058	.026	—.042	.041	—.084	.108
Hawaiian cousin terms	6	**.400**	.295	—.034	—.316	—.161	.249
Uto-Aztecan language family	7	.205	.115	—.141	.007	—.144	.181
Great Basin culture area	8	.176	.088	—.120	.004	—.135	.177
Bilocal or neolocal residence	9	.060	.159	.022	.025	.034	—.207
Western Arctic culture area	10	.035	.051	.045	—.058	—.003	—.111
Eskimo language family	11	.019	.034	.003	—.053	—.026	**—.661**
Central and E. Artcic culture area	12	—.007	—.002	—.039	—.005	—.030	**—.795**
Eskimo cousin terms	13	.120	—.001	—.125	.037	—.028	**—.576**
Bifurcate collateral avunc. terms	14	.221	.020	.094	**.602**	.138	.014
Oasis culture area	15	.046	—.034	—.146	.361	—.119	.019
Hokan language family	16	.062	.125	.060	**.555**	.133	—.053
E. Subarctic culture area	17	.093	.052	.022	.052	—.066	—.012
Algonkian language family	18	—.152	.004	.036	—.065	—.022	.017
Iroquoian cousin terms	19	—.097	.047	—.053	.315	—.078	.142
Generation avuncular terms	20	—.058	—.124	—.080	.015	—.084	.032
Caddoan language family	21	—.021	—.062	.187	—.046	—.083	.012
Avunculocal residence	22	—.057	—.168	.103	.075	—.073	.080
Northwest Coast culture area	23	.115	.070	—.074	—.237	—.048	.066
Wakashan language family	24	.038	.049	—.064	—.121	—.015	—.002
Yukon Subarctic culture area	25	.022	—.119	—.088	.079	—.024	.058
Mackenzie Subarctic culture area	26	.048	.075	.061	—.128	—.011	—.034
Athapaskan language family	27	.075	.015	.005	—.005	—.054	.077
Matrilineal descent	28	—.087	**—.730**	—.010	.134	—.161	.065
Circum-Caribbean culture area	29	.059	.055	—.039	—.051	.003	.086
Other language families	30	.127	—.116	—.041	—.028	—.071	—.008
Matrilocal residence	31	.016	**—.441**	.081	.038	—.197	.164
East culture area	32	.090	**—.652**	—.017	—.124	.051	—.051
Muskogean language family	33	.083	**—.608**	.053	—.081	.060	—.035
Crow cousin terms	34	—.105	**—.667**	.175	.082	—.124	—.013
Bifurcate merging avunc. terms	35	**—.438**	**—.428**	.104	—.151	—.072	.078
Plains culture area	36	—.068	.024	.193	—.159	—.192	.084
M-S avoidance	37	—.284	—.136	**.660**	.065	.239	.108
F-D avoidance	38	—.110	—.094	**.675**	.059	**.416**	.079
F-S avoidance	39	—.080	—.074	**.790**	.051	—.054	.010
M-D avoidance	40	.152	.029	**.728**	—.011	.157	.046
Souian language family	41	**—.711**	.015	.145	—.101	—.140	.025
Prairies culture area	42	**—.765**	.039	.079	—.066	—.038	.041
Omaha cousin terms	43	**—.588**	.030	.005	—.048	**.517**	.035
California culture area	44	.071	.097	.245	.240	**.624**	—.009
Californian Penutian language family	45	.000	.002	.197	—.010	**.673**	.036
Patrilineal descent	46	**—.504**	.066	—.188	.160	**.421**	.127
Mayan language family	47	—.040	.002	—.045	—.094	—.015	.065
Meso-America culture area	48	.089	.086	—.072	—.212	—.041	.000
Patrilocal residence	49	—.033	.276	—.096	—.075	.158	.017
Baja California-N.E. Mex. cult. area	50	.042	.069	—.003	.074	—.023	—.027
Proportion of total variance		.102	.101	.095	.076	.072	.067

VII	VIII	IX	X	XI	XII	XIII	XIV	XV	Com.
—.013	—.046	.268	.009	.047	.000	.011	.014	.005	.093
—.164	.080	.008	.044	.187	—.222	—.169	.048	—.140	.648
—.074	—.056	—.212	—.099	.198	.179	—.036	.078	.023	.775
—.115	.140	—.107	—.071	**.622**	—.147	.138	.052	—.022	.586
—.048	.002	—.014	—.067	**.622**	.133	—.021	—.023	.096	.448
—.220	—.060	.062	—.019	.265	.157	.029	.223	.020	.637
—.187	—.331	—.095	—.268	—.352	.143	.359	.021	.108	.639
—.122	**—.448**	—.096	—.234	—.256	.106	.356	—.013	.045	.588
—.022	**—.723**	.011	.011	.027	.099	—.031	.041	.095	.619
—.027	—.004	—.024	—.018	.004	.014	—.023	**—.802**	—.019	.666
—.054	—.035	—.030	—.006	—.021	.037	.093	**—.621**	—.011	.843
—.044	—.043	—.015	.010	—.026	.035	.143	—.063	.006	.665
.051	—.072	—.036	—.125	—.129	.048	—.110	—.024	.021	.420
.225	—.088	—.025	.024	.091	.205	.227	—.088	.114	.622
.139	—.029	—.044	—.008	—.168	.048	—.159	.105	—.123	.273
—.087	.056	—.016	—.050	.004	.027	.010	.092	—.045	.376
.769	.060	—.034	—.047	—.040	.011	.033	.025	.034	.622
.805	.009	—.076	—.065	—.058	.082	.048	.017	.028	.701
.298	.277	—.081	.134	—.255	—.221	.052	—.283	.075	.532
—.068	.030	.198	—.049	—.091	.054	—.139	.017	—.381	.256
—.008	.006	—.071	—.026	—.026	.083	.026	—.011	**—.527**	.340
.000	—.108	.053	.059	—.073	**—.567**	—.127	—.054	.148	.444
—.092	.202	—.121	—.017	.217	**—.639**	.078	.066	.003	.616
—.017	.106	—.083	—.034	—.089	**—.408**	.074	.013	—.001	.222
—.040	.036	—.011	**.460**	—.013	.014	.044	—.046	.094	.260
.003	—.083	—.015	**.599**	—.024	—.046	.024	.028	—.090	.408
—.062	—.008	—.060	**.801**	—.069	.047	.052	.036	.059	.678
—.086	—.030	—.025	.227	—.137	—.257	—.198	—.004	.034	.774
—.007	—.041	—.103	—.028	—.053	.107	—.394	—.062	—.040	.206
—.096	—.029	.096	—.151	—.001	—.084	**—.593**	.093	—.003	.446
—.121	—.022	—.198	.147	—.236	.259	—.227	—.055	—.341	.638
.092	.044	—.071	—.077	—.012	.072	.005	.005	—.155	.504
.005	—.010	—.028	—.035	.089	.083	.114	.023	.044	.423
—.128	—.033	—.029	.012	.005	—.066	—.098	.080	—.150	.570
—.047	.046	.047	.009	—.261	—.025	—.004	.013	.199	.534
.018	.037	—.060	.019	—.136	.199	—.004	.068	.286	.262
.020	.013	—.120	.089	—.065	.096	—.126	—.004	.177	.691
—.024	.016	—.041	—.035	—.028	.115	.031	.039	.056	.682
.037	—.004	—.008	—.036	—.029	—.030	.051	—.012	—.068	.653
.041	—.072	.032	—.014	—.029	—.040	.073	—.076	—.208	.645
—.121	.138	—.086	—.068	—.033	—.048	.053	.050	.144	.632
.091	—.033	—.078	—.069	.011	.049	.075	.030	—.229	.682
.062	—.069	.082	—.078	.004	.070	.058	.015	.002	.646
—.102	—.016	—.006	—.037	—.042	.052	—.014	.063	.094	.551
—.049	.075	—.035	—.023	—.060	.036	.023	—.027	.064	.513
.171	.117	.283	—.094	—.105	.011	.227	—.101	—.054	.720
—.034	.041	**.742**	—.018	—.063	.055	.085	—.019	—.031	.585
—.067	.138	**.706**	—.099	—.088	.072	—.108	.045	—.011	.625
.096	**.660**	.123	—.141	.195	—.089	.252	.031	.140	.726
—.039	.116	.004	—.067	—.020	.035	—.069	.069	.027	.044
.064	.060	.059	.059	.058	.054	.048	.047	.038	

the factor with the highest proportion of the total communality in Table 3, opposes two patricentered variables, bifurcate merging, a culture area, and a language family to two bicentered variables. Factor V (Table 3) repeats the same two patricentered variables, drops bifurcate merging, adds F-D avoidance, and adds another culture area and language family, but has no medium or high opposing loadings. Thus the patricentered cluster is split into two factors corresponding to the two areas where it occurs most dominantly. The split in matricentered variables of Tables 1 and 2 is also altered in Table 3. Factor II in Table 3 includes most matricentered variables, bifurcate merging, a culture area, and a language family, and opposes them to one bicentered variable. Factor XII lumps avunculocal residence with a culture area and a language family, but has only a light loading of matrilineal descent and no medium or heavily loaded opposing variables. The only factor loaded at the medium level or higher with two culture areas is X, and here the signs are the same. No factor is loaded at the same level with two language families.

As in Table 2, the four avoidances dominate factor III, but in Table 3 they are less isolated because F-D avoidance shows a medium-level loading on factor V in addition to its high loading on factor III.

Conclusions

The requirement of factor analysis that all variables be independent is not completely satisfied by ethnological data with classes of variables that contain mutually exclusive categories. Nevertheless, we believe that computing all relationships among all categories is preferable to dichotomizing each class of traits and thus arbitrarily reducing the number of variables to one for each class. The results obtained here are congruent in every respect with the more transparent clusterings and the results a mature ethnologist would expect. The ratio of factors to variables is about 1 to 4 when the artifactual factors are eliminated. We have made a serious effort to find some new major insight into explanations of avoidances and the other variables from the factor loadings, but have failed to do so. At the same time we admit that the factors sometimes sharpen details; for example, the lumping of bifurcate collateral avuncular and Iroquoian cousin terms together in factor VI of Table 2 when their ϕ coefficient (Table 1) was only 0.17.

We hold that clusters and factors are more meaningful when presented together and collated by listing the variables in the table of factor loadings in the same order, and when the factors are presented in order of greatest to least proportion of the total communality. Correlation coefficients and factor loadings combined are still insufficient expressions of the relationships among variables localized in time and space.

* Grateful acknowledgment is made to Bert Green and Garley Forehend of Carnegie Institute of Technology for their help in ironing out some of the problems related to the factor analysis. The final decisions and conclusions concerning the factor analysis are, of course, not their responsibility. The factor analysis was first run by Sanday as a member of the 1964 Summer Institute for Cross Cultural Research at the University of Pittsburgh. It was rerun with some changes in technique in the summer of 1965.

Too little is known about time differences among nonliterates who have left no documentary records, but spatial relations may be shown on maps. Every comparative (cross-cultural) study should map as much of its data as possible.

References

Dixon, W. J.
1964 *Biomedical Computer Programs*, Health Sciences Computing Facility, School of Medicine, University of California, Los Angeles.

Driver, Harold E.
1966 "Geographical-Historical Versus Psycho-Functional Explanations of Kin Avoidances," *Current Anthropology* 7: 131–160.

Driver, Harold E., and Peggy R. Sanday
1966 "Factors and Clusters of Kin Avoidances and Related Variables," *Current Anthropology* 7: 169–176.

Fruchter, Benjamin
1954 *Introduction to Factor Analysis* (Princeton, N.J.: D. Van Nostrand Company).

Harman, Harry H.
1960a "Factor Analysis," in *Mathematical Methods for Digital Computers*, H. S. Wilf and A. Ralston, eds. (New York: John Wiley & Sons), pp. 204–212.
1960b *Modern Factor Analysis* (Chicago: University of Chicago Press).

Kaiser, Henry F.
1959 "Computer Program for Varimax Rotation in Factor Analysis," *Educational and Psychological Measurements* 19: 413–420.

Nerlove, Sara, 200

Pitman, E. J. G., 215, 218
Pittendrigh, C. S., 147
Prais, S. J., 188
Pribram, K. H., 3

Randolph, R. R., 136
Roberts, J. M., 164n, 219, 223, 242, 245n,
    247n, 262, 266
Romney, A. Kimball, 50, 55–56
Roy, S. N., 218–219

Sanday, Peggy R., 226–228, 230, 236–239,
    269, 275
Sargent, W., 164
Sathe, Y. S., 218
Savage, L. J., 248
Sayles, L. R., 160, 163
Schneider, D. M., 67, 245n
Schuessler, Karl F., 239
Seki, Keigo, 119
Smith, Marshall S., 117
Smith, R. J., 219, 223, 245n
Sneath, Peter H. A., 227, 229, 231, 235
Snell, J. Laurie, 232
Sokal, Robert R., 227, 229, 231, 235
Spitz, R. A., 164
Stevens, S. S., 248, 249
Stone, Philip J., 117
Stuart, A., 216, 218
Suppes, Patrick, 10
Sutton-Smith, B., 245n

Terry, M. E., 217
Thatcher, James W., 57
Thompson, Gerald L., 232
Thompson, W. E., 245n
Torgerson, W. S., 247n, 248, 249
Tukey, J. W., 214, 215, 219

Volterra, V., 162
Von Neumann, J., 248

Wallace, Anthony F. C., 50, 55-56, 222–223
Wallace, D. L., 220
Wallis, W. A., 215
White, Harrison C., 209
Williams, G., 45, 127
Wright, H. F., 164n

Accountability, 15–16, 25
Affines, 43, 45
Age grades, 181–190
Aguacatenango, 200–202, 207–208, 211
Algorithms,
  and factor analysis, 274
  and information processing systems, 28
  in measuring endogamy, 192, 202–203, 207, 210
  and numerical classifications, 236
Ambrym, 53–54
Americans, 55–57, 214, 223, 246–264
Arrays, 169, 186–187, 242
Assessment, 3, 6–7, 9–12, 14–8, 233–35, 36
Autonomic nervous system, 143–145
Axiomatic method, 3, 7–34

Behavior
  and the axiomatic method, 3
  and code rules, 4
  and the construction of ethnographies, 43–45, 47
  and interaction, 142–144, 147, 160
Behavioral dictionary, 79, 80, 86
Biochemistry, 165
Biology, 142, 143, 147, 161, 170
Bisayan, 29–35
Blocks, 51–55
Boolean algebra, 240

Calculus, 189–190
Cameroun, 246–264
Carriers, 226, 232, 234–235
Cartesian product, 51, 147, 242, 262
Categories, 7, 9–10, 30–32
Categorizations, 8–10, 30–32, 36
Chiapas Drinking Project, 127
Chile, 246–264
Clusters, 227–231, 236–239, 269–278
Codes
  cultural, 4–5, 12n, 37, 48
  high-concordance, 245
  linguistic, 245, 246
  and preferential pattern analysis, 265
  rules, 4–8, 10, 12, 16–29, 36
  segment, 11–21, 24–27
Coefficients
  of associations, 227
  correlation, 227, 229–230
  of similarity, 231
  and numerical classification, 231, 239
  of Rogers and Tanimoto, 231, 235
Cognates, 43
Communality, 273–278

Communication, 145, 166, 169–172, 174
Complementarity, 147–149, 151, 153–165, 172–174
Componential analysis, 16n, 37, 40
  and the construction of ethnographies, 38, 43
  and information processing systems, 4
  and the substitution property, 50–58
Componential solution, 54–57
Computers
  anthropological use of, 127–137
  and factor analysis, 275
  multiprograming, 129
  and preferential pattern maps, 251
  programing, 47, 86–88, 128–137
  and scope viewing, 127, 129, 136, 137
  subroutines, 47, 86
  timesharing, 127, 136
Concordance, 214–223, 245–246, 260–262
Conditioning, 171
Consensus, 215, 222
Constant-sum method, 248
Constraints, 141, 145, 169–172, 174, 176
Contrast, 9–11, 38, 43–46, 242–266 passim
Correspondence, 7, 9–11, 12n, 14, 19–21, 28
Cross-cultural studies, 143, 279
Cross distinctions, 61–64, 66–67, 69–72
Cross-references, 42, 129–130
Crow, 62–63, 68, 236–237, 269–278
Culture,
  area, 269–278
  evolution of, 182–185, 187–190
  sharing, 215, 222–223
  stability of, 181–190
Cumulants, 216
Curves,
  die-away, 165
  indifference, 251, 266
  J-shaped, 160
  normal, 161
  sine, 159
Cybernetic hunting, 149, 154–155

Descent
  and cluster analysis, 269–278
  and factor analysis, 269–278
  and numerical classification, 236–239
  in predicting kin terms, 60, 66–71
Determinism, 145, 149, 182–184
Dichotomies, 227–228, 231–235, 278
Dictionaries
  behavioral, 79, 80, 86
  computer, 134–135
  construction of, 83

Dictionaries (continued)
Santa Fe, 118–119
and tags, 117–118
Distance
and the construction of ethnographies, 38–48
and interaction, 158, 166–168
in measuring endogamy, 211
measures, 226
in numerical classification, 227–236, 238–240
Dominance, 119, 122, 141, 148–176 *passim*
Druz Arab, 203–207

Egypt, 246–264
Eigenvalues, 274
Emotion, 144, 160
Endogamy, 191–213
English (American), 55–57, 214, 223
Equilibrium points, 66, 73
Eskimo, 62, 219, 236, 269–278
Ethiopia, 181–190
Ethnography, 3
construction, 37–48
formalism in, 36
and information processing systems, 4
and nonzero concordance, 222
structure of, 37–38
Exponentials, 156, 160–161, 165

Factor analysis, 227, 230, 238, 269–278
Field, 127, 128, 130, 135–137, 221
Flow charts, 36
in the construction of ethnographies, 38–42, 46, 48
in information processing systems, 21–22, 25, 27
Formalization, 3–38
France, 246–264
Frequency
in interaction, 147, 148, 151, 157, 160–161
and Markov chains, 187
in measuring endogamy, 197–198, 201, 205, 210
and numerical classification, 226, 230–231, 238
in predicting kin terms, 66, 68–72
table, 60
and thematic analysis, 117, 118, 122, 124

Galla, 181, 182–190
Genealogical data, 127–138
Genetics, 165
Graduate students, 135, 137

Grammar, 80, 82, 172
Graphs, 51, 54, 55–57, 64
Guttman scale, 39–40

Hawaiian, 62, 236–237, 269–278

India, 246–266
Information processing systems, 3–35
Information storage, 129, 187
Initiative, 141, 148–175 *passim*
Iroquois, 62, 68, 236, 269–278
Iteration, 192, 195–198, 200–297, 212–213
Ixil Maya, 125

"Jackknife," 214, 219–221
Japanese, 119–125, 214, 219–221

Kariera, 51–53
Kendall's *W*, 260
Kinship, 127, 128–136, 219–221
Kin terms
and cluster analysis, 269–278
and the construction of ethnographies, 43
and contrast, 265
and factor analysis, 269–277
and nonzero concordance, 219–221
prediction of, 60–74
Kroeber's *W* and *T*, 231–232, 235
Kwaio, 38–48

Language
computer, 128, 133, 137
families, 269–278
and interaction, 144
Latent roots, 274
Learning, 171
Lexemes, 4, 79
Linguistics, 223, 245
Linkage, 36, 38, 45, 48
Logarithms, 168, 249–250
Loop-free analysis, 54

Magic squares, 208–209
Majority response, 74
Mapping
and information processing systems, 6–7, 12–19, 25–26
preference, 242
in preferential pattern analysis, 246–248, 258–260, 262–264
Marginals, 192, 195, 201–210
Markov chains, 181, 189–190
Matrices
and age grades, 186–190

Scale
  Guttman, 39–40
  and interaction, 170
  interval, 170, 248
  and preferential pattern analysis, 242, 247–249
  ratio-, 247–249
Semantics
  and the axiomatic method, 3, 8
  and computers, 79–115
  and the construction of ethnographies, 46, 47
  and interaction, 172
  and utility, 266
Sets
  events, 174–176
  theory, 3, 232, 240
  truth, see Carriers
Signals, 166
Similarity, 79–87, 226, 227–229, 239
Spanish, 79, 81–83
Squared multiple correlation (SMC), 273–277
Stability, 182–190
State, 10–17, 186, 189
Statistical process control, 170
Stimuli
  and interaction, 168
  in predicting kin terms, 64–67, 72
  and preferential pattern analysis, 242
  sampling, 60, 65, 72–74
Stochasticism, see Models, stochastic
Substitution property, 50–58
Symbolic logic, 41
Symbols, 144, 170–172

Taxonomy, 3
  folk, 46
  numerical, 226, 227–240
Termination, 141, 157–158
Thematic analysis, 117–126
Traits, 221
Translations, 80, 129
Trukese, 37–38, 45
Turkey, 246–264

Utility, 218, 245, 248, 266

Variables
  and the axiomatic method, 11
  cluster analysis of, 269–278
  factor analysis, 269–278
  and information processing systems, 7
  in interaction, 142, 145–146, 149–165, 173

in kinship studies, 130, 136
and Markov chains, 181
and nonzero concordance, 216, 218
numerical classification of, 226, 227–228, 230, 236–239
in predicting kin terms, 66
in preferential pattern analysis, 245, 247, 261
Varimax criterion, 274
Venn diagrams, 240

Waves
  random, 149
  sine, 159
  square, 147, 159, 161
Word class, 79–80, 83, 86, 117
Work flow, 168

Yucatec Maya, 79, 81–83

Zuni, 223